MW01076748

UNFIT FOR DEMOCRACY

Unfit for Democracy

The Roberts Court and the Breakdown of American Politics

Stephen E. Gottlieb

NEW YORK UNIVERSITY PRESS
New York and London

NEW YORK UNIVERSITY PRESS
New York and London
www.nyupress.org

References to Internet websites (URLs) were accurate at the time of writing. Neither the author nor New York University Press is responsible for URLs that may have expired or changed since the manuscript was prepared.

Library of Congress Cataloging-in-Publication Data
Gottlieb, Stephen E., author.
Unfit for democracy : the Roberts court and the breakdown of American politics /
Stephen E. Gottlieb.
pages cm   Includes bibliographical references and index.
ISBN 978-0-8147-3242-7 (cl : alk. paper)
1. United States. Supreme Court. 2. Roberts, John G., 1955- 3. Political questions and
judicial power--United States. 4. Democracy—United States. 5. Constitutional law—
United States. I. Title.
KF8742.G684   2015
347.73'26--dc23   2015027832

New York University Press books are printed on acid-free paper, and their binding materials are chosen for strength and durability. We strive to use environmentally responsible suppliers and materials to the greatest extent possible in publishing our books.

Manufactured in the United States of America

10 9 8 7 6 5 4 3 2 1

Also available as an ebook

To a nation that pioneered democracy
and invited our ancestors to enjoy
the blessings of liberty and justice for all
and to my wife, our children, grandchildren,
and others we hold dear,
for a better world

CONTENTS

ACKNOWLEDGMENTS

One of my teachers, Thomas I. Emerson, wrote some wonderful studies of the First Amendment. By the time he passed away, the Supreme Court had moved from his focus on the needs of speech, to a focus on the needs and behavior of government. A better approach would incorporate the insights of each. I have spent a good deal of my career thinking about how to recalibrate American constitutional law more in line with Emerson's insights. With this book, I hope to repay a bit of the intellectual debt I owe him. He was a wonderful, generous human being and I am supremely lucky to have known him.

I owe a large debt to David Schultz. We collaborated on two articles and then planned and started a project on democracy and constitutional law before we both moved on in different directions. Nevertheless David's insight, knowledge, and generosity added immeasurably to the result of this book. David also read two very different drafts of this book and gave me the benefit of most helpful comments and criticisms.

The survival and demise of democracy concerned me since I was in college. One of my first guides was the late Professor Wilbert Moore who took time to chat with me around campus on innumerable occasions and helped steer my thinking. I am still indebted to him for his encouragement, generosity, and insight.

I benefitted enormously over many years from working with political scientists on a variety of projects: William Crotty and Roman Hedges, former colleagues on panels and clients on a brief to the Supreme Court, taught me a great deal; James Ceaser, Jerome Mileur, John White, Sarah Morehouse Jewell, Bernard Grofman, Steve Wasby, Byron Nichols, Gerald Pomper, Robert Nakamura, and the late Herbert Alexander and Joseph Board who pulled me into a variety of meetings, panels, and organizations or otherwise saw to my continuing education in the science of politics, as well as others too numerous to name who have been both kind and helpful. I owe them all a considerable debt. And I owe an enormous debt to the teachers who tried to inculcate in me the foundations I would need to follow and take advantage of developments in political science, especially Alpheus Mason, Walter Murphy, Harold Lasswell, and Karl Deutsch.

Friends and colleagues at faculty seminars at Albany, Akron, Boston College, Cleveland-Marshall, Marquette, and Suffolk law schools, participants at panels of the American, International, Midwest, New England, and New York Political Science Associations engaged with the issues I was raising and helped me see at least some of the gaps in my work, and participants at Rockefeller College Policy Conversations, especially Julie Novkov, Bob Nakamura, Rebecca Hamlin and Jason Pierce gave me the benefit of astute suggestions, criticisms, and encouragement. Thanks also to Jennifer Holmes, Ashutosh Varshney, and Kim Lane Scheppele for valuable suggestions in informal conversation. And thanks to my classmate and friend, Tyll van Geel, who made sure I was abreast of important work in the field.

Frank Donegan went over my first draft, helping me improve the book's readability; and my research assistant Tracie D. Rozhon, former news reporter turned law student, edited the manuscript closer to fruition and kept pushing me to make it better—for their help I am extremely grateful. My colleagues and friends James Gathii, Vin Bonventre, and the late John Baker read drafts and gave me the benefit of helpful comments and criticisms. James has been a font of knowledge and suggestions that took me past numerous barriers. Dr. Mark Sakitt read and commented on a draft on one of the relevant issues. I shudder to think what this book would have looked like without the benefit of their friendship, support, insight, and suggestions.

Anne Jelliff, one of my research assistants, grew up in Germany, is bilingual, and gave me a very helpful window into German cases as well as astute help on other issues.

Thanks to Azizah al-Hibri, Rabbi Donald Cashman, Massoud Mafi, and Firdos Abdul-Munim for their insights into religious traditions; my colleague Timothy Lytton for his insight and suggestions; and my student Diana Ng and research assistants over the years this book was germinating, Firdos Abdul-Munim, Renee Albaugh, Thomas M. Bevilacqua, Deborah Buchanan, Stephen Buckley, Emily Drazan, Lindsay Florek, Joe Frandino, Christopher Hahm, Milena Hanukov, Chris Kimball, Sarah Merritt, Vanessa Murphy, Kelly O'Donovan, Roxana Phillipson, Jennifer Ploetz, Brittany Strier, Alissa Sugerman, Mitch Tarighati, and Lindsay Thomas who delved into the materials with enthusiasm, efficiency, strong minds, and discerning eyes.

Library staff at the Albany, Akron, and Suffolk law schools made a huge difference: Bob Begg, Nancy Lenahan, and Mary Wood at Albany, Ellen Delaney at Suffolk, and Paul Reichert at Akron went to a great deal of trouble to help me and I appreciate their efforts enormously. Bob Emery's research magic has been legendary at Albany Law School, and I have been the frequent and deeply grateful beneficiary.

The John F. Seiberling Visiting Chair in Constitutional Law at the University of Akron School of Law gave me the opportunity to begin work on this project as well as an audience for early ruminations. Albany Law School supported it with a research semester and several research grants.

My wife, Jeanette, as always, made writing this easier for me and went through a draft to spot passages too cryptic for nonspecialists. As the writing dragged out, she became my cheerleader and provided the necessary prods to keep going.

Our children, BettyAnne and Eli, daughter-in-law, Karen, and granddaughters, Maggie and Rebecca, are much of the motivation for the book. Their world will be most affected by the trends described. For them—as well as for Ivana, our exchange student, and Fabiola, who lived with us while going to college, and their loved ones, and many others we hold dear—I want a decent and democratic world. I hope this book contributes in some small way.

Portions of this book are revised versions or draw on several prior publications: *Does What We Know about the Life Cycle of Democracy Fit Constitutional Law?* 61 RUTGERS L. REV. 595 (2009); *Law and the Polarization of American Politics*, 25 GEORGIA STATE L. REV. 339 (2008); *What Federalism and Why? Science Versus Doctrine*, 35 PEPPERDINE L. REV. 47 (2007); *Brown v. Board of Education and the Application of American Tradition to Racial Division*, 34 SUFFOLK U. L. REV. 281 (2001); *The Passing of the Cardozo Generations*, 34 AKRON L. REV. 283 (2000). I am grateful to the editors of each of those journals for making it possible to use those materials.

Thanks to Deborah Gershenowitz and Clara Platter at NYU Press. The proposal came out of lengthy conversations with Deborah, after which I was rewarded with consistent enthusiasm and encouragement, plus her gracious reception of the news that the manuscript would be late. She made the work a great deal easier, and certainly more fun. Clara picked up when Deborah moved to another press. Clara's editorial requests led to a much tauter, more focused manuscript.

Any work of value stands on the shoulders of innumerable wonderful and insightful people. Here and in what follows I have indicated debts of which I am aware. For mistakes, I claim sole responsibility.

PART I

Traditions

1

Legacies

The question at the root of this book is whether history and political science have a message for the courts about how to treat American democracy. It turns out they do and what they say is extensive, important, and systematic. They put individual decisions in more significant contexts, and bring to the fore cases little thought about in their relationship to democracy.

Criticism of the Supreme Court need not be a matter of pure politics. This study looks for clear and shared premises that are deeper, more enduring, and important before evaluating the Roberts Court. This and subsequent chapters examine the Court's work against the background of history, comparative law, political and social sciences, and jurisprudence.

The argument is simple. Since the founding of the United States, Americans have thought deeply about how to protect democracy in America and developed a set of prescriptions about how to do it. America projected those ideas onto the world stage, particularly after World War II, and many of them have been adopted as part of the constitutions of democratic states. As a result, they have been considered by foreign courts. That gives us the opportunity to review what happened to those ideas when they became part of constitutional law and whether those developments are encouraging—not out of any belief that we are bound to follow foreign courts, but in the scientific sense that their treatment provides a basis for predicting what similar choices would mean here. Political scientists have confirmed, modified, and added to those ideas while systematically examining the rise and fall of democratic governments. I examine what the Roberts Court has done against that background. Finally, I turn to the heated debate over how the Court should do its work, reaching the conclusion that the Court is bound by our Constitution to take these issues seriously. It is that combination of American thinking, foreign testing, scientific confirmation, and legal analysis of the role of the Court that provides a basis for evaluating the Roberts Court and seeing how seriously astray that Court has gone and the danger this poses to American democracy.

The implications for constitutional law, of what we can learn from history and political science after the Constitutional Convention, runs straight into arguments about the proper method of constitutional interpretation. Although that question has been debated at length, the answer here is simple and direct: everyone who participates in the American debate over constitutional interpretation uses some system or method that is based on assumptions about the demands of democracy—Scalia, Breyer, the conservatives and interpretivists, as well as the liberals and noninterpretivists. In effect the argument is based on false pretenses.

On that basis, the book challenges every aspect of conservative legal thought, its history, its ethnocentrism, its method of interpreting the Constitution, its values, and its democratic bona fides. Out of the chaos of the twentieth century, the book is designed to build a stronger vision of constitutional law that better accounts for the future of democracy in America, as well as the Founding Fathers' thoughts, firmly grounded in a realistic understanding of the world we have been bequeathed.

The most basic definition of democracy is elective government. The question addressed in this study is what keeps elective government alive. Those who have addressed that question, however, have concluded that much more stringent standards are necessary. Since the different forms of democracy are parts of vicious as well as virtuous circles, it will become clear that not a lot depends on the definition. As electorates become less inclusive, pressures increase to turn democracies into more coercive and autocratic systems.

Part I explores American ideas about how to nurture and protect democracy so that it would survive. Once those ideas were exported and adopted abroad, much of the democratic world constrained at least some aspects of law by what may be necessary for democracy. Nevertheless, the Roberts Court and its predecessor, the Rehnquist Court, have not done so. Looking at other countries as well as our own will give us a basis for understanding what it would mean to constrain law by what is necessary for democracy and how those principles, with strong American roots, might have worked if the Roberts Court had been loyal to them.

Part II addresses what political scientists are telling us about why it is important to shape law by what democracy needs. Political and social scientists have studied the successes and failures of the many nations that have had some experience with democratic institutions. They have produced penetrating studies of individual countries, as well as comparative and statistical ones with large datasets. The results are as interesting and surprising as they are important.

Part III focuses on the Roberts Court and the Constitution. In chapter 9, based on the foundations laid in parts I and II, I address what the Roberts Court has actually done, consider how different its record could have been if it had taken our democratic legacy seriously, and assess the impact of the difference against the findings of political and social scientists about what leads democracies to fail. Sadly, it turns out that the Roberts Court has taken this country in directions that have proven deeply destabilizing to democratic governments elsewhere. Chapter 10 addresses what the Constitution has to say about taking the future of democracy seriously, and whether it is proper to interpret the Constitution with this information in mind.

Thus I will offer a tour of history, science, and law to evaluate the Roberts Court.

Forecast at the Founding

The rest of this chapter is devoted to ideas on protecting democracy from our earliest days as a nation.

As the Constitutional Convention of 1787 was finishing its work, a woman asked Benjamin Franklin whether the American people at the time had a republic or a monarchy. "A republic," he responded, "if you can keep it."[1] The founders went well beyond faith in a bill of rights. They had to figure out how they could bring the country together and shape the population into one capable of managing self-government. They believed in the need to disperse both wealth and power and provide for an educated people. And they assumed that they needed unity, to encourage the population to mix, interact, and work together to develop the country for the benefit of all.

Success did not seem inevitable. Thirteen sparsely populated states were surrounded on three sides by British and Spanish forces and Native American tribes. The loyalty of settlers west of the mountains was in doubt. Those in power sought to keep it; the states were run by people with wealth, land, and connections who governed in an aristocratic manner, though in tension with revolutionary principles .

Wealthy patriots in Boston used armed criminal gangs to trigger the American Revolution. Participation by honest patriots made the demonstrations seem democratic, "the people out of doors," a legitimate expression of popular will. After the war, wealthy men feared armed mobs. Shays's Rebellion of farmers in western Massachusetts addressed the threat to their livelihood by judicial enforcement of stringent contract terms. It started as a demonstration, blocking or occupying buildings and closing courts so the farmers' grievances would be heard. In their minds, government should respect popular sovereignty. Those with an aristocratic mind-set, however, perceived popular sovereignty as dangerous.

Many understood that Governor Bowdoin's armed response had turned a relatively traditional popular attempt at self-rule into a shooting war. But

Shays's Rebellion became an organizing tool for a new, stronger union to control mobs, hotheads, and rebels. The aristocrats would get a promise of help against domestic insurrection in Article IV of the Constitution,[2] while the French Revolution soon showed that popular revolution need not lead to democracy. In eighteenth-century thought, nothing was certain.

The overriding issue was to keep the new nation from shattering. Small states feared their larger neighbors; Southern states feared slaves, Native Americans, Spain, and westerners. They wanted guarantees against rebellion and invasion. But southerners also feared northerners would give away rights to the Mississippi by treaty, preventing southern expansion. Northerners feared the South would use the new nation to expand slavery, undermining liberty and "free labor." Each feared commercial rules, fees, and taxes designed to favor a different region.

Their first assumption therefore was that they needed unity, to make one people out of many—*e pluribus unum*. In response they used politics, commerce, finance and education to bind the nation together.

Anti-Federalists argued that the country was too large and complex for a single central government. Differences of religion, language, national origin, ethnic background, and geography were enormous.[3] Religious sects lived separately. Schooling was organized through churches. Towns and regions were settled by distinct language groups; English was far from universal.[4] African and Native American slavery were increasingly divisive. James Madison and the Federalists replied that the size of the nation was an advantage because its diversity would force enlightened leaders, if not everyone, to rise above the pettiness of parochial interests. Integration at the electoral level would improve the politics of the new nation.[5]

But the Constitutional Convention did not rely on politics to integrate the nation. The Constitution protected citizens when out of their home states and supported commerce with post roads, uniform currency, weights and measures, commercial regulation and national courts.[6] Educated colonists would have read Montesquieu's remark that "commerce cures destructive prejudices."[7] It certainly forges ties. Aided by some theologians, commerce was also breaking down religious exclusiveness.[8] The founding generation understood the advantages of these provisions for building the new nation.

The founding generation used education both to build democracy and tie the country together. It was the so-called Age of Enlightenment when people believed in the perfectibility of human institutions through education. By the end of the eighteenth century, a new American college opened its doors every two years. The founders thought training civic-minded people crucial because a democracy could be no better than its citizens. Education would help produce public-spirited citizens. Madison proposed a national university in the Constitutional Convention but it was left to the states. Franklin had already helped found the University of Pennsylvania and Jefferson would soon help found the University of Virginia.

Hamilton added finance: to make them loyal, he wanted the wealthy to rely on the new nation's credit and make the new government central to commercial success. To do that, he created a national banking system and a federal debt. Both would tie investors to the success of the new nation.[9] It was brilliant but partisan, powerful and contested—raising the specter that wealth could also be used against the general welfare.[10]

Focusing on travel, commerce, finance, and education, the founders consciously built the new nation and knit together its disparate parts.

Power Shreds Paper

The Constitutional Convention voted for a strong government. They chose a president rather than a cabinet or parliamentary system, and authorized lower federal courts to serve as our first federal bureaucracy. Nevertheless, they sought to control the powerful government they created by dispersing power within it. Their tools included elections, a broad suffrage, two houses in Congress, a president, and courts, each able to control the others. Checks and balances gave everyone a stake in the new nation and a defense against other regions.

Slavery dominated checks and balances. White Southerners got the ability to vote three-fifths of their slaves for representatives. Eighteenth-century calculation that an agricultural population would grow in proportion to the physical size of the states meant probable southern control of the House of Representatives. With two senators for each small New England state, the North got probable control of the Senate. Those two formulas were put together in the Electoral College for president, almost guaranteeing southern control of the White House. The census was the arbiter.[11]

Divide and conquer became high craft. The Constitutional Convention took the prejudices of language, faith, economics, and geography and enveloped them in the larger nation. Large electoral districts encouraged broader perspectives. Different constituencies for the two houses, the president, and the courts fostered different perspectives. The misbehavior of any branch of government met a complex system of checks and balances.[12]

Thus their second assumption was that dispersing power would prevent abuse. It was brilliant, and later generations would extend their effort to disperse power in order to deal with new forms of concentrated power—

although we would later learn how checks and balances can be used to entrench autocratic power.

As states deliberated over ratification of the Constitution, they focused on the powers of the new government. Urging ratification in a New York paper, James Madison wrote that it is necessary, "first [to] enable the government to control the governed; and in the next place oblige it to control itself."[13] Unsatisfied, several states requested a Bill of Rights, which was adopted shortly after and states some of the conditions for a properly functioning democratic system. As Charles Black famously wrote, Americans would have had to invent a First Amendment to make democracy work if it were not already there. Justice Hugo Black decided that democracy required equally apportioned congressional districting, regardless of whether the equal protection clause applied. Their view is functional; these protections are necessary for elections to do their job. Widely used definitions of democracy in political science, the international community, and famous indexes of democracy include respect for the kind of political freedoms found in the American Constitution because we understand they are necessary for a truly democratic system of government.[14]

The founding generation understood that the most fundamental freedom was the right to vote, that democracy is impossible without political rights. The phrase *right of association* had not yet been created but they clearly understood the rights of speech, press, assembly, and petition were crucial political rights. They would have added freedom of conscience, including religious freedom, as essential for democracy. In succeeding centuries, it has become clear that freedom of speech and association help secure the loyalty of diverse groups. We owe the founding generation the understanding that these individual rights are collectively essential to the working of a democracy.[15]

The due process clause of the Bill of Rights—later also included in the Fourteenth Amendment—requires action according to law, passed by the legislature, not by whim, decree, vigilantes, or mobs. It offers protection against torture and coercion, seizures of persons and property, "disappearances," and political murder, all of which are sometimes aimed at altering political power.[16]

The Bill of Rights responded to British censorship and abuse[17] in favor of the public and against any authority that would seek to control it.[18] After the Civil War, Congress reacted to political repression and the abuse of the criminal process in the defeated states, writing and passing the Fourteenth Amendment to make the provisions of the Bill of Rights applicable throughout the country. The Bill of Rights was still a fighting faith, a political cause.

Modern democracies have lived through eras of enormous corruption that undercut protected rights, including tampering with the ballot box and political parceling of jobs and economic benefits. Corruption waxes and wanes with the ethics of partisan political officials, but it becomes too much when it threatens ordinary citizens with retribution for their political choices or locks up the political process in favor of one party.[19]

Federalists, supporters of the new Constitution, dismissed bills of rights as mere parchment guarantees, impotent against tyrants and demagogues. When the Adams administration passed the Alien and Sedition Acts, Jefferson and Madison turned to the state legislatures and the election of 1800 for repeal, rather than to the courts, which were staffed by Adams's Federalist appointees. Those paper guarantees helped people rally around their principles. The Constitution was protected by democratic culture and the dispersal of power. Supreme Court enforcement of the Bill of Rights was still a century in the future.

Thus the founders' third assumption was that it remained a question whether a bill of rights would help to protect freedom and democracy.

The legal tradition is important; it represents a glowing galaxy in the American science of democracy and a major legacy of the great eras of American Constitution-building in 1787–91 and 1866–71. But the legal tradition is not sufficient. Protecting constitutional rights, and the willingness of the republic to keep and honor those rules, goes well beyond declarations of rights. It requires people with the honor and the courage to enforce them. It requires those with power to stay their hands rather than hold democracy hostage to their own personal or partisan gains.

Harnessing good motives was part of the struggle over federalism. Nationalists feared loyalty to state governments. Madison urged that a cosmopolitan, diverse public, created strong incentives to treat all with respect, often favoring national over local politics. Slavery was his prime example of how unfair state politics could be. Yet it is easier for most of Americans to have their say in towns, cities, and state governments. For many Americans, state government seemed closer, more democratic, and trustworthier than a distant federal one.[20]

Rather than resolve this argument, the Convention gave us both. Yet the delegates in the Convention had little to say about principles of federalism. They argued endlessly about how states would be represented in the new government, but were almost mute about the meaning of national powers and laid down no principles of federalism except the set of overlapping grants of largely undiscussed and unexplained powers. The only principle enunciated was in the draft that instructed the Committee of Detail what powers to insert and that became the familiar powers of Congress. Those instructions read: "Resolved, That the Legislature of the United States ought to possess the legislative Rights vested in Congress by the Confederation; and moreover to legislate in all Cases for the general Interests of the Union, and also in those Cases to which the States are separately incompetent, or in which the Harmony of the United States may be interrupted by the Exercise of individual Legislation."[21] Thus their fourth assumption was that they could get the benefits of both national and state governments with something like a functional division of responsibilities, so that each level of government could accomplish what it needed to do.

Among their largest concerns was the threat of standing armies. Their principal hope was that standing armies would be minimal except in wartime. Guns might be necessary against slaves, Native Americans, French, Spanish, or British soldiers.[22] Guns, however, could also be turned on the people, on local, state, and national governments, or on men of wealth and their estates. Elbridge Gerry suggested limiting the size of armies that the country could maintain in times of peace. Tradition credits George Washington with suggesting in response a limit on the number of troops a foreign enemy would be permitted to land on American shores. Gerry's proposal failed. But the delegates tried to disperse military power by giving Congress (as part of civilian control) the power to regulate the state militia,[23] to control the privatization of warfare,[24] and to decide whether to wage war.

Thus their fifth assumption was that they could control the military by shifting power to civilian authorities. But the survival of democracy depends in large part on whether civilian control survives. The problem is to assure that the military, the folks with the firepower, will obey civilian commands. A military so inclined could oust civilian authorities, the secretary of defense and the president. Or it can support an executive coup d'état ousting the legislature. The president can promote officers. By choosing officers based on individual loyalty, presidents of some countries were able to scrap their constitutions. In some the military became so incensed by executive choices that it deposed the president. Either way, democracy lost.

Instead of a standing army, the founders championed a trained and organized citizen militia, which could respond when needed, over the fulltime soldiers whom the founders thought dangerous. Sam Adams thought an inclusive militia much safer than standing armies or a select, upper-crust militia, either of which would "feel a distinct interest from that of our fellowcitizens at large." He argued for mixing people together: "No man I should think, who possesses a true republican spirit, would decline to rank with his fellow-citizens, on the fancied idea of a superiority in circumstances: This might tend to introduce fatal distinctions in our country." Adams wanted an integrated militia for the sake of America: "The great principles of our present militia system are undoubtedly good, constituting one simple body, and embracing so great a proportion of the citizens as will prevent a separate interest among them, inconsistent with the welfare of the whole."[25]

The new nation did create a regular army, but its officers reflected a broad cross section of America, which many credit with helping keep the army out of party politics.[26] Militias and private armies outside of government authority posed serious risks in the eyes of the founders. They could turn into mobs that would threaten the peace and good order of the society. Only "well-regulated" militias were part of the constitutional design, and Congress was given the power to specify how. The founders had no romantic notion of men under arms in any form.

In simple language that the founders would have applauded: power, in all its forms, needs to be accountable, monitored, and controlled.

The Leveling Spirit

Gouverneur Morris, whose family owned much of the Bronx, rose on his peg leg to warn his fellow delegates in the Constitutional Convention that he feared the *absence* of property qualifications for voters *would lead to an aristocracy*: "Give the votes to people who have no property, and they will sell them to the rich who will be able to buy them." Political parties would prove something like that point in the nineteenth century, paying the poor and immigrants for their votes. Morris went on: "The time is not distant when this Country will abound with mechanics & manufacturers who will receive their bread from their employers." He feared that their employers would control their votes. "The man who does not give his vote freely is not represented. It is the man who dictates the vote."[27]

Freedom depended on economic independence, particularly before the secret ballot. Jefferson famously celebrated yeoman farmers as central to democracy. The independence of farmers meant they would vote their own opinions instead of their masters' and would resist excessive government.[28]

Control over the votes of others concentrates power. Madison worked to moderate holdings of property; "unnecessary opportunities . . . to increase the inequality of property by an immoderate, and especially unmerited, accumulation of riches . . . [should be avoided] [b]y the silent operation of laws, which, without violating the rights of property, reduce extreme wealth towards a state of mediocrity, and raise extreme indigence towards a state of comfort."[29] Tyranny was concentrated power; the founders feared it.[30]

Speculators sought large fortunes by gobbling and colonizing western lands. Large colonial land grants affronted Americans who believed land belonged to those who worked it. Still, enough land remained to challenge Old World–style aristocracy and buttress government by consent.[31] Just in case, tax, inheritance and other laws, were designed to meet Madison's injunction to "reduce extreme wealth towards ... mediocrity, and raise extreme indigence towards ... comfort." Despite inconsistencies, parts of the Constitution made little sense except on the understanding that all men are created equal.[32]

While the Constitutional Convention was underway in Philadelphia, Congress—working under the Articles of Confederation and meeting in New York—passed the Northwest Ordinance, shaping the future states of Ohio, Michigan, Indiana, Illinois, Wisconsin, and part of Minnesota. The ordinance laid the new lands into small plots with provision for a school in each new town. Some might get rich on the development of the western lands, but settlement and ownership would be in small holdings of ordinary Americans.[33]

Meanwhile, the Convention addressed private economic power in Philadelphia. Some wanted to tax luxuries; others thought it was included in the power to tax.[34] The Convention protected property against state, but not federal, "Law[s] impairing the Obligation of Contracts," a restriction understood very narrowly.[35] It prohibited aristocratic positions, authorized restriction of the slave trade and some state monopolies, and prohibited some legislation targeted at states, sections, or individuals. Meanwhile, states quickly eliminated provisions of English common law which kept large familial estates intact.[36]

Later the federal Homestead Act of 1862 promoted still wider distribution of property by offering federal land for the price of working a farm across the Mississippi to people whose only capital was their bare hands and the will to clear and settle the territory. The statute also provided for land grant colleges, which would spread the benefits of education around the country.[37]

Farming interests now often conflict with the needs of other Americans; and the independence of small farmers has been undermined both by large farm corporations and the highly leveraged financing of agriculture. The distinctive value of independent farmers for Jefferson and Morris was their role in eighteenth-century America. Their more enduring point was the importance of financial independence to the maintenance of democratic institutions. Dispersal of property helps balance power.

The founders' sympathy toward property qualifications now seems elitist, creating government of, for, and by property. Reality is more complex. Eighteenth-century property qualifications often expanded suffrage by including owners with modest holdings. The majority of the white male population could vote and states continued to extend the ballot to more of the voting age population. By 1825 property qualifications had largely disappeared.[38]

Thus the sixth working assumption of the founders was that dispersion of wealth as well as power was important for the democratic process. Disparities of wealth threaten the democratic process, both by motivating rebellion, and by facilitating the misuse of impoverished and dependent masses for rigging, buying, and stealing elections.

The founders left us a legacy of antagonism to large aggregations of power, and an effort to give the great mass of Americans control over their governments, in the face of repeated counterefforts to keep the money flowing. The founders' legacy included their insight on the relation of economics and democracy but they left no generic constitutional language on the "inequality of property." Subsequent generations would fight over economic issues without constitutional rules, to free the slaves, make suffrage universal, provide living wages, and substitute a safety net for the opportunities of the frontier and party patronage.

The founders' concerns about dispersing power gave rise to competing traditions. The deliberative tradition seeks wise public officials, who are beholden to none. The egalitarian tradition favors wide distribution of resources so that voters can act independently. Pluralism is the hypothesis that the more different groups compete in politics the more likely that politics will be fair. With fluid alliances, politics becomes the art of compromising and sharing benefits and burdens. When allegiances harden and polarize, politics becomes a contest of dominant and subjugated groups.[39]

For the founding generation, liberty was shared, social, and nearly synonymous with self-government.[40] To be a free man was to have the right to self-government—not freedom from government, but freedom to participate in government. Constitutional protections were designed to prevent using the criminal and civil laws to distort the political system, as England had. Liberty protected the people from domination by usurpers; it was not private.

Character Fit for Democracy

Delegates to the Constitutional Convention described the "genius of the people" as "republican" and realized they had to respect popular feelings about who could vote. Hamilton's promonarchy speech fell on deaf ears. But the delegates knew democracy would prove only as good as its people. A selfish public would not support a joint effort for the general welfare, instead of individual and short-term gains. Dispersion of power, loyalty of the wealthy, and a legal tradition alone would not protect democracy.[41]

The "genius of the people" was not a genius gene. It was a product of the context in which they found themselves. Able to govern themselves, why would people be fair? That problem haunted the founders. Rivalries abounded among competing economic and religious groups. Legislative seats were routinely malapportioned and gerrymandered to benefit those in power. What would prevent one faction from oppressing or disenfranchising another?

Because the people are the masters, the survival of self-government and respect for the rights of temporary or long-standing minorities depend on public virtue. Therefore the people's character was better protection for democracy and liberty than lists of legal rights. Subsequent generations must be brought up as republicans and imbued with republican principles, including commitment to representative government and respect for its decisions, commitment to public service and dedication to the general welfare, together with an egalitarian, antiaristocratic spirit.[42] To preserve that character and protect the nation the founders had created, subsequent generations had to have appropriate education, which required more and better schools.[43] Their seventh basic assumption was that dedication to republican principles and the education to sustain them were necessary to the success of popular government.

Along with public virtue, the founders expected education to teach the skills needed for people to take a responsible part in public discussion. The tools for thought and argument that they described included philosophy, logic, and an appreciation of the fundamentals of sound and unsound arguments.[44] Educated men were also expected to speak several languages.

Indoctrinating students remained important but changed as the assimilation of immigrants became a major issue in the late nineteenth century.[45] Rituals, pledges, songs, and history were increasingly scrutinized to ensure that children would not question America's superiority to other countries and cultures. In the twentieth century, schools were charged with providing every child with equal opportunity and training them to obey the law. Many school systems lost sight of the founders' purpose to educate students to take part in democratic government, in favor of educating students not to make trouble.[46]

Republican Equality as Tocqueville Saw It

Alexis de Tocqueville, a French nobleman, traveled through the United States in 1831 and 1832 to understand the implications for France of the growing popularity of democracy. Tocqueville feared that Europe would lose its greatest assets in the process of democratization. Yet he predicted that America would become a preeminent world power, and predicted its twentieth-century conflict with Russia. Tocqueville's concerns did not cloud his vision.[47]

In DEMOCRACY IN AMERICA, Tocqueville described four factors as essential for democracy: widespread economic well-being, independent organizations to channel public opinion sensibly, decentralization, and a democratic political culture.

He kept coming back to the political culture's rarely deferential leveling spirit, although slavery remained a challenge to republican ideology. Everyone thought himself a judge of everything. Egalitarianism prevented money and power from taking over and the development of an inherited aristocracy; it also unleashed the energy, productivity, and ability of the great mass of Americans to govern themselves. The few could not control America because all American institutions and customs attacked power as democracy's enemy. The Frenchman absorbed the American view that the relatively equal distribution of land supported democracy. He believed that for men to be reasonably equal in any respect, they had to be equal in all.[48]

Tocqueville wrote at length about what he called "self-interest rightly understood." Americans understood that their individual interests were bound up with the whole. To understand one's self-interest "rightly" required concern for the general welfare; that provided a kind of altruism in action that Tocqueville admired.

Although egalitarianism and individualism were essential, they were also dangerous.[49] Tocqueville wondered what kept equality in check. Without the guiding hand of an aristocracy, America would function like a mob. Without the training to deal with complex issues, it would decide based on trivia and threaten to destroy the very institutions that protected it. In effect, too much individualism could render everyone equally impotent against the passions of others, until they surge with the confidence of a hotheaded multitude.

Tocqueville noticed that Americans were joiners who believed in collective action, and created associations for almost every object in life. He hoped those associations would be the steady hand America needed, and break the mass down from a mob to more thoughtful voices. The America he observed was collectivist as well as individualistic. It had conquered government in order to use it. Tocqueville celebrated them all: American individualism, the collectivism that tempered its faults, and the equality crucial to both. He might have added that liquor was the necessary solvent, as large southern planters like Washington, Jefferson, Madison, and others, entertained their neighborhoods in exchange for votes.

Many of the participants in Jefferson's victory in 1800 saw it in egalitarian terms. Jefferson understood the political advantages of merchants and manufacturers: "Their wealth is . . . greatly superior. . . . They all live in cities, together, and can act in a body readily and at all times. . . . The agricultural interest is dispersed over a great extent of country [and] have little means of communication with each other."[50]

Parties balanced their power, so he joined Madison to create the Democratic-Republicans. He worried that the commercial classes had become "Monocrats" who opposed republican principles and might attack the representative system or disenfranchise most of the population in order to control elections and policies in favor of the very wealthy. Farmers, tradesmen, and others with local callings would be largely unrepresented and unheard without parties. Thus Jefferson and Madison turned a struggle between northern and southern elites into a referendum on the concentration of power.

Wealth also mattered at the polls. In many states, people originally voted aloud. Where people placed paper ballots in a box, political machines learned to hand out visually distinct, often color-coded printed ballots to make identifying voters easy so they could be rewarded with bribes or punished with beatings.[51] Large landlords in the Hudson Valley controlled their tenants' votes before the so-called rent wars ended their power.[52]

Benjamin Leigh told Virginians in 1829, either "property will purchase power, or power will take property."[53] The wealthy tell themselves their privileges are good for everyone. Slaveholders described slavery as good for the slaves, and the slaves as happy.[54] Landowners, politicians, businessmen, and corporations rise not by sharing power but by seizing it. Their perquisites continually challenge Americans who have a more egalitarian, republican spirit.

In the first half of the nineteenth century, Horace Mann and his generation remade American education to integrate people, especially rich and poor, effectively using schools to educate students in republican principles of equality. The "genius of the people" was partly a conscious effort.[55] Racial integration was the end product of this lengthy tradition.

Southern states challenged republican ideology in order to protect slavery. They attempted to interpose states' rights and a theory of concurrent majority, actually a veto by a minority of states. Southern resistance to majority rule and equal rights led to Civil War and the civil rights movement (although generations of American children were indoctrinated in a different understanding of the Civil War designed to whitewash the Southern and blacken the Northern roles).

Americans repeatedly challenged tools of concentrated wealth or power. Originally, specific legislative grants awarded monopolies and corporate charters for schools, bridges, or banks. In the Jackson era states substituted general corporation laws specifying rules for who could have a corporate charter. Corporate charters no longer implied monopoly. Nicholas Biddle, running the U.S. Bank, threatened economic implosion if it was attacked.

Jackson terminated the bank. Jackson's ideological point was rejection of the bank's concentrated power.

Jacksonians took credit for democratizing government service, believing it required no special expertise, and that too much power had been placed in the hands of wealthy elites.[56] In response, Jacksonians built on the political use of patronage in government offices, and so are blamed for the spoils system. At the same time, political parties started making decisions in large open-air gatherings of supporters, replacing meetings among officeholders.

The party system developed before the Civil War to counterbalance economic elites. At the time of his death during the war, former President Martin Van Buren was writing a book in support of the two-party system. Expanding on Jefferson's insight, Van Buren explained that if one party dominates, everyone joins, blurring friends and opponents, and it would be dominated by the wealthy elites who would rule in the absence of parties. Contest drives the parties to define positions and supporters.[57]

The parties changed what social scientists refer to as the collective action problem. Large unorganized masses have no good way to exert power. Parties created organizations that people could use to exert power. Madison had asked who guards the guardians. By the late nineteenth century, parties had themselves become nodes of corruption. As parties learned to control the franchise and the ballot box, Americans sought to democratize them. The primary system became one of the main legacies of the Progressive movement.[58]

Americans in the late nineteenth-century Gilded Age fought a parallel battle over economic power. Stockholders of the Union Pacific bribed congressmen with shares in their construction company, Credit Mobilier, in return for federal subsidies and huge profits. Corporations created company towns and hired boatloads of immigrants to dig in the mines or work in the factories. Workers had to vote by paper ballot, with supervisors looking at their ballots. Voting against the company risked losing a job. Where employers owned their homes, jobless workers would be homeless. If workers were paid in scrip— that is, company money redeemable only at a company store—anything left in their pockets was useless elsewhere. So they voted their employers' preferences. What corporate power had not decided at the polls, it finalized by cutting politicians in on the wealth. In states like Kentucky and West Virginia, a single corporation or industry controlled the land, business, and politics. In such circumstances, company preferences became state policy; wealth dominated politics.[59] Even short of that level of control, many found it difficult to turn their bosses down because there could be repercussions.

When West Virginia separated from Virginia during the Civil War, it originally abandoned the Virginia practice of voting aloud precisely because "open

voting gave advantages to persons in positions of power, such as employers and creditors, and intimidated those of lesser means or weaker fabric." A
decade later West Virginia restored open voting. To avoid a public outcry, it
made an "open, sealed, or secret ballot" optional. The West Virginia Constitution still preserves the "right" to vote by open ballot, although it also asserts
that one also has the right to vote by secret ballot. Whether that right is enforceable depends on the pressures tolerated in the community.[60]

The battle against concentrated power is continuous. New protections for
the secret ballot were enacted around 1900, especially preprinted ballots listing all candidates and parties and not easily distinguishable at the polls. Still,
party machines figured out how to identify voters' choices, based partly on
the availability of economically vulnerable people as enforcers or supporters.
Numerous provisions in state law to prevent violation of ballot secrecy testify
to the continuing threat to bribe or threaten voters.

Efforts to regulate corporate abuse grew through the nineteenth century.
Regulation of working conditions and child labor were thwarted by competition from businesses in states without similar regulation, but the Supreme
Court largely blocked national intervention before 1937. Railroads with local
route monopolies charged farmers heavily but states had little power over
interstate rails. In 1887, Congress established the Interstate Commerce Commission with control over rates of interstate carriers. It was abolished in 1995
after being accused of favoring trucking over railroads and being captured by
industry.[61] The growth of corporate conglomerates and holding companies
called trusts led to antitrust law that prohibited combinations and conspiracies in restraint of trade. The Sherman Antitrust Act of 1890 pioneered the
control of corporate power. Subsequent legislation attacked price discrimination that lessened competition and created the Federal Trade Commission to
regulate unfair practices.[62]

On the eve of World War I, Americans responded to "the curse of bigness."[63] Progressives like Louis D. Brandeis, a Wilson Supreme Court appointee, wanted to preserve American creativity through small, flexible enterprise;
he attacked large business for using its power to eliminate competition and
for being a menace to democracy, threatening to overwhelm citizens, and
even states and political parties. President Theodore Roosevelt argued for an
estate tax because concentrations of wealth ran counter to the ethos and the
health of American democracy.[64]

Once the objections of the Supreme Court were overcome in 1937, the federal government played a larger role in controlling corporate power and defending the economic rights of ordinary citizens.[65] Unions became a popular

means to counter corporate power. Later, when unions seemed to wield inordinate power, Americans became disenchanted with them as well.

New Deal and subsequent legislation attempted to defend family farms. Individual farmers still appeared to fit Jefferson's characterization as the backbone of democracy; although, once major corporations learned to get most of the funds, federal subsidies no longer served family farms well. Americans continue to challenge ever-changing and apparently never-ending subsidies for large business, from the infamous oil depletion allowance to a smorgasbord of other tax benefits.[66]

In the late twentieth century, public attention returned to the role of money in politics. States attacked the purchase of votes as early as 1776. Prohibition of corporate donations to political campaigns dates back to 1890. In 1907 the federal government prohibited campaign contributions by federally chartered banks and corporations. Other campaign limitations were passed in 1910. Senator Tillman argued that members of Congress should not be "instrumentalities and agents of corporations." Economic power was out of place in self-government.[67]

New campaign finance regulation was passed in the wake of the burglary of the Democratic campaign headquarters by people working with the campaign to reelect President Nixon. The Supreme Court originally accepted most of the legislation to prevent money from corrupting American politics. Discovery of loopholes alternated with rounds of legislation to close them. Congress's regulatory efforts never entirely banished opportunities to make politicians feel indebted.[68] In 2010, the Court recognized a constitutional right for corporations to use their corporate treasuries on political campaigns, making a century of restrictions unconstitutional.[69]

Americans have not attacked all inequalities. Hard work and good ideas justify reward. Americans internalize a balance between inequalities and their uses that seem fair and those that do not. The extremes—communism and corporate control of politics—are unacceptable. Those whose economic arithmetic sees only one set of benefits, equality or corporate freedom, erase this American tradition.

Americans repeatedly lecture other countries that democracy cannot take root where land is so concentrated that nations are divided into powerful landholders and powerless peasants. African poverty has led men to rebel armies for food, booty from victims, or the oil, diamonds, or ivory they can seize. The defense of privilege has led men to make war and murder political opponents in Latin America, while poverty has led some to declare war on the privileged and others to staff so-called death squads and torture their own people in order to make a living. Poverty and privilege have repeatedly defeated self-government. Looking abroad, Americans have seen that most clearly.

At home, Americans have found that the balance of power is dynamic, unstable, and always changing, so that the battle for a republican society has to be continually refought; there is no permanent solution.

In one tradition or another, character, democracy, ideology, and the structure of the American economy were all bound together with the spirit and the extent of equality. Tocqueville, who came to the United States specifically to study its government, had put his finger on a major constituent of American democracy, and a large part of Americans' understanding of their own condition. The democratizing urge that drove American education, the party system, the Homestead Act and the Progressive movement, also underlay antitrust and other legislation designed to control the growing power of large corporations. In each case, a part of the reasoning was political: concentrated power was politically both unfair and dangerous.

Conflict Management for a Diverse Republic

America has dealt with difference since the founding of the republic.[70] Anti-Federalists opposed ratifying the Constitution because the nation was too big to be governed from the center. Geographic, religious, ethnic, and language differences were so large that any attempt to subject them to a single set of laws or decision-making process seemed quixotic. English was far from universal and slavery just one of many enormous divisions. James Madison and the Federalists, however, answered by reversing the argument that the nation was too big and too diverse to be governable. They insisted that the nation's size was an advantage—its diversity would force enlightened leaders to rise above the pettiness of parochial interests. Integration would improve the new nation's politics.[71]

They had already seen the process at work. Nascent capitalism not only brought commercial interests together from across the nation, but had led previously sectarian institutions to integrate in order to survive in a religiously, as well as linguistically, diverse culture.[72]

Integration quickly became an ideology. In 1782, French immigrant Hector St. John de Crèvecœur famously wrote that immigrants wanted to become Americanized. They "melted" easily into Americans, and freed themselves from the slavery of the Old World. Historians have challenged his claims, but the ideology endured, became a self-fulfilling prophecy, and led Americans, sometimes grudgingly, to keep the paths of assimilation open. In a 1909 novel,

British writer Israel Zangwill put immigrants into "the great Melting-Pot where all the races of Europe are melting and reforming!" He added: "Into the Crucible with you all! God is making the American."[73] Americans long ago came to believe that integration was crucial to creating the republican society that could manage the democratic system, their eighth important assumption.

Common Schools

Public schools were originally called *common schools*. Horace Mann, who died just before the Civil War, saw emerging class differences challenge the nation's egalitarianism. Mann wanted to improve education, prepare lower classes for business and improve mutual understanding across classes. Integration would benefit everyone.[74] *Common* expressed an ideology, bringing Americans of all kinds into the same buildings and schoolrooms where they would meet, learn from, and learn to get along with each other. Think of Bill Bradley, a Missouri banker's son, future Princeton and New York Knicks basketball star and U.S. senator from New Jersey, going to and playing for Crystal City High. Bradley grew up comfortable with people unlike himself, an example of Mann's hope for America.

Bringing schoolchildren together that way was a major American innovation. Other countries pour public dollars into separate schools for each religious community. Ours has required religious communities to use their own funds. Public schools are for everyone.

Actual mixing has varied. In some areas where groups have lived more segregated lives, private or parochial schools have been more feasible or acceptable avenues for mixing. But the principles underlying the common public school—openness to all and bringing people of all backgrounds together—has been a matter of American exceptionalism and pride.[75] Indeed, during the Virginia desegregation trial, Robert Carter read, for the record, official publications of Virginia's Department of Education "all of which called for . . . encouraging cooperation among students of all types."[76]

Women and Girls

Boys were schooled as soon as the Mayflower landed. Harvard schooled young men less than three decades later. Women's education followed slowly.[77]

Separate seating by gender in church and school crossed the Atlantic with the first settlers. By the eighteenth century, families sat together in church and both parents educated their children. Puritans wanted girls to read the Bible because they had souls, needed to understand the moral law, and as women were expected to educate the next generation of men. In the colonial period, girls would be taught at home or so-called dame schools, run by women for small children, often both boys and girls. Although law required education for girls, parents either had to pay for it or teach the girls themselves. Schooling offered to girls was minimal, in off-hours, or in the summers.

After the American Revolution, women were expected to teach the virtue needed to protect and preserve a republican society. Gradually, ideology, religion, and economics expanded women's role as teachers. Thus, the early development of American coeducation had nothing to do with integration, nor with equality. Often it was just economics—schools were safe for young girls, and separate schools were too expensive except in the largest cities.[78] The Charlestown, Massachusetts, committee on coeducation reported: "We do not find [sexual segregation] in the organization of Sunday Schools or Primary schools" and "in all the social gatherings of the young, whether in the domestic circle, in parties of pleasure, or in rural or other excursions, it is desired and expected that both sexes will be brought together to participate in, and add to the enjoyments of the occasion."[79] Still, girls were treated differently, separately, and somewhat gingerly, because it was not clear why they needed more than the most basic education.

Once coeducation took hold in the countryside, cities began to grapple with it. But then, equality and integration became an issue. Coeducation was justified because boys would be restrained by and would learn to respect girls, while girls would learn respect for "manly" virtues.[80] Boys and girls would learn from and about each other.[81]

Many saw coeducation ideologically: republican values mandated equal treatment and respect for merit and ability. The latter emphasis ran in the girls' favor, as their school records tended to surpass their brothers'.[82] (Relative scores have seesawed for many reasons other than innate ability.) As well-known scholars of coeducational history put it: "The ideal of the common school decreed that public education should deliberately mix different kinds of people in order to create a unified nation of people who shared similar civic values."[83] Some argued that the girls would meet the wrong sort of boys. That objection ran squarely into conflict with the ideology behind so-called common schools.

Seth Thomas, on a schools committee in Charlestown, Massachusetts, wrote: "the law has provided that these schools shall be public and common. . . . The rich and the poor, the high and the low, the polite and the vulgar, all have an equal right in them." Thomas added that objections to allowing daughters to share classrooms with members of lower classes were "an attack upon the common school system."[84]

Debates over coeducation paralleled later debates over integrating black and white children. Women's advocates preferred coeducation because girls were often given inferior separate schools, just as advocates for African Americans later argued quality schooling would only be provided if they were educated with white students.[85] Concern that wealthy parents would remove their daughters from coeducational common schools if many students were boys from immigrant or poor families was repeated by concern over white flight from schools with many black students. Flight of wealthier girls would have eliminated many of the benefits of the common school movement.[86]

Some saw equality as an objective, but others saw it as the problem of co-education. Educating women, especially with boys, threatened to make them "unfit" mothers and homemakers. Integration would tend to wash away the differences between boys and girls. School administrators tiptoed around the issue, assuring everyone coeducation did not make girls unfit for proper gender roles.

The press was filled with hand wringing about feminizing boys and exhausting or toughening girls if men taught girls and women taught boys. The vastly increased presence of women on both sides of school desks worried some. Educators, however, concluded that same-sex teachers were not necessary, and would be too expensive to arrange. Women teachers eventually took over several of the educational associations, although they often continued to elect male officers. And the schools rode out the gendered storm.[87]

Business

Assimilation and integration were also tools toward other goals. With large-scale immigration early in the twentieth century, the different customs, languages, and attitudes of foreign-born workers concerned industrialists like Henry Ford, as well as educators and social workers. For industry, these differences were expensive sources of conflict, turnover, and resistance to traditional rules. Celebrating Eastern Orthodox Christmas thirteen days later than most Americans disrupted production. Differences made communications difficult and relationships testy.[88] Labor's efforts to organize were throttled by corporate-financed police and local political machines. Educators feared that foreign-born Americans were a threat to democracy and might undermine sacred American institutions.

Schools quickly became a means to prepare workers for industrial life, with regimented schedules that would Americanize the children. Large schools with students in age-graded lock step replaced one-room schoolhouses with children of diverse ages gathered together. Big schools were more efficient. To instill American cultural values, national civic education replaced the Bible as a fundamental text. The objective was to make new Americans less different from their older neighbors. Schools shifted from supporting an older nation of skilled craftsmen responsible largely to themselves, to supporting a new nation of industrial workers.

Major corporations developed Americanism classes, which included distaste for socialism and trade unionism. Ford created a graduation ceremony for its school, which included a huge incarnation of the melting pot—in went foreign nationals and out came Americans.[89]

Americanization was coercive. The post–World War I "patriotic" attack on foreigners (i.e., Germans, Jews, and Asians), race riots, revival of the Ku Klux Klan (directed against African Americans, Catholics, and Jews), and the Red Scare (against Old World anticapitalist views), defined *American* narrowly and challenged the Progressives' efforts at Americanization. Still, many believed assimilation was unavoidable, regardless of deliberate efforts. Crèvecœur's concept of "melting" supported America's faith that the vicious intergroup struggles of the 1920s would be overcome.[90]

Military Service

Militia service was already required of all free men in the colonial period. Americans have attached great importance to the idea that the army was composed of people from all walks and stations of life who had to work together on terms of equality.

The common militia mostly served a training function. Select and volunteer militias grew alongside it and did most of the actual fighting. They were based mostly on social status, and functioned like men's clubs. By contrast, the regular army was drawn from those so poor that military pay and food were attractive. Thus, Americans feared standing armies, drawn from the least substantial members of the society.[91]

Returning to Sam Adams's point in his farewell address as governor of Massachusetts, the common militia seemed safer than a standing army or more elite militias, which might not have everyone's interest at heart. As late as the Spanish-American War, local guard units kept the informality of their towns, using first names, regardless of rank and rules, and punishing anyone who put on an airs. Egalitarianism was strong despite social differences, and soldiers expected to be treated as independent, valuable human beings. The regular army had become strictly hierarchical and did everything according to rules. Officers and soldiers tended to come from different classes and there was considerably less mixing across classes in the army.[92]

Before the twentieth century, the military was based on local units—the First Massachusetts, the Fourth Indiana, the Rough Riders. But when Uncle Sam wanted you to join the army in the twentieth century, the idea was to enlist recruits without regard to origin. Farm boys from Iowa fought beside city slickers, hillbillies, and southern gentry. Before the United States entered World War I, "conscriptionists believed that military training would help restore harmony, order, and vitality to a society that they believed was becoming fragmented and debilitated by individual selfishness, class and ethnic divisions, and local and regional parochialism." They were "appalled" by "the lack of assimilation of millions of immigrants from southern and eastern Europe." Echoing Horace Mann, they wanted to "teach rich and poor to understand each other."[93] Theodore Roosevelt proclaimed, "the military tent, where all sleep side-by-side, will rank next to the public school among the great agents of democratization."[94]

Objections to the draft included the financial imposition on poor families, the assault on traditions of local control and individual responsibility, and hostility to a military establishment headquartered on the East Coast. Immigrant groups were divided both over the war itself and over conscription because the military bureaucracy would threaten their diverse sympathies, lives, and identities.

The American belief in the alchemy of living and working together threatened southern race relations. Mississippi Senator James K. Vardaman feared "arrogant strutting representatives of the black soldiery in every community."[95] Some black leaders thought the draft would improve the position of African Americans. But the administration segregated the military by race and the draft administrator suggested "a plan to keep blacks working in the cotton fields during the war."[96]

By the end of World War II, towns like Castroville, Texas, where European languages were spoken to the virtual exclusion of English, began to lose their Old World tongues. Soldiers had comrades across the country who introduced them to wives, business opportunities, and new cultures. War was homogenizing the culture of the United States.

The army deliberately "Americanized" immigrants by mixing them,[97] as well as by teaching them about "American" habits and beliefs, including sanitation, enlistment, success, American heroes, and obedience, but not fighting, Bolshevism, or strikes.[98] During World War I, some high-ranking Army officers wanted to break up units that had been segregated by language to facilitate learning.[99] Brigadier General Henry Jervey wrote, "it is not the policy of the United States Army to encourage or permit the formation of distinctive brigades, regiments, battalions or other organizations composed exclusively of the members of any race, creed or political or social group."[100]

President Wilson changed the policy to segregate the races and to recruit aliens.[101] There was no opportunity for black officers except in black regiments, and only under white command.[102] In World War II, blacks began to be sent as replacements for losses in battle. By 1951 both black and white troops in integrated units expected race relations to improve, although whites in segregated units did not.[103]

Race

Integration had been tried before the Civil War. In Ohio, it was sometimes a local option, sometimes required. Massachusetts originally required and maintained integrated schools but black students felt so badly treated in Boston that the community petitioned for a separate school. When the request was denied, the black community set up a private school of their own. Eventually, the city accepted some responsibility, but its segregated schools were poorly maintained, far from where the black students lived, and run by insensitive, often abusive, administrators and teachers. In response, a portion of the black community stressing racial pride, reestablished a private black school with an exclusively black staff. They feared any return to inhospitable, integrated schools, pointing to the failure of integrated schools decades before which had led to the establishment of separate black schools.[104]

Some blacks moved to the towns outside Boston to attend integrated schools. In 1849, Charles Sumner, future abolitionist senator from Massachusetts, argued in the Massachusetts Supreme Judicial Court, that the Massachusetts Constitution required integration of Boston's schools, using many arguments quite similar to those used a century later in *Brown v. Board of Education*. Sumner was assisted by a well-respected and capable black attorney, Robert Morris Jr. Chief Justice Lemuel Shaw was a well-known abolitionist. Nevertheless, in 1849 the Massachusetts Supreme Court denied the claim and sustained separate schools in Boston.[105] With white allies, however, blacks secured integrated schools by statute.[106]

In the post–Civil War South and some Northern states, the KKK and others "taught" blacks to submit by widespread violence and intimidation. More recently, resistance to the civil rights movement was written in blood—of children in bombed churches, of blacks who tried to vote or sue, of civil rights workers who sought to improve the position of blacks in the segregated South.[107] Some successful black communities were destroyed by murder, mayhem, arson, and a coup d'état in Wilmington, North Carolina (1898), Tulsa, Oklahoma (1921), Rosewood, Florida (1923) and other cities.[108]

The battle within the black community was fought again between the two world wars. Many thought "mixed" schools would subject black children to worse mistreatment and rob them of knowledge of black accomplishments and, by extension, their own potential. Others were convinced segregation was the root of white prejudice and black self-doubt.[109]

In his 1931 report to the National Association for the Advancement of Colored People (NAACP), Nathan Margold offered a strategy to make segregation unconstitutional. It would be less inflammatory to focus first on graduate schools because southern whites feared that integrated elementary schools would lead to intermarriage and "mongrelize" the race. As Margold pointed out, integrated elementary schools were the eventual goal because "contacts in childhood would have a tendency to arrest the development of prejudice and its evils."[110]

The country changed radically between *Plessy v. Ferguson* and *Brown v. Board of Education*, the 1954 decision that overturned it. A stunning example was CBS broadcast of the "Ballad for Americans" on national network radio in 1939, before the television era, on the eve of World War II. Paul Robeson starred, singing and narrating the ballad. Robeson was a chocolate-black son of a slave, and a Phi Beta Kappa and Rutgers valedictorian with a Columbia law degree. Robeson was a very public figure, a star of stage, screen, and opera, internationally acclaimed from London to Moscow. On Broadway, he introduced "Old Man River" in the original Broadway production of *Showboat*. The public response to Robeson's appearance with the "Ballad for Americans" led CBS to repeat it. An in-theater audience of six hundred applauded for fifteen full minutes. The song was recorded later and became a major hit in the 1940s. In the "Ballad for Americans" this well-known black man described himself as an Italian, Pole, Jew, lawyer, doctor, and accountant—he covered the litany of all origins, professions, skills, and occupations that made up the fabric of America society. The "Ballad for Americans" opened the 1940 Republican Convention. Honorary degrees followed. World War II propaganda celebrated the American melting pot, versions of which, like Robeson's portrayal, celebrated the participation of blacks in that national stew.[111]

Propaganda of that era, depicting people of all kinds working shoulder to shoulder, was all the more powerful in contrast to the racism of fascism. Even so, improvement came at great cost. KKK members worked in sheriff's offices or for the Federal Bureau of Investigation (FBI), were active in the White Citizens' Councils movement, or owned local businesses. To force African Americans to reject the NAACP and desegregation, segregationists threatened their homes, lives, and livelihoods. Parents who joined lawsuits or sent their children to previously white-only schools exercised real courage. Many paid dearly for their victories.[112]

Although integration has not come close to realizing the hopes of blacks, Native Americans, and many whites, it has been the principal American ideological response to difference and discrimination—and it has worked for many people.[113] In a fascinating set of interchanges on cross-examination in the Virginia trial of one of the cases that were consolidated as *Brown v. Board*, NAACP lawyer and later Judge Robert Carter got the state's expert witnesses to admit that segregation harms those who are segregated.[114] His answer was an amazing testament to the power of American ideology in the teeth of segregationist Virginia.

The Founding Generation's Working Assumptions on How to Keep Democracy Alive

These then were working assumptions of the architects of the country. The founders sought to secure republican government both for the nation and the states. They understood self-government as the essence of liberty, and general welfare the encompassing object of government.

To run their government safely, they tried to disperse power, provide civilian control of the military, questioned the impact of bills of rights, and expected benefits from the partly national, partly federal character of the new nation.

The founding generation believed that to keep republican government alive the country would need more than constitutional rules distributing power among governmental bodies. To keep the republican character of the country, the new nation needed unity—to forge one nation out of its many parts. It needed education to inculcate republican principles. It needed wide dispersion of wealth to support republican government. It needed integration to forge republican society. In short, it needed a republican community, equality, and character for the security of their new democracy. Despite sectional differences and plenty of room to debate particulars, these assumptions were part of the founding generation's understanding of what would be necessary to keep their country republican.

They gave a great deal of thought to the survival of their governmental child. Time and distance have gradually separated us from our founding generation's understanding of their own creation.

2

In the Shadow of War

This chapter is devoted to exploring how the U.S. Supreme Court grappled with democracy in the face of the destructive events of the first half of the twentieth century. In the 1930s, the Court reacted to the threat to democracy with explicit protection for self-government, protection against abuse of the criminal process, and embrace of the underlying republican and democratic ideals. The country returned to its egalitarian roots, extending the vote to all adults, dispersing resources widely, reintegrating the population to reforge a single union. For the next half-century the Court's jurisprudence built on those developments, which have now been abandoned by the Roberts Court.

Contrary to the earlier assumption that a healthy democracy depended on dispersion of wealth and power, entrepreneurs claimed after the Civil War that America had been founded on laissez-faire principles, that businesses should have unimpeded and unregulated freedom to make contracts for what they wanted.[1] The Supreme Court had embraced commercial liberties by 1900 in its interpretation of the due process clauses, which prohibit deprivation of "life, liberty, or property, without due process of law." Instead of limiting due process to the judicial process, the Court interpreted the due process clauses to require reasonable legislation, and often found both federal and state regulation of business unreasonable. Populist and Progressive movements succeeded in many legislatures. But laws to protect workers, ban child labor, and protect public health and safety met the judicial axe.

Everything was reshaped in the cauldron of World War I, which was fought by soldiers from every inhabited continent and resulted in thirty-seven million casualties, including sixteen million soldiers and civilians killed by the war. The war, immigration from abroad, and African American migration northward led to renewed thinking about the meaning and requirements of democracy.[2] The NAACP (formed in 1909), the American Civil Liberties Union (ACLU, founded in 1920), and the growth of the labor movement all reflected those changes. War also led the military to experiment with mixing soldiers from different backgrounds.

But so-called patriotic private vigilantes attacked German Americans like Robert Paul Draper, a German immigrant and coal miner, lynched in Collinsville, Illinois, on rumors he was a saboteur.[3] German was yanked from school curriculums and banned in Iowa and Nebraska.[4] Race riots followed victory.[5] Religious prejudice incited laws requiring children be educated exclusively in public schools through the eighth grade.[6]

After World War I, many wanted to insulate America from events abroad but failed. Russia overthrew the Czar in 1917 and the Communists took over within months. The Russian Revolution triggered the Red Scare in the United States. Americans discredited, deported, and prosecuted Communist sympathizers. Those fears contributed to the appointment of J. Edgar Hoover in 1924 to create what became the FBI. A succession of congressional committees investigated "un-American" activities, and created blacklists of liberals, leftists, and those who stood up for the right to free speech, hire attorneys, and advocate peaceful change. Loyalty became an issue and, with it, freedom of speech.

The stock market crashed in 1929, putting a quarter of the American labor force out of work by 1933. Stockbrokers jumped from windows. The homeless congregated in "Hoovervilles," with no livelihoods or possessions. Veterans came to Washington, D.C., seeking to move up payment of bonuses earned for service in World War I, but President Hoover and General MacArthur treated them as threats and ran them out at gunpoint.[7] Labor violence grew. America had become desperate and afraid of itself. Jonathan Alter put various measures together in a picture of disaster: unemployment officially was 25 percent, but more than 37 percent of nonfarm workers had no jobs. Unemployment reached 80 percent in cities like Toledo, Ohio. Business lost 90 percent of its 1929 investment. Average income was lower than it was in 1900. If your bank failed, your savings and deposits were gone.[8]

The devastation made the political system vulnerable both here and abroad. John Steinbeck, formerly a reporter, encapsulated people's desperation in THE GRAPES OF WRATH, following refugees from the Dust Bowl, where giant black clouds of dry soil struck in the middle of the Great Depression. Unable to plant or harvest and barely able to breathe, farmers, sharecroppers, and their workers were suddenly thrown into the army of jobless Americans looking for any way to feed themselves and their families. Their poverty made them seem useless; their desperation made them seem dangerous.

Scapegoating and extremism spread. Roosevelt was attacked for addressing economic issues. The Hearst press proclaimed, "Whenever you hear a prominent American called a 'Fascist,' you can usually make up your mind that the man is simply a loyal citizen who stands up for Americanism."[9] First on a Detroit station, then CBS and, when kicked off the network, syndicated on some sixty stations, Father Charles Coughlin used his air time to attack Jews, vilify the New Deal as the "Jew Deal," and plagiarize the canards of

Joseph Goebbels, Nazi Germany's minister of propaganda. Coughlin told his audience there would be "more bullet holes in the White House than you could count with an adding machine." His supporters attacked Jews on the streets. Some planned terrorist attacks, which were foiled by the FBI.[10]

Huey Long inspired Robert Penn Warren's ALL THE KING'S MEN. As governor of Louisiana he provided infrastructure, education, and health care that also benefitted the poor and blacks. But his use of bribery, threats, and other illegal behavior made him feared as well as loved. By 1932 he had become dictator of Louisiana with power to declare election winners. Long taxed newspapers that attacked him. A unanimous U.S. Supreme Court condemned it as "a deliberate and calculated device . . . to limit the circulation of information to which the public is entitled" under the First Amendment.[11] When challenged under the Louisiana Constitution, Long responded, "I'm the Constitution here now," and boasted, "I can frighten or buy ninety-nine out of every hundred men." The other 1 percent did not stand a chance. Long's methods had been used by political machines before but he raised the scale. Already feared in national politics when he took his seat in the U.S. Senate in 1932, his populist message resonated with those down and out. Long was preparing to challenge Roosevelt for president in 1936 when he was killed by the son of a judge whose career Long had destroyed.[12] The future of democracy looked uncertain.

Breakdown of Democracies

Nazi depravity set off waves of postwar legal changes in constitutions, treaties, and international institutions to enforce them and prevent repetition of the damage the Nazis had done. The 1917 Russian Revolution, however, was the polarizing event of the twentieth century. The Bolsheviks conducted waves of violence, expropriation, and collectivization, aimed at both the former aristocracy and the peasantry which had not supported the revolution. Americans had celebrated equality as the key accomplishment of the Revolutionary War, but would soon distinguish god-fearing Americans from atheist Communists. Red Scares followed both world wars, even though neither socialism nor communism appealed to the majority of Americans. In Europe, however, the old aristocracy had much to lose. Fear had disastrous consequences.

Most Europeans were committed to democracy when the Nazis took over. But the Russian Revolution raised the apparent stakes as aristocrats and leftists feared and questioned each other's loyalty to democracy.[13] Before his takeover, less than 1 percent of the population joined Mussolini's party and they had 6 percent of the seats in the National Assembly. But Mussolini's paramilitary army terrorized political opponents and the violence exacerbated distrust. His infamous 1923 March on Rome has been characterized as a bluff—the army vastly outnumbered Mussolini's Black Shirts. Nevertheless the threat worked. As their mutual anger and distrust grew, Italian officials left Rome, the military refused to defend the government, which abdicated in frustration, and the king invited Mussolini to form a government.

The Nazis, too, took power in Germany without gaining a majority of the people's votes. Throughout the 1920s, German leadership supported competing paramilitary armies. Conservatives in government prosecuted left-wing paramilitaries, while protecting their right-wing equivalents. In 1932, only a third of Germans voted for Hitler and the Nazis, yet Field Marshall Paul von Hindenburg appointed Hitler chancellor. A disloyal German aristocracy had abandoned democracy, more afraid of a liberal victory than dictatorship. Too much wealth made the wealthy fearful.

Dictators were invited to rule Italy, Germany, Greece, Romania, and Yugoslavia. Right-wing groups seized control of Austria, Bulgaria, Estonia, Latvia, Lithuania, Poland, Portugal, and Spain. None of these countries fell to a popular uprising; popular forces instead challenged Spanish dictatorship. Dictatorship was imposed at the top, by the misnamed "right wing," claiming fear of the left. As Nancy Bermeo summarized the 1936 Greek surrender to dictatorship, "The trigger for this change—as for so many others—was an electoral outcome that frightened the Right."[14]

The Reichstag building, seat of the German legislature, burned down shortly after Hitler became chancellor, probably on his orders. He used it as an excuse to arrest Communists, including elected legislators, and take full control of government. Within months he outlawed all but the Nazi party, organized the first concentration camp for his opponents, ordered a boycott of Jewish businesses, and began removing Jews from universities and entertainment. The exodus of scientists, intellectuals, Jews, and other persecuted minorities began.

These events shaped the U.S. Supreme Court's understanding of democracy and its role toward it. With millions out of work, hate and scapegoating in the air, many Nazi supporters and admirers in the United States, the threat to American institutions was clear. But this country took a different path. Before the end of the decade, Congress reduced the violence in labor disputes in 1937 with a statute creating procedures for collective bargaining, approved the Social Security program, unemployment compensation, and welfare for those unable to provide for themselves. These programs had important political consequences, not least by reducing some of the incentives for the legions of low-level workers required to intimidate, bribe or fix ballots. During the Great Depression, and for many years thereafter, Americans saw a common stake in each other's welfare. By the end of World War II, American democracy no longer appeared to be under significant stress, and political machines were in steep decline.

The 1930s Supreme Court

The justices were aware of world events. But no cases addressing the barbarity of Hitler,[15] Lenin, or Stalin,[16] nor their violation of human rights, reached the Supreme Court in the 1930s. The Court considered cases arising from the Red Scare in the United States, and it resisted punishing peaceful advocacy. Germany was involved in property and commercial cases arising from World War I, especially the War Claims Act of 1928 and the Trading with the Enemy Act of 1917. German legal practices were sometimes treated as examples for proper handling of domestic legal issues. Hitler's name does not appear in Supreme Court opinions before June of 1943 when the United States had been at war with Germany for a year and a half.[17]

Justice Louis Brandeis had a major labor-management practice, trusted by both sides, while deeply involved in Progressive politics. He famously feared "bigness"—the power of large, governmental or private institutions to dominate individuals. When a large employer told Brandeis, "We can't run the risk of our property being destroyed by these 6,000 men," Brandeis responded, "How can the 6,000 men run the risk of their lives being destroyed by you?"[18] His well-known book, OTHER PEOPLE'S MONEY, impressed President Wilson. The book sought to break up the trusts, attacked their support among the bankers, urged bank regulation, and contributed to the founding of the Federal Reserve System.

Brandeis also urged industrial democracy. In 1915, in testimony to the Commission on Industrial Relations, Brandeis said:

> We are as free politically, perhaps, as free as it is possible for us to be. Every male has his voice and vote; and the law has endeavored to enable, and has succeeded practically, in enabling him to exercise his political franchise without fear. He therefore has his part; and certainly can secure an adequate part in the government in the country in all of its political relations. . . .
>
> On the other hand, in dealing with industrial problems the position of the ordinary worker is exactly the reverse. The individual employee has no effective voice or vote.[19]

In the two years prior to his Supreme Court appointment in 1916, Brandeis became leader of the American Zionist movement, heading a committee to assist endangered European Jews. He would found the American Jewish Congress, the Palestine Endowment Fund, and the Palestine Cooperative Company. Zionism expressed Brandeis's understanding of American values: the same right for Jews to a homeland as other nationalities have, in order to strengthen their claim to equality among the world's peoples. Palestine, he argued, must not be claimed by war but by purchase and settlement,[20] "with clean hands . . . [so] as to ennoble the Jewish people. Otherwise, it will not be worth having."[21] He compared Zionism to the recent independence and unification of Italy, Greece, Bulgaria, Ireland, and the more short-lived Servia.[22] For Brandeis, support for justice, fairness, and democracy everywhere, in service to "the brotherhood of man," makes one a better American.[23]

Long before Hitler came to power, Brandeis studied the burdens imposed on Jews in Europe—from the Dreyfus affair in France to the pogroms in Russia; from German curbs on Jewish access to university, bureaucratic, and military careers to their continued social disadvantages in England and, despite the opportunities in "this hospitable country," even in the United States.[24] Brandeis attributed much of the risks and restrictions imposed on Jews to the common assumption that people necessarily had either to dominate or be dominated by others.[25]

For Brandeis, Progressivism and Zionism were entwined in a unified concept of democracy and justice, allowing everyone to flourish both for their own and society's benefit.[26] "Democracy . . . insists that the full development of each individual is not only a right, but a duty to society, and that our best hope for civilization lies not in uniformity, but in wide differentiation."[27] At the time, Jews could fulfill neither their democratic rights nor their duties.

Hitler's racism stung Brandeis's American, brotherly, democratic, and Jewish instincts. In November 1933 he warned his daughter that America needed to curb the size of institutions or "we are apt to get Fascist manifestations."[28] On June 13, 1934, Brandeis wrote in a letter to Rabbi Stephen Wise "how deeply perverted German Jewish judgment" is for trying to stay in Germany during Hitler's rampage, and expressed hope that "Palestine will purify the refugees."[29] With anti-semitism rife in America, he told Rabbi Wise to "[c]ompare Father Coughlin's talk [with] the praise of Jews by Cardinal McConnel [sic] of Mass." A year later, referring again to Europe, he wrote, "there is no hope for anyone who does not emigrate" from Germany.[30]

When Benjamin Cardozo took his seat on the Supreme Court in 1932, the era's racial prejudices reached the court almost immediately. California had prosecuted George Morrison, alleging he allowed a noncitizen of Japanese ancestry, identified only as Mr. K. Osaki, to cultivate land. Stipulated facts recited that California had shown no evidence that Mr. Osaki was a noncitizen. The state argued that his racial appearance was sufficient to shift the burden of proving Mr. Osaki's citizenship to the defendant, Morrison, without any evidence by the state. The Supreme Court dismissed the appeal without considering the merits, letting stand the decision of the lower court finding no constitutional violation.[31] But when the case returned the following year, Cardozo wrote that the court had now discovered that one of the defendants was white, implying he could not easily have proven Mr. Osaki's citizenship. His opinion concluded that it was unfair to shift the burden of proving citizenship to the defendants.[32]

A month after his opinion in *Morrison*, Cardozo wrote in a letter to future Justice Felix Frankfurter about Hitler's behavior, "the United States has its own record of brutalities, as the poor negroes know, but nothing quite so bad as this."[33] And early in 1936, Cardozo sent another note to Frankfurter in which he emphasized, "[w]e need another [William Lloyd] Garrison who will cry out unceasingly until all the world shall hear" about what Hitler and the Nazis were doing.[34]

Justice Harlan Fiske Stone, on the Court since 1925, was also blunt: "I have been deeply concerned about the increasing racial and religious intolerance which seems to bedevil the world, and which I greatly fear may be augmented in this country."[35] Depression and inequality aggravated the problem. Stone expressed concern with "the unequal distribution of national income" in the United States and feared a crisis.[36] He alternately ridiculed and condemned the Führer.[37] His former clerk, Louis Lusky, adds that after 1937 Hitler "probably . . . deserves much of the credit" for increased "sensitivity" to abuse of political and religious freedoms, racial equality, and the constitutional protections of criminal procedure; Hitler "and his fellow dictators revealed the ghastly consequence of drowning those values in a sea of conformist fervor" so that acts infringing those rights in the United States were increasingly likely to be "seen as symptoms of the same killing disease."[38]

Palko—Essential Freedoms

In 1926, Justice van Devanter wrote: "The due process of law clause in the Fourteenth Amendment . . . require[s] . . . that state action . . . shall be consistent with the fundamental principles of liberty and justice which lie at the base of all our civil and political institutions."[39] In context the language was conservative—*only* such principles would be protected. Cardozo rephrased Van Devanter's phrase for a similarly exclusive purpose, to protect only those "principle[s] of justice so rooted in the traditions and conscience of our people as to be ranked as fundamental."[40] Their language shortly acquired a different meaning. The Weimar Republic that Hitler shattered was itself built on a longer history of constitutional monarchy. Before Hitler, Lenin had suppressed Russia's brief democratic experience. Between those despots, democracy fell in much of Europe. Some sought a dictator in the United States. Van Devanter's and Cardozo's language began to assume prophetic proportions.

Cardozo delivered the Court's opinion in *Palko v. Connecticut* shortly before the heart attack and stroke that ended his service on the Court, and soon his life.[41] Palka—the Court misspelled his name[42]—claimed a privilege against self-incrimination. He died because the Court refused to overturn his death sentence. But Cardozo's opinion was about liberty and democracy. Without the privilege, Cardozo wrote, "there would remain the need to give protection against torture, physical or mental." Cardozo wanted to be sure to protect those freedoms without which "neither liberty nor justice would exist." He regarded "freedom of thought, and speech . . . [as] the matrix, the indispensable condition, of nearly every other form of freedom."[43] And, quoting van Devanter, he wanted to protect "those 'fundamental principles of liberty and justice which lie at the base of all our civil and political institutions.'"[44]

Palko was all but unanimous. The Court's conservatives believed the Court should review the reasonableness of legislation; they were not troubled by the discretion inherent in *Palko.* Cardozo's language could be read either as defining freedom or as a statement about cause and effect, about what could unravel freedom. In context it was conservative. But the standard was capacious. With *Palko* as its guide, the Court could look out for democracy, free government and a free society. Cardozo's opinion put essential liberties and the system of free government within the Fourteenth Amendment's protection. In that way, *Palko* symbolized much of what the Hughes Court did in response to significant failures in the legal system.

But the Court had not yet embraced the Bill of Rights, protecting only what was essential. Justice Hugo Black, in his first term, joined the opinion. He would later insist on the Court's responsibility to enforce the entire Bill of Rights, arguing *Palko* gave the Court too much discretion. Black wanted to constrain the Court by interpreting the Fourteenth Amendment due process clause to incorporate only the Bill of Rights. In 1937, *Palko* marked the Court's direction, but not with clarity.

Flash forward. *Palko* would suit Justices Felix Frankfurter, William Rehnquist, and John Marshall Harlan II. For them, *Palko* imposed few Fourteenth Amendment obligations on the states, certainly not the entire Bill of Rights.[45] Instead they would be able to pick and choose whatever they thought necessary to "ordered liberty."

Harlan and Black thought the states were much more constrained by the Fourteenth Amendment than Frankfurter or Rehnquist. For Black, the problem with *Palko* was the discretion it allowed.[46] For Harlan, discretion was the advantage of *Palko*.[47] But the standard, what is essential for free society, could mean either more or less than these justices assumed. It is, in effect, open to the lessons of subsequent history.

Carolene Products—Democracy at the Center

The Supreme Court deepened protection for democracy in the 1930s, protecting speech, press,[48] and the right to vote,[49] attacking the White Primary,[50] and broadening protection of minorities.[51] But the Court also began to practice judicial restraint, deferring to the legislature about whether policy was reasonable. In *United States v. Carolene Products Co*,[52] the Court simply decided it was Congress's job to decide whether skimmed milk could be shipped in interstate commerce with additives to resemble regular milk or cream. Writing the decision in *Carolene Products*, Stone was concerned that judicial restraint could reverse the Court's progress on speech, press, voting, and equal protection. He wanted to prevent that from happening.

Stone explained to Judge Lehman, "I was greatly disturbed by the attacks on the Court and the Constitution last year, for one consequence of the program of 'judicial reform' might well result in breaking down the guaranties of individual liberty."[53] At stake was the protection of democracy.

Stone added a footnote to the *Carolene Products* decision.[54] The first paragraph was suggested by Chief Justice Hughes: "There may be narrower scope for operation of the presumption of constitutionality when legislation appears on its face to be within a specific prohibition of the Constitution, such as those of the first ten amendments, which are deemed equally specific when held to be embraced within the Fourteenth." Their language focused on the text; a year after *Palko*, however, it suggested protecting the entire Bill of Rights aggressively. The full paragraph cited two First Amendment cases that went beyond the word "speech" to the silent display of a red flag and a licensing scheme. Those citations made clear the First Amendment protects the people from censorship. Cardozo had treated the First Amendment as "the indispensable condition, of nearly every other form of freedom." In the succeeding paragraphs, Hughes and Stone made it the foundation of democracy.

The second paragraph focused squarely on protecting democracy:

It is unnecessary to consider now whether legislation which restricts those political processes which can ordinarily be expected to bring about repeal of un-
desirable legislation, is to be subjected to more exacting judicial scrutiny under
the general prohibitions of the Fourteenth Amendment than are most other
types of legislation . . . [citing cases on] restrictions upon the right to vote . . . ;
on restraints upon the dissemination of information . . . ; on interferences with
political organizations . . . ; as to prohibition of peaceable assembly.

Stone chose citations protecting the democratic process of political change,
including rights to speak, publish, assemble, associate and vote—all of which
were under stress in 1938. Protecting the process of change required protecting access to ideas and prohibiting censorship. And the logic of democracy
required that all citizens be included, even marginalized groups like blacks,
Jehovah's witnesses, and leftists—*e pluribus unum* applied to democracy, the
process of change, and First Amendment freedoms; all were intertwined.
Stone added a citation to a rousing Brandeis defense of free speech, which
made clear that democracy is not for sissies; it takes courage and principle.[55]
The third paragraph addresses inclusiveness directly:

Nor need we enquire whether similar considerations enter into the review of
statutes directed at particular religious . . . or national . . . or racial minorities . . . : whether prejudice against discrete and insular minorities may be a
special condition, which tends seriously to curtail the operation of those political processes ordinarily to be relied upon to protect minorities, and which may
call for a correspondingly more searching judicial inquiry.

Stone cited decisions protecting parents' rights to send children to religious
schools or teach them German or Japanese in an era when mobs attacked
Germans, states barred Japanese from jobs, and the federal government
would soon "intern" Japanese Americans on the West Coast. After referring
again to the voting cases that emphasized continuing racial injustice, Stone's
final citations made clear that democracy provides states no right to burden
those outside their borders or not allowed to vote. Democracy depends on
inclusion and representation; anything less is seriously flawed. Stone thereby
channeled the patriots' "no taxation without representation," broadening it
to all kinds of legislation and articulating it as a statement of a fundamental
principle of democracy: inclusion matters; *e pluribus unum.*

Stone's point goes further. The third paragraph refers to discrimination—
"statutes directed at particular . . . minorities." People have the right to govern
themselves, but democracy provides no justification for governing others,

those not included in the voting, speaking, deciding, and self-governing population. *E pluribus unum* matters for self-government.

Other decisions also suggest that members of the Court already understood that segregation would eventually be held unconstitutional.[56] The right to speak is not enough; integration matters as it had in the working assumptions of the founding generations.

Stone's former clerk, Louis Lusky, wrote that paragraphs 2 and 3 "assume . . . two national objectives—government by the people, and government for the whole people." Legislatures should "be controlled by the people . . . and . . . weigh impartially the competing needs of all segments of the population" to reach a "fair compromise among such needs."[57] Legislatures may never be that good, but several constitutional provisions prohibit exclusion from the process.

The Court decided *Carolene Products* without Cardozo, terminally ill, and Justice Reed who recused himself. Hughes, Brandeis, and Justice Owen J. Roberts joined Stone's opinion. Justices Pierce Butler and Black concurred only in the result. Butler preferred aggressive review of economic regulation. Black became a strong advocate for enforcing the Bill of Rights and protecting democracy, but on grounds closer to the textualism of paragraph 1. His note to Justice Stone suggests he supported the rights Stone wanted to protect, but objected to language suggesting increased judicial power.[58] Only Justice James C. McReynolds dissented, although without opinion.

Beginning early in the twentieth century, the Supreme Court's work showed growing awareness of legal interconnections. The Equal Protection Clause and First Amendment alone cannot protect minorities and dissenters. Their protection is tied to voting, labor, and commercial rights,[59] and protection of life and liberty from imprisonment, lynch mob, vindictive officials, or prejudice.[60] By the time World War II broke out in Europe, the Court had developed a relatively sophisticated understanding of democracy and its links to various other areas of the law.

Carolene Products has been read more broadly than *Palko*. Both cases addressed self-government, but *Carolene Products* was more precise in its commands. The mechanisms of democratic governance had to be protected, including but not limited to speech and voting rights. Racial, religious, and ethnic groups had to be protected lest they be not merely disenfranchised but also abused. The *Carolene Products* Court had no doubts that some of those groups were being abused as they wrote.

Carolene Products would yield a sharp ideological division between supporters and critics. John Ely termed the Warren court a *Carolene Products* Court, although that designation would apply as well to a good deal of the groundwork laid by the Hughes, Stone, and Vinson Courts. Justices Brennan and Marshall carried the spirit of *Carolene Products* with them throughout their service on the Court. The Rehnquist Court unequivocally rejected it. Rehnquist preferred the *Palko* formula—it allowed him more discretion about what not to protect.[61]

Neither case fully defined either free or democratic. Americans are so used to the terms that their meanings seem obvious, and definition unnecessary. But democracy is a continuum, from elections as a minimum, provided that they actually determine who runs the government, to maximally competitive, participatory democracy. The science of democracy applies to the continuum with different outlooks at either end. The range matters—a subject we will return to.

Both decisions, however, reflect some of the working assumptions of the founding generations, the importance of a Bill of Rights, the essential unity of the people, the importance of inclusion and integration of the population, to which the Court added a clear understanding of the morality of democracy, while its deference to Congress and state legislatures supported their thrust toward workers' rights and the wide dispersion of economic resources.

3

Export

In this chapter and in chapter 4, we trace the influence of American ideals and solutions abroad, in an attempt to find out how they have been understood and applied. To blunt some opposition to looking abroad, we will focus on values with clear American roots, and follow them in American hands to the international stage. Chapter 4 examines the implications courts abroad found in those American values. This argument will not satisfy Justices Scalia or Thomas but it should inform reasonable minds.

World War II affected everyone in the United States who was serving in the military, producing for the war effort, supporting the troops, or making do with rationed foodstuffs and products made from the iron, steel, rubber, and other components needed for the military. Democracy needed to be defended territorially against foreign enemies and against sabotage and revolution at home. War pushed the United States toward unity, repression, control, and both tolerance and prejudice.

Squelching freedom and murdering millions, Hitler and Stalin dramatically altered what it meant to protect democracy. Injustice abroad led to a redefinition of what it meant to be democratic. Strong currents in U.S. law rejected the German model and protected human rights, equality, and democracy. In the 1940s and well into the 1980s, the Supreme Court expanded freedom, protected the people, and shaped a vision of a more perfect democracy. Germany turned "law" into a route to the gallows but the Supreme Court rejected the "third degree," then the main technique for criminal investigation across the world, and insisted on careful criminal procedures.[1] The Court connected prejudice and the powerlessness of young black men with the likelihood of unjust convictions. Members of the Court understood that criminal justice, equal rights, and democracy depend on each other. In a wide variety of cases the Court made the protection of human rights fundamental to American democracy, and largely led global development of humanitarian law, to great worldwide admiration.

While the Nazis persecuted Jews, the U.S. Supreme Court developed the protections of the First Amendment religion clauses; but not at first. In 1935 Lillian and William Gobitis, aged twelve and ten, were expelled from the Minersville, Pennsylvania, public schools for refusing to salute the flag.[2] To the children, who were Jehovah's Witnesses, saluting the flag violated the biblical injunction against idolatry. In 1940 Frankfurter wrote for seven justices in *Minersville School Dist. v. Gobitis*, that the legislature should decide what "program or exercise will best promote in the minds of children who attend the common schools an attachment to the institutions of their country," that is, lead them to be patriotic. National unity justified coercion. He argued their decision complied with the teaching of *Carolene Products* because members of the Jehovah's Witnesses could try to change school rules politically.

Justice Harlan Fiske Stone wrote years before, "all human experience teaches us that a moral issue cannot be suppressed or settled by making its supporters martyrs."[3] Dissenting now, Stone touched on the threat of war: "Government . . . may compel citizens to give military service . . . and subject them to military training despite their religious objections. . . . It may suppress religious practices dangerous to morals, and presumably those also which are inimical to public safety, health and good order." But: "The very essence of . . . [constitutionally protected] liberty . . . is the freedom of the individual from compulsion as to what he shall think and what he shall say, at least where the compulsion is to bear false witness to his religion." *Gobitis* generated criticism along with violence directed at Jehovah's Witnesses. West Virginia then required the flag salute. Officials expelled children who were Jehovah's Witnesses and threatened to confine them in reformatories for "criminally inclined juveniles" and to prosecute their parents for causing delinquency.[4] By then the United States was at war with Nazi Germany, which had already overrun most of Europe. Religious intolerance would no longer find a home in the Court .

West Virginia State Bd. of Ed. v. Barnette,[5] overruled *Gobitis*. Justice Jackson explained why, in language that has become an icon of First Amendment jurisprudence: in America "no official . . . can prescribe what shall be orthodox in politics, nationalism, religion or other matters of opinion."[6] Speech could not be coerced for unity.

Both unity and religious tolerance led to the wall of separation between church and state. *Everson v. Board*, decided in 1947, addressed state-provided nondiscriminatory free school bus service to public, private, and religious schools. The Court connected the Establishment Clause to the history of religious strife, explaining that religious war, persecutions, torture, and murder had been going on for centuries before and during the colonization of America. Punishments were inflicted for speaking disrespectfully, nonattendance at church, expressions of disbelief in church doctrine, and failure to pay taxes or tithes to support them.[7] Given that history, the Court held the First Amendment required a wall between church and state, separating governmental from religious functions. While strongly endorsing separation, the Court pointed out that nondiscriminatory provision of nonreligious, public services like busing, do not breach the wall.[8]

A year later, in *McCollum v. Board*,[9] the Court applied *Everson* to reject a multifaith arrangement for separate religious classes in public schools during the school day to children with parental consent. The First Amendment prohibited funds for religious education itself.[10] The Court's decision was crucial for the common school movement. If nondiscriminatory policies alone satisfied the First Amendment, state support for religiously segregated education would have been constitutional. Instead, public funds supported unified education in community schools.

The Court's most spectacular wartime failure was in sustaining convictions under the Japanese exclusion orders.[11] Fear and prejudice contributed to the internment of Japanese Americans—imprisoning them in camps or housing them in horse stables or similar accommodations for the duration of the war—without charges, hearings, or the ability to secure their businesses or goods and effects. Most had to start over after the war. Documents have since been uncovered showing that the government lied to the Court, concealing evidence showing no military need for rounding up and incarcerating 120,000 Japanese Americans from the Pacific states.[12] Decades later Congress appropriated funds as compensation, though they were meager. The decisions are now remembered as a shameful error on the way toward the systematic rejection of Nazi racism.

Nazi beliefs about genetics labeled Jews, Gypsies, homosexuals, and others as "unfit," except for slaughter or medical experiments in concentration camps, testing the effects of torture and weapons on prisoners. German doctors injured, infected, and operated without anesthetics to test so-called cures. They tried to alter people physically, or change the orientation of homosexuals.

Nazi atrocities ended American infatuation with eugenics, sterilizing, or executing the "unfit." In 1942, the Court used a sterilization case, *Skinner v. Oklahoma*, to reinstate protection for fundamental rights under the due process clause. *Skinner* overturned an Oklahoma law, which required sterilization of some prisoners who had been convicted three times. After expressing disapproval of distinctions in the Oklahoma law, the Court addressed the significance of the sterilization remedy. Its language fairly smoked with disgust at Nazi forays into biological "purity": "We are dealing here with legislation which involves one of the basic civil rights of man. Marriage and procreation are fundamental to the very existence and survival of the race. The power to sterilize, if exercised, may have subtle, far-reaching and devastating effects.

In evil or reckless hands it can cause races or types which are inimical to the dominant group to wither and disappear."[13] Germany flaunted a theory of racial superiority, and snubbed Jesse Owens, the African-American who won gold at the 1936 Olympics in Berlin. The Supreme Court soon handed down groundbreaking civil rights cases addressing intolerance and inequality. African Americans had been barred from voting in southern primary elections. The Court attacked racially exclusive primaries in the so-called white primary cases, beginning in the 1920s,[14] although stagnating in the 1930s.[15] Before the war ended, the Court denied that a state could merely repeal its discriminatory statute and let political parties do as they pleased; states bore responsibility to provide actual equal access to the voting booth.[16]

Shelley v. Kraemer held courts could not constitutionally enforce racially restrictive real estate covenants.[17] Without court action, private contracts may be unenforceable. Attorneys recognized immediately that private individuals can often do what government officials, including judges, cannot. Judicial enforcement of such decisions would not violate the Constitution. An additional premise beside court action must determine which private actions or agreements could be enforced. This is known to lawyers as the "state action" issue, and a satisfactory distinction has eluded the courts. Nevertheless, no court has suggested that racial covenants, or racially restricted primaries, are ever going to be enforced.

Another series of decisions between 1938 and 1950 held that African Americans could not be segregated in state institutions of higher education because the education offered was not equal. Inequalities that mattered included school reputation, faculty quality, and the ability to get to know other future local practitioners of one's profession.[18] Those decisions demonstrated that separate could not be equal, although it still took courage in 1954 for the Warren Court to announce the logical conclusion in *Brown* that segregation is "inherently unequal."[19]

Apportionment of seats in the Illinois legislature had not changed since 1901, although the proportion of people living in cities had changed drastically. That affected all urbanites—immigrants who had flocked to cities, blacks who had come north, and workers in big urban factories; all of whom were represented in much lower proportions than farmers and rural residents. Similar malapportionment affected legislatures all over the country. Despite the importance of the vote to democratic government, and the Court's other efforts to update its treatment of democracy, the justices would not budge on malapportionment. Justice Frankfurter described it as a "political thicket" inappropriate for courts.[20]

The Court had resurrected the equal protection clause, protecting equality in graduate schools, housing and most pertinently in primary elections. It had made clear that African Americans had the same right to vote as whites, but, apparently, they had no right to have their votes counted equally with people in other districts. Logic is one of the drivers of the law and this was contradictory. The Court would follow the logic of what it had already done. But democracy would continue to elude those who remained underrepresented for nearly two more decades.

The Supreme Court also delayed making the Bill of Rights applicable to the states. That issue was raised in *Adamson v. California*, which reached the Court in 1947.[21] On the basis of the historical work of Horace Edgar Flack,[22] Justice Black explained how the Thirty-Ninth Congress incorporated the Bill of Rights in the "privileges or immunities" clause of the Fourteenth Amendment, thereby requiring the states to live up to national standards.[23] The Court rejected Justice Black's argument.[24] Led by Frankfurter, the Court would only apply the Bill of Rights if it were essential to ordered liberty, the test designed in *Palko*. Although Justice Black lost the historical argument, beginning a decade after *Adamson*, the Court incorporated the vast majority of provisions of the Bill of Rights within the prohibitions of the Fourteenth Amendment.[25]

Global Standards

International legal developments, like developments in the United States, moved in opposition to the Nazi experience. The Nuremberg Trials, the formation of the United Nations, and the preparation of the Universal Declaration of Human Rights were all aimed to assure that Nazi totalitarianism would never happen again and that no other power would inflict such damage on the world. Rather than reluctant guests at an American party, countries that had joined the Allied powers were enthusiastic participants.

Treasury Secretary Henry M. Morgenthau Jr., a confidant of President Roosevelt, returned from Europe seeking retribution. U.S. government lawyers wanted formal trials that would demonstrate Nazi transgressions unequivocally. They questioned, however, whether Nazis could legally be tried for crimes that hadn't previously been defined by international or other relevant law, and struggled to construct charges that would pass those strict standards, in order to establish the legitimacy of the proceedings. Barely a month before the German surrender and before their plans could be readied for the president's approval, Roosevelt died. The lawyers would have to take their concerns to President Harry S. Truman and respond to the flood of moral concerns that came with the end of the war.

In the 1940s, movie houses showed Movietone and Pathé News clips between double features. They were my first images of the concentration camps. GIs from all races, creeds, and parts of the country liberated survivors at Auschwitz, Dachau, Bergen-Belsen and other camps. Newsreels showed piles of stiff, naked bodies. Those who survived were so emaciated they looked more like the walking dead. America and much of the world were outraged. Nazi racism spared few minorities. They were particularly venomous toward Jews, but gays, Gypsies, dissidents, and so-called non-Aryans as well felt the brunt of their murderous rampage throughout central and Eastern Europe. The Soviets, having sustained huge losses fighting the Nazis, were determined to see them punished. The Allies shaped the Four Power London Charter out of which came the Nuremberg Principles, to be applied at the Nuremberg Trials of Nazi war criminals from 1945–46, later codified by the International Law Commission of the United Nations in 1950. The principles were limited to crimes with a connection to peace or war, "war crimes," and "crimes against humanity." War crimes included "murder, ill-treatment or deportation to slave-labour or for any other purpose of civilian population . . . [and] murder or ill-treatment of prisoners of war . . . killing of hostages, plunder of public or private property, wanton destruction of cities, towns, or villages, or devastation not justified by military necessity." Crimes against humanity included "[m]urder, extermination, enslavement, deportation and other inhuman acts done against any civilian population, or persecutions on political, racial or religious grounds . . . in execution of or in connexion with any crime against peace or any war crime." Both provisions included specifics alongside the generic "ill-treatment" and "inhuman acts."

Nazi depravity temporarily united the United Nations, from its founding in 1945 and across the emerging Iron Curtain, to prevent a Nazi or similar regime from rising from the ashes of the Third Reich. Hitler and the Nazis, along with Stalin and the Soviets, had been responsible, directly or indirectly, for the death of some sixty million people. Nazi slaughter accounted for some two-thirds of the Jewish population of prewar Europe. The entire world was affected by the war and German and Russian war crimes. Germany had occupied almost all of continental Europe, from France through much of European Russia. Troops throughout the world suffered casualties. Delegates shared the hope that this new international organization and its work could help to prevent the reemergence of such a regime.

Moral Revulsion

The UN Universal Declaration of Human Rights (UDHR) reflects the world's reaction to Nazism and determination to prevent its repetition. It took two years, two General Assembly sessions, and many commissions and committees to translate revulsion into the Declaration. Eleanor Roosevelt chaired the seventeen-member UN Commission on Human Rights, with representatives from every continent, all major religious blocks, and countries at various stages of development. UN staff provided a report relating draft sections to provisions of then existing national constitutions. The UDHR would be tied to both preexisting and subsequently enacted constitutional language of member states.

The delegates were quite familiar with Nazi brutality. One high official described Nazism as "applied biology," referring to the Nazi's differentiation between the "master race" and "useless eaters"—the old, infirm, and terminally ill in nursing homes, asylums, and hospitals who were starved or executed along with despised minorities, and those who opposed or showed little attachment to the regime. Brutality toward non-Aryans extended to labor and sex slavery. And Nazi differentiation between German Aryans and everyone else brought delegates from the rest of the world together. Virtually every clause in the document reflected those reactions. It was drafted in the hope that specifications of liberties and protections for human rights would help sustain free and democratic government and block the brutality of tyrants.

Nazis thoroughly perverted law. Crimes were vaguely stated; guilt often depended on the courts' and prosecutors' whims.[26] Delegates, by contrast, were determined to ban so-called *ex post facto* laws, which punished actions that were legal at the time they were taken. Delegates also wanted to eradicate evils addressed by the war crimes trials in Nuremberg and Japan. However, it was not clear whether prior law incorporated the Nuremberg principles. The Nuremberg principles state fundamental rules whose violation was inherently wrong, a concept that is known to lawyers as *malum in se*, that also means that everyone, Nazis included, should have understood the wrongfulness of such acts. But that justification of the Nuremberg rules would be controversial. To protect both the trials *and* the *ex post facto* prohibition, the delegates stated fundamental rights which predated the UDHR in the law of some countries, if not all, put a form of *ex post facto* clause in Article 11, and condemned acts or omissions which were illegal "under national or international law"—a compromise that arguably but ambiguously incorporated the Nuremberg principles. They also drove home requirements of fairness and procedural regularity in Articles 9–11, prohibiting "arbitrary arrest, detention or exile" and requiring "a fair and public hearing by an independent and impartial tribunal" and "all the guarantees necessary for his defence."

American courts had long gone further than the UDHR in finding unwritten fundamental rights,[27] later grounded on the Fourteenth Amendment. Although that became controversial by the early twentieth century, three areas of unwritten or at least inexplicit fundamental rights remain constitutionally protected: the rights to travel, privacy, and vote. Delegates were wary of the American approach. Instead of privacy, they addressed marriage and procreation by requiring gender equality and consent. Muslim delegates objected; Saudi Arabia abstained.

In the UDHR, equality is a moral imperative underlying the entire document. Twenty-eight of the thirty articles begin with "all," "everyone," or "no one." Article 30, applies to "any State, group or person." Article 16, about marriage, uses "men and women," "the intending spouses," and "the family" as implicitly universal. In doing so, the UDHR explicitly entitles everyone to all the rights outlined. The Declaration also asserts "[a]ll are equal before the law," proscribes discrimination, and requires "equal protection of the law."[28]

The Nazis treated non-Aryans as "legally dead," without rights or claim to their goods, contracts, jobs, or persons. That led to Article 6, which protects the right to be recognized "as a person before the law." "Code" countries, whose laws were loosely based on a Roman code, once recognized "civil death," but it had largely disappeared.[29] In reaction to Nazi practices, the UDHR made it clear that one's personhood could not be denied or abolished.

Other Nazi abuses are similarly condemned in language adjusted to incorporate new and different experience. Slavery, servitude, and the slave trade are prohibited "in all their forms."[30] "Cruel, inhuman, or degrading treatment" are prohibited whether common or unusual.[31] "Arbitrary interference with [one's] privacy, family, home, or correspondence" are prohibited but the Declaration adds "honor and reputation," which receive no constitutional protection here.[32] Protection for "freedom of movement" is analogous to our right to travel,[33] and the UDHR explicitly protects property.[34] Protections for asylum, and "nationality" respond to Nazi dislocation.[35] Article 18 protects freedom of religion, without addressing religious establishment, but protects the right, in public or private, "to manifest one's religion . . . by teaching, practice, worship, and observance," thereby limiting what established religions can require. The right to change one's faith, controversial because of views expressed by Muslim representatives, was included by majority vote as a part of religious freedom.

American wartime propaganda stressed the "four freedoms," including freedom from want. The Constitution, however, is silent on welfare rights.

State constitutions have incorporated welfare rights, beginning with a right to education. During the Great Depression, states took responsibility for the needy. During the war, caring for the needy became a war aim, contrasting with Nazi efforts to eliminate the frail and vulnerable. The UDHR made caring for the needy obligatory. It adopted neither a socialist version of collective responsibility, nor a free market stance that left welfare entirely to individuals. The UDHR protected rights to education and to work—including the rights to choose where to work for a fair wage with reasonable hours, holidays, and vacations, as well as the right to organize and to protect those rights—and it made the state responsible to assist where those necessities were otherwise out of reach.[36]

Thus the UDHR went beyond the U.S. Constitution, although without tying political rights or the democratic form of government to any degree of economic equality.

Soviet definitions of *democracy* made the word nearly unusable in the UDHR. Nevertheless the Soviet delegates agreed that people are entitled to self-government. By World War II, the general rule had become universal adult suffrage, although still racially limited in the United States. The UDHR stated explicitly: "Everyone has the right to take part in the government of his country" and "elections . . . shall be by universal and equal suffrage and . . . by secret ballot."[37] Each of the articles dealing with self-government begins with the pronoun *everyone*.

When the UDHR was adopted in 1948, separate but equal was still the general obligation under the equal protection clause as defined by the U.S. Supreme Court. But the Court continued to make progress against racial exclusion in southern primaries,[38] home ownership,[39] and education.[40] By clarifying the contradiction between separation and equality, it continued undermining *Plessy v. Ferguson*.

Delegates disagreed whether enemies of democracy were entitled to advocate their ideas. Russians questioned whether Nazis had speech rights. Some, including the Soviet Union, did not accept electoral competition. Nevertheless, the UDHR protected democratic rights by which voters choose—whether as an individual right to make up one's own mind, the people's collective right to self-government, or aspects of electoral competition which had somewhat different implications in the delegates' minds. It also protected freedom of expression and information,[41] freedom of association and assembly,[42] and access to public office[43] as well as against some hate speech,[44] as did many postwar constitutions, particularly in deeply divided countries like India. Overall, despite Russian objections to some democratic language, the UDHR condemns devices that entrench power and deny popular control.

Two principles underlie the structure of the self-government provisions, universal inclusion in the governing electorate and political competition.

The word *democratic* appears only in Article 29, which prohibits restricting rights except to "secur[e] . . . the rights and freedoms of others and of meeting the just requirements of morality, public order and the general welfare in a democratic society." Similar language has been incorporated in the constitutions of Germany, Canada, Greece, Japan, South Africa, Sweden, and Turkey.

Finally, Article 8—protecting "the right to an effective remedy" for violating fundamental rights—is unique. Rights without remedies are mere prayers. The UDHR insists on the reality. The UDHR and the principles it adopted remain part of international law.

By the late 1940s, law reflected global moral revulsion to the Nazi war crimes. The legal standards established in Washington, DC, and in Nuremberg, and the UDHR developed by the UN Commission on Human Rights and adopted by the United Nations—then meeting in Lake Success, New York—would have a long reach.

Postwar America

The UDHR mirrored the founders' emphasis on dispersion of power, education of the entire population, and hostility to monopoly. Noteworthy examples of economically egalitarian thinking in the United States include the war and excess profits taxes, which treated war as a common obligation and not as a business opportunity.[45]

Scientists began studying the relationship of democracy to the melting pot in World War II. Black regiments served in World War II; many distinguished themselves with courage and skill. By the end of the war, black soldiers served in white regiments to meet shortages of available manpower.[46] The military deliberately mixed white soldiers regardless of the language they spoke, where they came from, or where they prayed. For the War Department, Samuel Stouffer polled soldiers during the war to discover the war's impact on the men, including attitudes toward men of different racial and religious backgrounds with whom they served. Through his tears, my father-in-law described witnessing a race war among American troops in France when a white soldier killed a black soldier crossing the white's ship even though the black soldier was acting under orders. Within moments soldiers of both races were shooting each other across the dock. Stouffer found incidents like that did not define what most of the troops brought home in their hearts.[47] Truman famously integrated both black and white troops during the war in Korea. By 1951, both black and white troops in integrated units expected race relations to improve while whites in segregated units did not.[48] Serving together changed the attitudes of many soldiers for the better.

The domestic moral universe was also changing. Baseball broke the color bar seven years before *Brown*, although it was not an easy victory. Jackie Robinson endured vicious racial attacks and took seriously his role as African American spokesman on political and racial issues.

Waves of refugees from Southern and Eastern Europe reinforced some prejudices. Severe quotas, from the 1920s through the 1950s, favored Northern European immigrants and virtually excluded Asians. Blacks, referring to the depth of racism, often remarked "they won't even let Jews in." In the 1950s, the Forest Hills Tennis Club, host of the national tennis tournament, refused membership to Victor Seixas, the Jewish 1950 national singles champion, despite roots in seventeenth-century New York. Sport and private clubs continued to bar blacks and women, including those who dominated their fields.

Nevertheless, America was becoming more open. More Americans of all races and backgrounds went to college. Colleges relaxed their Jewish quotas. Many northern colleges accepted both black and white students, and well-respected and established Negro colleges and medical schools continued to provide opportunities. Women's education gradually extended beyond teaching and nursing. The Servicemen's Readjustment Act of 1944, informally known as the GI Bill, vastly increased the mobility, education, and productivity of American workers.[49] These new paths to college gave many the chance to improve their social status after World War II, leading to middle-class, sometimes distinguished, lives, and a much broader distribution of income in America.[50]

However, while blacks moved to northern cities after World War II, the Federal Highway Administration built roads that opened the suburbs. The Federal Housing Administration then guaranteed mortgages for whites but not blacks, and discouraged banks from lending to blacks living in the suburbs and in the cities.[51] Whites but not blacks could realize the American dream of a house in the country, making the suburbs white.

Meanwhile the Truman and subsequent administrations managed "slum clearance"; blacks just called it "Negro clearance." Poor and black areas looked dilapidated to whites, who tore them down. Black businesses were cut off from their customers. Under eminent domain rules, businesses received no compensation for the loss of loyal customers—the backbone of the sales value of any retail business. Forced out, they had to start over. Black America went down two divergent tracks—college-educated blacks became the new black middle class. Once factories moved to the suburbs, working-class blacks were headed for oblivion. The consequences of that side-by-side integration and segregation were powerful, driving American politics to decades of new extremes.

In 1945, those consequences were well in the future. Veterans changed America immediately. Before the war, local officials regularly used bribes and threats, zoning variances, tax assessments, and other government benefits and burdens for political gains or favoritism.[52] Soldiers coming back from World War II had less taste for dirty politics and the courage to resist, and the GI Bill proved to be a more powerful tool to a better life.[53] Politicians needed new ways to hold on to power.

The economic changes in this period influenced the quality of American politics and American democracy changed radically.

Constitution Building

Mid-century constitutions embody contemporary views of democratic government while pulling people out of the depression, war, colonial and Nazi racism, and abuse, and building on the UDHR, the Nuremberg principles, and the Four Freedoms.

Constitutions historically specified the distribution of governmental powers, and protected human rights. The twentieth century added economic concerns, although with eighteenth-century origins. The French Constitution of 1791 provided for public aid for abandoned children, the infirm poor, and "to furnish work to the sturdy poor who have not been able to procure it."[54] The French Constitution of 1793 proclaimed: "Public assistance is a sacred duty. Society owes subsistence to unfortunate citizens, either by procuring them work, or by ensuring those who are unable to work the means of existence."[55]

By World War I, prolabor ideology had gained strength in much of Europe, partly in reaction to the Russian Revolution. The 1919 Weimar Constitution of Germany shows dual capitalist and communist influences, promising combined employer-labor management on "collectivist principles," a labor code, the right to organize for better wages and working conditions, and forms of labor and management negotiation and cooperation.[56] It also provided individual, family, child, and education rights, building on nineteenth-century traditions.[57]

Social welfare provisions abroad invite comparison to the long-held American belief that dispersion of wealth was important to protect democracy as well as to twentieth-century developments in the United States that culminated both in domestic policy and the Four Freedoms. Social welfare provisions in foreign constitutions also provide a basis for exploring in chapter

4 how courts have interpreted that language and how their interpretations relate to democracy.

1937 Ireland

In Ireland, the Great Depression led lawmakers to include in the Irish constitution a statement of "principles of social policy . . . intended for the general guidance of the . . . [the legislature which] shall not be cognisable by any Court."[58] The principles sought "a social order in which justice and charity shall inform all the institutions of the national life," including "an adequate means of livelihood" for "men and women equally . . . through their occupations." The Directive Principles subordinated unrestrained capitalism to distributive justice "to subserve the common good," via competition but not monopoly, and via management of credit for "the welfare of the people as a whole," all to the end of "economic security." The state should supplement "private initiative" for "efficiency . . . and . . . to protect the public against unjust exploitation." Ireland pledged "to safeguard with especial care the economic interests of the weaker sections of the community, and, where necessary, to contribute to the support of the infirm, the widow, the orphan, and the aged" and to protect workers and children from abuse, being "forced by economic necessity to enter avocations unsuited to their sex, age, or strength." The manner and extent of implementation were left to the legislature. Ireland would not be alone.

1939 New York and State Constitutions

American state constitutions require public schools.[59] Relief for the poor is traditional in the United States but not generally incorporated in constitutional language.[60] New York's 1939 Constitution required the legislature to provide for the needy. Although it lacked the Irish language barring court implementation, the clause directed legislative action and, like the requirement of a school system, lacked specifics—the legislature had to decide what it could and should do—implying that it was primarily for legislative consideration. Seventeen other states have similar welfare language.[61]

1946 Japan

Japan's Meiji Constitution of 1889 created a legislature and protected rights to relocate, to criminal trials, and regarding entry, searches, property, religion, speech, association, and petition.[62] All were limited as provided by law, paralleling the Magna Carta's restriction of the executive to the legislatively approved "law of the land." Japan in the 1920s had a vibrant political culture based on universal manhood suffrage.[63]

Japan's 1946 Constitution was jointly designed by General McArthur's team and Japanese leaders. Japan used the British model for parliamentary government, with judicial review but judges approved by voters decennially.[64] It reduced the emperor to ceremonial powers under the Cabinet or the Diet.[65] Article 9 renounced war, aggression, and military forces capable of war. With a catalogue of rights that are generally linked to democracy, their bill of rights makes "fundamental human rights . . . irrevocable and inviolable," including equal, political, criminal, judicial, expressive, and religious freedoms.[66] Article 15 defines elements of popular control over government, including the people's right to choose and dismiss public officials, universal adult suffrage, a secret ballot, voter independence, and the obligation of "[a]ll public officials . . . [to] the whole community and not of any group thereof."[67]

Notable provisions addressed workers' rights,[68] matrimonial equality,[69] the right to an education, and a ban on child labor.[70] Property rights are protected as "defined by law, in conformity with the public welfare."[71]

Article 25, "Welfare Rights," had European sources and Japanese support to protect "the right to maintain the minimum standards of wholesome and cultured living," and obligates "the State . . . [to] promotion and extension of social welfare and security, and of public health."[72] Like the clauses in the Irish and New York constitutions, Article 25 set important objectives for legislative and administrative implementation.[73]

1948 Italy

Italy's 1948 Constitution gave government the responsibility "to remove all obstacles of an economic and social nature which . . . [limit] the freedom and equality of citizens, prevent the full development of the individual and the participation of all workers in the political, economic, and social organization of the country."[74] It "recognizes" a right to work and governmental responsibility to "[promote] those conditions which render this right effective,"[75] to "[safeguard] health as a fundamental right of the individual . . . and [guarantee] free medical care to the indigent,"[76] a living wage,[77] and social insurance or public assistance "in case of accident, illness, disability, old age, and involuntary unemployment."[78] By "recognizing" obligations, the Constitution may be merely wishful, but Italy did not adopt the Irish Constitution's specific bar to judicial action and used much more specific language.

1949 Germany

Germany similarly protected popular sovereignty, personal rights, and economic position. As the Allies took control, the United States required that Germany be democratic and federal, defining the essentials of democratic government as competition, popular control, and civil liberties.

In April 1945, the Joint Chiefs of Staff ordered the military governor "to promote the development in Germany of institutions of popular self-government" and federalism. They told the military governor:

> Your Government does not wish to impose its own historically developed forms of democracy and social organization on Germany and believes equally firmly that no other external forms should be imposed. It seeks the establishment in Germany of a political organization which is derived from the people and subject to their control, which operates in accordance with democratic electoral procedures, and which is dedicated to uphold both the basic civil and human rights of the individual.[79]

The Joint Chiefs, obviously determined to avoid regeneration of German military power, repeatedly stressed their opposition "to an excessively centralized government," insisting that a central authority have only "carefully defined and limited powers."

In 1945 at Potsdam, President Truman, Soviet Premier Stalin, and British Prime Minister Clement Attlee agreed to decentralize Germany in a democratic state with competitive political parties, representative and elective principles, and freedom of speech, press, religion, and, subject to military security, trade unions.[80]

In Moscow two years later, U.S. Secretary of State George Marshall stated that a properly democratic German state meant popular sovereignty, frequent popular elections with freely competing, voluntary parties treated equally, together with the kinds of political rights reflected in our First Amendment and "other equally basic rights of man," including "equality under the law" and protection from arbitrary criminal processes.[81]

Similar ideas were already present in the 1919 Weimar Constitution, except that it had a strong executive with emergency powers.[82] The constitutions of the individual *Länder*, or German states, which were drafted by Germans with minimal interference before the *Grundgesetz*, or Basic Law, of the Federal Republic of Germany, also make clear that Allied notions of democracy were quite compatible with native German ones.[83] They stressed democracy, liberty in the Kantian tradition, and fraternity in the Rousseauean tradition of mutual dependence and support. The Bavarian constitution stressed both liberty and fraternity: "Schools shall not merely convey knowledge and ability, but shall also develop sympathetic hearts and character. The highest objectives of education are reverence for God, respect for religious convictions and human dignity, self-control, a keen sense for and ready acceptance of responsibility, a willingness to help others, and receptiveness for all that is true, good, and beautiful."[84]

The Hessian constitution announced, "Concepts which endanger the foundations of the democratic state must not be tolerated" in the schools, and "The teaching of history must be directed towards a true, unvarnished presentation of the past. Special attention is to be paid to the great benefactors of mankind, to the development of the State, economics, civilization, and culture, rather than to warlords, wars, and battles." Both mutual responsibility and individual rights are protected by the "right to make an adequate living by means of his [sic] labor" and the "right to adequate housing."[85]

All Länder constitutions "allow for state planning and some socialization, especially of utilities and transportation, and provide for land reform."[86] They explicitly rejected Nazism and militarism, but denied protection to those tried or disfranchised under the denazification and demilitarization laws.[87] They entrenched democracy in clauses barring constitutional amendments that would change the basic democratic character of the governments.[88]

The Länder followed the earlier Weimar Constitution in providing emergency powers[89] but barred the legislatures from delegating powers, in reaction to Hitler's misuse of that opportunity.[90]

Germany's 1949 postwar constitution, called the Basic Law, shows the influence of the Weimar Constitution and incorporates some of its language, rather than the language or structure of the American Constitution.[91] It declares, "The Federal Republic of Germany is a democratic and social federal state."[92] All three—democracy, social welfare, and federalism—had roots in German history.

The Basic Law elaborates on Germany's self-definition as a "democratic ... state," with popular sovereignty: "All state authority is derived from the people. It shall be exercised by the people through elections and other votes and through specific legislative, executive, and judicial bodies."[93] Popular sovereignty organizes the Bundestag, the lower house of the German legislature, which "shall be elected in general, direct, free, equal, and secret elections." The sovereign public includes the entire population: "Anyone who has attained the age of twenty-one years is entitled to vote," a provision that later was changed to eighteen.[94] Furthermore: "In county and municipal elections, persons who possess citizenship in any member state of the European Community are also eligible to vote." The constitution apportions power by popular strength,[95] although it leaves the details of elections to legislation by the *Bundestag*, subject to the requirement of equality. The *Bundesrat* represents the *Länder*, but the number of seats is weighted by population.[96]

The Basic Law protects the political rights of competition and expression,[97] specifically including unions and parties.[98] Elections are held periodically— the *Bundestag* serves no longer than four years.[99] The president and the chancellor are selected by the legislature.[100]

Like the European Convention on Human Rights and the constitutions of Canada and South Africa, the German Basic Law explicitly incorporates the concept of democracy in mandatory language in several provisions and thereby clearly puts it before the courts for interpretation. To protect German democracy from Nazism, the Basic Law declares parties unconstitutional that "seek to undermine or abolish the free democratic basic order" or threaten "the existence of the" country.[101] Restrictions on constitutional protections are only permissible "to protect the free democratic basic order," Federation or *Länder* security.[102] Protections of "the free democratic order" run through the Basic Law, requiring the courts to protect democracy.[103] Conversely, using rights "to combat the free democratic basic order . . . forfeit[s]" them.[104] The courts must protect "the essence of a basic right."[105]

The Four Freedoms and welfare state traditions reappear protecting economic justice and welfare, including a mothers' right "to the protection and care of the community," protection of "illegitimate" children, "the right freely to choose . . . [one's] occupation or profession . . . place[s] of work and . . . training," and the right to form unions.[106] Public schools are provided along with the right to found and operate private ones.[107] Property rights are restricted: "Property entails obligations. Its use shall also serve the public good."[108] The public may own "land, natural resources, and means of production," conditioned only on just compensation to prior owners.[109]

Länder constitutions must follow "principles of a republican, democratic, and social state governed by the rule of law."[110] Authority over public welfare and economic regulation, labor, social security, and unemployment insurance is concurrent,[111] while other social insurance is federal.[112]

In addition to political and economic rights, an extensive set of civil rights—including freedom of religion, "free development of . . . personality," "life and physical integrity,"[113] privacy, and freedom of movement—are protected.[114]

The entire set of "basic rights" is grounded in the Kantian principle of "human dignity"; human rights are "inviolable." Moreover, "inalienable human rights . . . [are] the basis of every community, of peace and of justice in the world." And they "bind the legislature, the executive and the judiciary as directly applicable law."[115]

Going further in several respects than the U.S. Supreme Court's understanding of the Fourteenth Amendment, the Basic Law requires equality regardless of "sex, parentage, race, language, homeland and origin, faith, . . . religious or political opinions [or] disability." It imposes an obligation to "promote the actual implementation of equal rights for women and men and take steps to eliminate disadvantages that now exist."[116]

The Basic Law includes fewer explicit protections for Germany's very different criminal process but its protections overlap many provisions of the U.S. Constitution, including the *ex post facto* and attainder provisions of Article I, judicial provisions of Article III, and procedural provisions in the Fourth, Fifth, and Eighth Amendments. Germany also abolished capital punishment, and requires notification of someone acting on a prisoner's behalf.[117]

Allied ideas about democracy, carried across European battlefields, are thus defined and elaborated in the postwar German Basic Law. In its use of the language of democracy it invites judicial construction, and its provisions for universal suffrage and popular sovereignty elaborate the concept of democracy in common with several other postwar constitutions.

1950 India

Many of the trends that had driven the constitutional language elsewhere came together with force in India. Millions of Indians fought in World War II, mostly on the side of the Allies, despite India's still unresolved drive for independence. Indians were keenly aware of the tragedy in Europe. In 1973, the Supreme Court of India explained:

> After World War II when the disastrous effects of the positivist doctrines came to be realized there was reaction in favour of making certain norms immune from amendment or abrogation. This was done in the Constitution of the Federal Republic of Germany. The atrocities committed during Second World War and the worldwide agitation for human rights ultimately embodied in the U.N. Declaration of Human Rights on which a number of the provisions in Parts III and IV of our Constitution are fashioned must not be forgotten.[118]

As the result of its organization in pursuit of independence, the Congress Party dominated Indian politics for decades, in contrast to the Federalists in America, who were ejected after only twelve years.[119] Congress Party leaders were less concerned with controlling the abuse of power than the founding American generation because its Indian leadership expected to be in control and wanted power to enact major social change.

Equally important, the Muslim minority was not large enough to force sufficient constitutional protections.[120] The creation of Pakistan as a Muslim nation at the same time that India became independent increased Hindu dominance in India.

The Indian Constitution, adopted in 1950, was drafted by a national elite that was schooled in the struggle for independence, familiar with legal developments across the globe, and led by lawyers educated in England. Determination to lift the lowest among the Indians socially and economically was shaped as well by Congress Party principles in the fight for independence.

Benegal Narsinga Rau, a career public servant and judge, became the constitutional advisor to the Constituent Assembly responsible for drafting the Indian Constitution.[121] Well educated in the constitutional law of many countries, he studied them anew; in 1947, he traveled to England, Ireland, Canada, and the United States—countries that either used to be or still were subject to the British Crown—to talk with experts in those countries. Of the U.S. Supreme Court, Rau met the present and former Chief Justices Vinson and Hughes, and Associate Justices Frankfurter, Murphy, and Burton. Frankfurter made a big impression on Rau with his insistence that courts be as restrained in civil liberties as in economic cases.

Rau described the dilemma facing constitutional draftsmen. If they created enforceable rights on the American model, they risked court decisions that intruded on judgments legislatures should make. Yet, language deferring to legislative judgment risked emasculating protections entirely. And language not judicially enforceable risked becoming a dead letter, an object only of derision. He illustrated each possibility with examples from American cases, all fresh in memory from recent battles over the courts' proper role. The British model was based on parliamentary supremacy with no judicially enforceable restrictions on Parliament. India, having been part of the British Empire, was familiar with that model. That left the Constituent Assembly with stark choices.

Before Frankfurter's appointment, the U.S. Supreme Court held major state and federal legislation "unreasonable," and therefore unconstitutional violations of the due process clause. Most of those cases were not about process but about economic policy that the Court disliked. The Due Process Clause in the Constitution improved on the Magna Carta, which promised merely that no one would be punished but by the law of the land, that is, by legislation. The Due Process Clause required that criminal process must be *due*, that is, appropriate, and reflect a search for truth. But Frankfurter persuaded Rau that due process was a capacious formula that allowed courts to do a great deal of damage.

In India, many disliked the absence of procedural protections available elsewhere. Rau countered that legislatures, not courts, should weigh protections against other concerns. To protect their social and economic program, Congress Party leadership backed Rau and rejected the phrase *due process of law*. The Assembly instead took the phrase *according to procedure established by law* from the Japanese Constitution. Like the ancient Magna Carta, it protected against the king, but not the legislature. That decision, repeated on many issues of criminal prosecution, left the Indian Constitution without many of the protections available elsewhere.[122]

Multiple clauses, however, require equality. British Fabian socialism influenced Congress Party leadership regarding India's impoverished masses. The Indian National Congress resolved in 1931 that "in order to end the exploitation of the masses, political freedoms must include real economic freedom of the starving millions, and that the organization of economic life must conform to the principle of justice."[123] The 1950 Preamble omitted "socialist" rather than tie the country to a particular economic solution.[124] Nevertheless, the Preamble described a broad-based social agenda. India would be a "DEMOCRATIC REPUBLIC," securing "to all its citizens":

> JUSTICE, social, economic and political;
> LIBERTY of thought, expression, belief, faith and worship;
> EQUALITY of status and of opportunity;
> and to promote among them all
> FRATERNITY assuring the dignity of the individual.[125]

According to Rau, "equality before the law" came from the Weimar Constitution and "equal protection of the law" from both the Weimar and the American constitutions.[126] That dual guarantee immediately precedes prohibition of discrimination on grounds of "religion, race, caste, sex, [or] place of birth," effective both against government and private places of public accommodation. Rau took Justice Frankfurter's advice "that legal provision might occasionally have to be made for women, for example, to prohibit their employment for certain periods before and after childbirth," an example suggesting no distinction between protecting and prohibiting action by women. India's Constitution permits "special provision for women and children."

Equality provisions continue. Discrimination in government service is prohibited based on "race, caste, sex, descent, place of birth, [or] residence" but affirmative action "in favour of the Scheduled Castes and the Scheduled Tribes" is authorized. Untouchability is abolished, its practice forbidden and criminalized, a provision that passed with shouts of "Mahatma Gandhi Ki Jai," which translates as "Hail victory to the Great Souled Gandhi" who had been assassinated by another Hindu as the nation was being established.[127]

The next article abolished titles, completing the section devoted to equality but the section on fundamental rights continues by protecting religious and linguistic minorities. And the Indian Constitution reinforces equality in the apportionment of legislative seats, proportional representation in Parliament and the right to vote for all adult citizens, although courts were barred from most electoral disputes. The Constitution also reserves legislative and administrative positions for members of the Scheduled Castes, Scheduled Tribes, and the Anglo-Indian community. In all, the Constitution has quite a bit to say about equality and affirmative steps to achieve it.[128]

The Indian Constitution adds sixteen articles to improve the welfare of the millions of impoverished Indians which, however, "shall not be enforceable by any court, but the principles therein laid down are nevertheless fundamental in the governance of the country and it shall be the duty of the State to apply these principles in making laws."[129] Rau explicitly borrowed the Indian Directive Principles from Ireland. He recommended making them judicially unenforceable because their guarantee depends on what may be practical and therefore they are "not normally either capable of, or suitable for, enforcement by legal action."[130]

Rau's approach was criticized as ineffective. He responded they would be educative. Dr. B. R. Ambedkar wanted the principles to be justiciable. Ambedkar—by caste an "untouchable," not a member of the Congress Party, and critical of many of its positions—played a major role in writing the Constitution, chaired the drafting committee, and served as the first law minister as well as on many relevant committees. Ultimately he supported the Directive Principles because he realized that no party was guaranteed to head the government, so those principles could help to steer the state toward public welfare.[131]

Before the Constitution went into effect, Ambedkar made the connection between economic and political rights and democracy. When the Constitution would go into effect, India would "enter into a life of contradictions." It would have equality in politics and inequality in social and economic life. He wondered how long that could continue. If too long, they would put "our democracy in peril . . . or else those who suffer from inequality will blow up the structure of political democracy which this Assembly has so laboriously built up."[132] Politically India would have one person per vote in 1950, well before the U.S. Supreme Court recognized that principle.

The Directive Principles were longer and broader than the Irish precedent, part of an ambitious blueprint for remaking Indian life, society, and economy from the bottom up. The Directive Principles address income inequalities, gender justice, workers' rights, the caste system, nutrition, public health, public welfare, and public assistance, plus the environment, historic places, separation of powers, and the promotion of international peace and security—a lengthy wish list. Although judicially unenforceable, the principles were backed up with enforceable injunctions on equality, education, and representation elsewhere in the Constitution.

Indian Supreme Court Judge H. R. Khanna was celebrated for decisions blocking the Parliament from undermining the democratic constitutional framework to keep Indira Gandhi in power, and for his 1976 dissent insisting that prisoners who had been detained without trial had the right of habeas corpus.[133] Speaking to the Indian Law Institute, Judge Khanna put Ambedkar's insight into a larger context: "Since the . . . French Revolution, there has been a growing awareness of the close link between political freedom and social justice." He continued: "[T]he content of political freedom can be impaired by the absence of social justice. Unless there was adequate protection for social and economic rights, classical individual liberties like the right to equality, liberty of person, and freedom of speech might lose much of their significance and even face a serious threat for their own survival." And he expanded the context to the formative events of the twentieth century: "The aftermath of the first World War also highlighted the fact that peace in the world can be established only if it is based on social justice. A number of modern Constitutions accordingly embodied within themselves declarations of principles which emphasize the duty of the State to strive for social security and to provide work, education and proper conditions of employment for the citizens."[134] The founding generation of America understood that democracy depends on a republican society with sufficiently equal and independent people. Ambedkar and Judge Khanna explained its centrality to the Indian Constitution. And Judge Khanna tied the Indian experience to European and American constitutions. Thus, American contributions to democracy were expressed halfway around the globe.

1950 European Union

The European Convention on Human Rights, adopted in 1950, incorporated many rights specified in the UN Universal Declaration of Human Rights adopted two years earlier, making them binding on members of the European Union and enforced by the European Court of Human Rights. The Convention makes explicit the connection between those fundamental freedoms, political democracy, justice, peace, and European unity.[135]

Articles 2–7 protect life and liberty in criminal and other proceedings and against slavery, including protections similar to those of the Fourth, Fifth, Sixth, Eighth, and Thirteenth Amendments to the U.S. Constitution. They are necessary for democracy so that the criminal process cannot be used for political ends, and to protect the welfare of the public.

Articles 8–11 use democracy as a standard for permissible restrictions on human rights. For example, Article 9 par. 2 allows limitations of rights only if they "are prescribed by law and are necessary in a democratic society in the interests of public safety, for the protection of public order, health or morals, or the protection of the rights and freedoms of others." Articles 8–11 all say "necessary in a democratic society" but add different considerations.[136]

Two years later the Council of Europe added Protocol No. 1 to the Convention. Art. 3 of the Protocol spelled out some requisites of democracy: "The High Contracting Parties undertake to hold free elections at reasonable intervals by secret ballot, under conditions which will ensure the free expression of the opinion of the people in the choice of the legislature." The courts will understand "people" to include universal adult suffrage.

1982 Canada

Canada and South Africa later adopted interesting and influential constitutions. By Canadian and U.K. statutes in 1982, the United Kingdom relinquished power over Canada, and Canada adopted the Charter of Rights and Freedoms.[137] Building on language in the German and Indian constitutions and the European Convention, the first section makes protected "rights and freedoms . . . subject only to such reasonable limits prescribed by law as can be demonstrably justified in a free and democratic society."

The Charter protects such rights as religion, speech, assembly, association, and other fundamental freedoms along with rights in the criminal process.[138] Section 3 guarantees the right to vote to "every citizen of Canada."[139]

The Charter treats equality at length, in ways reminiscent of the Indian Constitution. It protects equality "before and under the law" and "to the equal protection and equal benefit of the law without discrimination based on race, national, or ethnic origin, colour, religion, sex, age, or mental or physical disability." Continuing, it protects efforts to "ameliorat[e] . . . conditions of disadvantaged individuals or groups including those that are disadvantaged because of race, national or ethnic origin, colour, religion, sex, age, or mental or physical disability."[140] And the Charter commits Canada to "promoting equal opportunities for the well-being of Canadians . . . economic development to reduce disparity in opportunities; and . . . providing essential public services of reasonable quality to all Canadians" as well as regional equality.[141]

1996 South Africa

American-influenced free world values also bore fruit in the South African Constitution, which expresses the democratic ethos throughout. As stated in the Preamble, the Constitution was designed to:

Heal the divisions of the past and establish a society based on democratic values, social justice and fundamental human rights;

Lay the foundations for a democratic and open society in which government is based on the will of the people and every citizen is equally protected by law;

Improve the quality of life of all citizens and free the potential of each person;

Build a united and democratic South Africa able to take its rightful place as a sovereign state in the family of nations.

Democracy was more than a method of counting votes. It was intended to reflect the will of the people, and was tied to social justice, human rights, equality, and improvement of the lives of all South Africans.

The first section continues the democratic refrain, connecting democracy with inclusion and competition in order to secure an accountable, responsive government: "The Republic of South Africa is one sovereign democratic state founded on the following values: . . . (d) Universal adult suffrage, a national common voters roll, regular elections, and a multi-party system of democratic government, to ensure accountability, responsiveness and openness."[142] The South African Bill of Rights links democracy with dignity, equality, and freedom: "This Bill of Rights is a cornerstone of democracy in South Africa. It enshrines the rights of all people in our country and affirms the democratic values of human dignity, equality, and freedom."[143] For South Africa, democracy includes all adult citizens in an open, competitive, and participatory process. The right "to vote in elections for any legislative body" and to campaign for or hold public office belongs to "every adult citizen,"[144] along with the rights of speech, press, assembly, demonstration, picketing, petitioning, association, "academic freedom and freedom of scientific research."[145] The South African Constitution provides for multiparty competitive democracy via proportional representation.[146]

The Bill of Rights includes elaborate provisions for equality,[147] and a set of economic rights including freedom of trade, occupation, profession, and fair labor practices; a healthful, sustainable environment; elaborate property rules which include consideration for the dispossessed, housing, health care, food, water, and social security; rights of children which include "nutrition, shelter, basic health care services, and social services"; and the right to education.[148]

Like Germany, India, Canada, and the European Convention, South Africa made democracy central to any limitation of rights protected "in the Bill of Rights [which] may be limited only in terms of law of general application to the extent that the limitation is reasonable and justifiable in an open and democratic society based on human dignity, equality and freedom . . . [as well as five other listed factors]."[149]

The 1996 Constitution reemphasizes the point in Section 39(1), which sets out how the South African Bill of Rights should be interpreted:

1. When interpreting the Bill of Rights, a court, tribunal or forum
   a. must promote the values that underlie an open and democratic society based on human dignity, equality and freedom;

It continues by requiring that courts:

   b. must consider international law; and
   c. may consider foreign law.

Then using the Bill of Rights for wider purposes, the Constitution adds:

2. When interpreting any legislation, and when developing the common law or customary law, every court, tribunal or forum must promote the spirit, purport, and objects of the Bill of Rights.

The Constitutional Court was given power to determine the constitutionality of acts of national, provincial, and local legislatures and to certify amendments of provincial constitutions for consistency with the national Constitution.[150] Democracy is a theme throughout the document.[151]

The Era of Constitution Building

In short, this era of constitution writing created documents that used democracy as a standard, provided for electoral competition, inclusion of all people, and incorporated social and economic rights as part of a democratic framework. The goal of social and physical integration was less clear abroad than in the United States where it was becoming increasingly powerful, often to the exclusion of economic rights deemed important abroad.

4

Foreign Courts

Courts abroad treat *democracy* and *democratic* as terms with real meaning that courts can and should enforce, in sharp contrast to the Roberts Court, for which democracy is largely an excuse for inaction, but not of rights or requirements.[1]

International developments, influenced by the United States after World War II, came together in an understanding of democratic majorities as "fluid," with citizens moving in and out of the majority. For that to be possible, they must "at all times enjoy a core of political rights that ensures effective participation."[2] Instead of understanding elections and democratic procedures as ends in themselves, judges have understood them as a way to ensure that the people can elect their leaders. As developed in the courts of many nations, popular sovereignty requires that all adults can actually vote. To protect the political freedom on which democracy depends, and also because human rights and welfare are central to the moral claim of democracy, they understand democracy to require economic justice, civil liberties, and protections in the criminal process. And they demand more than the Roberts Court does.

Foreign examples are not new to American law.[3] But they became a flashpoint in cases holding that the death penalty could not be applied to juveniles, the mentally retarded, or those guilty of serious crimes but not murder,[4] and cases protecting the private, consensual relations of gays and lesbians.[5] Justice Thomas shot back "this Court . . . should not impose foreign moods, fads, or fashions on Americans."[6] In 2003, Justice Scalia added, "constitutional entitlements do not spring into existence because . . . foreign nations decriminalize conduct."[7] Two years later, he made plain his objection to "the Court's conclusion that the meaning of our Constitution has changed over the past 15 years."[8] The Court should not have taken "guidance from the views of foreign courts and legislatures."[9] This battle continues on the Roberts Court.[10]

One might respond that other versions of originalism are more receptive to foreign law,[11] and closer to the understanding of the founders,[12] or that neither Scalia nor Thomas are consistently faithful to eighteenth century behavior. More important, however, the purpose here is not to copy but to learn from foreign courts. Americans will want to know what might happen if, in fact, the U.S. Supreme Court took the concept of democracy as seriously as it takes the concepts of the separation and division of powers. And we want to explore the logic of taking democracy seriously, to uncover what democracy can mean and has meant to others.

Decisions by foreign courts are not binding precedent in the United States. American judges adopt or reject what they do based on their understanding of American law. However, American state courts and the high courts of many countries look to treatment of similar issues in the sister courts of other states or countries, including the United States. In exploring, we consider the possibilities. This is particularly appropriate at a time when many countries and courts are, for better or worse, learning from each other.[13]

In this chapter we explore what courts have said about what makes democracy work properly and what helps it survive. In subsequent chapters we will explore what political scientists have added to our understanding of the requisites of democracy.

In the following pages, we do this without assuming that principles adopted elsewhere can or should be adopted here. Foreign courts are more limited than the U.S. Supreme Court. All other national constitutional courts are much younger. The European Court of Human Rights (ECtHR), founded in 1959, applies rules to governments that are in fact sovereign. ECtHR member countries can withdraw from treaties, conventions, and international institutions. They each possess formidable and independent armed forces. The ECtHR cannot count on supranational leaders to enforce decisions the way U.S. presidents have sometimes enforced judicial judgments. Finally, the legitimacy of the Court, the general sense of obligation to obey, that characterizes American attitudes toward the Supreme Court, is lacking for many other courts with constitutional or international authority. Generally, therefore, they have less power to work their will than the U.S. Supreme Court does.

Many legal issues are not strictly comparable either. Voter equality raises very different issues in proportional systems than in our geographic system, with problems of districting, apportionment, and gerrymandering. Issues like voter registration, that bedevil U.S. elections, are resolved in many other countries by mandatory registration and voting, although the United Kingdom may be moving toward more exacting forms of voter identification, similar to some U.S. jurisdictions.[14]

These differences are mitigated somewhat because the focus in this book is on the proper standard rather than actual behavior. No nation implements democracy perfectly. Each makes idiosyncratic choices about its representative system that make comparisons difficult. Although examples will clarify some points, we will focus in this book on what democracy means instead of the precise arrangements or compromises each country has made.

Language in some national constitutions explicitly makes democracy a criterion of legality. I looked for interpretations of democracy in those constitutions. The U.S. constitution has no such language. Whether the meaning of democracy is relevant to constitutional law in the United States depends on whether the Constitution implies a democratic principle much the way the courts have concluded it implies federal and separation of powers principles. Those issues will be discussed in the concluding chapter. This chapter does not trace or examine the strength of inferences judges have drawn from their own constitutions, but focuses instead on judges' understanding of the explicit requirement of democracy in their constitutions.

German Constitutional Court

On the heels of Nazi dictatorship, and bordered by two Iron Curtain countries, West Germans felt their democracy threatened by totalitarians both internally and on its eastern border. Membership in the European Union pulled West Germany and then the unified country toward more open and inclusive democracy.[15]

The German Constitutional Court promptly made democracy fundamental to law in 1951, concluding that even constitutional language must be consistent with fundamental principles of democracy and human rights; some "constitutional principles that are so fundamental . . . [have] precedence even over the Constitution." The Court added, "it follows that any constitutional provision must be interpreted . . . [so] that it is compatible with those elementary principles" as well as "the basic decision of the framers of the Constitution."[16]

The German Constitutional Court looks at cause and effect to protect democracy, quoting Cardozo's *Palko* opinion in English, that freedom of opinion is "the matrix, the indispensible condition of every other form of freedom" and "basic to a liberal-democratic constitutional order."[17] The Court nevertheless limits free speech to protect privacy.[18]

Part of the German response to the threat of totalitarianism was defensive.[19] Following Article 21, the Court found it "simply inconceivable that the Constitution . . . in the wake of the bitter experience of Weimar's democracy . . . should also permit the surrender of this state to its enemies."[20] The unapologetically Nazi Socialist Reich Party was dissolved.[21] The Communist Party's relationship to Warsaw Pact forces across the West German border also threatened German democracy, and it too was dissolved.[22] But Germany's commitment to "militant" democracy can be double-edged.[23] The power to dissolve political parties has been abused in many countries regardless of expressed intent.

The Court defines democracy based on popular sovereignty: "all public authority emanates from the people" who exercises authority "by means of elections and voting."[24] The constitutional designation of Germany as a democratic state means parliamentary control of government and that the right to vote of all German citizens is critical.[25] Democracy, the Court explained, is a fluid "process that requires constant renewal and in which all citizens of voting age share equally."[26]

Citizenship and voter eligibility, however, had been restricted to those with German blood. Foreign guest workers were excluded from citizenship because of their ancestry, and therefore left without a vote. The Court found that allowing foreign nationals living in Germany to vote in local elections conflicted with the right of German citizens to self-government.[27] That has been changed because EU law now requires some birthright citizenship and German law has been amended to conform.[28]

Proportional representation in the legislature is designed to include Germans of all persuasions. "The proper standard . . . [for] parliamentary organization and procedure . . . is the principle of universal participation."[29] However, to encourage coalition and make government manageable, it does not seat small splinter parties. These opposite purposes clashed after unification of the former East and West Germany. In *Re-Election Processes in Unified Germany*,[30] the Court wrote: "Democracy cannot function—as a matter of principle—if the parties are unable to enter an election campaign under the same legal circumstances." The East German party primarily responsible for unification expected but failed to win the 5 percent of the electorate required for representation in the new unified country. The Court recognized that it had less opportunity to develop in a democratic political process and permitted a one-time reduction of the percent required for representation from the former East Germany.[31]

Nevertheless, minor parties are crucial for competition and for equal citizen participation. So their role in the legislature is protected:[32] "[P]arliamentary opposition . . . [is] in the interest of the democratic state."[33]

Historic American concern with a republican distribution of wealth is incorporated in the notion that Germany is a "republican, democratic, and social state" and in German constitutional law, which makes public economic welfare a significant consideration and provides some protection for economic welfare.[34]

Germany is less focused than the United States on using the schools to build unity among students of all ranks, races, and faiths. Students are permitted to take religious classes in interdenominational state schools, or to go to religiously based schools supported by the government.[35] Local authorities, however, tried to exclude a teacher from a state school because she wore an Islamic headscarf, claiming it conflicted with her obligation of religious neutrality toward her students. The Court overruled her ouster but decided she could be excluded if her action "conflicted with purposes of constitutional legal protection, and if this restriction of her free exercise of religion were based on a sufficiently definite statutory foundation."[36] The Court's examples suggested the law could easily be rewritten to exclude Muslim women who wore the Islamic headscarf.[37] Two-thirds of German states banned headscarves categorically after the decision and the prospective teacher eventually gave up her fight, saddled as she was with substantial legal expenses.[38]

The founders of the United States thought many procedural rights were necessary to protect democracy from abuse of the criminal law for partisan or other improper purposes. Procedural protections of that type are based in Germany on the generic concept of the rule of law.[39]

German federalism differs radically from U.S. federalism. Germany has not created a federal bureaucracy in most areas, so that national legislation is implemented by the states unless the federal government is better able to address the problem.[40] But federal law sets boundaries. States as "member[s] . . . of a federation [are] not autonomous and independent." Instead they are "part of a federal order which restricts [their] sovereign power in various respects." The Court found that the government could even abolish a state as part of a reorganization plan.[41]

Internally, the German states are required to "conform to the principles of a republican, democratic, and social state." County and municipal governments must be "chosen in general, direct, free, equal, and secret elections."[42] And mimicking the guarantee clause of the U.S. Constitution, the German Basic Law requires the federation to protect those principles.

The German Constitutional Court decided that, unlike U.S. constitutional law, the Basic Law creates values to which law relating to private disputes must conform. In much of the free world, this is known as the direct horizontal effect of the constitution.[43] In the United States, the doctrine of state action generally eliminates private responsibility to conform to constitutional standards or requirements, sometimes protecting private interference with political efforts against federal action.[44] The German approach expands democratic obligations.

Germany thus pioneered in using the concept of democracy as a tool of interpretation, both in constitutional language and judicial decision. It would prove both influential and controversial.

Supreme Court of India

Indian democracy faced different problems. Although British response was often quite violent, the nonviolent revolution led by Mahatma Gandhi spared India the militarization that leaves democracy under the heel of strongmen. The unity of India's leaders at independence and their confidence in each other led to a constitution that placed few restrictions on the new government and left its courts with few tools to keep India on a democratic course. But it would nevertheless develop a strong view of the requirements of democracy.

From the date of independence, segregation was facilitated, though not required by Indian law, leading to India's own bath of fire. The British Parliament's Indian Independence Act of July 1947 partitioned the territory into India and Pakistan. Partition led to the flight of ten to twelve million people crossing the new border in both directions, largely becoming homeless. Partition and migration led to riots and mass killings and many more died fleeing for safety. A Hindu nationalist who thought Gandhi was favoring Muslims over Hindus assassinated him shortly after partition. Estimates vary but probably a million people lost their lives within months of partition. Nevertheless, many stayed and India's Muslim population remains one of the world's largest.

Tribal and caste conflict are other sources of communal violence.[45] Politicians, aided by criminal gangs, have initiated violence to foment communal rage so that people would vote for them at elections.[46] Trains, villages, shrines, mosques, and temples have been attacked and violence has often leapt out of control. Results have been tragic. The Supreme Court of India quoted Jonathan Swift in 1994, "We have just enough religion to make us hate, but not enough to make us love one another." Referring to demolition of a mosque, the Court wrote: "What was demolished was not merely an ancient structure; but the faith of the minorities in the sense of justice and fair play of majority." Casualties included "faith in the rule of law and constitutional processes."[47]

Secularism, Justice Verma wrote for the Court, "treats all religions alike and displays a benevolent neutrality towards them"; but it also "should connote the eradication of all attitudes and practices derived from or connected with religion which impede our development and retard our growth into an integrated nation." This was crucial "to the stabilisation of our democratic State and the establishment of a true and cohesive Indian nationhood."[48] Justice Verma continued: "In a pluralist, secular polity law is perhaps the greatest integrating force." Justice Verma's majority opinion described a "cultivated respect for law and its institutions and symbols; a pride in the country's heritage and achievements; faith that people live under the protection of an adequate legal system" as "indispensable for sustaining unity in pluralist diversity."

With Harvard's John Rawls's recent work in mind, Verma wrote: "Rawlsian pragmatism of 'justice as fairness' to serve as an 'overlapping consensus' and deep-seated agreements on fundamental questions of basic structure of society for deeper social unity" described a "political conception of justice" necessary for a pluralist society.[49] "Law should not accentuate the depth of the cleavage and become in itself a source of aggravation of the very condition it intends to remedy."[50]

In that strife-riven environment, the justices valued education for democracy. Although the Preamble declares that India will be a "secular republic" and Article 28 bars "religious instruction in any educational institution wholly maintained out of State funds,"[51] the Court saw value in the comparative study of religion. Religious education could convey "moral character and . . . the inherent virtues of human-being [sic] such as truth, love and compassion" necessary to the survival of democracy.[52] Delivering the judgment, Justice Shah, wrote: "Bereft of moral values secular society or democracy may not survive."[53]

The point of these justices was not to indoctrinate, focus on a single faith, or dilute differences to reach a common denominator. They sought secular but neither anti- or nonreligious education. As Justice Shah put it: "Value-based education is likely to help the nation to fight against all kinds of prevailing fanaticism, ill-will violence, dishonesty, corruption, exploitation, and drug abuses."[54]

On the advantage of comparative study of religion, Justice Shah wrote: "Let knowledge, like the sun, shine for all and then there should not be any room for narrow-mindedness, blind faith, and dogma. For this purpose also, if basic tenets of all religions over the world are learnt, it cannot be said that secularism would not survive."[55] Justice Dharmadhikari agreed that education about religion in schools "fully maintained out of state funds" must be "different from religious education" offered in schools "maintained by minorities or those established under any endowment or trust."[56]

The U.S. Supreme Court long since approved comparative or historic study of religions.[57] Those whose goal was the promotion of a specific faith have often misunderstood the U.S. Supreme Court, especially in the Warren years, as against religion, instead of for broad and comparative knowledge of different faiths. The Indian Court is somewhat clearer.

The same concern with the risk of fanaticism and the reality of intercommunal violence led toward regulation of speech more like German law, with the same downside of potential abuse. The Indian Constitution permits "reasonable restrictions" on free speech for "the sovereignty and integrity of India, the security of the State, friendly relations with foreign States, public order, decency or morality, or in relation to contempt of court, defamation or incitement to an offence."[58] Similar restrictions are permitted on assembly, association, travel, and settlement.[59] The Court set aside an election because a candidate appealed to religious hatred and used the candidates' faiths to seek election. The Court held that seeking votes because of religion was properly prohibited, without needing to assess the likely impact.[60]

Nevertheless, the biggest threat to Indian democracy came from the top. The Court rejected several land reform measures of Prime Minister Indira Gandhi, daughter of Jawaharlal Nehru who had been a founder and the first prime minister of India. Gandhi overturned the Court's rulings with amendments to the Constitution, and moved the Court leftward with new justices. The Court retreated but landmark decisions denied that amendments could change the "basic structure" of the Constitution.[61] Some amendments, though procedurally correct, were unconstitutional.

U.S. Supreme Court decisions are often based on inferences from the structure of the Constitution, its federalism, and separation of powers. The Indian Court's decision was more radical. The crucial 1973 *Kesavananda Bharati* case arose out of a contest over land reform but in explaining their conclusion that constitutional amendments designed to overturn prior judicial rulings were themselves unconstitutional, the justices used the democratic provisions of the Constitution to explain why some amendments would be illegitimate. In the process they announced a number of conclusions about democracy itself.

Justice Khanna's opinion made the fundamental point: "It would not be competent under the garb of amendment, for instance, to change the democratic government into dictatorship or hereditary monarchy nor would it be permissible to abolish [the two houses of their legislature]." Equally fundamental, "[t]he secular character of the state" which prohibits it from "discriminat[ing] against any citizen on the ground of religion only cannot likewise be done away with." Justice Khanna added: "Provision regarding the amendment of the Constitution does not furnish a pretence for subverting the structure of the Constitution . . . or provide sanction for what may perhaps be called its lawful harakiri." Constitutional suicide is not an "amendment."[62]

Justice Khanna recounted Hitler's use of emergency powers under the Weimar Constitution "to issue decrees suspending the rights guaranteed by the basic law and to make direct use of the army and navy." But "almost from its beginning the government found itself in one emergency after another, so that rule by executive decrees . . . supplanted the normal functioning of the legislative branch of government." As a result, "[i]n less than two years, the Weimar Republic was transformed into a totalitarian dictatorship."[63] Hitler had not taken power by constitutional amendments, but the justices made clear that democratic government would not be sacrificed.

For the dissenters, elections and executive responsibility to the legislature sufficed for democracy.[64] But for the majority, democracy implements popular sovereignty and "enabling an authoritarian system . . . [is] the negation of parliamentary democracy."[65] Instead, the Constitution's democratic structure required "legislative, executive and judicial organs,"[66] a democratic parliament and state participation in the amending process.[67]

The justices went beyond the specifics of the governing system; the "democratic ideal" also "assures . . . the dignity of the individual and other cherished human values" for full personal development.[68] Fundamental rights help "ensure the ideal of political democracy and prevent authoritarian rule."[69]

The Court's linkage of democracy with widespread economic welfare was equally groundbreaking. In describing that linkage, The Court articulated an understanding of democracy accelerated by World War II and reflected in the Indian Constitution. Justices K. S. Hegde and A. K. Mukherjea wrote: independence "from foreign rule . . . [is] only . . . an opportunity to bring about economic and social advancement." Tying that directly to the Indian Constitution, they wrote, "this liberty to do better . . . is the theme of the directive Principles of State Policy in Part IV of the Constitution."[70] They added, "Representative democracies will have no meaning without economic and social justice to the common man." Justice Reddy emphasized their point in a history of the Directive Principles.[71]

Perhaps to mollify the prime minister about the fate of India's impoverished millions, the justices emphasized the Constitution's "mandate to build a welfare State" as part of the basic structure, which could not be sacrificed.[72] The Constitution barred the courts from applying them, but Justices Shelat and Grover announced, "the court may not entirely ignore these directive principles" when "determining the scope and ambit of the fundamental rights." Instead it "should adopt the principle of harmonious construction and should attempt to give effect to both as much as possible."[73]

Meanwhile, the Allahabad High Court banned Gandhi from Parliament for six years for misconduct in the 1971 elections. She responded with a constitutional amendment overturning that result. That suit arrived in the Supreme Court of India in 1975, two years after *Kesavananda Bharati*.[74] By then, Gandhi had declared a state of emergency. Legislators were jailed during what Indians refer to as "the Emergency," probably altering the vote in Parliament on the amendment.[75] The Court retreated regarding her seat in Parliament but four of the five justices who heard the appeal held the amendment inconsistent with the basic structure doctrine of *Kesavananda Bharati,* although they differed in their reasoning.[76]

The crisis culminated in rule by decree from June 1975 to March 1977, and violent suppression of opposition. Sankaran Krishna reported that Indira Gandhi suspended the Constitution, "imprison[ing] all key opposition leaders and Congress dissidents, and . . . [running] roughshod over the democratic rights of citizens." The Emergency led to "the arbitrary arrest and imprisonment of more than a hundred thousand citizens . . . a campaign of forced sterilization . . . the disappearance of hundreds of individuals, and produced the complete demoralization of the bureaucracy," doing lasting harm to Indian democracy.[77]

A stronger judiciary emerged from the chaos but at great cost.[78] Only the Preamble mentions democracy, but the Court repeatedly decided that the Constitution protects what democracy requires, including respect for individual dignity, political competition, universal suffrage, civil liberties, and economic justice as envisioned in the Directive Principles on welfare, always emphasizing universalism.

The Court starts with "government by the people."[79] That principle mandates "adults [*sic*] suffrage, that is to say, every person who is citizen of India and who is not less than 18 years of age . . . shall be entitled to be registered as a voter at any such election" unless "disqualified . . . [by] non-residence, unsoundness of mind, crime or corrupt or illegal practice."[80]

Democracy means "government by the people . . . a continual participative . . . appeal to the people after every term." To do that, India has "adult franchise and general election as constitutional compulsions." Indeed, "the heart of the Parliamentary system is free and fair elections periodically held, based on adult franchise, although social and economic democracy may demand much more."[81] The Court repeatedly stresses "free and fair periodical elections based on adult franchise" are necessary for democracy."[82] Everyone must be included: "True democracy cannot exist unless all citizens have a right to participate in the affairs of the polity of the country."

Participation is "meaningless unless the citizens are well informed" and "a farce" when media are "monopolised."[83] Therefore the Court protects the "[v]oter's (little man-citizen's) right to know" as "fundamental and basic for survival of democracy."[84] The Court added, "The right to get information in democracy . . . [is a] natural right flowing from the concept of democracy."[85] The Court also added its weight to the drive for voting machinery that facilitates verification of the accuracy of the recorded ballot.[86]

The Indian Court understands competition is essential to a democratic system and courts as barriers to devices that entrench officeholders against the wishes of their constituents. As the Court put it, the "essence" of "parliamentary democracy . . . is to draw a direct line of authority from the people through the legislature to the executive."[87] The "legislature, thus, must owe their power directly or indirectly to the people."[88]

By contrast, interreligious violence especially around elections, led the Court to extensive restriction of speech, and that attitude limiting speech to proper behavior extended to criticism of the courts' own work. "Bonafide criticism of any system or institution including the judiciary cannot be objected to as healthy and constructive criticism are tools to augment forensic tools for improving its function"; but "[n]obody has a right to denigrate others right of person and reputation"[89] to "impair or hamper the administration of justice,"[90] and "society . . . is entitled to regulate freedom of speech or expression by democratic action."[91] Judges and courts can properly be criticized but only "if reasonable argument or criticism in respectful language and tempered with moderation [are] offered."[92]

In the face of Justice Frankfurter's advice to omit a due process clause, the Indian Supreme Court balances freedom and security: "[L]iberty . . . must give way" when it conflicts with state or public security; but "[i]n a democracy governed by the Rule of Law, the drastic power to detain a person without trial for security of the State and/or maintenance of public order, must be strictly construed."[93] An early decision of the Supreme Court of India overturned a statute that allowed the dissolution of an association that assisted the then banned Communist Party. The Court invalidated the statute for lack of adequate procedural safeguards.[94] And the Court is also prepared to hold the police accountable.[95]

The *Kesavananda Bharati* majority agreed that India is a federal state, and that federalism is a part of the basic structure of the Indian Constitution that could not be abolished.[96] But they did not make the connection between federalism and democracy, so common in American thinking, or discuss any relation between them. Their point was not a specific conception of federalism or its functions, but rather that some federal role had to be retained. Beyond that fundamental point, their approach was positivist—federalism is whatever the Constitution provides.[97] Those in the minority denied "the theory [that federalism imposed] implied or inherent limitations" on national power.[98] Justices on both sides were at pains to demonstrate the general supremacy of the federal government.[99]

The Indian Court demonstrated a great deal of courage in protecting Indian democracy and has won respect from jurists worldwide for its work. It took strong stands on constitutional structure, elections, equality, and religious tolerance. Its rhetoric on economic welfare was reflected in another group of cases that, while not repeating the connection to democracy, required consideration of the needs of the poor.[100] Indian positions on free expression are troubling because of vague standards, the Court's preference for its own self-interest and the difficulty of defining respectful interfaith dialog or criticism. Perhaps like all courts, its record is mixed but nevertheless inspiring.

Supreme Court of Canada

The Supreme Court of Canada understands "the values and principles essential to a free and democratic society" as including "respect for the inherent dignity of the human person, commitment to social justice and equality, accommodation of a wide variety of beliefs, respect for cultural and group identity, and faith in social and political institutions which enhance the participation of individuals and groups in society."[101] In its "commitment to social justice and equality," the Court appeared to be referring to the kind of economic rights developed in the Universal Declaration and in the Indian Directive Principles. Quoting the same language in a later decision, the Court held that hate speech had no place in a democratic society.[102]

Looking at several equality provisions of the Canadian Charter of Rights and Freedom, the Court held that promoting equality is not just one of many constitutional requirements, but "an undertaking essential to any free and democratic society." The Court held that speech can "undermine our commitment to democracy" when it attacks democratic values and therefore it was appropriate for a statute to protect equality and democracy from the promotion of hatred.[103] "Hate propaganda" argues "for a society in which the democratic process is subverted" and people "are denied respect and dignity simply because of racial or religious characteristics." So the Court concluded such hate speech is "wholly inimical to the democratic aspirations of the free expression guarantee."[104]

In reaching those conclusions, the Court upheld the prosecution of James Keegstra, a high school teacher in Alberta who was charged "with unlawfully promoting hatred against an identifiable group by communicating antisemitic statements to his students."[105] He had taught anti-semitism in class and graded the students on how well they learned it.

In other cases, the misuse of prosecutions for abusive language against the very people the statute was designed to protect has been troublesome.[106] Narrower judgments restricted to the obligations of teachers might well have reached similar conclusions while leaving less room for abuse. The Court's response that the requirement of intent would protect against misuse seems inadequate. Nevertheless, the *Keegstra* decision reflects the feeling of commitment by members of the Canadian Supreme Court to protect and advance democracy, to treat equality as an essential part of democracy, and to keep hatred out of the schools. As the Court wrote in another decision, "hate propaganda . . . erod[es] the tolerance and open-mindedness that must flourish in a multicultural society which is committed to the idea of equality."[107]

When the issue of the possible secession of Quebec heated up in the late 1990s, the government asked the Court to advise it on three questions: whether the Constitution of Canada permits Quebec to secede unilaterally, whether international law gives Quebec that option, and whether the Constitution or international law would take precedence in the event of a conflict.[108] Those questions led the Supreme Court of Canada to make an extensive examination of the concept of democracy under both the Canadian Constitution and international law.

The Court started by returning to section 1 of the Canadian Charter of Rights and Freedoms, which uses the term *democratic* as a limitation on how rights and freedoms can be circumscribed. The Supreme Court concluded that "there are four fundamental and organizing principles of the Constitution which are relevant to addressing the question before us." The Court then listed "federalism; democracy; constitutionalism and the rule of law; and respect for minorities."[109] The Court decided that these principles are constitutionally fundamental, "[a]lthough these underlying principles are not explicitly made part of the Constitution by any written provision." The Court concluded: "[I]t would be impossible to conceive of our constitutional structure without them. The principles dictate major elements of the architecture of the Constitution itself and are as such its lifeblood."[110] As the Court explained: "These principles . . . are the vital unstated assumptions upon which the text is based" and therefore "inform and sustain the constitutional text."[111]

This of course is familiar to U.S. lawyers as "structural" interpretation. It is the same logical step that the U.S. Supreme Court has taken through much of its history in discussing federalism and the separation of powers.[112]

The Canadian Supreme Court explained that the concept of democracy includes the entire population, rather than justifying the rule of one portion of the population by another. The Court saw a Canadian tradition of "evolutionary democracy moving in uneven steps toward the goal of universal suffrage and more effective representation. Since Confederation, efforts to extend the franchise to those unjustly excluded from participation in our political system—such as women, minorities, and aboriginal peoples—have continued, with some success, to the present day."[113] The Constitution and the Court treat popular sovereignty and the right to vote as coextensive. Institutionally, "democracy means that each of the provincial legislatures and the federal Parliament is elected by popular franchise." Individually, "the right to vote in elections to the House of Commons and the provincial legislatures, and to be candidates in those elections, is guaranteed to 'Every citizen of Canada.'"[114] Democracy includes "the right of citizens to participate in the political process as voters . . . and as candidates."[115]

The "notwithstanding power" permits "Parliament or the legislature of a province . . . [to] expressly declare . . . that [an] Act or a provision . . . shall operate notwithstanding" its violation of a number of other protections in the charter. The Supreme Court of Canada noted that the significance of the "democratic principle," however, which requires regular parliamentary elections, "is not subject to the notwithstanding" power; neither is the right to vote.[116]

"[D]emocracy is [also] fundamentally connected to substantive goals, most importantly, the promotion of self-government."[117] The Court "articulated some of the values inherent in the notion of democracy" and "essential to a free and democratic society." To spell them out it returned to the language of *Oakes* listing human "dignity . . . social justice and equality, accommodation of a wide variety of beliefs, respect for cultural and group identity, and . . . institutions which enhance the participation of individuals and groups in society."[118]

The Court's assertion of the importance of the connection between democracy and human welfare is reminiscent of Germany, India, and the UN Universal Declaration of Human Rights. In making that connection the Supreme Court of Canada implicitly drew a philosophical connection between the inclusiveness of the right and the purposes of democracy, as in Lincoln's "of . . . by . . . and for the people." Though the Canadian judgment appears to have been based on moral principles rather than empirical connections, a strong causal relationship is verified by empirical work, to be discussed below.

"Universal suffrage and more effective representation," the rule of law and the protection of minority rights are all related to core democratic concepts of providing opportunity for discussion and change.[119] Thus it is inconsistent with democracy for a majority to decide to exclude a portion of the population in the future. The position of the province of Quebec depended on resolving minority rights with respect to both language and religion throughout Canada, not on the exclusion of English or French speakers from portions of Canada.[120]

The Court concluded that all of the principles involved—federalism, democracy, constitutionalism, the rule of law, and respect for minorities— enveloped Quebec in wider structures that barred unilateralism, but that also imposed a duty on the federal government to bargain in good faith with Quebec over the issues and incidents of secession if the Quebecois voted to secede.[121]

Many international agreements protect self-determination but, the Court added, treat it as a counterpart of the democratic principle.[122] Democracy, under those agreements, belongs to the nation state as an entity. Parts of the state have the right to secede only if they are oppressed. Quebec had been well represented in Canada, the source of many prime ministers, and not oppressed, despite the desire of some Quebecois for their own state.[123]

Shortly after the Quebec case, the Court reconsidered the exclusion of prisoners from voting in Canadian elections and reinforced its conclusion that democratic rights must be universal.[124] A prior statute had been found unconstitutional two decades earlier. Section 3 of the charter declares "[e]very citizen of Canada has the right to vote." The Supreme Court held that a statute denying voting rights to people "imprisoned in a correctional institution serving a sentence of two years or more"[125] violated the voting rights provision of the charter.

Once again the Court considered the charter requirement that any limitation of a protected right is permissible only if "demonstrably justifiable in a free and democratic society." The Court held it was not. "The right to vote is fundamental to our democracy and the rule of law." Therefore, the Court held, "[a]ny limits on it require not deference" to the judgment of the legislature, "but careful examination."

Having no counterpart, the Canadian Court had no occasion to examine the language of the Fourteenth Amendment section 2 providing an electoral penalty "when the right to vote at any [federal and most state] election[s] . . . is . . . in any way abridged, except for participation in rebellion, or other crime." Instead, the Canadian judgment examined equality and the vote as central aspects of democracy.

The Court concluded: "The Crown failed to establish a rational connection between denying the vote to penitentiary inmates and its stated goals of promoting civic responsibility and respect for the rule of law, and enhancing the general purposes of the criminal sanction."[126] The Court wrote that denying "prisoners the right to vote is to lose an important means of teaching them democratic values and social responsibility." In fact, the Court found it "more likely to send messages that undermine respect for the law and democracy than messages that enhance those values.[127]

At a deeper level, the Court found that disenfranchising "penitentiary inmates [of] the right to vote misrepresents the nature of our rights and obligations under the law and consequently undermines them."[128] Basic democratic principles require more: "In a democracy . . . the power of lawmakers flows from the voting citizens." The "lawmakers act as the citizens' proxies." Law receives "its legitimacy or force" from "[t]his delegation from voters to legislators."[129]

Both "the legitimacy of the law and the obligation to obey the law flow directly from the right of every citizen to vote."[130] Those conclusions "[flow] from the fact that the law is made by and on behalf of the citizens."

In language reminiscent of the founding of the United States, the Court wrote: "This connection, inherited from social contract theory"—which Americans took from Hobbes, Locke and others at the time of the American Revolution—was "enshrined in the Charter," and "stands at the heart of our system of constitutional democracy."[131] Equality is central to the social contract, and central to democracy: "The government's . . . political theory . . . would permit elected representatives to disenfranchise a segment of the population." It "finds no place in a democracy built upon principles of inclusiveness, equality, and citizen participation."[132]

The Court also rejected the notion that the inmates lost the right because of their own misbehavior: "Denial of the right to vote on the basis of attributed moral unworthiness is inconsistent with the respect for the dignity of every person that lies at the heart of Canadian democracy and the Charter. . . . It also runs counter to the plain words of s. 3, its exclusion from the s. 33 override, and the idea that laws command obedience because they are made by those whose conduct they govern. For all these reasons, it must . . . be rejected."[133] Everyone's vote counts.

In 2006 Gurbaj Singh Multani, an orthodox Sikh, challenged school tolerance when he was about twelve and accidentally dropped his kirpan, a metal religious object resembling a dagger. School authorities, Gurbaj Singh, and his parents agreed he could wear the kirpan if sealed inside his clothing but the board refused. The Court returned to section 1 of the Canadian charter to harmonize the competing interests and pointed to the importance of religious tolerance: "Learning respect for . . . [the constitutional] rights [of all members of society] is essential to our democratic society and should be part of the education of all students." Schools "have a duty to foster the respect of their students" for the rights of others and "these values are best taught by example and may be undermined if the students' rights are ignored by those in authority."[134] By contrast, "an absolute prohibition would stifle the promotion of . . . multiculturalism, diversity, and . . . an educational culture respectful of . . . others."[135]

Principles entail risks and other students might think it unfair that they cannot carry knives, but it is "incumbent on the schools to . . . instill" multiculturalism in students because it is "at the very foundation of our democracy."[136]

In these and other cases, democracy matters to the Supreme Court of Canada. Because it matters, many things follow. Democracy requires and is based on popular sovereignty, including the entire adult population in the voting electorate. They are expressed through discussion and an electoral process that makes the government accountable to the public. They require concern for public welfare, civil liberties, and minority rights. All are inherent in the concept of democracy and are mutually supportive.

Constitutional Court of South Africa

The Constitutional Court of South Africa inherited an unusual responsibility—to decide whether the yet unwritten 1996 Constitution complied with Constitutional Principles negotiated in 1993 as white-run South Africa became the new multiracial South Africa.[137] Equality and universality were touchstones of virtually every provision. The shift to black majority power made equal rights important to white, tribal, and Asian South Africans.

Under the Constitutional Principles, the Court would determine whether the new Constitution (a) provided one state, common citizenship and "a democratic system of government committed to achieving equality between men and women and people of all races"; (b) created a "representative government embracing multi-party democracy, regular elections, universal adult suffrage, [and] a common voters' roll"; and (c) assured minority participation in the political system with "proportional representation" and "participation of minority political parties in the legislative process in a manner consistent with democracy" and "democratic representation" at "each level of government."[138] These principles required the Court to consider the meaning of democracy before the new Constitution could take effect.

The Court issued a single opinion signed "By the Court" to emphasize its unity at the unprecedented task.[139] It held the text largely complied with the Constitutional Principles.[140] The new document created a "democratic system . . . founded on openness, accountability and equality." It provided for equality and inclusion of all in the political system "with universal adult suffrage . . . regular elections" and "representative government." The principles required, and the Court held, that the proposed Constitution embrace "multi-party democracy, a common voters' roll and, in general, proportional representation."[141] Voters choose parties, not individuals, in proportional representation systems, and the number of votes for the party determines the number of individual candidates who would be seated. Proportional representation would make the new South African government more like European than U.S. models, and it would permit representation of regional minorities, including white South Africans as well as regional tribal minorities.[142]

The Court commented that "the drafters of the . . . [Constitutional Principles], having . . . established the principle that the state they contemplated would be a democracy, immediately proceeded to describe one of its key attributes," namely that "[e]veryone shall enjoy all universally accepted fundamental rights, freedoms and civil liberties." The Constitutional Principles required that those rights, freedoms, and liberties "shall be provided for and protected by entrenched and justiciable provisions in the Constitution." In other words, courts should be able to protect those rights and the legislature should not be able to abandon them.

Quoting the Preamble to the Interim Constitution, which accompanied the Constitutional Principles, the Court explained that the drafters were determined "to create a new order in which all South Africans will be entitled to a common South African citizenship in a sovereign and democratic constitutional state in which there is equality between men and women and people of all races so that all citizens shall be able to enjoy and exercise their fundamental rights and freedoms."[143] In addressing the content of what rights are "fundamental," the Court surveyed the major international documents of the years since World War II. It rejected a search for complete consensus, which would leave little content. Instead they wrote: "What the drafters had in mind were those rights and freedoms recognised in open and democratic societies as being the inalienable entitlements of human beings."[144] The court viewed the Constitutional Principles as seeking "those rights that have gained a wide measure of international acceptance as fundamental human rights" and requiring that those "must necessarily be included."[145]

The constitutional text permits fundamental rights to be limited or infringed only if the "relationship between the right to be protected and the importance of the objective to be achieved by the limitation" were appropriately balanced, including an examination of alternative means to accomplish the government's purpose. That is known in South Africa and other countries as *proportionality* and is similar to a strong version of what is known in the United States as *strict scrutiny*.[146]

The Court was sensitive to the constitutional bargains reached to maximize support for the new government. The requirement that the Constitution protect democratic values while preserving "traditional leadership, customary law and, at the provincial level, traditional monarchy" presented a major challenge.[147] The Court recognized that "[i]n a purely republican democracy, in which no differentiation of status on grounds of birth is recognised, no constitutional space exists for the official recognition of any traditional leaders, let alone a monarch."[148] The 1993 Principles, however, required recognition of traditional institutions. "The non-derogation section thus opens the way for traditional leadership to be involved in democratic government," although without prescribing how.[149]

Preservation of traditional codes also conflicted with "equality before the law" if the 1993 Principles "presuppose[ed] a single and undifferentiated legal regime for all South Africans."[150] However, the 1993 Principles "authori[zed] . . . recognition of indigenous law."[151]

Reconciling the Constitution with the required democratic participation in government presented the Court with several issues, one group of which revolved around the role of political parties. The 1993 Principles required "[p]rovision . . . for participation of minority political parties in the legislative process in a manner consistent with democracy." The draft constitution, however, gave each province a single vote in the National Council of Provinces (NCOP) decided by each delegation's majority. Provincial minority parties would not be reflected in the NCOP. Noting provisions "for the full participation of minority political parties" in the National Assembly, the Court decided that "to involve the provinces" and "provide a forum [for] . . . provincial interests," one vote per province was acceptable.[152]

Another question revolving around the representation and participation of South Africans in government through minority parties arose over the requirement that "legislators . . . vacate their seats if they cease to be members of the parties that nominated them."[153] The Court wrote that the antidefection clause "meets the expectations of voters who gave their support to the party" and therefore promotes accountability to the electorate.[154] It held that legislators' freedom from such restraint is not universally accepted.[155]

As in the United Kingdom, the proposed constitution permitted executive officers to be members of the legislature. Against the charge that it provided an insufficient separation of powers, the Court responded that no countries completely separate powers.[156] It found that "the overlap provides a singularly important check and balance on the exercise of executive power" which "makes the executive more directly answerable to the elected legislature."[157]

The Court concluded that the 1996 draft largely met the standards of the 1993 Principles. But several protections for fundamental, individual, and minority rights were found wanting and not sufficiently protected from abridgment, and the 1996 draft did not entrench judicial jurisdiction to protect those rights, nor the right of individual employers to engage in collective bargaining. The Court required more protection for minorities from the amendment process through "special procedures involving special majorities." And it held the 1996 draft did not safeguard the independence and impartiality of the Public Service Commission, Auditor-General and Public Protector. Regarding federalism, the Court decided that the 1996 draft failed to provide the provincial autonomy, fiscal and other powers required by the 1993 Principles and failed to provide formal legislative procedures for local legislatures.[158]

As the Court predicted, those problems were quickly solved and the Constitution went into effect as amended a little over two months later.

The following year, the Court linked democracy with human welfare.[159] Suffering from irreversible renal failure, forty-one-year-old Thiagraj Soobramoney sought dialysis based on the 1996 Constitution which provides: "No one may be refused emergency medical treatment" and stipulates "[e]veryone has the right to life."[160] The Court decided against ordering dialysis because choices on the use of scarce resources were inevitable and the medical protocols appropriate. But President Chaskalson's opinion for the Court focused on the Constitution's economic aspirations. He noted South Africa's "great disparities in wealth" and the millions "living in deplorable conditions and in great poverty" with high unemployment and inadequate security, and without "access to clean water or to adequate health services"; he added the "commitment to address" these conditions "and to transform our society into one . . . [with] human dignity, freedom and equality, lies at the heart of our new constitutional order."[161]

President Chaskalson emphasized the point with words of the Preamble: "We therefore . . . adopt this Constitution . . . to—Heal the divisions of the past and establish a society based on democratic values, social justice and fundamental human rights . . . [and] Improve the quality of life of all citizens and free the potential of each person." This commitment to democratic values, social justice, and fundamental human rights is "reflected in various provisions of the bill of rights." In addition, "human dignity, equality and freedom" are specifically described as "democratic values" in the Constitution.[162] "Some rights in the Constitution are the ideal . . . to be strived for . . . amount[ing] to a promise . . . and an indication of what a democratic society aiming to salvage lost dignity, freedom and equality should embark upon."[163]

Justice Sachs, concurring, added that the Court's opinion "does not merely 'toll the bell of lack of resources.'"[164] In "open and democratic societies based upon dignity, freedom and equality," principled and consistent decisions about care are preferred to merely arbitrary ones.[165] And he elaborated on the necessary "framework based on . . . interdependence." Sachs explained that we depend on each other for a "healthy life . . . : the quality of air, water, and sanitation which the State maintains for the public good; the quality of one's caring relationships, which are highly correlated to health; as well as the quality of health care and support furnished officially by medical institutions and provided informally by family, friends, and the community."[166]

The justices linked a free and democratic society with programs for the welfare of the public, including health care, as twin inferences from the same fundamental human values, to which they added that one is a goal of the other.

Four years later, the Court provided limited relief, declaring that the government had not satisfied its obligation to house those without decent places to live:[167] "Mrs Grootboom and . . . other[s] . . . lived in an informal squatter settlement . . . in shacks . . . [with] no water, sewage or refuse removal services and only 5% of the shacks had electricity. The area is partly waterlogged and lies dangerously close to a main thoroughfare."[168] They tried to move onto better land but were evicted. Because their former places were now occupied, they had nowhere to go. The government objected even to providing "tents, portable latrines and a regular supply of water (albeit transported)."[169] The problem stemmed from the apartheid era when government evicted Africans from areas near available jobs. But the Constitution promised efforts to improve the lives of those forced to live in conditions the Court described as "appalling."

The Court understood that allocating resources involves complex trade-offs but concluded that government had not acted appropriately. "Our Constitution entrenches both civil and political rights and social and economic rights," the Court said. "All the rights in our Bill of Rights are inter-related and mutually supporting." It added, "human dignity, freedom and equality, the foundational values of our society, are denied those who have no food, clothing or shelter."[170] Welfare rights affect everyone because until "the plight of these communities is alleviated, people may be tempted to take the law into their own hands in order to escape these conditions" as Mrs. Grootboom and those with her tried to do.[171]

Government, the Court held, "failed to make reasonable provision within its available resources for people in the Cape Metropolitan area with no access to land, no roof over their heads, and who were living in intolerable conditions or crisis situations." Instead "the Constitution requires the state to devise and implement within its available resources a comprehensive and co-ordinated programme progressively to realise the right of access to adequate housing."[172]

While it is difficult to measure the impact of the Court's declaratory relief, Theunis Roux reported "a slow but inexorable shift in national housing policy towards the position preferred by the Court."[173]

Meanwhile, the Court made good on its conclusion that "[e]veryone has the right to have access to . . . health care services."[174] The manufacturers had offered Nevirapine free at birth for babies of HIV-infected mothers but the government refused to provide it at public hospitals despite a World Health Organization recommendation because it prevents transmission to the children. The Court ordered the government to make it available "without delay."[175] The Court's handling of constitutional welfare rights was thus cautious but positive.

The democratic principle of universal suffrage was challenged by the refusal to allow prisoners to vote. The first of two suits was brought before any legislation on the subject.[176] After the decision in favor of the prisoners, government passed legislation leading to a second suit brought by the National Institute for Crime Prevention and the Reintegration of Offenders (NICRO). It concluded that prisoners have a right to vote and government had to make it possible.[177]

The Constitution bars any limitation on protected rights that are not "reasonable and justifiable in an open and democratic society based on human dignity, equality and freedom," and requires analysis of the "proportionality" of the means chosen to the objectives and alternatives.[178] The Court in NICRO quoted its earlier opinion stressing the importance of "the universality of the franchise . . . for nationhood and democracy . . . [and as] a badge of dignity and of personhood. Quite literally, it says that everybody counts."[179] The court later added: "[T]he right to vote is foundational to democracy which is a core value of our Constitution . . . denial of the right to vote was used to entrench white supremacy and to marginalise the great majority of the people of our country. . . . [I]t is for us a precious right which must be vigilantly respected and protected."[180]

The systematic deprivation of voting rights observed in South Africa parallels the incarceration of blacks and Latinos by the American criminal system out of all proportion to their participation in criminal activity, resulting in extensive disenfranchisement of minorities in the United States.[181]

After discussing the Canadian cases on prisoners voting rights, the Court tactfully added that the government in South Africa had not provided information that would justify denying the prisoners' rights and ordered that the prisoners be allowed to vote.[182]

Saying voting laws "must be interpreted in favour of enfranchisement rather than disenfranchisement,"[183] the Constitutional Court decided that the African Christian Democratic Party should be allowed to contest a local election. The party had been barred because of a late deposit to cover costs. But the Court wrote that a previous general deposit was sufficient and should be used.[184] The "foundational values" in the Constitution, including universal adult suffrage, require the courts and the Electoral Commission "to seek to promote enfranchisement rather than disenfranchisement and participation rather than exclusion" when interpreting electoral statutes.[185]

The Court also decided democratic principles required enfranchising voters in a case involving a change in provincial boundaries. The changes stemmed from the intentional resettlement policies of the prior apartheid regime. The case raised issues that resemble the combination of gerrymandering with zoning and other American suburbanization policies. The Court saw the risk of "undermin[ing the South African] multi-party system of democratic government." Although "the national legislature could alter provincial boundaries and any [necessarily included] municipal boundaries," the Court found "there were good reasons to exclude legislatures from changing [any other] municipal boundaries and giving that power exclusively to an independent body" in order to avoid "political interference." The independent board was set up for that reason.[186]

In a sequel, the Court held that municipal hearings were required for its role in the process of changing boundaries,[187] in order to provide "participatory democracy, accountability, transparency and public involvement," because the South African "conception of . . . democracy" requires more participation than merely voting.[188]

The antidefection clause returned to the Court when the national legislature amended the Constitution to permit legislators to change parties and still keep their seats in national, provincial, and local legislatures.[189] As parties forged alliances and ran under new banners, it led to difficulty and confusion, and the Constitution was changed.

Crossing the floor to join another party has the effect of changing the proportion of legislators for the relevant parties. The Court was asked to decide whether the change undermined the basic structure of the Constitution and was therefore impermissible as the Indian Supreme Court sometimes found. The South African Court held it did not undermine the basic democratic structure. Many electoral systems, the court wrote, "are consistent with democracy, some containing anti-defection clauses, others not; some proportional, others not. . . . [The changes are not] so fundamental to our constitutional order as to preclude any amendment of their provisions."[190]

Nor was an antidefection clause essential to proportional representation. The "link between voter and party" is "closer" in proportional systems. "But even in constituency-based elections," the link between legislators and parties is close and defectors are "equally open to the accusation" of betraying the voters.[191] The nondefector rule therefore "is not an essential component of multi-party democracy . . . [or] proportional representation."[192]

The Court did not think the change required the special procedures applicable to a change in the founding values, specifically the requirement of multiparty democracy.[193] Nor did the mere shift of partisan advantages make it unconstitutional. All electoral systems favor one or another political party or position to some degree. "For instance, the introduction of a constituency-based system of elections may operate to the prejudice of smaller parties," but it is still a democratic system.[194] And "accommodat[ing] mid-term shifts in political allegiances" appeared to be a valid purpose.[195]

The Court refused to look at motives or consequences.[196] It focused only on whether the procedural rules, founding purposes, and Constitutional Principles left the legislature power to make the change. The Court ultimately invalidated one of the four acts on the ground that it could only have been passed as a constitutional amendment, not as ordinary legislation.[197]

Democratic requirements for participation in government returned to the Court regarding appointments to mayoral committees.[198] Johannesburg's mayor appointed only members of the African National Congress (ANC) to his mayoral committee. The ANC had spearheaded the struggle against apartheid and won the majority of seats on the municipal council, to which the Constitution gave executive authority.[199] The Constitution required that "parties and interests reflected within the Council . . . be fairly represented" on committees of the council.[200] The impact of exclusion would be racial, tribal, and ideological. The Court adopted a separation of powers argument, holding that minority parties had to be fairly represented on legislative but not executive committees.[201] The majority wrote that the constitutional goal "to provide democratic and accountable government for local communities" meant "ensuring that the will of the majority prevails and also that the views of the minority are considered."[202] Thus their language supported both popular sovereignty and inclusion of contrasting views. And the Court linked inclusiveness to democracy. But in their judgment that concept was limited.

Justice O'Regan dissented, writing: "The fundamental constitutional purpose is to undo the separation, exclusion and inequality of the past by ensuring that there is shared involvement in deliberation subject, of course, to the right of the majority to make decisions."[203]

Justice Sachs, concurring, agreed with much of O'Regan's "eloquent and forceful reasoning . . . particularly . . . [on] the importance of . . . inclusivity at the local government level."[204] Justice Sachs put the argument for inclusion in both international and traditional terms:

The requirement of fair representation . . . contemplates a pluralistic democracy where continuous respect is given to the rights of all to be heard and have their views considered. The dialogic nature of deliberative democracy has its roots both in international democratic practice and indigenous African tradition. It was through dialogue and sensible accommodation on an inclusive and principled basis that the Constitution itself emerged. It would accordingly be perverse to construe its terms in a way that belied or minimised the importance of the very inclusive process that led to its adoption, and sustains its legitimacy.[205]

Like some U.S. states, legislation regulated approval of abortion facilities together with what the Court collectively described as health legislation.[206] Doctors for Life complained that the "[obligation] to facilitate public involvement" in the legislative process had not been honored on abortion facilities and other pieces of health related legislation.[207] Reviewing the issue of participation, the Court described it as "at the heart of our constitutional democracy," and "crucial" to it and overturned some of the legislation.[208]

In support of its decision, the Court cited international documents describing the right of participation as "a general right to take part in the conduct of public affairs; and a more specific right to vote and/or to be elected."[209] The International Covenant on Civil and Political Rights (ICCPR) provides: "Every citizen shall have the right and the opportunity . . . [t]o vote and to be elected at genuine periodic elections . . . by universal and equal suffrage and . . . by secret ballot, guaranteeing the free expression of the will of the electors."[210] Justice Ngcobo emphasized that the ICCPR "guaranteed . . . the 'opportunity'" as well as the right. Suffrage must be both "universal and equal."[211] Summarizing the ICCPR, he wrote: "Taken together, they seek to ensure that citizens have the necessary information and the effective opportunity to exercise the right to political participation."[212] He found similar provisions in African and inter-American documents which protected the right to take part and participate in self-government, though realized in different ways.[213]

South Africa, like much of the world, protects less speech and expression than U.S. doctrine. Their rules became an issue when the Department of Correctional Services continued to hold Mr. Terre Blanche, the leader of the Afrikaner Weerstandsbeweging (African Resistance Movement, a white supremacist, neo-Nazi group), despite an order granting him bail. Mr. Russell Mamabolo, spokesperson of the Department of Correctional Services, told a local paper that the order granting bail was in error. He also told the reporter that the department had documents that showed that the order granting bail was erroneous.

The judge was furious and directed his anger at Mr. Mamabolo.[214] The following Monday morning, applicants for the state and the prisoner appeared before him, though the nature of the proceedings was not clear to the Constitutional Court. The judge questioned them about the facts and gave them an opportunity to comment. Mr. Mamabolo's counsel was not given the opportunity to comment "or explore any of the factual material."[215] Counsel did, however, tell the judge that "the Constitution has overtaken the court's previous powers to summarily order people before court to give an explanation of any kind whatsoever."[216]

The judge held Mr. Mamabolo in contempt. It is somewhat unclear from the judge's comments whether he was held in contempt for ignoring the bail order, although as the department's public affairs representative there was no indication that he had power to order the release of Mr. Terre Blanche, or whether he was held in contempt for saying the judge was wrong.[217] The judge declined to hold a commissioner in contempt because he may not have known about the statements to the press, although he might have had more to do with the actions of the department holding Mr. Terre Blanche.

The Constitutional Court unanimously set the contempt order aside, but the justices were disturbed by the position taken by the department: "It would have been a very serious matter indeed, calling for speedy and decisive action, if the order had actually been defied. The spectre of executive officers refusing to obey orders of court because they think they were wrongly granted, is ominous. It strikes at the very foundations of the rule of law when government servants presume to disregard orders of court."[218] And the Court took the opportunity to assert a judicial right of self-protection. The Court's opinion initially challenged the power to condemn criticism: "Why should judges be sacrosanct? Is this not a relic of a bygone era . . . ? Are judges not hanging on to this legal weapon because it gives them a status and untouchability . . . ? Is it not rather a constitutional imperative that public office-bearers, such as judges, who wield great power, as judges undoubtedly do, should be accountable to the public who appoint them and pay them?"[219] To which Justice Kriegler added, "vocal public scrutiny . . . [is] a democratic check on the judiciary."[220] Indeed, "[f]reedom of expression . . . is of the utmost importance in the kind of open and democratic society the Constitution has set as our aspirational norm."[221] It is especially important in South Africa because of the country's "recent past of thought control, censorship and enforced conformity to governmental theories, freedom of expression," Justice Kriegler continues, "[an] open market-place of ideas is all the more important . . . because our democracy is not yet firmly established. . . . Therefore we should be particularly astute to outlaw any form of thought-control, however respectably dressed."[222] But because the courts are weak, their answer was sometimes, not never.[223] They resisted the American approach because the power "of invalidating any law or governmental conduct . . . [that courts find] inconsistent with the Constitution . . . could involve the judiciary in public contention."[224]

"[H]aving reposed such trust in the judiciary," the Court concluded, the Constitution shields the courts.[225] It requires the government to "assist and protect the courts to ensure" their "independence, impartiality, dignity, accessibility and effectiveness."[226] That language protects courts against slander, since "the crime of scandalising aims to protect" the courts' dignity.[227]

Justice Sachs, concurring, also thought the courts' dignity sometimes needed protection, but he resisted the majority's language. After quoting warnings from the Indian Supreme Court, he wrote: "If respect for the judiciary is to be regarded as integral to the maintenance of the rule of law, as I believe it should be, such respect will be spontaneous, enduring and real to the degree that it is earned, rather than to the extent that it is commanded."[228] A year later the Court addressed a complaint against the broadcast of an interview with a Holocaust denier. The complaint claimed the broadcast was likely to strain relations between Jews and other communities, in violation of Broadcast Authority regulations, which barred the broadcast of "material . . . likely to prejudice . . . relations between sections of the population."[229] While it was being processed, the Islamic Unity Convention sought an order declaring that the rules were unconstitutional.

South Africa protects freedom of expression but does not include "propaganda for war . . . incitement of imminent [violence] or advocacy of hatred that is based on race, ethnicity, gender or religion, and that constitutes incitement to cause harm."

The Court decided the case on the law without reference to the facts in the original complaint.[230] On the one hand, the Court described freedom of expression as part of "a 'web of mutually supporting rights,'" including the rights to religion, belief, opinion, dignity, association, assembly, and vote as well as the right to stand for public office; these rights "implicitly recognise the importance, both for a democratic society and for individuals personally, of the ability to form and express opinions, whether individually or collectively, even where those views are controversial."[231] Freedom of expression "lies at the heart of a democracy," is "a guarantor of democracy," recognizes "the moral agency of individuals," and "facilitat[es] . . . the search for truth."[232]

Reemphasizing "our recent past of thought control, censorship, and enforced conformity to governmental theories," the Court declared that "the open market-place of ideas is all the more important to us in [South Africa] because our democracy is not yet firmly established and must feel its way."[233]

The Court was not willing to follow the U.S. example because "[t]he pluralism and broadmindedness that is central to an open and democratic society can . . . be undermined by speech which seriously threatens democratic pluralism itself." Therefore "open and democratic societies permit reasonable proscription of activity and expression that pose a real and substantial threat to . . . [the] values [of dignity, equality, human rights and freedoms] and to the constitutional order itself." Many countries limit speech to protect the fairness of trials and elections.[234]

The Court's endorsement of protecting democracy by restricting expression assumed both the discernment and good faith of the deciding body. Ultimately the Court decided the regulation was both vague and overly broad, avoiding a choice on free speech grounds.[235]

One distinguished commentator described the conception of democracy embodied in the South African Constitution as "deep" rather than "shallow." Their concept goes well beyond elections, to participatory, multiparty, representative, and constitutional democracy, with a set of values emphasizing "human dignity, equality, and freedom."[236] It has been part of a recent wave of democratization—with "a common set of political institutions, including universal adult suffrage, regular elections, the right to free political participation and freedom of the press"—in which universal adult suffrage is "a necessary precondition for democracy."[237]

European Court of Human Rights

The European Court of Human Rights (ECtHR) takes cases under the European Convention of Human Rights, both products of the 1950 Convention of Rome. The Court opened in 1959 and sits in Strasbourg, France. With jurisdiction now over forty-seven member nations, it has become a very important court and window on developments throughout Europe.

The 1648 Treaty of Westphalia accepted state control over religious affiliation and Europeans continue to give states a large role in their lives. Nazi and Communist totalitarianism devastated Europe and caused Americans to fear state power; but Europeans blamed the Nazi and Bolshevik parties and paramilitaries for empowering Hitler and Stalin. Hence, Europe remains friendlier to government authority, and European agreements limit personal rights by what is necessary to protect a free and democratic order.[238] The ECtHR supports some preventive measures against political parties "deemed dangerous," because "political parties have more power over the people."[239]

As the court explained in a 1995 German case, it "takes into account Germany's experience" and Germany's wish "to avoid a repetition . . . by founding its new State on the idea that it should be a 'democracy capable of defending itself.'"[240] To Europeans, protecting democracy often meant defending it from its opponents or from issues that could tear apart democratic societies, like the former Yugoslavia. "These circumstances understandably lent extra weight to this underlying notion and to the corresponding duty of political loyalty imposed on civil servants."[241] That background creates a duality in European democratic thought: a full understanding of what democracy needs and a felt need to play with fire.

European courts emphasize that human rights law is an aspect of democracy.[242] Protocol 1 of the European Convention of Human Rights binds the members to "hold free elections at reasonable intervals by secret ballot, under conditions which will ensure the free expression of the opinion of the people in the choice of the legislature." The ECtHR held that "the opinion of the people" requires universal suffrage and participation. International covenants emphasize universality—"every" citizen has the right to vote, and suffrage is "universal."[243] What people have equally, they have universally, and vice versa. Equality plays an important part in the Court's decisions in many areas, from the settlement of land claims[244] to the right to vote[245] and freedom of religion.[246]

The Court's commitment to equal and universal adult suffrage was tested in *Hirst v. The United Kingdom*,[247] which was decided twelve to five and dealt with prisoners' rights to vote. The ban categorically barred voting by prisoners.[248] The judgment related to the indiscriminate ban on voting by prisoners, not individual justice. The applicant, John Hirst, was not a sympathetic individual.[249] Latvia intervened, lest a judgment affect it and other countries that barred all convicted prisoners from voting.[250] The Court summarized its survey of the parties to the European Convention on Human Rights: "a minority of Contracting States" imposed "a blanket restriction on the right of convicted prisoners to vote" or made "no provision allowing prisoners to vote."[251] It quickly added that the Convention, and therefore the sufficiency of the reasons behind the restriction, governed, not the numbers.[252]

The ECtHR examined the logic and experience of courts outside its jurisdiction which had similar democratic language. The Court described the 2002 *Sauvé* decision of the Canadian Supreme Court, which found its voting ban undermined the objectives of the policy. In the words of the ECtHR, the Canadian court had found that it "undermined respect for the law and democracy." Morally, according to the Supreme Court of Canada, "[t]he legitimacy of the law and the obligation to obey the law flowed directly from the right of every citizen to vote." Remedially, "[t]o deny prisoners the right to vote was to lose an important means of teaching them democratic values and social responsibility." Crucially, it "ran counter to democratic principles of inclusiveness, equality, and citizen participation." Thus, it "was inconsistent with the respect for the dignity of every person that lay at the heart of Canadian democracy and the Charter."[253]

The ECtHR agreed that the Canadian denial of voting rights had not been appropriate punishment, but "arbitrary" insofar as "it was not tailored to the acts and circumstances of the individual offender" so that it "bore little relation to the offender's particular crime."[254] And the Canadian ban had served no "valid criminal-law purpose" because "disenfranchisement [neither] deterred crime [n]or rehabilitated criminals."[255]

Turning to South Africa, the ECtHR discussed the first of the two major cases involving voting rights in South Africa, *August v. Electoral Commission*. The second case, *NICRO* (discussed in the previous section), was heard at nearly the same time as *Hirst* in Strasbourg. The court noted the significance the Constitutional Court of South Africa attached to the right to vote: "Quite literally, it says that everybody counts."[256] After apartheid, that was a significant achievement. The court noted that the South African Court "recognised that limitations might be imposed upon the exercise of fundamental rights, provided they were, *inter alia*, reasonable and justifiable."[257]

Then the ECtHR undertook its own analysis. It "highlight[ed] the importance of democratic principles underlying the interpretation and application of the Convention."[258] Those principles mean that "the right to vote is not a privilege"; instead "the presumption in a democratic State must be in favour of inclusion. . . . Universal suffrage has become the basic principle" of democracy.[259]

Differences "in historical development, cultural diversity and political thought within Europe" limit the power of an international treaty court.[260] But the European Convention of Human Rights bans limits on election and voting rights that "impair their very essence and deprive them of their effectiveness." It also requires any limitations "imposed [be] in pursuit of a legitimate aim; and that the means employed are not disproportionate."[261] The criterion for the Convention's guarantee of free elections is "an electoral procedure aimed at identifying the will of the people through universal suffrage."[262] The Convention warned: "Any departure from the principle of universal suffrage risks undermining the democratic validity of the legislature."[263]

Prisoners still have rights; they "continue to enjoy all the fundamental rights and freedoms guaranteed under the Convention save for the right to liberty."[264] The "Act remains a blunt instrument," disproportionate to any valid purpose. It "imposes a blanket restriction on all convicted prisoners in prison" and "applies automatically . . . irrespective of the length of their sentence and irrespective of the nature or gravity of their offence and their individual circumstances."[265] That indiscriminate ban on voting could not be well tailored for deterrence, retribution, or other significant purposes. Therefore, the Court concluded that "[s]uch a general, automatic and indiscriminate restriction on a vitally important Convention right must be seen as falling outside any acceptable margin" for national choice.[266]

Universal inclusion also led the Court to describe "pluralist democracy" as "the only political system . . . compatible with the Convention."[267] In Germany and South Africa pluralist democracy implied inclusion of opposition and most minor parties both in the election process and on legislative committees, a common result of systems of proportional representation.[268]

Tănase v. Moldova[269] dealt with Moldova's exclusion of those with dual nationality from the national legislature unless they renounced their other nationality. In a section of the Romanian-Moldovan border, many had dual citizenship. The ECtHR held they were improperly excluded "from participating in the political life of the country," with a "disproportionate effect" on opposition parties.[270]

Loyalty to the nation can be required of members of parliament, consisting of "respect for the country's Constitution, laws, institutions, independence and territorial integrity."[271] But, the court held, "there can be no justification for hindering a political group solely because it seeks to debate in public the situation of part of the State's population and to take part in the nation's political life in order to find, according to democratic rules, solutions capable of satisfying everyone concerned." That is true even where Moldovan members of Parliament wish to pursue an agenda which some believe incompatible with "the principles and structures of the [existing] Moldovan State." Disagreement on important issues, including "the way a State is currently organised" is "A fundamental aspect of democracy . . . provided that they do not harm democracy itself."[272] National security can be adequately protected, without restricting political rights, by "[s]anctions for illegal conduct or conduct which threatens national interests . . . [and] security clearance for access to confidential documents."[273]

Yumak & Sadak v. Turkey addressed the threshold percentage for party representation in the legislature.[274] The ECtHR began with the basic standards of Protocol No. 1 to the Convention which "prescribe[s] 'free' elections held at 'reasonable intervals' 'by secret ballot' and 'under conditions which will ensure the free expression of the opinion of the people.'"[275] In turn "the will of the people" depends on "universal suffrage" and "[a]ny departure from the principle of universal suffrage risks undermining the democratic validity of the legislature."[276] The Court "emphasized" that the state is the "ultimate guarantor of pluralism" and is "obligat[ed] to adopt positive measures to 'organize' democratic elections 'under conditions which will ensure the free expression of the opinion of the people in the choice of the legislature.'"[277]

Parties are crucial. "Expression of the opinion of the people is inconceivable without the assistance of a plurality of political parties representing the currents of opinion flowing through a country's population."[278] Their "contribution . . . political debate" is "irreplaceable" in part because they are "an instrument which citizens can use to participate in electoral debate and a tribune through which they can express their support for various political programmes."[279] To ascertain "the free expression of the people" it is crucial "to maintain the integrity and effectiveness of an electoral procedure."[280] To do that, "the Court has established that [the Convention as amended] guarantees individual rights, including the right to vote and the right to stand for election."[281] Nevertheless the Court agreed that Turkey, with a system of proportional representation, could deny seats in the national legislature to parties with less than 10 percent. The Court ruled that, in "context," and with "correctives and other guarantees which have limited its effects in practice," the threshold has not impaired the "essence" of those rights.[282]

Aware of the limits of its power, the ECtHR sometimes accepts results that are inconsistent with the Convention and its own judgments, particularly toward recent members whose political systems are more distant from Convention ideals than the original members. Perhaps for those reasons, and in deference to the sovereign states that submitted to its jurisdiction, the Court noted that rights are "not absolute"[283] and legitimate aims are "implied limitations."[284] The "[c]ontracting States must be given a wide margin of appreciation" for aims that are compatible with the objectives of the Convention, and for measures that are not arbitrary, disproportional, and do not impair the "essence" or "effectiveness" of the right or interfere with free expression of opinion or "thwart the free expression of the people in the choice of the legislature."[285] The Convention as amended only prescribes "'free' elections held at 'reasonable intervals' 'by secret ballot' and 'under conditions which will ensure the free expression of the opinion of the people.'"[286]

According to the ECtHR, "[F]air representation of the parties in parliament," "avoid[ing] a fragmentation of the party system and encourage[ing] the formation of a governing majority of one party in parliament" are legitimate competing objectives.[287] Such "limitations" can easily undo the principle of fair representation. But the Court explained that "[a] low threshold excludes only very small groupings, which makes it more difficult to form stable majorities, whereas in cases where the party system is highly fragmented a high threshold deprives many voters of representation."[288]

The ECtHR also found that "no electoral system can eliminate 'wasted votes.'"[289] Independents had succeeded in Turkey with party support.[290] The proportional system generally allows for the free expression of the people's views even when a high threshold disadvantages small parties.[291] And Turkey "had the legitimate aim of avoiding excessive and debilitating parliamentary fragmentation and thus of strengthening governmental stability."[292] Thus the Court ultimately blessed the 10 percent rule in Turkey while stating both strict standards and potentially loose excuses.

Juxtaposed with the ECtHR's prodemocracy rhetoric is its flirtation with censorship of political parties. The great threats to European democracy came from religious, national, and ideological flames and bigotry that ravaged the population over several centuries. Those threats led to limits on speech, especially by political parties—limits that could protect or squelch democracy.

In 1998, the European Commission for Democracy through Law, known as the ECD or Venice Commission, reported a survey of the treatment of political parties by member nations and several with observer status.[293] Of the forty countries that responded, six had banned or dissolved a party since World War II. The report concluded that sanctions against parties were rare and unnecessary since individuals could be punished. If it did seem necessary, courts should judge it according to the principle of proportionality. In 1999, the Venice Commission adopted guidelines, which found it may be justifiable to prohibit or dissolve "parties which advocate the use of violence or use violence as a political means to overthrow the democratic constitutional order."[294] The essence of that guideline was retained in a 2009 document on political parties.[295] Thus the European position has converged on two conclusions: prohibition or dissolution of a party is rarely necessary, and only violence or advocacy of violence justifies such measure. Nevertheless several countries have challenged that position.

The ECtHR repeatedly points to "the free expression of the opinion of the people" as its standard for judging electoral rules and practices.[296] Eliminating a party conflicts with principles of free speech, yet the court treats both the principle and the restrictions as necessary for a democratic society.[297] Whether the Court is true to the *Hirst* principles depends on what leads the Court to accept local practices that vary from universality. One scholar at a Turkish university has described the Court as protecting prominority but not antisecular parties, and protecting separatist parties unless they had proven links to terrorist organizations.[298]

For example, the ECtHR protected a party seeking extensive regional autonomy against dissolution by the Bulgarian Constitutional Court and had a lengthy dispute with Turkey about the Kurds' ambitions.[299] Turkey dissolved the United Communist Party (TBKP) for espousing the Kurdish cause. By law there was only one "Turkish nation."[300] Turks believed the difference between Kurds and Turks was a product of political agitation. By distinguishing "between the Kurdish and Turkish nations, the TBKP had revealed its intention of working to achieve the creation of minorities which . . . [threatened Turkey's] territorial integrity." The Court noted that Turkey's Constitution proscribed both self-determination and regional autonomy."[301]

Issacharoff argues that Turkey's dissolution of earlier Islamic parties brought the Islamists into the mainstream of Turkish politics.[302] Turkey made changes to its statutes but continues to prohibit parties. The Human Rights Association (İnsan Haklari Derneği) catalogued an extensive list of bans and dissolutions through 2008.[303]

The ECtHR responded that "political parties are . . . essential to the proper functioning of democracy."[304] They do not lose protection under the convention "simply because . . . national authorities" believe their democratically pursued objectives "undermin[e] the constitutional structures of the State."[305] Instead, the possibility "of resolving a country's problems through dialogue, without recourse to violence, even when they are irksome" is a principal characteristic of democracy. The Court held: "[T]here can be no justification for hindering a political group solely because it seeks to debate in public the situation of part of the State's population and to take part in the nation's political life in order to find, according to democratic rules, solutions capable of satisfying everyone concerned."[306] The ECtHR found Convention guarantees violated in "seven more cases where the applicant parties had discussed possible solutions to Turkey's Kurdish issue at the domestic level and were therefore dissolved by the Turkish Constitutional Court."[307] The ECtHR defended parties that raised questions of "autonomy, federalism, self-determination . . . [and the treatment] of minority culture and language."[308]

The ECtHR has little sympathy for parties that attack secularism or seek to promote applications of Islamic law. Battles over secularism and Islam reached the Court in *Refah Partisi v. Turkey*,[309] on dissolving the party, and *Leyla Şahin v. Turkey*,[310] on a headscarf ban.

The ECtHR accepted Turkey's dissolution of Refah Partisi, known in English as the Welfare Party, the largest member of a center-right coalition ruling Turkey when the court ordered dissolution. Among those banned from politics was Necmettin Erbakan who had been prime minister in the mid-1990s.

The Court treated the Refah Partisi as attempting to replace democratic government with theocracy for some areas covered by law; it treated theocracy as inconsistent with democracy, and the Refah Partisi as seeking to introduce theocracy to Turkey.[311] The Court held that introducing religious courts that bind individuals according to their faiths would "do away with the State's role as the guarantor of individual rights and freedoms and the impartial organiser of the practice of the various beliefs and religions in a democratic society. Instead it would oblige individuals to obey, not rules laid down by the State in the exercise of its above-mentioned functions, but static rules of law imposed by the religion concerned."[312]

There are at least three different ways to consider the compatibility of Shari'ah with democracy. One is whether Shari'ah condemns democracy or denies that it is proper for Muslims to adopt a democratic regime. There has been a lively debate about the compatibility of Shari'ah with democratic authority. Some scholars point out that "[e]lections (in their old form) are mentioned in the Qur'an itself," suggesting therefore that Shari'ah is not in conflict with democracy.[313]

The compatibility of Shari'ah and democracy can also be addressed regarding the means of making binding decisions. The authority of those who interpret Shari'ah differs from elected political authority. The court's discussion is somewhat unclear, but it focused on process, suggesting that it was treating Shari'ah as a source of binding authority rather than whether Shari'ah is generally hostile to an electoral system.

Finally, the compatibility of Shari'ah and democracy may reflect particular rules, which the Court believes Shari'ah requires. This includes its treatment of the role of women and their rights in society. Many interpreters of Shari'ah deny that restrictions on the rights of women are proper interpretations of the sacred texts. So one must distinguish between Shari'ah as tradition in given locations and Shari'ah as the meaning of the sacred texts. Conflict with rules of human rights may not be integral to Shari'ah but traditional interpretations of Shari'ah may be linked with those restrictions in certain societies. This appears to have been part of the Court's reasoning although its language was both more general and less clear.

The ECtHR concluded that Islamic law, or "sharia is incompatible with the fundamental principles of democracy."[314] The Grand Chamber of the ECtHR (similar to an American appellate court sitting en banc), quoted the chamber opinion (similar to a panel opinion) finding that Shari'ah law is static: "the Court considers that sharia, which faithfully reflects the dogmas and divine rules laid down by religion, is stable and invariable."[315]

Despite the age of the sacred texts, the claim that Shari'ah is "static" is in tension with actual practice, since there is no grand chamber that interprets Shari'ah. Shari'ah law is promulgated by experts versed in the texts and traditions more in the manner of the common law by judges, individually, looking at the work of others, which does not produce a static body of religious law.[316]

Putting aside the question of the accuracy of its understanding of Shari'ah, the Court, still quoting the chamber opinion, explained why it understood Shari'ah as incompatible with democracy. First, regarding process, "[p]rinciples such as pluralism in the political sphere or the constant evolution of public freedoms have no place in it."[317] And substantively, "[i]t is difficult to declare one's respect for democracy and human rights while at the same time supporting a regime . . . which clearly diverges from Convention values, particularly with regard to its criminal law and criminal procedure, its rules on the legal status of women and the way it intervenes in all spheres of private and public life in accordance with religious precepts."[318] Those aspects of the party's proposals were not limited to Shari'ah but would restore practices under the Ottoman Empire, and similar practices in much of Europe, giving religious groups authority over their own faithful and the social practices they enforced.[319] Thus, the Court saw a deeper tension with elevating religious law to obligatory status and the doctrinal implications of the Court are clearly broader than, although occasioned by, disputes involving Islam.

The harsh reaction in those cases to Islamic dress or to parties which advocate Islamic views on religion or culture, are in tension with European practices acceptable to the Court. Many European institutions and courts are relatively tolerant of government entanglement with religion. Pluralism, in both speech and entangled institutions, is valued by much of the European community, but these cases treat the claims of Muslims as outside the perimeter of European pluralism.

The dissolution of political parties also reached the ECtHR where parties were associated with violence. The Court calls for legal, necessary, and proportional responses.[320] For example, a party representing separatist Basques in Spain was dissolved with the Court's blessing based on a finding of links to Basque terrorists.[321]

Concerns about hate, violence, loyalty, and the Nazi past also play significant roles in speech cases. Concerns about loyalty to the free democratic constitutional system "are certainly relevant," but the bare fact of membership in the German Communist Party was not "sufficient to establish convincingly that it was necessary in a democratic society to dismiss" a teacher.[322]

Sensitive about anything that might glorify the Nazis, France started a transatlantic legal battle over its attempt to block access to an internationally available auction of Nazi memorabilia on AOL.com.[323] In another case, the ECtHR wrote that efforts to rehabilitate the memory of Marshall Petain who had been convicted for working with Hitler remain "very painful in the collective memory, given the difficulties . . . in determining . . . whether isolated individuals or entire institutions . . . [were responsible] for the policy of collaboration with Nazi Germany."[324] Nevertheless, the Court held that free speech applies to "'information' or 'ideas' . . . that offend, shock or disturb."[325] Exposure to such messages "forms part of the efforts that every country must make to debate its own history openly and dispassionately."[326] Making the connection to democracy, it added: "Such are the demands of that pluralism, tolerance and broadmindedness without which there is no 'democratic society.'"[327]

A 1999 judgment arose out of competing libel suits between researchers and police, over studies by academics and the Ministry of Justice alleging significant police brutality in Bergen, Norway, and a competing investigation initiated by the prosecutor general which reached the opposite conclusion and resulted in a prosecution and conviction of some accusing witnesses that was later overturned. The ECtHR agreed with the Norwegian courts that police claims that the researchers had deliberately lied was defamatory. It otherwise reversed, finding factual support for police claims at the time statements were made which were within "limits of permissible criticism" in a democratic society in the context of an angry public debate.

Judges Kūris, Türmen, Strážnická, and Greve dissented and would have found additional statements of the police against the researchers actionably defamatory. They emphasized the "vital need for every society to exercise strict supervision over all use of force in the name of society." Their point was that critics of official abuse need to be protected against groundless charges. They referred to the 1984 United Nations Convention against Torture and other Cruel, Inhuman or Degrading Treatment or Punishment, which specifically protects the right to complain. In the dispute over brutality in Bergen, the Court held, the "purpose of these attacks [by the officers] was to suppress the debate on this issue." The government, however, has "a monopoly over force . . . [which] also entails the danger of force being abused to the detriment of the very values it is meant to uphold." Therefore "abuse of force by officials is not just one of many issues of broad general interest, it is . . . a matter of primary concern in any society." Keeping authorities in check is particularly important for a democracy. And the ability to hold a state's use of force in check requires protecting those who raise the alarm. The European Commission for Democracy Through Law observed that in "numerous states . . . [there is a] general ban on the creation of para-military formations."[328]

In *Ceylan v. Turkey*, a union president was indicted for inciting "hatred and hostility" by protesting the treatment of Kurds. The ECtHR held that "Mr Ceylan's conviction was . . . not 'necessary in a democratic society'" and therefore violated the Convention; "there is little scope . . . for restrictions on political speech or on debate on matters of public interest" especially with regard to "criticism . . . [of] government." This is essential. "In a democratic system the actions or omissions of the government must be subject to the close scrutiny not only of the legislative and judicial authorities but also of public opinion." The power of government "makes it necessary for it to display restraint in resorting to criminal proceedings, particularly where other means are available for replying to the unjustified attacks and criticisms of its adversaries." Only special circumstances, such as "where . . . remarks incite to violence," could justify curtailment and then only if government reacts "appropriately and without excess."[329] The Court sustained the conviction of a pro-PKK speaker for supporting some forms of violence. But concerns about violence did not justify shutting down discussion of the treatment of a minority, including the Kurds.

Some writers have suggested that prohibiting speech that encourages hate or division will be misused to exclude minority complaints. The ECtHR cases suggest that happens often, as in the Turkish indictment and conviction of Ceylon for attempting to air Kurdish grievances. This happens even though the Court distinguishes hate speech from complaints and resists blaming minorities for airing their grievances.

On the other hand, the Court treats freedom of religion as inherent in democratic society. When Bulgaria's government chose religious leaders, the Court responded that "pluralism [is] indissociable from a democratic society," but could not exist if the government could select who runs religious institutions and such a power would therefore weaken democracy.[330]

With ECtHR support, European nations restrain groups from taking positions that might upset religious peace,[331] even if only to protect national majorities.[332] In majority Christian parts of Europe that policy creates anti-Islamic discrimination, in which their critiques and their religious expression or wearing of religious garments are suppressed in favor of religious peace,[333] and their feelings are unprotected in favor of others' free speech.[334] On those and other issues, individual or minority group critiques or complaints are often lost in the process.[335]

The Court supported the secularists position against Muslim religious garb in the case of *Leyla Şahin v. Turkey*, holding that Turkey could bar religious clothing, including Muslim headscarves in universities.[336] The secularist policy dates to the 1923 establishment of the Republic of Turkey. More recently, there has been a lengthy debate within Turkey about the role of Islam in the state and the freedom of Muslims to wear Islamic dress.[337] The Court agreed that the regulation interfered with religious freedom. Therefore it addressed whether the limitation was "necessary in a democratic society" under the Convention. That issue required a balance to protect the rights of all:

"In democratic societies, in which several religions coexist within one and the same population, it may be necessary to place restrictions on freedom to manifest one's religion or belief in order to reconcile the interests of the various groups and ensure that everyone's beliefs are respected."[338] The headscarf ban prevented "certain fundamentalist religious movements from exerting pressure on students who did not practise their religion or who belonged to another religion."[339] Dress would disclose belief, making religious garb a flash point. Turkey could be trying to diffuse tensions on the street; the ban "served to protect the individual not only against arbitrary interference by the State but from external pressure from extremist movements."[340] The Court also worried about "the proselytizing effect" of religious garb.[341]

The Court noted no consistent approach to religious garb among the member nations.[342] The same restriction may have different meanings in France, a majority Christian nation, and Turkey, a majority Muslim state. Turkey's historic commitment to secularism could have been to protect minorities, because of hostility toward religion, due to a judgment that modern states work better when religious forces are constrained, or to facilitate change in gender relations (by doing away with such symbols as the headscarf, for example). Each of those reasons has secular and religious components. Religion sometimes has to give way to important secular purposes.[343] For the Turkish court, secularism prevented government from showing a preference for one faith, guiding government as "impartial arbiter," and protecting freedom of religion and conscience.[344]

The ECtHR concluded that the headscarf regulations were not directed against Islam, but for "the legitimate aim of protecting order and the rights and freedoms of others and . . . to preserve the secular nature of educational institutions."[345] The history and contemporary situation of Turkey appeared to require that result.[346] And for the ECtHR, secularism may be "the guarantor of democratic values . . . the meeting point of liberty and equality."[347] It is "consistent with the values underpinning the Convention." Indeed, it "may be considered necessary to protect the democratic system in Turkey."[348]

According to the ECtHR, pluralism is "indissociable from a democratic society" and depends on freedom of religion.[349] Protecting everyone, however, requires reconciling the freedom of each with the interests of others to "ensure that everyone's beliefs are respected."[350] Without "eliminating pluralism" in order to "remove . . . tension," the task is to "to ensure that the competing groups tolerate each other."[351]

Democracy does not imply that the "majority must always prevail." A balance is needed to ensure "the fair and proper treatment of . . . minorities" and avoid "any abuse of a dominant position."[352] Conflicts among the "'rights and freedoms' . . . guaranteed by the Convention or its Protocols" may require that the state restrict one in favor of the other. For the Court, "this constant search for a balance between the fundamental rights of each individual . . . constitutes the foundation of a 'democratic society.'"[353] And a "margin of appreciation" or deference to the member states is necessary "to protect the rights and freedoms of others, to preserve public order, and to secure civil peace and true religious pluralism, which is vital to the survival of a democratic society."[354]

The dissent by Judge Tulkens also expressed support for the principle of secularism.[355] She argued, however, that "[o]nly indisputable facts and reasons whose legitimacy is beyond doubt—not mere worries or fears" justify infringing on religious freedom. In her assessment they were not needed.[356]

The subsequent erosion of Turkish secularism suggests that repression can bring about the consequences it was supposed to prevent. Repression may also have blocked consideration of Kurdish complaints within Turkish politics while simultaneously stimulating Kurdish nationalism in Turkey, Iraq, and other countries in the region.

The rule of law itself is basic for a democratic society.[357] In *Hasan and Chaush v. Bulgaria,* the ECtHR described the government's intervention in religious affairs as standardless, and it therefore violated the rule of law, a fundamental principle "inherent in all Articles of the Convention," as well as violating religious freedom.[358]

The rule of law was a major issue in *Segerstedt-Wiberg v. Sweden.*[359] For the ECtHR, and European law in general, the rule of law is not limited to following whatever the legislature or other lawmaking bodies may have proscribed; "settled case-law 'in accordance with the law' not only requires the impugned measure to have some basis in domestic law, but also refers to the quality of the law in question."[360] To be "compatible with the rule of law . . . it must provide a measure of legal protection against arbitrary interference by public authorities."[361] The case involved intelligence files and the Court commented that the "risks of arbitrariness are evident" where powers are exercised in secret. The Court explained: "Since the implementation in practice of measures of secret surveillance is not open to scrutiny by the individuals concerned or the public at large, it would be contrary to the rule of law for the legal discretion granted to the executive to be expressed in terms of an unfettered power."[362] The law must provide "the individual adequate protection against arbitrary interference."[363] The "law must indicate the scope . . . and the manner of its exercise with sufficient clarity" to protect the individual.[364] The Court held it did.[365] It nevertheless held that storage of some of the information interfered with their right to private life under the Convention.[366] The

Court explained that, while intelligence services have a legitimate role, "powers of secret surveillance of citizens are tolerable under the Convention only in so far as strictly necessary for safeguarding the democratic institutions.[367]

As a former president of the ECtHR points out, the covenant and the Court also address unlawful detention and cruel treatment in prison.[368] Officials do not have unlimited power to arrest people for questioning.[369] The object is security within "a substantial measure of procedural justice."[370]

Combating terrorism creates "difficulties" for democracy.[371] Following 9/11, the United States argued that the United Nations and international agreements authorized and required executive action to pursue terrorists without the usual procedural protections. That met resistance from the European Court of Justice.[372] Luzius Wildhaber, then president of the ECtHR, commented that no derogation is possible from absolute guarantees like the prohibition of torture or inhuman or degrading treatment.[373] He quoted former Israeli Chief Justice Aharon Barak that even the "ticking time bomb" does not justify torture and that democracies still have the "upper hand" because the rule of law and the protection of liberty strengthen democracies.[374] He also quoted former Indian Chief Judge Anand: "State terrorism is no answer to combat terrorism. State terrorism would only provide legitimacy to 'terrorism.'"[375] Yet, effective measures to counter organized terrorism will not be found disproportional.[376]

Democratic Ideals in Foreign Courts

The decisions of these courts interpret democracy as a set of principles and as cause and effect—what causes democracy to survive or collapse. They stress universal suffrage and equality but take little account of integration and protect less expression than our own courts. Those conclusions of these foreign courts can be either warning or encouraging.

How should this be evaluated? One could conclude that competing traditions offer little reason to adopt any foreign ideas. People like different things leading to a draw. There are, however, other ways of thinking about the handling of democracy abroad.

Competent courts and intelligent people, interpreting concepts found in our own constitutional traditions, reached conclusions about the logic of democracy—what it means and requires. Though the Declaration of Independence has not been treated as controlling authority, "a decent respect to the opinions of mankind requires" that we consider their insights.

One can read these materials as a test. As much as the U.S. Supreme Court interprets the Constitution based on its federal structure and separated powers, one might also read it based on its democratic structure. The record of these foreign courts then tells us something about the ways democracy is likely to be understood. It is hardly conclusive. We have selected examples from countries that were demonstrably influenced by American ideals, whether directly, through British influence, or because of shared reactions to Nazi terror and World War II. Even a statistical sample would be only a prediction that our courts would behave like other courts, not an argument for it. Still, foreign judgments provide some idea about whether interpreting the U.S. Constitution in compliance with the spirit of its structurally democratic provisions is a good idea.

Foreign constitutional courts inferred the importance of universal suffrage and participation, competition, equality, and dispersion of resources from democracy. But they also accepted parallel worlds in schools, although rejecting them in communities, and failed to protect the voice of dissenters in states like Turkey. I would be a very selective cheerleader for their conclusions.

However, if we ask what difference the courts made, the results look somewhat better. Lawyers and judges often describe courts as counter-majoritarian because they sometimes reject what the people or their representatives have voted for. Cases in which courts were most deferential to government made the least difference; they merely confirmed what the political system did. Where the courts made a difference was in their instinct to protect everyone's participation in the democratic process and the rights of minorities; that suggests a prodemocratic difference.[377]

Their interpretation of their own constitutions and the European Convention on Human Rights also led foreign courts to address the consequences to democracy—cause and effect, not merely definition. The question about the consequences of these differing interpretations for democracy is also addressed by political scientists. While politicians have steered their states by their hunches, political scientists have investigated causal relationships with increasingly robust data and methods. Their work tests the ideals explored both in the United States and abroad since the ratification of the U.S. Constitution. The legal connections made by these jurists can be rejected at any moment. But the empirical consequences studied by political scientists are less pliable.

PART II

Political Science

5

Rules of Democracy

So far, we have discussed the competing traditions about what counts as democratic. However, while politicians steer by their hunches, and judges by concepts, traditions, and philosophies, political scientists examine the consequences of choice for the present and future of democratic governments. Their research invites us to ask whether the founders' prescriptions stand up to the test of modern science or are challenged by it.

Before the twentieth century, elective government was so rare that it was almost impossible to study scientifically. England, France, and the United States spread democracy in the first half of the twentieth century, first as examples and then by control over Western Europe, Japan, and territories abroad. Elsewhere, democracy was occasional and unstable.

With increasingly robust data and methods, political scientists have investigated causal relationships, why some democracies broke down and became authoritarian, and why others successfully changed from monarchy, aristocracy, or dictatorship to democratic rule. Those studies give us an opportunity to address the future of American democracy.

Elective Government: An Initial Definition

What makes elective government survive or fail? Elective government is a minimal definition of democracy; but to avoid arguments about whether some definitions are too stringent or too political, we use a basic definition and let political scientists address the requirements of democracy. Some researchers organize their work around the degree of democracy, others around more elaborate definitions.[1] Their work leads in the same general direction.[2] This should not be surprising—compromising the foundations of democracy makes elective government vulnerable.

Basic Rights

Rights are essential. Without basic freedoms, democracies shrivel and die. Sometimes freedoms are lost after dictators have taken power; sometimes the loss of freedom allows dictators to seize power.

Nazi inhumane perversions of law led to worldwide agreement on protections in the United Nations Universal Declaration of Human Rights. The U.S. Supreme Court's defense of basic freedoms quickly became an international beacon. Core rights in the U.S. Bill of Rights defined ways government protects or abuses its population.

The Constitutional Convention listed guarantees against government subordinating, suppressing, or terrorizing its people, specifically blocking methods then used in England: an expansive definition of treason, denial of habeas corpus, and abuse of the criminal process to reach foreordained conclusions.[3] Two years later James Madison proposed a Bill of Rights with protection to speak, publish, assemble, and petition, plus procedural protections to forestall the abuse of the criminal power of the state.[4] He was explicit about the instrumental character of the latter.[5] Later the Reconstruction Amendments filled out the promise of the Declaration of Independence that "all men are created equal," now requiring equal treatment.[6]

The founders, not confident written rights would protect anyone, referred to them disparagingly as "parchment" guarantees, out of skepticism that fallible and sometimes malicious people would honor them when they had motives to do otherwise.[7] The Constitution's guarantees rest on the backbone of U.S. citizens, not the stiffness of the paper they are written on. Protections are weak when they seem unimportant to or for political opponents.

What Bills of Rights Cannot Do

Rights would not have stopped the Nazis. Once in power they ignored or perverted existing rules. Dictators abuse the criminal process in order to put opponents away and stifle revolutionary movements, like the imprisonment of Nelson Mandela on Robin Island, Aung San Suu Kyi in Myanmar, mass arrests of dissidents in Iran, and too many others.

Bills of rights do not protect democracies from external threats, civil war, or internal deterioration; from misusing or squandering their armies,[8] closing themselves off from the rest of the world,[9] or destroying their industrial base.[10] Bills of rights cannot protect democracies if authorities can sidestep them by claiming to counter other threats. As the ACLU puts it, "freedom cannot protect itself."

The Bill of Rights has not stopped American governments from tracking antiwar demonstrators and questioning who they voted for, in the name of national security.[11] The FBI's well-known effort to crush Martin Luther King and cripple the civil rights movement was cut short by Presidents Kennedy and Johnson. It harassed Americans whose politics were unpopular with FBI

Director J. Edgar Hoover. The participation of FBI agents in the KKK and other racist organizations was sometimes lethal. Frank Church, former Senate Intelligence Committee chair, said the resources of the National Security Agency (NSA) "could be turned around on the American people" leaving no privacy because it could "monitor everything." Church added that if a dictator came to power, the NSA "could enable it to impose total tyranny, and there would be no way to fight back."[12] His point, in part, was that the ability of government agencies to gain business and personal information can be used to target or crush disfavored individuals. Recent revelations of NSA tapping and storing of phone and digital records underscores his point.

The use of drones to execute people abroad takes life without any defense, let alone due process. Restriction to the field of battle once offered noncombatants some protection, but the find-and-execute policy obliterates it. Used against Americans abroad, the policy short-circuits the Bill of Rights, and invites more targets at home to enemies abroad.[13]

Detention without due process is no longer merely foreign behavior, based on the 2012 National Defense Authorization Act. President Obama denied some implications in a signing statement but defended the law against a suit by well-known journalists. On September 12, 2012, District Court Judge Katherine Forrest, an Obama appointee, held that portion of the Act unconstitutional.[14] The administration immediately requested that her order be delayed pending appeal. On July 17, 2013, the Second Circuit decided that the plaintiffs did not have standing, that is to say the legal right, to challenge the law.[15]

The Bill of Rights depends on the backbone of legislators and judges, the compliance of the authorities, and the means to protest. After 9/11, the administration rounded up Muslims who lived in the United States and refused to identify those in custody, for the benefit of relatives, friends, or lawyers. The administration blocked access to phones and moved detainees, convicted of nothing, to sites far from their families.[16] Many Americans appear to have accepted those risks and to have been convinced that such risks are essential for "security," even as the tools used by the administration threaten security from within.

Unfortunately America has had dictators. The slave-holding South before the Civil War treated slaves tyrannically and violently suppressed antislavery dissent.[17] Open warfare in the post–Civil War South killed Republicans and removed an elected biracial government by coup d'état.[18] Until the late twentieth century, roving bands of white enforcers, the Ku Klux Klan, and similar organizations enforced a code of total subservience throughout the former Confederacy, many border states, and sometimes well beyond. They infiltrated all levels of law enforcement.[19] At the same time, big city machines controlled elections with a combination of intimidation, bribery, mayhem, the machinery of public administration, police, and the courts so that one had little choice but to cooperate.[20]

Abuse by law enforcement officials is more serious than most Americans realize. It includes using the power of office and weapons for illegal purposes, framing the innocent, and covering the officials' own misbehavior. Serious official abuse is continuous,[21] in the East,[22] the West,[23] rural areas,[24] police labs,[25] prosecutors' offices[26] and at the FBI.[27] Weapons are used inappropriately,[28] and people are injured or killed for reasons known only to the officers involved.[29] Minor crimes like breach of the peace or interfering with a police officer are prosecuted to cover official abuse of people they believe are not respectful enough.[30] And racial abuse is ubiquitous.[31] Dealing with it has so far proved unsuccessful.[32]

Available statistics are notoriously difficult to interpret, but Kami Chavis Simmons described excessive force, perjury, and racial profiling in Los Angeles, New Orleans, Atlanta, Chicago, and New York, among others.[33] Documented abuse runs the gamut from quotidian but collectively damaging abuse of minority communities[34] to wonton shootings—"New Orleans police officers opened fire upon several citizens as they were crossing Danziger Bridge to flee . . . [Katrina's] devastation."[35] Simmons reveals that "nearly 30% of the officers surveyed believed that 'the use of excessive force is a serious problem facing the Department.'" And almost 4.6 percent of officers believed they were justified in physical punishing suspects with "a bad or uncooperative attitude."[36] In effect as Simmons, among many others, has noted, this is not merely a few "bad apples" in police departments, but a culture that protects the officers and defends their behavior.[37]

Investigations intended to stop flagrant abuse of power are recurrent, including the Wickersham[38] and Mollen Commissions[39] in New York, the Christopher Commission[40] in Los Angeles, and congressional hearings,[41] among others. The scholarly literature about the problem is lengthy, from Paul Chevigny's pathbreaking study in the late 1960s[42] to Michelle Alexander's in 2012.[43]

Torture used to seem foreign. But America introduced waterboarding to the Philippines during the Spanish-American War; later it would torture Iraqi, Afghan, and other detainees for information—despite moral and practical reasons not to do it, and against the advice of experienced interrogators to avoid torture altogether because the "information" it yields is untrustworthy and because they have more effective ways to interrogate prisoners. The Bush administration refused to describe "detainees" from Afghanistan as prisoners of war precisely because that would have called for the application of specific legal rules governing their detention and treatment, effectively making it illegal to hold them in hot, open cages, hooded, blindfolded, masked, chained, or kneeling for extended periods—as well as incommunicado, and without access to attorneys. Prisoners were deprived of sleep and many were placed in bindings that compress and make limbs swell.

Americans are not angels. When the Bill of Rights and Reconstruction Amendments have not been enforced, Americans experience serious mistreatment.

What Bills of Rights Can Do

Freedom cannot protect itself; democracy cannot survive without freedom.[44] Political scientists describe countries as democratic if they protect core rights including the right to vote, and autocratic otherwise.[45] Elections are insufficient if people can be otherwise controlled.[46] Regardless of description, societies that abandon civil liberties to search for terrorists sink into autocratic rule. Jennifer Holmes documented the way military reign drove Peru and Uruguay into dictatorship, while Spain, defending itself against the Basque insurgency, restrained itself and remained democratic.[47] Paul Wilkinson added postwar Germany, France, and Italy as countries that maintained both freedom and democratic government while fighting terrorists.[48] British courts fought back at attempts to imprison people without charges, hearings, or trials.[49] Without the restraint of courts and due process, petty tyrants are empowered to pillage and control their own people and governments become as debased as the guerillas; both groups sell out democracies.

Voting Rights

Elections define the people's choice if the people can vote. Keeping people out of the electorate gives some people the power to rule others. That might be described as colonialism, apartheid, or occupation.

Inclusiveness—Universal Suffrage

Those in office are generally satisfied with prior voters; new voters threaten their power and they often try to prevent them from voting. Whatever magnifies the time, effort, and cost to vote tends to exclude the poor—costs for transportation; special forms of identification required by new voter ID laws; lost wages while they wait in lines, respond to spurious challenges at the polls, or go to court to seek their right to vote can be prohibitive for the poor but are minimal or nonexistent burdens for more economically secure voters. Other methods exclude immigrants, students, and those caught in or abused by the criminal justice process.[50] This is not about democracy but about attempts to control the results.

Equally important, inclusive electoral systems are more likely to remain democratic than uninclusive ones. The smaller the group of people to whom the leadership owes its power, the fewer the leadership need to pay off; the fewer people a ruler needs to satisfy, the less he needs to do for the people at large, and the easier to satisfy his crucial supporters. That kind of society collapses into a kleptocracy. Stealing from the poor and giving to the favored few has been the method of tyrants in all generations.[51] One way to accomplish this is by excluding people from the polls. Conversely, the larger the group of electors and the larger the group of people who can keep the leaders in power or put them out, the more the leadership is driven to adopt policies that serve the public, and not merely the friends of those at the top.

The Struggle for an Honest Election

Inclusiveness is only partly about election rules. The world struggles for honest elections. Criticism of dishonest elections abroad is nonpartisan here. Honest elections are the *sine qua non* of democracy for judges and political scientists. Yet domestically clean elections have often been a casualty of politics.

Stuffed ballot boxes can take over democratic government. For much of our history, election results had the security of gold shipped on stagecoaches through narrow valleys in movie westerns. Armed mobs and state militia faced off at the Pennsylvania capital in 1838 over disputed election returns and determined the winners.[52] Landowners and their overseers controlled the votes of many white tenant farmers in New York's Hudson River Valley until the antirent wars of 1839–46 changed their relationship.[53]

Landowners, employers, and local leaders prevented blacks from voting in southern states well into the twentieth century and carefully picked those few who were allowed to cast ballots.[54] The Civil Rights Act of 1957 authorized appointment of federal registrars to register black voters where discrimination had been rampant, and the 1965 Voting Rights Act gave the Justice Department new powers to secure the right to vote. Nevertheless, those in power continue to intimidate, disqualify, and block many blacks from voting.[55]

Large-scale, effective election chicanery starts at the top. Big city machines intimidated and bribed voters well into the twentieth century.[56] Voters responded by demanding secret ballots and enclosed voting booths.[57] Political bosses then sent people to watch whether voters spent enough time in the voting booths to split tickets instead of casting a straight party line vote, to assist voters inside the booths, or to rig the machines.[58] Small-town registrars did not bother to count some ballots.[59] Political bosses and their henchmen were well-practiced masters at stealing elections, miscounting votes, stuffing ballot boxes, and other chicanery.

In the late nineteenth century, mining and similar companies with isolated work forces in one-industry states gained all-encompassing economic power over employees, coerced their votes, and gained control over entire states like West Virginia and Montana.[60]

In the twentieth century, the New Deal safety net, which included Social Security and unemployment insurance, reduced the attractiveness of jobs for the legions of people required to intimidate, bribe, or fix ballots. And it rebalanced employer-employee economic power by substituting a system of labor negotiation for preexisting violence. Soldiers returning from World War II had less taste for dirty politics, more courage to resist, and the GI Bill to find a better life.[61] We rely on those improvements at our peril; attacks on the safety net and growing economic insecurity make many people more vulnerable.

Seventeen states made it impossible to check election equipment to verify the 2012 count.[62] Hurricane Sandy wrought havoc with the election, creating lines of voters, discouraging some, and making the wait impossible for those with inflexible obligations such as work or family care.[63] Equally devastating, misallocation of polling places and equipment, photo identification laws, limits on early voting, electrical and other failures and decisions make it difficult, prohibitively expensive, or impossible for some people to vote, skewing elections.[64] Voting machines misfire, whether by accident or design.[65] Election administrators are politically selected, leading New York Mayor Bloomberg to object that party leaders "should not be . . . picking their buddies to supervise the basis of our citizenship."[66] New voting technologies bypass the need to employ large numbers of people for voter fraud by making the count itself insecure and unverifiable.[67] People get used to abuse of election machinery.[68]

Each new weapon or strategy in the battle for honest elections is eventually met and defeated by another. There is no known unanswerable protection for elections and no substitute for vigilance. The United States has had relatively clean elections only since World War II in the North and the civil rights movement in the South. But the jockeying continues.

For most living Americans, discomfort with the 2000 presidential election tally was a new experience. The *New York Times* examination of the handling of absentee ballots made it clear that partisan differences in the acceptance of illegal ballots in Florida were sufficiently large to affect the results—George Bush's election would have been confirmed if a recount examined only those counties which Al Gore requested, but Al Gore would have been elected if the entire state had been recounted.[69] Others studied Florida's systems for disqualifying and discouraging likely Democratic voters and reached the same conclusion.[70] Questions have also been raised about the 2004 presidential election.[71]

If the ballot count can be gamed, then the voting process is ineffective. Had the secretaries of state been judges in battleground states like Florida and Ohio, they would have been disqualified by their stakes in the outcome from supervising the elections and affecting the result.[72] The political culture and the risks of exposure are not strong enough to protect everyone's right to vote. Skepticism about the accuracy of the count and doubt about the seriousness of the risk of trying to game it are corrosive.[73]

Apportionment

Malapportionment corrupts democracy. Delegates to the 1787 Constitutional Convention criticized British elections as having been corrupted by rotten boroughs, those boroughs with few voters.[74] The delegates also understood that malapportionment had poisoned state representation. Settled western portions of the thirteen colonies had fewer representatives in state legislatures in proportion to population than the older seaboard communities. The seaboard was unwilling to readjust inland representation. At the Convention, delegates criticized the unfairness to western counties. They insisted on a census for allocating seats in the House of Representatives among the states, with the crucial exception of slavery.[75]

Predetermining power by apportioning representatives was crucial to the North-South compromise at the Convention. By eighteenth-century calculations, delegates expected southern states to control the House. Their calculations assumed that the potential population base in an agricultural society would be proportional to the size of the states. Southern states were much larger. It dawned on northern representatives that their protection against the slaveholding states was in the Senate where the tiny New England states would each have as many senators as Virginia, then the most populous state. So the distribution of seats in the two houses of Congress in the original Constitution confirmed both southern power in the House and northern power in the Senate.[76] Of course, the eventual path of population growth did not work as expected. But the "Connecticut compromise" governed national power for decades, regardless of voters' preferences.

Congress soon decreed that states could not elect representatives at large, a method in which state representatives are elected as a block, similar to how the electoral college works.[77] Instead, each state must elect representatives by districts. That produced a vote more in keeping with the balance of forces within each state, although the shape of districts became vulnerable to partisan manipulation.

As population growth shifted from farming communities to cities, legislatures ignored the changes. The shift left rural districts with fewer people per representative than urban and suburban districts, and therefore, more representatives and greater clout in legislative halls than their voting population would have warranted. Representatives of farming communities continued to dominate the malapportioned Congress and state legislatures.

The Warren Court required "one person, one vote," or, more precisely, that each legislative seat should represent the same number of people. If not, then people from favored regions would have more legislators than their numbers justified.[78] The Warren Court's reapportionment cases—from *Baker v. Carr* in 1962 to the final 1969 quartet at the end of Chief Justice Warren's service on the Court—shifted considerable legislative power from rural to suburban parts of the United States on the basis of their relative population strength.[79] None of us are, in Orwell's famous words, "more equal than others."[80] The Burger Court, however, in its last year, 1986, came to the conclusion that two to one was sometimes equal enough.[81]

The Court is often described as undemocratic because the justices are not elected. But the Burger, Rehnquist, and Roberts Courts have been increasingly undemocratic in a different way—their decisions have been dismissive of malapportionment, gerrymandering, miscounting, and other ways to minimize the voting rights of qualified voters.[82]

Gerrymandering

Gerrymandering survived the reapportionment rules. The word comes from the name of Elbridge Gerry, member of the 1787 Constitutional Convention and governor of Massachusetts, when a strangely shaped district was created to increase his party's representation.

The way lines are drawn can make a legislature safe for one party, regardless of voters' preferences. Using census, statistical, and political data, line drawers waste opposition votes by "packing" or "stacking" opposing voters into a few districts and "cracking" the remaining pockets of opposing voters so they can be defeated easily—divide and conquer by drawing maps. Line drawers sometimes call legislators to tell them their careers are over; one called a prominent congressman and classmate of mine, whose district was carved up to enable the Hispanic community to elect a person of its choice.

Courts rarely intervene. Justices Clarence Thomas and Antonin Scalia long since denied there is any useful concept of democracy.[83] Their Court decided it is permissible to draw lines for the purpose of protecting incumbent legislators' seats.[84] Strong opponents can be isolated. The Court upheld a 2004 redistricting plan that gave Republicans victories in twelve of nineteen Pennsylvania congressional districts even though the statewide vote for Congress substantially favored the Democrats.[85]

Incumbents are protected by designing districts with overwhelming support for them or their parties. In turn so-called safe districts encourage political extremism. Freed of competition, middle-of-the-road independent voters can be ignored. Victory means pandering to party activists; no district residents have the clout to make objections stick.

Legislators in competitive districts must appeal to centrist voters who hold the balance of power. Squeezing out competitive districts makes independent and centrist voters impotent, leaving the primary the only mechanism of voter choice. Primary elections, however, are contests for more partisan, ideological candidates. The primaries forced Romney closer to the right wing of his party. American voters now have more of what Barry Goldwater termed "choice; not an echo," with intransigent Tea Party members facing ever more determined Democratic opponents. As moderates willing to compromise were forced out, legislative politics shifted from compromise to conflict, although the resulting Congress is deeply unpopular with American voters.

Gerrymandering is undemocratic—because incumbents pick their voters, protecting themselves against political accountability, and because it determines the partisan outcome of voters' choices at the polls. Gerrymandering diminishes the incentive of elected officials to produce the kind of public goods that would broadly benefit the population.[86]

Proportional representation gives legislative seats to parties in proportion to votes and usually provides seats across the spectrum, from moderate to extreme. Such systems are sometimes thought to raise the political temperature because individual legislators have no incentive to moderate positions. Statistically, democracy may survive equally well with proportional representation as with the single-member districts, commonly used in the United States. However, extremism has led to the breakdown of democracy and played a role in the demise of democratic governments in countries like Italy, Germany, and Austria between the world wars.[87] Although single-member districts are often more moderate, they become problematic when safe districts polarize the country.

The politicization of the districting process and the appeal to the courts to evaluate the lines is a peculiarly American problem. Other democratic countries with geographical districts like ours have used nonpolitical commissions to draw the lines.[88] Nevertheless, courts could deal with gerrymandering. Political scientists have been using *symmetry*, also described as *neutrality*, to measure bias for decades. Symmetry requires treating both parties the same way so that a given percentage of the statewide vote should give either party approximately the same number of seats. (By contrast, packing and cracking of voters are reflected in deviations from the statewide average of expected party voters. Predictions are based on comparing expected deviations.) Symmetry does not guarantee what voters will do. Symmetrically designed districts, however, are not a stacked deck. A mathematical formula allows measurement that approximates the precision of the one person, one vote standard for reapportionment.[89] Despite questions around the edges, the central concept is hard, clear, and powerful.[90] Districting can be done in such a way that losing parties are highly unlikely to win the majority of the seats.

Symmetry is consistent with preferences for homogenous or for diverse district populations, but not with unequal treatment of supporters of different parties—what's sauce for the goose is sauce for the gander. As Justice Kennedy explained in another gerrymandering case, there are fundamental rights involved.[91] The parties have a constitutional right to equal treatment. Symmetry measures it with considerable precision, using the same data that the parties use to rig elections.

Partisan management of election outcomes is particularly virulent where it has the support of prosecutors and courts, both here and abroad.[92] Democracy is only as secure as the people who work it.

Misplaced Confidence in the Separation of Powers

There are two issues here: One is whether the separation of powers excuses us from worrying about threats to American democracy; the short answer is not much. A separate issue is how best to understand the value of separating the powers of the branches.

To much of the world, the American model is summed up by a powerful president and a powerful court. All democracies have legislatures so long as they last. The separation of powers among the three branches creates checks and balances.

The separation of powers was the French Baron de Montesquieu's inaccurate description of British government, which many in America's founding generation admired.[93] Most European democracies have followed a parliamentary model where the ruling coalition, often led by a powerful executive, dominates all branches. The separation of powers is not a good description of the checks and balances of that system. But few European democracies seem in any danger of collapse into autocracy.[94]

American constitutional law is bathed in the light of the Federalist Papers.[95] Written as an argument for the adoption of the Constitution in 1788, they embodied the best eighteenth-century thinking about democracy. American courts have assumed in turn that the success of the Constitution is sufficiently explained by its structure as explained in the Federalist Papers.[96] Empirical science, however, tells a different story.

Gauging the effectiveness of the separation of powers suggests comparison between the failure of many parliamentary systems in Europe between the two world wars, which fell to the Nazis, with the presidential systems in Latin America since World War II, which have repeatedly fallen to dictatorship, often at the hands of their presidents.[97] On average, parliamentary systems have lasted longer than presidential ones.[98] Many other differences among those countries and regions may account for those outcomes, but they certainly cast doubt on the belief that our separation of powers has much to do with the stability of our democratic system.

Should we blame the model or the culture? Political scientists dispute whether presidential and parliamentary systems are an important cause of the short or long lives of democracies. Juan J. Linz, a Spanish political scientist who recently passed away after a long and distinguished tenure at Yale, was born shortly before Generalissimo Franco defeated the Spanish Republic and made himself dictator. Linz devoted his life to understanding why democracies rise and fall, and he believed presidential systems more likely to succumb to takeovers, with Latin-American countries his prime examples.[99] G. Bingham Powell, an award-winning political scientist at the University of Rochester, discounts Linz's observation about Latin America, saying the difference is essentially the result of economic factors.[100] Either way, the system of checks and balances that go with presidential systems have not prevented coups d'état and takeovers by chief executives. Fear of executives is well justified. Democracies are likely to be taken over by their presidents and prime ministers.

Both presidential and parliamentary systems reflect and react to the distribution of wealth and power. Where political and economic power is concentrated around the executive branch and its supporters, the country will function as a dictatorship. Similarly, a powerful aristocracy may offer little protection for the rest of the population. Social and economic hierarchies prove more crucial than the choice of presidential or parliamentary systems.

Nevertheless, two centuries of tradition have shaped our practices and expectations and they matter here even if the separation of powers is not exportable for the purpose of controlling executives. They create, and were intended to create, checks and balances and to enable the departments to act with "energy" where appropriate. Some courts have treated the separation of powers as a method for protecting certain powers as independent privileges of one branch of government beyond the oversight of the others.[101] Treating separated powers as independent tends to exceed historical understanding—Madison thought *blended* a better description of the powers than *separated*[102]—and treating separated powers as independent conflicts with the purpose of distributing power so that executives are not dictators.[103]

Federalism

The Constitution's federal structure is quite important to the way American democracy functions.[104] The overwhelming subjects addressed by federalism are coexistence of people in different places, the effectiveness and fairness of their governing structures, and, in turn, the survival of democracy. A separate issue is the kind of federalism that matters. There is little or no evidence that the differences about which American courts have spilled so much ink matter.

Federalism typically comes about by means of a deal among the powerful, designed to protect their control over territory, people, or issues or to protect themselves against control by those they fear. Political scientists refer to constitutions that come about in that way as pacted constitutions. Federalism, then, may be an unavoidable compromise or a wise one—either an efficient way to get things done by decentralizing power or an inefficient duplication of resources. It may reflect tolerance for different cultures or it may be an invitation to intolerance by segregating people and maximizing the differences among them. If travel (sometimes called "exit"[105]) is less threatening than staying put, people may segregate themselves as they did in India and Pakistan and in many recent conflicts in response to racial, religious, and ethnic attacks. If there are opportunities that cut across federal units, people may be inclined to learn to work and live together. If different sections share problems they may be inclined to work together in solving them. How federalism turns out is determined by history—there may be no universally right way to divide populations, although there may be wrong ways that lead societies to threaten their members with mayhem.

With federalism designed to solve so many different problems in so many different ways, there is no single correct definition of federalism for political scientists. Germany is federal although the *Länder* (federal subunits somewhat like American states) are required to carry out national policy,[106] and the United States is federal although it has a powerful central bureaucracy unlike Germany.[107] National and local politics determine what is constructive, what diffuses power or conflict, and what hobbles government or threatens minorities.[108]

Yugoslavia functioned as a federal republic.[109] It may not have been possible to create that state other than as a federal one.[110] The various Yugoslavian states had a great deal of power.[111] But Yugoslavia became a poster example of federalism gone awry.[112] When international and economic conditions worsened in the 1980s, the federal government had little power to deal with its problems. So the politicians in the various Yugoslavian states blamed each other's states for their predicament; and they sank their country into civil war.

That is one of the biggest issues for political scientists—federalism either relieves political stress or makes it much worse; and it either strengthens or weakens democratic government.[113] As in Yugoslavia, the consequences can be disastrous.[114] Local allegiances can breed resentment and distrust of the nation and eventually lead to dismemberment or civil war.[115] Switzerland has held together,[116] but Belgium,[117] Canada,[118] and other countries have gone through great internal turbulence related to their federal structure. Our own country nearly came apart when the eleven states of the Confederacy seceded from the Union. Political scientists point to whether federal borders follow or cut across ethnic or other fault lines in society.[119] Borders that follow fault lines can exacerbate problems; crosscutting borders may calm them down.

Political scientists are somewhat divided on how best to make deeply divided societies democratically governable.[120] The coincidence of ethnic and provincial boundaries may be too simple an explanation for strife and violence, given that we are learning that identities can be reshaped and, as in the birth of Pakistan, ethnic groups can be exchanged—to use a very sanitary word for a very nasty business.[121] And the distinction between federal boundaries that do and do not cut across ethnic lines may be particularly unhelpful when the political bargains demanded as the price of a unified democratic state depend on boundaries that follow deeply felt distinctions.[122]

Federalism that enacts a political bargain may have to define political boundaries very sharply in order to engender trust. And as long as the society remains deeply divided, there may be no alternative to sharp boundaries among groups and between federal and national powers. It makes sense in such societies for courts to police such bargains. The French Constitutional Court, for example, was developed as part of a political bargain to protect the Gaullist Constitution.[123]

As democracy ages, however, issues that could have erupted and torn the state apart are likely to dissipate. Judicial supervision of the antique federal-state line becomes increasingly irrelevant. Moreover, outdated distinctions can throw monkey wrenches into the machinery of democracy. Slavery is one such outdated distinction, but it cast a strong shadow on the eighteenth century world in which the American constitutional language of federalism was written.[124] Judicial "benign neglect" is not likely to undermine a two-century-old democracy, but judicial activism, using federalism to make policy, can do a great deal of damage. Precisely because federalism is a method of conflict resolution, its contribution changes with the conflicts and therefore is not permanently defined by stone tablets.

Federalism may be the midwife of emerging democracy.[125] It may help to develop talent and inculcate democratic attitudes.[126] It offers opportunities for participation in which people can learn and develop skills. And it offers people the opportunity to solve local problems as well as an escape valve for strong local feelings. Those advantages, however, depend on contemporary problems and not on ancient distinctions. It is best treated as a political problem, not a judicial one.[127]

In a mature democracy, a clear division between federal and state powers may be precisely the problem, encouraging extremists and aggravating conflicts where candidates think they can benefit from stirring the hornets nests,[128] or where the national institutions become incapable of dealing with common problems because of jurisdictional issues.[129] In those situations, political organs may police the proper boundaries better than courts.[130] More permeable bargains may actually assist in defusing conflict by moving conflicts to arenas in which they can be handled more successfully. In such societies courts would be better advised to keep out.

Federalism may contribute more to a mature democracy if national and state powers overlap, keeping all political actors in check and preventing a slide toward autocracy.[131] Ian Shapiro has described freedom as the "multiplication of dependent relationships" (in stark contrast to slavery which imposes dependence on a single other).[132] Federalism can reduce freedom by simplifying government jurisdiction. Juan J. Linz[133] and Robert A. Dahl[134] describe decentralization as moving problems to smaller units that may be less able to handle them fairly.[135] A more flexible federalism may alleviate some of those problems.

Madison and Hamilton described important ways in which the two levels would restrain each other.[136] Describing the Constitution as partly national and partly federal,[137] Madison argued for a blending, rather than a clear division, of powers. Similarly, in the context of the separation of powers among the branches he also argued that blending was the more effective guarantee.[138] He told us that by blending powers we would enable the constituent parts of government to control each other.[139] It was precisely the overlapping of powers that created the possibility of protecting liberty. Overlap between state and federal jurisdictions permits each to investigate the other, to compete for public support, and to provide a staging ground for opposition as the Virginia and Kentucky resolutions did in 1798 and 1799.[140] Opponents of our Constitution wanted the kind of clear division of powers the Court has advanced. But those who wrote and supported it had a more sophisticated understanding of federalism.

Political scientists are also concerned by the impact of federalism on the quality of democratic government and on the extent to which government reflects and responds to the governed.[141] Madison famously argued that a larger republic would be fairer;[142] for example, it would be fairer to the slaves than the southern states were. Martha Minow described the same problem of fairness with respect to several modern conflicts.[143] Majorities can be thwarted by federalism in the same way that gerrymandering can thwart them. State, county, and municipal boundaries stack and crack groups just as gerrymandering of election district lines do. Majorities can be defeated, submerged, and subordinated by empowered cultures or groups.[144] There is no automatically appropriate federal division of the population that reflects democracy best.

Robert Dahl, a foremost student of democracy, has explained this problem at length. The majority principle and the principle of fairness may, or may not, require ever-greater inclusiveness so that the needs of the larger population are met.[145] There is no principled point at which one can stop enlarging or dividing the borders.[146]

Beyond the fairness of geographic lines, clear division of powers between federal and state governments makes some problems unsolvable, thus frustrating democracy. This is true wherever the source of the problem extends beyond state borders and requires regulation of external entities, such corporations, businesses, or other states. Democracy can be frustrated when the state political machinery is too corrupt to clean itself up.

In short, for political scientists, there is no morally better level of government—which level of government is or will be fairer and better depends on the distribution of people and prejudices.

The Court's explanations and its inferences of federal structure from the Constitution are virtually unrecognizable to political scientists. State sovereignty is a problem, not an explanation.[147] Clarifying the lines of authority has a nice ring to it, but poses important trade-offs for democratic government. The Court's clarification of authority eliminates much of the mutual restraint that provides checks and balances.

Different versions of federalism make different trade-offs among various measures of fairness. Local control can mean democracy to the anti-

Federalists or "faction" and unfair treatment to Madison and Federalist supporters of the Constitution.[148] Political scientists find that localities use power to keep "classes, races, ethnic groups, genders, and life-style groups in their places."[149] Against a standard of just government, federalism can be cited by both sides. In effect, the definition of federalism is political and contextual rather than a subject of universal, unchanging principles.

Federalism can thwart liberty; many groups around the world look to more cosmopolitan entities to protect them.[150] It was that threat to liberty that led Congress to propose and the states to ratify the Fourteenth Amendment to change federal relations.[151]

Justice Blackmun agreed that federalism can protect personal liberty: "Federalism secures to citizens the liberties that derive from the diffusion of sovereign power."[152] Justice Blackmun, however, meant that federalism is valuable when and if it advances liberty, but not otherwise. He made the comment in a case where the petitioner was being denied any review, state or federal, of a conviction for murder. His point was that deference to the states does not automatically advance liberty. "Federalism," as Blackmun put it, "has no inherent normative value."[153] In *Lopez*, the Court barred federal power to ban guns from schools.[154] It prevented the federal government from protecting children from weapons in their schools. How that protects liberty is much less clear.

Was James Madison right when he told the Constitutional Convention in Philadelphia that a larger republic would be fairer than a smaller one?[155] The government of the larger republic would have to consider different perspectives, and people in a larger republic would be less likely to gang up on small or weaker groups, African Americans included. So it would be wise to give central authorities the powers they need.

Or was Madison wrong? Political scientists find support for decentralized systems, and the data indicate that decentralization can sometimes increase stability.[156] But scientists are appropriately agnostic on the fairness of federalism.[157]

Courts focus on definitions, and sometimes on objectives defined by their understanding of the founders. Political scientists, by contrast, have focused on the ambiguous relationship of federalism and democracy. Federalism often helps secure democracy but also deepens conflicts that tear it apart.

Political scientists' theories of pluralism suggest that clarity of boundaries will also have an ambiguous relationship to democratization and the stability of democracy—possibly reducing stress and strengthening democracy when regions do not trust each other, but potentially weakening democracy by emphasizing regional competition and differences. In other words, whether the boundaries need to be sharp depends entirely on political circumstances. There is no reason to believe that the courts will prove themselves wiser than the politicians in discerning whether and where the tensions are in fact so sharp and what resolution would calm them. And there is good reason to believe that an aging conceptual federal-state boundary will make it harder to resolve contemporary disputes. The Court may have had it right, from an empirical perspective, in *Garcia*, when it left that issue to the political process.[158]

Federalism doctrine as the Rehnquist Court left it in 2005 at Chief Justice Rehnquist's death paid careful attention to eighteenth-century feuds—indeed it "protected" states from exercises of national power that were sought by the vast majority of states.[159] Despite all those issues, all branches of government can use federal structures for better or worse. If managed pragmatically, with an eye toward the context of needs and problems, federalism can contribute to democracy: It can be part of a compromise necessary so that people can agree to a democratic government; it can be handled as part of a system of checks and balances, limiting abusive behavior wherever it happens; it could be part of self-government, making it more efficient, effective or improving people's satisfaction with their government; and as many political scientists address it, federalism could be constructed as a system for managing (that is, cooling and moderating) conflict.

Federalism is about statesmanship, not lines in the sand.

Conclusion

A healthy democracy depends on protecting its people from the kinds of abuse that can be used to break or intimidate them, protecting the procedures of democracy, from speaking and joining to voting, and including the whole population. Morally, the right to govern depends on self-government and therefore on universal and equal treatment and inclusion of the population. Pragmatically, that becomes an important protection and predictor of the health of democracy.

By contrast, whether government follows a presidential model with the separation of powers or a parliamentary system where executive and legislative powers appear more blended has no convincing relationship to the survival of democracy, except, and this may well be important, to the extent that they bring out the best in their peoples. Stability may be more important than the supposed virtues of a different system.

Federalism is a tool that can be as damaging as it can be helpful; it needs to be used and managed with intelligence.

6

General Welfare

Does it matter whether the Roberts Court's reputation as a business court is accurate or what the Roberts Court's theory of the rights of business is? Does that have anything to do with democracy? And does it matter that American wealth has become more skewed toward ever fewer people than it has been since the eve of the Great Depression of 1929? What does that have to do with the Supreme Court?

Poverty and Education

The seminal insight came from Seymour M. Lipset in 1959.[1] Lipset presented a correlation: wealthy, well-educated countries were much more likely to be democratic; poor countries and poorly educated countries were quite unlikely to be democratic. Since public opinion polls had suggested that support for democratic values increased with education, the solution was to develop and educate the world.

Two outliers were difficult to explain. Germany was at the center of European civilization. In the recent past it had given the world its finest music, its most compelling philosophers, enormous scientific breakthroughs, and the whole new field of psychiatry. Germany was Christian, civilized, wealthy, educated, capitalist, and developed. Neither poor nor uneducated, Germany's surrender to fascism made little sense and called for a different explanation, though the country was going through hard times when President Paul von Hindenburg rolled out the red carpet for Hitler to become chancellor.[2]

India was another problem. India was very poor; its people largely illiterate. If democracy rested on education and wealth, Indian democracy should have failed. Nevertheless, its Western-educated leaders—Mahatma Gandhi, Jawaharlal Nehru, and their colleagues in the Congress Party who led the effort toward independence, as well as Dr. B. R. Ambedkar who led the movement to empower India's "backward classes"—brought a Western model of democracy to a poor Eastern country. The Constitution they wrote committed India to a policy of massive affirmative action for the most despised peoples of the subcontinent, the "untouchables" or, as Gandhi relabeled them, the Harijan, the blessed. Preferences in India dwarfed America's later attempt at affirmative action. India encompassed enumerable languages, peoples, castes, and all the conflicts that go with them. When Lipset wrote, it seemed one could just count the days until the collapse of democracy in India. Students of democracy are still counting. Except for a brief period in the 1970s, India has remained a democracy against what seemed like solid odds against it.

To political scientists who do empirical work these are challenging facts. At best, they meant that wealth and education are influences that compete in the real world with other factors. Waves of democracies created and lost in the twentieth century have gradually been unraveling the relationships.[3]

The Historical Record

A second, complementary strand of research has been historical. In a four-volume set, Juan Linz and Alfred Stepan brought together historical descriptions of the breakdown of democracy in European and Latin American countries. They found a common theme in the way that the deep gulf in resources led powerful elites, fearing attacks on their wealth, to circle their wagons against more popular parties.[4] Nancy Bermeo followed with a powerful reinterpretation of the data. Most people, she found, remained committed to democracy. But they voted for more redistribution than the powerful were willing to accept. Wealthy aristocrats lost tolerance for democracy and questioned the loyalty of their competitors. Partisan wrangles then greased the path to authoritarian rule.[5]

In Italy after World War I, aristocrats had much to fear from seizures of farms and factories and the political leadership on both sides refused to work together to find acceptable common ground, eventually losing the will to resist a takeover. Italy's prime minister responded to Mussolini's threat, or bluff, to march on Rome by leaving. The military refused to defend it, and King Victor Emmanuel asked Mussolini to form a government.[6] In effect the leadership of the country abdicated in frustration.

In Germany throughout the 1920s an increasingly polarized leadership supported competing paramilitary armies. Conservatives in government took action against left-wing paramilitaries and blocked or refused to take action against right-wing paramilitaries. In 1932, most Germans believed in democracy; Hitler and the Nazis won only a third of the vote before Field Marshall Paul von Hindenburg handed Hitler the reins of government. German democracy was abandoned by an aristocracy, more afraid of a liberal victory than of dictatorship. Too much wealth makes the wealthy fearful and the rest needy. Every election in pre-Nazi Germany seemed too liberal to satisfy the landed aristocracy and wealthy entrepreneurs.

Between the world wars, dictators were invited to rule Italy, Germany, Greece, Romania, and Yugoslavia. Leaders disloyal to democracy took over via coups d'état in another eight states—Austria, Bulgaria, Estonia, Latvia, Lithuania, Poland, Portugal, and Spain. None fell as the result of a popular uprising, although Spain suffered a bloody civil war between forces supported respectively by Hitler and Stalin. Leaders on both sides abandoned democracy well before the 1936 attack on the Republic by Generalissimo Franco and others ended Spanish democracy for decades.[7] Dictatorship in Europe and Latin America was largely arranged at the top, by the Right, in fear of the Left. Nancy Bermeo, a political scientist then at Princeton, describing the loss of Greek democracy in 1936, wrote, "The trigger for this change—as for so many others—was an electoral outcome that frightened the Right."[8] Working together to solve their differences did not appear to be more attractive than giving up on democracy. Too frequently, the Left also viewed dictatorship as less to be feared than trying to find a political middle path. In Spain, political stalemate led to breakdown and violence.

The narratives assembled by this group of scholars from Linz to Bermeo evidence the importance of the leadership's loyalty to the survival of democracy. Mutual allegations of disloyalty became self-fulfilling prophecies, and threatened aristocracies who circled their wagons against change and against a democratic system that could produce it. The Left responded with equal distrust.

The pattern was repeated in Latin America after World War II. Violence in the Colombian countryside was periodic. In the 1940s it was tied to new labor organizations that seemed to promise or threaten change in political arrangements. Both parties began to find ways to rig the electoral system in their favor—liberals by adding voters, conservatives by using force at the polls. With loss of trust in the electoral system, democracy broke down. The experience of the various countries in which democracy foundered on efforts to manipulate elections suggests the potential dangers of *Bush v. Gore*.

In Chile, the military rejected any notion of a coup just two months before the overthrow of Allende and the installation of Pinochet. In those two months, a couple of mutinies were nipped in the bud, and paramilitaries, prepared to defend against each other's violence, grew. In 1973, Salvador Allende's policies went too far for Chilean landed and military elites, who seized power in a coup d'état, with support from the Nixon administration in Washington, DC. In each case, wealthy elites and powerful generals decided that this elected government should not be allowed to survive.[9]

Scholars studying the sequence of events in countries where democracy broke down argue that breakdown is not an automatic process; human decisions matter. In country after country, the large mass of people remained committed to democracy but the leadership became so divided that they could not work together or act to deal with the country's problems until they eventually became complicit in the breakdown of democracy. Only people dedicated to the dream of democracy could keep India from the dictatorial experience of neighboring Pakistan. The gulf between those with and those without power makes subjugation likely. But the powerful may make different choices.

Westerners often treat countries that are ruled by a few well-placed families as undemocratic. The Philippines have long been governed by a small minority of wealthy families. Philippine "democracy" has seemed closer to aristocracy.[10] The same has been true for many Latin American governments. Americans profess to see the origins of their insurgencies in the huge inequalities of landholding even while many in the United States quake at the thought of any of those insurgencies succeeding. The majorities in those countries are ruled by small, wealthy, and entrenched minorities. And most of us rightly condemn it. Democracy is government by and for the people, not rule over them.

Amy Chua, who experienced personally and tragically the strains and struggles of Philippine politics, wrote about it in her book WORLD ON FIRE. She explains that small elites feel besieged by large hostile populations and become defensive. They surround themselves with armed guards in private compounds and are ready to seize power if necessary.[11] From personal experience she confirmed what political scientists have found: power corrupts. With power in few hands, few dare oppose them. Those who collude in the government share the spoils.

A new group of comparative historical analysts describe the choices of economic aristocracies to protect themselves from the dangers of holding great income and wealth in an otherwise impoverished population. They look for allies, sometimes allying with a rising middle class and sometimes against it. Noneconomic factors like religion and ethnicity affect what alliances are possible. Those alliances are driven in part by the distribution of human capital among the population, including skills, literacy, education, and mobility.[12] Democracy developed slowly if at all in the face of slavery, serfdom, or other immobile and constrained supplies of cheap labor.

By the Numbers

Late in the twentieth century, democracy began an exciting march into new areas during what Samuel Huntington termed "the third wave."[13] In 1974

Portugal overthrew the autocratic regime of António de Oliveira Salazar and his successor, Marcello Caetano, and soon joined the ranks of relatively stable European democracies. In 1976 King Juan Carlos de Borbón set Spain on a path to democracy after decades of autocratic rule by Generalissimo Franco. The Soviet Union crumbled in 1991 and nascent democracies struggled to hang on in parts of what had been the USSR.

Suddenly it became possible to investigate the emergence and the stability of democratic systems, with much more sophisticated statistical tools that could not have been used when democracies were rare events.

Despite the powerful counterexamples of Nazi Germany and independent India, third-wave and post–World War II data reaffirmed the importance of wealth. Per capita wealth has been one of the strongest predictors of democracy.[14] The poorest countries provide the least fertile soil for democracy and rising income stabilizes their democracies.[15] Contests over political systems in more economically developed countries are usually less deadly.[16] Democracy has been very stable in the richest countries. The relationship between poverty and democracy has been confirmed both in comparative studies of democratization and its breakdown in individual countries, and in large-scale statistical studies of modern democracies.[17]

In 1994, Vice President Al Gore convened a State Failure Task Force, a group of political scientists both inside and outside of the government, working with the Central Intelligence Agency. The group's goal was to figure out the chances that countries would "fail," that is, whether they would become engulfed in civil war, be taken over by a coup, or have their governing system displaced.

The Task Force reanalyzed its own data to focus on the thirty-five cases in its database from 1955 to 1996 in which democratic governments had been replaced by autocratic ones.[18] When they took a closer look, two variables stood out, accounting for 75 percent of all the instances in which democracy had been replaced by autocracy. Infant mortality turned out to be an accurate index of the breakdown of democracy.[19] The Task Force interpreted that as an indicator of widespread poverty and serious infrastructure problems.[20] The other was the length of time in which the country had been governed as a democracy.[21] That finding could be interpreted as inertia or that democracies that provided a decent quality of life survived.[22]

Political scientists understand infant mortality not as a cause but as a symptom of important but less easily measured factors. There are competing explanations for why infant mortality predicts state failure. It could be the result of poverty, governmental incompetence, civil war, or other state failure. Competent states can provide the sanitation and health services necessary to bring death rates down. States that do not take care of their people and provide necessary services are incompetent. Incompetence breeds dissatisfaction and incompetent states may be unable to control violence. Hence they fail.[23] Infant mortality could reflect civil wars that decimate the population through starvation and disease. In that case too infant mortality reflects state failure and poverty. Each of those interpretations fit the long-standing finding that poverty is one of the best predictors of autocracy. The Task Force data do not pinpoint a specific connection between poverty and the failure of democracy. The strength of the correlation with mortality, however, suggests that the disparity of resources plays an important part.

To understand why democracy survives or breaks down one has to dig beneath the correlation between democracy and national or per capital wealth. Robert Dahl, one of the century's most renowned students of democracy, wrote that "we indeed do find an extraordinarily strong correlation between economic well-being and democracy,"[24] but he went on to explain that more was involved than merely wealth: "We must not misread the evidence. . . . Democracy requires . . . a widespread sense of relative economic well-being, fairness, and opportunity, a condition derived not from absolute standards but from perceptions of relative advantage and deprivation."[25] In other words, Dahl concluded that disparity plays a crucial role.

Whether wealth, as Lipset initially described it, or disparity, as Dahl discussed it, makes a bigger difference for the survival or breakdown of democracy, also has important implications for constitutional law. If the question is whether United States is wealthy enough, then, unless the country quickly declines relative to the rest of the globe, it seems unlikely that there is cause for concern; and even if there were, it seems unlikely that constitutional law would have anything to contribute. However, if the issue is disparity, neither conclusion follows. America may be headed toward considerably greater disparities in wealth, and there are ways that constitutional law does deal with such disparities. So how this issue is resolved in political science can make a difference in how issues of constitutional law should be resolved.

Murphy's Law and the Concentration of Resources

The work of the Finnish political scientist Tatu Vanhanen has received a lot of criticism,[26] but he had an often overlooked insight. Recently, Bruce Bueno de Mesquita, a widely admired political scientist now at New York University, has been making a related point from a different vantage point. The intersection of their work can be summarized as Murphy's Law of Democracy—whoever can suppress democracy and rule, will. Their explanations, which bring us back to disparity of resources, are powerful and complementary.[27]

Vanhanen, father of a former prime minister of Finland, has long argued that where the resources needed to exercise power are very concentrated, they will be exercised undemocratically and democracy will not persist.[28] Whether the power is held by wealthy landowners in Latin America, oil rich royalty in the Near East, or those who control the trade in crucial African mineral resources, their power is or seems too great to challenge. Vanhanen's basic hypothesis is well stated in his 1984 study: "Democratic institutions cannot be expected to succeed in circumstances in which power resources are highly concentrated, whereas the emergence of democracy is highly probable in societies in which crucial power resources are widely distributed among the competing groups and sections of the population."[29] That is, whoever can take power, reflected in the resources they have, probably will. The distribution of power in society, therefore, determines whether democracy survives. Vanhanen's point incorporates the findings of many scholars about the correlations between national wealth and democracy and the findings of other scholars about the behavior of leadership. Where historical studies have focused on elite motives and actions, Vanhanen focuses on relative power.

It is very difficult to measure power or the concentration of the necessary resources to wield power and that poses a difficulty for Vanhanen and for the interpretation of his data. His empirical work has been subject to well-deserved criticism.[30] Nevertheless his underlying explanation is powerful. What he has tried to do is give statistical support to Amy Chua's description of the corruption of elites. If people can control the nation, odds are they will.

Groups protect their perks and tell themselves it's good for everyone. "They like it this way." Slaveholders kept describing slavery as necessary for the blacks, and described the slaves as happy.[31] Politicians and corporations do not rise because of their willingness to share power. They rise because of their desire to seize it. What makes them stop short and accept rules of engagement that we can fairly call democratic?

Because power corrupts, the crucial problem is to identify when, where, or how power becomes too concentrated. The possibilities change over time. Americans largely invented the first mass political parties. That changed the ways people could exert power in our political system. In business we describe power with terms like monopoly or oligopoly.[32] We have many names for power in politics—dictatorship, aristocracy, or sometimes just corruption or machine politics. Pinochet exerted control in Chile through the military and Ayatollah Khomeini exerted control through the clergy in Iran. In such places, dissenters are cowed by beatings, imprisonment, or torture. In other places, dissenters are silenced by the aristocratic patrons they need for the success of their own projects, businesses, or survival.

A degree of power is inevitable and valuable. The ability of police, businessmen, editors, and planners, to make the society we live in manageable reflects a degree of power. We depend on government to be able to govern, for which it must exercise power. But when power becomes too concentrated, government becomes less democratic, or democracy is eliminated altogether.

Bruce Bueno de Mesquita and his colleagues offer us another glimpse of Murphy's Law in action with an up-close look at how leaders can stay in office.[33] Let's call their version Murphy's Law of Dictatorship. They argue that rulers generally have an incentive to shrink the number of people they need to rely on in order to stay in power, so that the rulers can lavishly reward their supporters and keep them in line. A small group that controls the selection of the leader can be rewarded regardless of what happens to the rest of the population. And so it is to the leaders' advantage to rob from the poor in order to provide lavish benefits to the few other powerful people the leaders depend on. Bueno de Mesquita and his colleagues call those people the "selectorate." The difference between what members of the leader's coalition and the public at large get must be large enough to assure their continued loyalty and determination to keep others out of power. This is similar to aristocracies circling their wagons to prevent the masses from sharing the wealth that Bermeo and others have described. But the Bueno de Mesquita group then explains the way the elites are corrupted. Elite success depends on denying the people a voice, and also on refusing to spend on productive public goods so that there is plenty of money to satisfy corrupt appetites. Money spent on productive public goods broadens the distribution of power and reduces the share that can be lavished on supporters. Or in the language of American politics, money spent on infrastructure leaves less room to reduce the tax share of the wealthy.

The Bueno de Mesquita group also reflects on the resource side. Who the leader needs to reward depends on who has the power to keep the leader on top, the "selectorate." However, if resources are widely distributed, the leadership will have too many people to contend with. In other words there is a cycle of power and one needs to look both at the incentives of the leaders and the way that power is distributed. Vanhanen would describe that side of the equation as resources for power. And that's why Murphy's Law is a fair description—elites and leaders do what is possible. They have an incentive to exert their power and take over, if they have the resources to do it. So as Murphy would have described it, what can happen, will happen.

The implications for democracy are straightforward. A group that can exclude everyone else from sharing power is likely to do it. The more resources are concentrated in a few hands, the less democratic we expect society to be. And the more dispersed resources are, the more democratic we expect society to be. In a vicious circle, concentrated wealth leads to concentrated power which leads to concentrated wealth. In a virtuous circle, broadly distributed resources lead to broadly distributed power which leads to broadly distributed resources.

Murphy's Law of Dictatorship is also a corollary of a point experts have begun to make about revolutions, that revolutions are generated by the resources to wage them.[34] Gary King and Langche Zeng at Harvard concluded that the Task Force could have improved predictions of state failure had they examined the percentage of the population in the military, the density of population, and the effectiveness of the legislature. The military population matters because "the larger the fraction of the population that has weapons and is trained in military conflict, the more risk there is that internal dissent may lead to state failure."[35]

James Fearon and David Laitin at Stanford University concluded that poverty, political instability, rough terrain, and large populations make insurgency and civil war more likely and facilitate the overthrow of regimes. In other words, in their analysis too, opportunity makes rebellion more likely. If people have the opportunity to take power, watch out. Everything else may be no more than an excuse.[36] Murphy rules. Political scientists refer to the ability to organize, so that many people can act together, as the collective action problem. Carles Boix points to solutions for the collective action problem as critical to the likelihood of revolution or takeover.[37] As resources and the people who control them keep shifting, the payoffs people can expect from democratic and undemocratic behavior, their motives to support or damage democracy, and the likelihood of action are always in flux. That makes focusing on power an important corrective to models focusing on motives. And as the resources mount in the hands of potential revolutionaries, elites, officers, or warlords, state failure and democratic failure loom.

Paths to Failure

Game theorists have tried to model the path by which democracies are put together or break down, as a sequence of behaviors. That is a more demanding effort than identifying factors, motives, and resources. Game theorists model specific ways or sequences of events that people with a given set of motives and resources would generate.[38] So far they have not found a single sequence of events by which breakdown can be described, and the existing measures leave many questions about the extent or power of resources.[39]

Breakdowns are generally easier to see and trace than the lengthy process of democracy building.[40] For that reason, the statistics available to show the path from inequality to the breakdown of democracy are clearer than they are to the creation or consolidation of democracy.[41] And in multiple ways, they reveal that fear of subordinated masses threatens democracy wherever there is a permanent underclass. Pursuit of security leads the fearful to accept a corrupt, repressive government.[42] The result is a cycle of increasing fear, protection, and repression. Arms create a police state. Confirming the conclusion of earlier historical work, scientists are finding again that great inequalities encourage the wealthy to circle their wagons against the public.[43] If they can control the population, it is likely they will.

Half a century after Lipset, it remains "conventional wisdom [among political scientists] that income per capita sustains democracy."[44] Disparity of resources defines who can control the state—an aristocracy, warlords, oligarchs, or the people.

Samuel Huntington identified different ways in which economic factors make democracy stronger or allow autocrats to take over. Economic development breeds trust. Entrepreneurs and other wealthy people need not fear majority rule as long as development equalizes and diffuses income. Starkly divided societies cannot develop that degree of mutual confidence. Democracies must, to a degree, function as communities.[45] Economic development also supports better education, which increases support for democracy and broadens the demand to take part in government. And economic development makes compromise easier, by enlarging the resources available to meet competing demands, especially in a growing economy.[46]

Conversely, people who are poor can be lured into doing things that others would scorn—living as soldiers of "revolutionary" movements for the booty it brings, manning so-called goon squads that once intimidated American voters and forced them to vote as ordered, or accepting bribes to vote as requested.[47] Poverty makes people vulnerable. Studies of social psychology confirm the result. Insecurity regarding basic human needs like food, clothing, and shelter are likely to produce violence.[48] Democracy is not a likely result.

This strand of research has focused on the ways that great inequalities make the poor more dissatisfied, and available for the kinds of activities that corrupt elections or overturn elected government—in short anything for the individual to survive but curtains for democracy.[49] Pathologies like those were extensively reflected in the heyday of American political machines prior to the New Deal.[50] It can happen here and often did.

To summarize, large disparities threaten democracy in multiple ways. Too much wealth makes people powerful and fearful. Too much poverty makes people vulnerable. Generalizing both, power corrupts, and too much power is terminal for whatever is left of democracy. Either way, democracy requires dispersion of resources among the population at large. All these strands of political science converge on the relationship between inequality and the likelihood that democracy will break down. The fact that such different approaches yield complementary results adds considerable weight to their findings.[51]

This work counsels against the self-satisfying conclusion that America is bound to remain "exceptional," that we are and will remain different from Germany and other European countries between the wars, or many Central American and southern hemisphere countries since then. It is important because it brings together the various and persistent observations that large economic inequalities endanger democratic government. These suggest an economic dimension to constitutional law that has been consistently denied in most prior scholarship and opinions on constitutional law.[52] Democracy is threatened by concentrations of power, economic or otherwise.

Capitalism

The founding generation would have equated freedom with voting rather than an economic system. Indeed state enterprise was an important part of their eighteenth-century economic world. Nevertheless, in the mirror of the Cold War, many believed that capitalism would protect both freedom and democracy. That has been a powerful strain in conservative ideology,[53] although some prominent conservatives have realized that capitalism can undermine both freedom and democracy[54] and others have understood that capitalism does not cause democracy.[55]

Given that increasingly common view, political scientists began to examine whether there was a relationship. There can be. Communism as practiced behind the Iron Curtain involved the concentration of resources, so that everything depended on the state; more precisely, everything depended on the blessing of party bureaucrats and leaders. Communist government monopolized economic as well as political power. Government power can be used to demand loyalty, restrict mobility, and limit opportunity.

Capitalism can counter that by offering people alternative ways to earn a living and flourish. It can offer political freedom. But capitalism does not necessarily do either. It too tends to monopolize. Private enterprise can exert monopoly power.[56] Company towns did;[57] they were like one-company states controlled by large extractive industries, which maintained deep control over every aspect of life, from shopping to religious and public life.[58] Aristocratic and plutocratic economies concentrate power, extracting what economists call monopoly rents, limiting what others can earn and do.

The crucial issue for democratic government is the extent of control or distribution of power and resources, not the name of the system. Many dictatorships are run by combinations of politicians with economic oligarchs. Mixed capitalist and socialist states, however, need not exert monopoly power; Europe provides many examples of this mix, as did the economy of the American colonies and early states. The issue is diversity; diversity of economic actors adds opportunity. So long as government remains one among many players in the economic system, its entry increases pluralism and the dispersion of power. People have more options, more tools to deal with problems.[59] The message of political science has been that concentrated wealth and power impose considerable stress on democracy, and it is as true of economics as for politics.

Should Americans Be Concerned?

Many Americans are convinced, although the facts do not back them up, that they live in the world's wealthiest society, and many economists suggest that the very size of the U.S. economy will make it hard for others to overtake. How quickly that could change has obviously been affected by globalization which now permits giant capital flows among nations, and capital has in fact been moving industries around the globe. The continuing effects of the 2008 depression confirms the speed with which conditions can change for a large portion of Americans.

Both income and wealth are now highly concentrated in the United States, and have become increasingly concentrated over the past three decades, reaching levels of concentration not seen since 1929.[60] Data also suggest slippage by comparison with the rest of the industrialized world on many measures, including income disparity. That disparity between rich and poor is now considerably greater than in the United Kingdom, France, Canada, and the nations of the industrialized world; greater than any of the other industrialized democracies in any hemisphere.[61] Economic mobility from one's circumstances at birth to opportunities later in life is no greater in the United States than in other industrialized countries and may now be less.[62]

Concentrated power and wealth creates incentives to undermine democracy and the tools to accomplish it. Antipathy toward democracy has already become a theme in much conservative rhetoric, theorizing, and activity.[63] The question is where it will lead.

Given both the absolute change in the disparity of income and wealth within the United States, and the change relative to other countries, it is difficult to predict that the U.S. economy will protect U.S. democracy. The future is contingent on how Americans will handle the U.S. economy as much as it depends on how Americans handle other challenges.

7

A Sense of *We*

Our national motto is *e pluribus unum*—Latin for out of many, one. Constructing that one, what Robert Putnam called a "sense of 'we,'" is an important task for democracy.[1]

The logic of a democratic system requires that people accept the legitimacy of contrary views and parties. The world's foremost students of our attitudes toward each other's views worry about the corrosive effect of intolerance on democracy. It saps support for the rights of those who disagree, limits the ability to raise issues, let alone solve them, and can lead to violence. Rolling over dissent, mob psychology can open democracy's door to dictatorship and tragedy.[2] In short, intolerance is dangerous, the autoimmune disease of democracy.[3]

Democracy, however, requires much more than our tolerance of each other's beliefs; it requires cooperation. Robert Putnam touched a chord in 1993 with a prize-winning book on the development of democracy in Italy. In MAKING DEMOCRACY WORK, Putnam concluded that historically there were a great deal more civic and social activities outside the family in northern than in southern Italy. Confining activity to the family stifles the broader connections needed to run a democratic government. Community activities, by contrast, helped democracy take hold earlier and more firmly in northern than in southern Italy.[4] He concluded that it is not enough that people be educated about democracy's virtues, want, or believe in it; economic incentives and enlightened self-interest are insufficient for democracy to take root. For democracy to thrive, people have to trust, cooperate, and care about one another across the broader community. Democracy is based on "social capital"—the things people do together that develop loyalties to each other, to a larger population, and to the greater good. Putnam used "bowling alone" as a metaphor for what he saw as the contemporary decline in routine social activities that build social capital.[5] His conclusion that social capital has declined is very controversial. But the need for social capital is fundamental.

Many encapsulated Putnam as saying democracy depends on mutual trust, although trust is only part of Putnam's point.[6] Trust enables cooperation and makes it possible to let political opponents govern whenever the people vote for them. It is crucial to be able to rely on basic fairness from opponents, on their respect for your vital interests, even while more peripheral matters may be decided against your views or interests. The decency of our behavior toward each other creates either a virtuous cycle that reinforces democracy or a vicious cycle that destroys it.

Social capital does not always cross party, class, gender, religious, ethnic, and racial lines.[7] When the population polarizes so that people despise or fear each other, it becomes harder to trust opponents' fairness when in power. Constitutions and bills of rights attempt to guaranty essential protections to the losers, but they too rest on trust that those in charge will respect the paper guarantees.[8]

An almost forgotten work adds a crucial thread through these relationships of tolerance, trust, and trustworthiness.[9] David McClelland, in a work much discussed when it appeared in 1961, concluded that the flowering of democracy depended on matching people's desire for power by their desire for the affection of others. People who care only for power would gladly destroy democracy to gain or keep control. Democracy depends on a culture that puts the rules of the political contest above one's own choices. Successful democratic societies put a high value on getting along and winning the esteem of others. By comparison with other countries, McClelland found that Americans cared deeply about both power and the affection of others. Americans want to be liked, as David Riesman classically described Americans in the "lonely crowd"; they crave affection.[10]

McClelland's methods were controversial but his insight was brilliant.[11] The politicians' creed—coupling their desire for power with their need to be liked—lies at the foundation of democracy. When we want the approval of others, it is easier to accept democratic values and to respect rather than threaten or coerce the public. The sense of community, of mutual concern and need for approval, is critical to the way power is shared in a democracy. Democracy demands concern for others.

Tolerance, social capital, desire for approval, and concern for the opinions and welfare of others are all part of the way people collaborate with others across society; they are critical for democracy to succeed. Looking around the world, it is clear those needs and relationships are neither genetic nor automatic, but cultural. They have to be nourished and protected.

These conclusions of modern social scientists corroborate the founders' insistence that democracy depended on a republican frame of mind defined by a shared sense of civic virtue and public responsibility. A republican education was crucial precisely because selfishness could easily destroy democracy.[12] A similar insight lay behind anti-Federalist resistance to the

Constitution because they doubted that people could develop the necessary loyalties beyond their own states.[13]

If tolerance, social capital, mutual care, concern and a need for approval are all necessary to sustain democracy, do we have a problem? If democracy needs to bring all of society under its wing, what builds the necessary relationships? And what do law and courts have to do with that?

Do Americans Have a Problem?

Alexis de Tocqueville noticed American intolerance in 1830 while touring the young nation: "I know of no country in which there is so little independence of mind and real freedom of discussion as in America."[14] Other great students of American politics have described the ways public opinion can censor and stifle thought.[15]

Polls revealed a surprisingly large percentage of Americans ready to silence those with whom they disagree.[16] That finding has been robust through significant scientific improvements in understanding tolerance.[17] Willingness to have government silence others goes well beyond constitutional and other appropriate limits.[18] Tolerance and compromise are in decline.[19]

Divided Minds

Political scientists have been concerned about those findings since they were documented more than half a century ago.[20] There is evidence that Americans are aware of each other's intolerance. Gibson found that nearly three-quarters of Americans would not put a political sign on their lawns because people might get upset, and a majority would not show their politics in public with a bumper sticker. Americans are reluctant even to take action in private, like writing a congressman.[21]

Although Americans claim pride in freedom of speech, they often find disagreement inappropriate, even rude, and they consider dissenters an embarrassment. Many resist allowing a forum to those who disagree. As Robert J. Samuelson put it, "Americans disdain fierce moral combat," and disdain protesters and their grievances.[22]

Attacking free expression is sometimes used as a "tough," honorable stance. Mayor Giuliani conducted a running battle with the New York Civil Liberties Union over whether taxi drivers or others could demonstrate in front of City Hall, or use a megaphone to be heard without his approval, though he mostly lost in court.[23] Mayor Bloomberg created holding pens for demonstrators, out of view of those they demonstrated against, with access blocked to many wanting to join the demonstration, and exits blocked for those seeking a rest-room.[24] For many, demonstrations became a violation against civil order and obedience. That too is a form of intolerance, and when officially enforced, a violation of the First Amendment. One has to assume that Giuliani and Bloomberg thought their actions would be popular among their supporters.

It may be indicative of our polarization that efforts have been made to impeach four of our last six presidents—Nixon, Reagan, Clinton, and Obama. The level of partisanship led a deeply divided Supreme Court to stop the 2000 presidential ballot count, lest it embarrass one of the candidates,[25] ignoring precedent and specific provisions of the federal Constitution which defined how a disputed presidential election should be resolved. Five justices feared leaving the republic in Al Gore's Democratic hands.[26]

A 2003 report of the Pew Research Center for the People and the Press found "[t]he extraordinary spirit of national unity that followed the ca-lamitous events of Sept. 11, 2001 has dissolved amid rising polarization and anger."[27] The report found the country "further apart than ever in its political values."[28] Andrew Kohut, the founding director of the Pew Research Center, described "the anger level [as] so high that if the demonstrators of 1968 had felt like this, 'there would have been gunfire in the streets.'"[29] Actually, some put up websites with gun-sight style hash marks for opponents while oth-ers lobbed bricks through the windows of congressional representatives; one malcontent shot Congresswoman Gabby Giffords, and several made attempts on Obama's life. Although clearly not typical, extremist behavior reflects the tension. The Pew Research Center reported that the partisan gap grew by 25 percent between 2003 and 2012, and it continues to deepen.[30]

The temperate middle ground now has dubious associations as opportu-nistic, lukewarm, compromising, and vacuous. Writing in THE CHRISTIAN CENTURY, Gary Dorrien described the loss of an appealing and principled Christian middle ground, leaving the religious in the hands of a variety of radical faiths.[31] "Maverick" congressmen in this polarized political world are Republicans whose support for George W. Bush reached only 96 percent, and ticket splitting at the polls has declined.[32] Richard Tomkins accurately pre-dicted that polarization would have a major impact "on Capitol Hill where changing party demographics and geographics have contributed to hardening partisanship on and off the floor."[33]

A Zogby poll portrayed both separate red and blue "nations" and "distinct moral world views"—a divide that continued through the subsequent elec-tions of Presidents Bush and Obama.[34] John White, a professor of politics at Catholic University, in a much-discussed essay, wrote, "Not since the Civil War and post-Reconstruction period has the country been so divided."[35]

Polarization in national politics—with standoffs over the debt ceiling, the "fiscal cliff," and executive appointments—brought the government to its knees, lowered the national credit rating, and extended the recession. The parties have alternated their control of Congress. But for all their talk about compromise, the geographical segregation of voters is magnified by the political system and shows no sign of changing.

Congressmen and senators have retired saying the atmosphere has become unhealthy. Their departure continues the trend. Compromise has come to mean selling out, resulting in indecision. As the title of Jim Hightower's book says, THERE'S NOTHING IN THE MIDDLE OF THE ROAD BUT YELLOW STRIPES AND DEAD ARMADILLOS.

More than the difficulty of legislating, this level of tension and partisanship reflects the loss of many forms of the social capital necessary to sustain democratic government: tolerance, trust, trustworthiness, empathy, and the need for the approval of fellow citizens. As Dr. Jean Twenge put it, "Income inequality seems to be a key predictor of social capital—and thus the health of our nation."[36]

The Human Divide Underneath

In 1950 my father put a five-hundred-dollar deposit on a home in Levittown, on Long Island. A few months later, when the Korean War broke out, he got cold feet, and we never made the move. Putting down that original deposit, however, had nothing to do with "white flight." There were no black families in our neighborhood to flee. If there had been, we would have welcomed them; many of us were already rooting for the Dodgers' new cleanup hitter, Jackie Robinson.

There were plenty of other reasons to flee the city. Some were trying to reconnect with their families' pasts, before the move to cities had taken them away from homes in the country. Arthur Miller immortalized the dream of a white house in the country in his DEATH OF A SALESMAN. It had nothing to do with race.

Cities were hot, muggy, and stifling in the summer. We spent our summers upstate. Before the Salk vaccine, our trip was also fueled by fear of polio. The city seemed to be where it spread. The March of Dimes collected coins in little boxes in almost every store. Occasionally, we would see pictures of children in iron lungs, unable to do anything except lie there, enclosed in the machinery that helped them breath. It was terrifying.

Suburbs separated people, white people, to an extent that cities did not. People from different economic strata typically rubbed shoulders in mid-twentieth-century city neighborhoods. In our neighborhood, apartment houses lined many avenues, while one- and two-family homes lined the side streets. Urban buildings had gone up independently or at most in small groups. Levittown, built right after World War II, encompassed virtually an entire town. When it and subsequent developers cleared large tracts and offered a limited number of designs in a single price range, they homogenized large areas by economic class. The Levittown model, built separately for lower, middle, and "upscale" homes, now dominates suburbia. My dad later spent twenty years living in a large, gated Florida retirement community built for people like him.

These new suburbs would be bedroom communities for the city before establishing their own economic cores. It was easy to establish separate lives in the suburbs, separate from people on a different rung of the income ladder, driven to different suburbs by the price, not fear or dislike, just money.

Local governments use zoning to wall people off by wealth, now with one and five acre tracts. Robert Reich, former secretary of labor, observed, "the fortunate fifth is quietly seceding from the rest of the nation," ticking off the myriad ways they separate themselves. Shopping malls ended the need to travel into the older cities. Private health, golf, tennis, and skating clubs replace the need to take advantage of public parks and playgrounds. Condominiums and residential enclaves provide internal streets, sidewalks, landscaping, swimming pools, and security guards for residents only. Wealthy children go to private schools and a large number of middle-class offspring now do the same. The revitalization of inner cities has also been aimed at making them attractive to those with considerable wealth, but the office complexes are self-sufficient—there is no need to leave. Even charity has now detached itself from the needs of the poor. Voluntary organizations often mirror geographical, gender, and class biases. Contributions go largely to the pleasures of wealth: art museums, opera houses, theaters, orchestras, ballet, private hospitals, and elite universities. The wealthy are increasingly unlikely to experience how other Americans live or be aware of their interdependence.[37]

The suburbs changed more than money. Some came to the United States with the intention to form separate, segregated, and often isolated religious communities. Mennonites, Amish, Pennsylvania Dutch, Chasidic Jews, and similar groups managed to retain that character. Either way people came and still come to America looking for people familiar from the old country—family, friends, or just people from the same places. That led to communities defined by nationality, ethnicity, and faith. For most, segregation broke down relatively quickly, partly influenced by the integrative traditions that we have described.

Nevertheless, Thomas Schelling, a Nobel Prize–winning economist, noticed that some suburbs that had originally been religiously mixed, soon resorted themselves so that each suburb was more homogenous. In a famous article, Schelling demonstrated that this could be true even if virtually everyone preferred to live in a mixed environment, so long as people's definitions of a comfortable mixture varied.[38]

Many reasons have in fact divided people by faith—some because of affinity for what became red and blue states[39]—to settle near their houses of worship, for convenience or because communities organize social activities around their places of worship. The religious revival now taking place in America leads people to organize activities around religious experience. Many children are schooled at home, or in religious schools, skipping whatever diversity public schools have to offer. Believers form networks and use the institutions they belong to in order to attract other believers. Prayer groups allow people to find each other.

Traditionally, Catholic Charities, Jewish Family Services, and similar organizations were nonsectarian, partly because it was legally required or encouraged by the tax code. But the faith-based initiatives of Clinton and Bush now allow religious groups to be much more explicit about their religious mission in delivering services than merely advertising their sponsorship of charitable activities. Thrivent Financial for Lutherans advertises for Lutheran investors and bars others.[40] For recreation we turn to private or religiously affiliated health clubs. Religion is not just about one's relation to God. It is also about one's relation to a community. These trends have undercut some of the purposes of the common, or public, school system.

African Americans, of course, were the last to benefit from the deliberate mixing of Americans in schools over the past two centuries, and their participation is still controversial. Some will be surprised that racial divisions grew after the celebrated decision in *Brown v. Board of Education*, especially in northern states. As blacks went north looking for jobs that opened up as a result of World War II, the Federal Highway Administration was building the roads that opened the suburbs. But those suburbs were "red-lined" by the Federal Housing Administration (FHA), which means that you could have your mortgage guaranteed, but only if you were white.[41] Federal officials made sure that blacks were not welcome. The suburbs became lily white—not because of white flight from blacks, but because only whites were now able to realize the American dream of a house in the country. Gradually, as whites left for the suburbs, they took their businesses, and the jobs they funded, with them. As the central cities deteriorated and minority areas became increasingly impoverished, later emigrants may well have had different reasons for leaving but the die had long since been cast.

The Truman and subsequent administrations oversaw a large effort at "slum clearance"; blacks called it "Negro clearance." Their parts of the cities looked dilapidated to whites who tore them down. Storied neighborhoods, alive with businesses, were torn down to make way for offices and white-owned stores. The demolition and renovation undercut all the work, social, and religious connections that make healthy communities. It would not be the first time white America eyed and took land from racial minorities.

Whether "urban renewal," "slum clearance," or "Negro clearance," tearing down their old neighborhoods cut black businesses off from their customers. Under the rules of eminent domain, business gets nothing for what lawyers and businesses call "good will"—loyal customers. As businesses and their customers were forced out, they had to try to start over.

Before *Brown*, there was an extensive black economy—from universities, hospitals, and insurance companies to skilled trades and a host of small businesses. For black businesses, the Civil Rights Act of 1964[42] was a mixed blessing as customers exercised their right to shop and eat at newly integrated white stores and lunch counters. Minority-owned mom-and-pop businesses declined by *half* from 1960 to 1980.[43] Whether forced out by "slum clearance" or loss of business to integration, switching to the white economy meant starting again at the bottom of the ladder, playing by white rules and customs, and hoping for white good faith in hiring, training, educating, and promoting blacks, but running instead into decades of resistance.[44] The black community followed precisely the pattern of ingenuity, savvy, and dedication to self-help that other immigrant groups did—but the fruits were repeatedly pulled out from under them. Blacks were caught in a dilemma: Discrimination by the FHA and others were segregating the north, while affirmative action, the most effective remedy for discrimination against blacks, was attacked as discrimination against whites.

Northern segregation, largely the result of official Washington, DC, decisions, has had enormous implications. It is easy to forget how recent the pathologies are that are now routinely associated with black ghettos. In the 1950s, street crime was a product of white gangs—in the street we feared black leather jackets, not black skin. In the 1960s, drugs were a medical problem. Crime in black communities came later. When school boundaries were changed in the early 1960s, teachers like my father reacted with relief because the black children assigned to their schools were easier to handle than the white toughs now assigned elsewhere. Skin color changed on the block of a wealthy friend. No problem—good neighbors came in all colors.

A group led by Gary Orfield, a Harvard professor and expert on desegregation orders, reported in 2003 that although "desegregation of black students . . . increased continuously from the 1950s to the late 1980s," it had "receded to levels not seen" since 1968. Orfield noted that the South had become "the nation's most integrated region for both blacks and whites," but "it is the region that is most rapidly going backwards as the courts terminate many major and successful desegregation orders."[45] Unfortunately that is similar to what the great historian C. Van Woodward described as "the strange career of Jim Crow" at the end of the nineteenth century when the Northern states lost interest, the KKK instituted a reign of terror, and the South used segregation to turn back the clock.[46]

Most black Americans live in racially segregated areas where they have little contact with whites.[47] Minority communities are "isolat[ed] from social networks," and "mismatch[ed]" by residence for job opportunities and for financing both for housing and business opportunities.[48] Immigration also has increased residential segregation for Asians and Hispanics. In turn, residential segregation in the United States contributes to the subsequent segregation of business leaders which becomes enormously important in guiding the interactions of the groups.[49] On average what the Bureau of the Census calls "non-Hispanic whites," that is whites without Hispanic surnames, have the least interracial exposure of any group in the United States.[50]

Steven Greenhouse documented workplace segregation of people of Vietnamese and Hispanic origin in different company departments, generating about a five-thousand-dollar annual differential.[51] *Wards Cove Packing Co., Inc. v. Atonio*[52] documented the complete segregation of original Alaskan peoples, employed only in assembly line jobs, from the rest of the workforce working in white-collar jobs, in separate buildings. The company accomplished that result by recruiting for the assembly line jobs only among the native peoples in Alaska and recruiting for the white-collar jobs exclusively on the West Coast of the lower forty-eight. The U.S. Supreme Court chose to look the other way, saying they did not mean it.

Elizabeth Anderson, at the University of Michigan, comments that: "Firms located outside black neighborhoods and beyond the reach of public transportation are significantly less likely to hire black employees." The same is true for Hispanics and other minorities. In other words, government policies that have shaped the suburbs since the 1940s have separated blacks from jobs. But nearly 60 percent of white-owned firms in major biracial metropolitan areas have no minority employees, and even in black neighborhoods, "one-third still have no minority employees." By contrast, nearly 90 percent of black-owned firms in those metropolitan areas employ minority workers for three-quarters of the positions. The extent of separation goes much deeper because "employers practice occupational segregation" within companies. One survey showed that half of all job titles were only occupied by whites, "and one-quarter of blacks worked in jobs to which only blacks were assigned." She gives the example of a "slaughterhouse in North Carolina [which] assigns the butchering jobs to black men, knife work to Mexicans, warehouse jobs to Indians, and mechanic and supervisor positions to whites."[53] White Americans may share the building but not much else.

Eleven o'clock on Sunday mornings has been described as the most racially segregated hour in America.[54] Curiously, the most mixed congregations are conservative, nondenominational Protestant congregations with little awareness of the systemic problems that face their black congregants. Michael Emerson, codirector of the Kinder Institute for Social Research at Rice University, and Christian Smith, director of the Center for the Study of Religion and Society at the University of Notre Dame, teamed up on an award-winning study of race and religion. They point out that whites in those congregations are unaware of the extent to which blacks lack the social ties that provide "[a]ccess to valued resources—such as jobs, prestige, wealth, and power."[55] Therefore whites believe that blacks are responsible for their own status and that the press is responsible for making an issue of it. According to Emerson and Smith: "[Those congregants] tend to be socially and culturally isolated. So they do not see the hurdles that our segregated society places in front of blacks."[56] By contrast, those congregations in which the membership does see and object to "the hurdles that our segregated society places in front of blacks" tend to be even more racially segregated. Religion does not seem to be playing a significant part in breaking down racial isolation despite the earnest efforts of a number of religiously based organizations of both liberal and conservative orientations.

It is possible that we could get to know each other just by moving around to different places. But two-thirds of those born in the United States live in the state of our birth.[57] Most who move, stay in the same county. Those who move across state boundaries are likely to be better educated and wealthier. They move for work-related reasons. Those with lower incomes and education are more likely to stay put and move for family rather than work-related reasons.[58]

Immobility is also generational. About half the men will have an income like their fathers.[59] The other half will move up or down a quarter of the income scale. Mobility for daughters has been a bit larger.[60] Much generational mobility is the result of the availability of a college education since World War II, but financial pressures make that harder to maintain.[61]

Americans do much less mixing than we want to believe. Most Americans stay put geographically[62] and financially[63] and remain segregated at work[64] and in prayer.[65] Solidarity across class lines is for political campaigns only. No American knows a representative cross-section of America.[66] Despite the polls that attempt to tell us what each other thinks, we remain divided by birth and by condition. That separation affects our tensions and our understanding.

The Connections

Some of the institutions on which Americans relied to unite as one people have unraveled. The draft brought together Americans from all regions and backgrounds; but it became a casualty of the unpopular war in Vietnam. Schools were designed to bring Americans together; but the growth of large urban areas with segregated suburbs and deteriorated city neighborhoods, plus the push to move students into charter schools or give them vouchers they can take to private schools, undermine the unification that schools used to provide. We have separated the communities we live in, the amenities we have sought outside of our homes and offices, and the people we work, worship, and play with.

Our differences, our red and blue states, urban, suburban and rural environments, ethnic, class, religious, and racial backgrounds—all contribute to mutual incomprehension. Destroying the bonds across families and communities can wreak havoc. The loss of social capital can hollow out the democratic system and corrode its mechanisms.[67]

Statistics systematically miss the impact of events not captured in prior data. As a result, statistics can underestimate the creativity of politicians and their ability to capitalize on changes in the political environment by trying new strategies. The future of clean elections depends on who thinks democracy more or less important than victory, and what opportunities they have to pursue power. It has been barely half a century since party "machines" functioned as vast vote-falsifying organizations and elections became relatively clean and accurate reflections of public choices. But that decent period is even shorter if one takes into account racial exclusions, the stopped count in the 2000 election, and the demise in 2013 of the crucial sections of the Voting Rights Act at the hands of the U.S. Supreme Court. If politicians choose to subvert the system, by falsifying ballots and counts, or by other means, much depends on the help they can expect from their supporters or the likelihood their fraud will be uncovered with criminal penalties to follow. Democracy has consistently taken second place to the promotion of capitalism by the

U.S. government in foreign affairs. It is not clear how well protected it will be domestically.

Conflict, over jobs, patronage, values, or principles can lead people to subvert democracy, particularly where means for acceptable resolution are not at hand or valued. Once polarized, people can behave like mobs. The scene of Bush supporters screaming in front of television cameras at the vote counters in Florida, in an obvious attempt to intimidate them, shows how politics have changed. Mobs used in politics were once poor, unemployed, and criminal gangs. The mobs in the 2000 election appeared upscale but they were mobs nonetheless—otherwise respectable people turned into a screaming mass to intimidate vote counters, seeking victory at any cost, as if they believed in a Manichean good versus evil contest in which God had decreed Bush should be president and the Devil was backing Al Gore. Supreme Court justices, tied by blood or marriage to people with much to gain from the election but refusing to recuse themselves, reflected the same determined partisanship. Such polarization threatens all the fundamentals of democracy, the trust and expectation of trustworthy behavior, the tolerance and willingness to accept defeat, the mutual care, concern, respect, and desire for approval on which democracy depends.

The Law's Role in Dividing America

The contemporary picture of American politics is very different from the Tweedledum-Tweedledee politics of the 1950s and early 1960s that Goldwater and many in his generation decried. Many echoed Goldwater's call for "a choice, not an echo" of the other party, and as early as 1950, political scientists called for "responsible parties" with clearly distinct platforms and the ability to enforce discipline on representatives, so that voters knew what voting for a party meant.[68] Both groups have finally achieved what they wished for even though many dislike the results. Some blame the Bush administration[69] or the Democrats[70] for polarizing America. Many writers focus on changes in religious leanings,[71] the culture wars,[72] the decisions of political leaders,[73] other national political voices, the availability of computers, and the balkanization of America into separate suburbs, jobs, and faiths.[74] Those explanations, however, are incomplete.

What has changed substantially is the way the public is sliced and fed back for political representation. Law organizes how we are informed and represented. Legal changes share the blame for the contentiousness of contemporary politics. They have piled on one another sufficiently to have a powerful effect on the political culture in the United States. They will help polarize politics as long as they remain on the books. Law shapes the bitterness in American politics.

Stanford political scientist Morris Fiorina comments that over the course of a century the substitution of civil service rules for government jobs, public services like garbage collection, and government procurement rules for much of the patronage jobs that had once been benefits of politics, led the majority of the public to withdraw from politics because they assumed that there was little left that affected their daily lives. Fiorina argued that their withdrawal left politics to the most committed and ideological among us.[75]

Let me add a few more legal changes over the last several decades that have made a difference. We have rewritten the law of speech and politics to substitute insanity for milquetoast. For much of the twentieth century, the rules governing the national media and the political nomination process favored broad appeals to the public. Following the 1968 Democratic Convention, that changed for the nomination process.[76] By 1980, that also changed for the national media.[77] Now American media and political institutions magnify the differences among us.

Law is a powerful tool; it alters what is possible, sometimes intentionally, sometimes in ways that are unanticipated. Law matters.

Legal Changes to the Shape of the Media

From the birth of radio, national policy created a broadcasting oligopoly. In the 1920s, then Secretary of Commerce Herbert Hoover, and later the new Federal Radio Commission, systematically stripped universities of their radio stations in favor of commercial broadcasters.[78] The Federal Communications Commission (FCC), which took over in 1934,[79] looked for middle-of-the-road ownership, sometimes with political ties, such as its award of broadcast licenses to newspapers that had supported Eisenhower's election.[80] The FCC prevented unions and political parties from owning or acquiring broadcasting stations, announcing that stations were henceforth to be apolitical.[81] It restricted broadcasting to a maximum of three national networks through a policy known as localism, which allocated station licenses with signals that had a short reach to as many different communities and congressional districts as possible. To prevent broadcast signals from interfering with each other, the policy of localism made it impossible until recently to give any but the largest cities more than three licensed broadcasters, and most had fewer.[82] The FCC later repeated those policy choices in setting up broadcast television. The result was a large set of locally centrist stations with near monopoly status in their broadcasting markets. In turn, by contracting with the big three networks for prime time and other parts of their daily schedules, they received the benefit of bigger budget national programs.[83]

Vying for a broad audience, networks excluded whatever would offend any part of their audience. They avoided politics except for equal time to candidates during campaigns and some Sunday news interview programs.[84] Network politics were distinctly centrist. Counterculture protest songs made the rounds attacking the war in Vietnam but rarely on the tube.[85] Extremism gained a foothold on marginal stations, in communities out of the mainstream and during the Great Depression of the 1930s,[86] but centrist incentives kept it to a minimum.

The FCC unintentionally reinforced bland television with the fairness doctrine, until abandoned in the 1970s.[87] It required broadcasters to provide conflicting points of view on controversial issues of public importance. Actually, it encouraged broadcasters either to stress conflict or avoid anything that looked or sounded like a point of view. Points of view required time for a response to make the opposite point. If the disagreement bored or antagonized the audience, ratings would plummet, advertising would leave, and the networks would foot the bill. So typically they did their best to avoid controversy.[88] Broadcast centrism shattered after the media were splintered by cable and the Internet.

The networks enlarged news broadcasts in the early 1960s just in time for the signature moments of national political coverage.[89] Americans mourned the Kennedy assassination together on national television. Network news covered civil rights demonstrations in the South, showing demonstrators kneeling in prayer where they were barred from registering to vote; kneeling by the Edmund Pettus Bridge in Selma, Alabama, where state troopers attacked with clubs and gas; or marching to protest segregation only to be attacked with dogs and fire hoses. The national network audience for these events played a large role in the bipartisan passage of the Civil Rights Acts of 1964 and 1965. Later in the decade the whole country saw dramatic images of riots across the United States and carnage in Vietnam. News organizations in this era made conscious efforts to be neutral; biases tended to flow from unexamined stereotypes rather than deliberate manipulation of news.[90] However, by focusing everyone on the same images, the same ideas, and the same people, these televised events had a huge impact on American values and politics.[91]

Beginning in 1976, legal changes boosted cable companies. Prior to 1976, the FCC sharply restricted cable carriage of broadcast signals.[92] The Copyright Act of 1976 provided for a compulsory license of broadcast signals on behalf of cable companies.[93] That statute conflicted with the FCC's protection of local broadcasters against cable importation of distant signals and led the

FCC to dismantle its regulations.[94] As cable reached an increasing proportion of American homes, television viewers soon had many more options than the three provided by the national broadcast networks. The FCC then finally authorized new broadcast networks.[95] In the 1990s the Internet added more options. As the viewing audience splintered, there was room for networks with strong political points of view. Differences between networks grew. Fox News and MSNBC do not duplicate CBS or ABC. The market for the center began to dwindle. American politics splintered along with the broadcast audience. Many refer to affirmative action as a "wedge issue" that split the Democrats.[96] The splintering of the media may have been just as important; it changed the incentive structure within the newsroom. Where the old three channel broadcast oligopoly tried to avoid angering any part of its audience, the new niche media seeks to excite its audience and deliberately insults others to dramatize disagreement.

Legal Changes to the Responsibility of the Media

Other changes in the law of media liability removed both incentives for and enforcement of responsible journalism. The first significant legal change dates from 1964 when several southern juries were poised to bankrupt the New York Times in a series of libel cases. In *New York Times v. Sullivan*, a southern jury found the New York Times Company guilty of libel because of several misstatements in an ad placed by leaders of the civil rights movement. The jury reported $500,000 in damages, a very large award in the 1960s, now equivalent to several million dollars.

The then existing law made the press responsible for any misstatement, regardless of how innocent. The sizable award was possible because the law allowed the jury to estimate the damage to the sheriff's reputation, regardless of whether he actually suffered any financial injury; indeed the errors probably improved his standing among the electorate.[97] The Supreme Court responded by blocking legal liability for misstatements about public officials, which was later expanded to public figures, unless they were made with knowledge of their falsity or reckless disregard of the truth.[98] The rule, however, immunizes innocent misstatements.[99]

The second major change, about a decade later, crippled the fairness doctrine, which had required all broadcasters to provide a balanced presentation of controversial issues of public importance.[100] Lack of fairness could put demerits in broadcasters' files to be considered when their licenses came up for renewal. Although nonrenewal was rare,[101] broadcasters took that threat very seriously.

NBC broadcast a documentary called "Pensions: The Broken Promise." It highlighted abuses of pension plans where workers were denied pensions after spending their careers working for a company that had promised retirement benefits. The documentary won awards and was part of the run-up to the passage of pension legislation in Washington, DC. The specific examples were neither controversial nor disputed. However, Accuracy in Media, a conservative watchdog organization, argued that NBC had not made a balanced presentation of whether pension plans were good or bad in general. NBC responded that it had not addressed that issue, and whatever anyone in the documentary said about the topic was balanced. The documentary's explicit point was that abuses took place and existing law made it possible.[102] On those examples there was no controversy—the facts were accurate. With nothing to balance, the fairness doctrine was satisfied.

The FCC sided with Accuracy in Media, and the network appealed. The court of appeals reversed. Any set of facts could cast light on a large number of issues, but it was unreasonable to require broadcasters to address every inference people might draw. The documentary dealt with a significant problem and performed a public service. To require more would discourage networks from addressing significant issues. They would have to take time from otherwise accurate and hard-hitting documentaries to face other issues or run another program. Either alternative would cost them some of the audience for documentaries.

The court of appeals' approach narrowed the fairness doctrine substantially. Henceforth, only explicit issues would be covered. Following the circuit court decision and questions about the constitutionality of the doctrine, the FCC eliminated the fairness doctrine entirely in 1987. As a result, broadcasters are no longer required to address issues in a fair and balanced way.[103]

Several years later, the FCC also withdrew from the comparative licensing process intended to license public-spirited broadcasters who would reflect the interests and needs of their communities.[104] Licensing had been abused, from official partisanship to favoring middle-of-the-road broadcasters and excluding racial and political minorities.[105] Terminating a faulty system was overdue. But that left quality totally dependent on the market. And the arrival of niche broadcasting changed the market's discipline from rewarding inoffensive broadcasting to rewarding deliberately outrageous programming.

With the development of the Internet, legal changes added additional dodges. One protects Internet providers from responsibility for material posted on an Internet service by someone else.[106] The courts held that Internet services are excused from responsibility for what they edit, pay for, or refuse to take down even if they know the content is false. An Internet posting directed people to call Ken Zeran for T-shirts and other memorabilia of the bombing of the Alfred P. Murrah Federal Building in Oklahoma City just six days earlier. The posting implied that Zeran had condoned the bombing. As the hoax spread, he received so many calls, including death threats, that he could no longer carry on his business. He asked AOL to take the hoax down but it did nothing while the story spread around the country. Eventually courts excused AOL from responsibility. When the media investigated the incident and reported that he had never offered such items, the angry calls declined to some eighteen per day.[107]

Litigation over inaccuracies in the Drudge Report and other Internet sources have been similarly fruitless; the courts almost routinely had found that the information was delivered by someone else, so no one was responsible who could be identified and held liable.[108]

As a result of these legal changes, the media marketplace has shifted from a highly regulated market toward one that is legally wide open, with remarkable websites alongside toxic swamps.

Nevertheless, the current marketplace was shaped by government decisions that favored commercial over public or educational broadcasting. The FCC spent half a century protecting the media oligopoly that Hoover had created.[109] It was finally forced to provide a spectrum for the public broadcasting system in the late 1960s. Most broadcasting, by decree, has been private, for profit, and dependent on advertising. When the era of niche media arrived and the wraps came off both licensing and content, commercial broadcasters were ready to advocate a point of view. However, in a segmented market there are few brakes on what people say.

Before his appointment to the Supreme Court, Justice Lewis Powell prepared a report for the U.S. Chamber of Commerce arguing that liberals (but not businesses) were getting their point of view across.[110] He urged corporations to organize to present their point of view to the public. Following his advice, conservatives funded think tanks to advocate economic *laissez faire* and other conservative causes. Politically inclined investors and religious institutions established new stations and networks, including several with substantial media interests.[111]

The market does not put a brake on the partisan use of segmented media.[112] Very large rewards are available through the political system. The economic benefits from redirecting the course of legislation—and convincing people to support claims for deregulation, tax exemptions, friendly legislators or other causes—can be enormous.[113] Segmented markets, however, are not effective in policing the use of the facts. Checking on information has large costs—in terms of time, effort, and sometimes money. Even if they are eventually self-correcting, the passage of time matters, just as water in the mountains is not instantly available at sea level just because it flows downhill. In a fractured marketplace, there is plenty of room for angry, partisan broadcasters, yet very little room for those who are annoyed to object to broadcasts, especially if they are not part of a loyal target audience, and those who want to discover competing views without taking the time and trouble to search for them.

The legal changes outlined above permit an organized and deliberate ideological use of the media, but there are many reasons for media bias: to persuade, to draw attention, and to save on the costs of news gathering.[114] Much of it is happenstance, from press releases, from whoever happens to be president, or from unexamined prejudices and stereotypes.[115] A study that appeared in the neoconservative journal, THE PUBLIC INTEREST, concluded that news had a conservative impact in the middle and late 1960s because of the riots in ghettos around the country, while the entertainment media had a liberal impact because of their concentration on stories about current social issues.

Jettisoning rules of responsibility makes it easier for portions of the press to move toward the extremes. There are always other factors. The press was highly partisan for much of the middle and late nineteenth century, yet it cannot be blamed for all the partisanship of that era. In the first half of the twentieth century, the press deliberately moved toward a "neutral," nonpartisan format so that advertisers could reach potential buyers on both sides of the political spectrum (although advertisers reinserted themselves in subtler ways).[116] The legal changes of the last decades facilitated another shift toward a press that is more partisan and less responsible. And that has an impact on our politics.

Many liberal voices urged a more diverse press and fought restrictions that led to oligopolistic control of the media in the name of free speech. That the changes fanned the flames of a conservative counterrevolution is partly the happenstance of a democratic system in which Americans do not believe in controlling the press. Nor are liberals urging that we return to the era of dominant broadcasters and squelch the Internet. The trend of change seems proper, but the justification does not erase the impact.

Journalistic Principles

Journalism also changed. At the start of the twentieth century, the so-called penny press sought a mass audience. Advertisers wanted to appeal to customers without regard to politics. Opinion was confined to the editorial page and news took on a hard facts approach, presenting a record of who said what and what happened where. Joe McCarthy upset that model by using it too well. By reporting his unsupported allegations of disloyalty without comment, the news media gave McCarthy enormous influence. In the wake of McCarthyism, the press looked for ways to report the news without being so vulnerable to unscrupulous allegations. The newsman's obligation was to get at the truth, to provide a more carefully digested record.

A liberal or a conservative truth was not supposed to exist. Truth should be independent of party and partisanship. But the news media came under attack. Nixon's first vice president, Spiro Agnew, attacked the national media as "effete" snobs before he was forced out of office for corruption. Bob Woodward and Carl Bernstein's investigation of the Watergate scandal brought Nixon down. The impeachment was bipartisan, but the reaction to it was highly partisan. Many on the right wing of the Republican Party blamed the press instead of Nixon for hounding him out of office.

Journalists increasingly settled on a new paradigm for reporting. Conflict provided drama, and drama became the engine to sell papers and win viewers. Get an allegation, and then ask someone on the other side for a response. Now you have conflict plus "unbiased" and "responsible" reporting, which does not always make clear what actually happened. The sides are easier to tell apart. But the ubiquitous combat storyline contributes to polarization.[117]

As a result, a splintered press, partly freed of responsibility, found its theme in the maximization of antagonism on paper, screen, and radio. That reorienting of press content would be matched by a reorientation of politics.

Legal Changes to the Nomination System

Mass meetings replaced nomination by elected officials in the Jackson era and radicalized politics. Political bosses reasserted control with a variety of tools, some legal, some not. Storied political machines—from Tammany Hall and Boss Tweed in New York to the Prendergast machine in Missouri—decided nominations in infamous smoke-filled back rooms of party conventions. In the late nineteenth century, Progressives backed legislation to require parties to nominate by primary elections.[118] Several decades later, primaries helped clean up American politics. Like many reforms, it had both intended and unintended consequences.

Conventions, and the professionals who ran them, looked for coalitions to win the general elections. They wanted competitive candidates. Primaries are relatively divisive, particularly where a plurality suffices to win the nomination. Where only party members can vote in primaries, winners reflect the party's base but not necessarily the general public that votes in general elections. Candidates elected by each party's base will be far apart. The late V. O. Key documented the pressure of primaries toward the extremes in work repeatedly corroborated since.[119] The mathematics is simple. If each party has close to 50 percent of the voting public, then it takes just above half of either party, and often less, to nominate a candidate who can go on to win the general election. Just over half a party, which is roughly half of the public, is equivalent to 25 percent of the general public. In a well-fought election, that 25 percent of the voting population, and often much less, is enough to control the political system.

Primaries were held for state offices until the Democratic Party changed its presidential selection rules in the 1970s.[120] The party wanted to secure black participation in southern state delegations and to take back the party from bosses like Mayor Daley, who used the police to abuse demonstrators during the 1968 Convention in Chicago. The Democrats determined to end boss control by substituting more democratic selection systems throughout the country. In practice this meant a national move to primaries for selection of state delegations to the national party conventions. In the wake of those changes, the Republican nomination process changed as well.

After those changes, party conventions lost control over presidential nominations, which now were decided in the primaries before the conventions opened. Use of primaries to nominate presidential candidates pushed both parties further from the center, driven by the mathematical logic of the primary nominating process. Both parties tried to alter the national conventions in favor of centrist delegates by adding so-called super delegates, who were existing office holders and not nominated in the presidential primaries. The primaries, however, dominated the conventions.

The percentage of the public that it takes to control presidential selection depends somewhat on whether the parties allow each state to use the winner-takes-all system to allocate the states' votes in the conventions. The controlling proportion has to be adjusted slightly upward to the extent that parties allow independents to vote in party primaries, or divide their delegates in proportion to the votes for each candidate.[121]

The mathematics are equally applicable to the Republican primaries. Primaries have been the battleground between liberal and conservative Republicans. The dominance of the right-wing Republicans over their party might have been achieved in other ways; they got their workers out and into every available party position. Nevertheless, the right wing has dominated many elections without the support of more than about a quarter of the general public.

So the extension of the primary process has tended to deepen the political divide.

Legal Changes behind Safe Seats

Law drives the political divide in yet another way. Gerrymandering proliferated after the Supreme Court held malapportionment unconstitutional in the early 1960s.[122] Malapportioned legislatures benefitted "geographically protected oligarchies of rural and small-town legislators" by assigning them more representation.[123] Gerrymandering works by designing districts that make elections safe from voter judgment, both in individual seats and in the complexion of the state legislative delegation.[124] Districts are made safe for one of the parties by excluding voters from the opposite party.[125]

The lack of competition in safe districts encourages politicians to move toward the extremes since nothing pulls them toward the center. "As a result, members speak more to their parties' 'bases,' which provide most electoral and financial support."[126] The move to the extremes supports a very bitter politics. As Samuelson puts it, "stridency is a strategy."[127] Partisan extremism is reinforced by the overall gerrymandered pattern protecting the safety of one political party's legislative wing.

That combination of the constitutional revolution against malapportionment, and the subsequent proliferation of gerrymandering to write incumbent and partisan protection into the laws shaping districts have helped stamp stridency on modern American politics. The Supreme Court has protected legislative gerrymandering, saying it has not found a "manageable, reliable measure."[128]

Legal Construction of Campaign Money

In the early 1970s, the federal campaign finance statutes were designed to equalize the positions of the candidates and give them more control over their own campaigns. The Supreme Court immediately denied the first and reversed the second. It sustained limitations on contributions but only on the ground that contributions could corrupt politics, functioning like bribes or at least appear to do so. The Court also overturned limitations on independent contributions saying they did not have the same likelihood to corrupt or appear to corrupt. By unleashing independent expenditures, it took control of the campaigns out of the hands of the candidates—a consequence that has been growing in the light of subsequent decisions overturning pieces of the campaign funding statutes coupled with the increased need for financial support for campaigns.[129]

The statutes created limits on what could be contributed to individual candidates, political parties, total annual political contributions to all recipients and other restrictions on how money could be raised and spent.[130] Coordinated expenses would be treated as contributions and would likely exceed contribution limitations or violate statutory prohibitions. Therefore, candidates and their committees had to do their own fundraising without coordination. Political committees that supported several different races also had to separate their state and federal fundraising.[131]

This combination of the Supreme Court decisions and the statutory provisions appears to have intensified the forces driving politics away from the center by splintering the campaign among many independent committees,[132] and increasing the importance of major donors.[133]

One consequence of the new campaign finance rules was noticed immediately—they made fundraising much harder, and therefore took much more of the time of members of Congress as well as presidential candidates than fundraising had taken before. The increased difficulty of fundraising guaranteed that those who could accomplish it would take on increased importance.[134]

A succession of legendary fundraisers in both parties kept upping the ante with new and different voter lists and techniques to reach them in both large and small amounts.[135] Everything was available for auction—a chance to meet the president, alone or in groups; a visit to the White House, including a stay in the Lincoln bedroom or a tour of other private parts of the building, each for a given size of donation or other service to the candidate or party.[136] In what became known as the K Street Project, congressional Republicans under the leadership of Tom Delay made lobbyist access dependent on exclusive contributions to and work for the Republican Party.[137] Fundraising became dominated by so-called bundlers, those who raise large sums from many different people, each of whose donations are within the statutory limits, but are then turned in together in large aggregates, often by bundlers who collect and turn over more than a million dollars.[138]

As noted earlier, the rewards of political success can easily be large enough to justify large donations. Significant changes in taxation and regulation create very large stakes large for many. Recent tax cuts, which reduced the progressivity of the tax code, rewarded large donors and shifted the burden further down the income scale.[139] The larger the gulf between the parties, the greater the stakes. As stakes appeared larger, the size of donations followed and their complexion became more ideological, with donors seeking to move politics further left or right. Two much discussed examples among many were the Koch brothers' support of the Tea Party and Sheldon Adelson's support of Newt Gingrich in the 2012 Republican presidential primaries.

Now a major donor who wanted to influence the campaign could not do it within the party or candidate campaigns. Independent expenditures became the legally required vehicle for major contributions. The statutory requirements also became the justification for donors to work independently of the candidates without earning condemnation for interference. The statute and court decisions changed the culture of campaign finance.

In other words, instead of taking money out of the political equation, political scientists found that money mattered more than it had before the statute was written. Powerful and independent donors—using statutory requirements for separate, independent organizations whose campaigns are uncoordinated with the candidates—have seized the political megaphone and now contribute to the polarization and splintering of American politics.

The polarization may have been increased by the anonymity of the new vehicles for independent expenditures because they have not been required to disclose their donors. That became possible as the result of a complex interaction of tax and federal election campaign law with Supreme Court, Federal Election Commission, and Internal Revenue Service decisions.[140] But the effect is to free the contributors from disclosure and any pushback as the result of their positions. In political terms, organizations may feel free to take more strident positions than some of them would if their donors were disclosed.

Legal Resegregation of the Landscape

Law has also played a significant role in separating us into communities by wealth, faith, and race. Those physical divisions make it harder to trust, collaborate, and empathize because we do not know each other. In those ways they contribute to political extremism. Because the housing market and other private construction projects are involved, people make the mistake of thinking that residential separation is all about private choice, what the courts call de facto segregation. American geographic politics aggravate the separation of Americans.

Government facilitates what Robert Reich called the "secession of the successful." Public roads make new communities possible, and then encircle and separate them from older, poorer ones.[141] State rules for municipal incorporation facilitate formal secession from older cities and communities and prevent central cities from expanding to include newly settled areas.[142] State law protects new communities from responsibility for the schools, pools, parks, and other amenities for the children of the people who clean, sweep, guard, and otherwise serve the wealthy, leaving their own communities to deteriorate.[143] Local governments zone to separate poorer from wealthier residents, requiring one and five acre tracts which force people to travel further for work and other needs.[144] In combination, roads and zoning protect residents' access to some jobs and block access to selected others. The physical divisions allow the wealthy to believe that everyone is on their own, as if they are citizens of separate countries, and not entangled in each other's fortunes.

Government has begun separating us by faith in the ways it handles schools, zoning, public funds, and discrimination. Religious service organizations, like Catholic Charities or Jewish Family Services, long operated in nonsectarian ways, partly to administer government funds and other legal requirements, including the tax code. The faith-based initiatives of Clinton and Bush now allow religious groups to be much more explicit about their religious mission in delivering services than merely advertising their sponsorship of charitable activities.[145] Federal law now forces cities and towns to loosen their zoning rules for the benefit of religion.[146] Vouchers and tax credits now ease exit from the public schools. Charter schools cannot discriminate, but they make it easier for communities to regroup within the public school system.

The government is also behind the racial resegregation of America. The Court likes to describe contemporary segregation as de facto, as if it were the natural result of lots of individual decisions, beginning with "white flight," but that is a white wash. As noted at the beginning of this chapter, people had many reasons to leave the cities that had nothing to do with race, and government legislation made sure blacks would (or could) not follow.

Decisions in the FHA were intended to ensure different treatment of African American would-be home buyers. Those were clear violations of the federal equal protection law even under the narrow definitions the Supreme Court gave it after Chief Justice Warren had left the Court. Contemporary with the decision to red-line black neighborhoods and bar blacks from obtaining mortgages in the suburbs financed by the FHA, were decisions to tear down black communities, scattering them into new neighborhoods in equally dilapidated housing less desired by whites or warehousing them in inhospitable "projects." States facilitated the incorporation of new towns with no responsibility for the old neighborhoods they abandoned, which zoned them out and blocked construction of housing blacks could have rented near jobs they might have held.

Contemporary segregation is the source of many present social ills. It has the imprimatur of government all over it. All the pathologies we associate with poor black ghettos are a product of the past half century and stem from decisions in the white world.

Consequences—A Perfect Storm

Journalistic conventions that emphasize conflict; media that now appeal to narrow segments of the public and are held by ideologically driven owners; gerrymandering that segregates the voting population into safe districts; primary elections and campaign finance rules that pass control to politically active portions of the parties; and a population segregated into separate communities—all come together in a bare-knuckles brawl of extremists. That is what the papers like, what people find on their screens, and the way primary election math adds up. The winners reinforce the point by demonizing everyone who disagrees. The two parties have become fighting faiths. That outcome is facilitated by government residential policies that obscure the stakes of large segments of the population in each other's welfare.

We have had fighting faiths before—before the Civil War, America's bloodiest, and perhaps holiest, conflict; during the Populist movement, when many died over the union movement; and the beginning of Jim Crow. In that period, segregation was designed largely to divide the Populists and keep power in wealthy hands.[147]

There are ideological divides behind these contemporary fighting faiths. Political systems can moderate divisions or make them worse. The legal changes support the latter. Changes in law and judicial opinions would not themselves suffice to cause all the polarization we have seen. But it would be foolhardy to conclude that the changes in the law played no part in facilitating and exaggerating the changes we have seen.

Democracy is in peril when the objectives of partisanship override respect for those opposed. It is in peril when the splits among us organize themselves so that the same people are so consistently opposed that we understand each other as enemies, with no stake in each other's welfare, so that we seek only to take advantage of others or defend ourselves, when progress is defined as someone else's sacrifice and there is no shared welfare toward which all jointly need to contribute and protect one another. Democracy is not only in peril when we are pitted against each other as our country's worst enemies, but also when we lose faith in the care and concern of our own governments, when sensible caution turns into outright hostility, and when "government is the enemy" rather than a friend. When totalitarianism comes to this country, it will surely come dressed in red, white, and blue, "saving" us from ourselves.[148]

The political process magnifies the differences among the public. No single person or politician has the power to change public opinion, but a chorus does. And the feedback loop continues. Once the public is on fire, it pushes politics further. Polarization becomes a self-aggravating feedback loop, and therein lies the danger.

There are contrary forces. Presidential politics, for example, can encourage centrifugal or centripetal forces and other changes can undercut the polarization encouraged by a splintered media, primaries, and segregated privilege and poverty. One can hope.

Risks to Democracy

Half a century ago, American political scientists would have welcomed greater polarization of the parties to give Americans a much clearer choice.[149] Half a century later, the entire political environment has undergone large changes and the effects on the polarization of the parties seems to have gone too far. For scholars of democracy and its history, polarization and intolerance threaten commitment to democracy.[150] The polarization of the leadership is even more threatening than the polarization of the masses.[151] Democracy has been brought down repeatedly when competing partisans came to believe each other disloyal to the democratic system.[152] Both the reality and the perception are dangerous. Mutual charges of fundamentally undemocratic behavior reflect the depth of modern distrust and have become a trope in modern politics.

Mutual distrust has led the political leadership of numerous countries to believe that winning was more important than respecting the wishes of the public, until the parties goaded each other in a kind of death spiral until one party seized the reigns. Sometimes that dance of death was initiated by economic policies, sometimes by violence, and sometimes both. In other words, polarization at the top endangers democracy.[153]

Americans have gone through periods in which they could not in fact trust each other. The election laws in all of the states reflect periods when political success was governed by dirty tricks, fraud, and intimidation. Americans are used to attributing those flaws to party machines of a bygone era.

The contested 2000 presidential election brought these issues back to the fore and the win-at-all-costs behavior reflected the underlying and poisonous malaise. Invalid absentee ballots were counted in some Florida counties but not others.[154] The procedure of voting and the form of the ballots dif-

fered by county, and in those counties that used punch cards, the much pub-
licized hanging chads (incompletely pushed through the card stock) were
scored differently, a difference the Florida Supreme Court tried to end with
consistent standards until the U.S. Supreme Court barred it from continuing.[155] A private computer data company with strong ties to the Republican
party was hired without competitive bidding to purge the Florida rolls of
people who should not vote, but their sloppy process purged tens of thousands who were qualified, most of them Democrats.[156] The counting of ballots itself was interrupted by a mob of screaming party workers reminiscent
of the goon squads that steered many an election at the turn of the twentieth
century.

Politics in Congress began to show serious cracks, with one party excluding the other from many traditional opportunities to examine legislation, participate in hearings, or gain access to information, and both parties changed
the rules and practice of filibustering. Bipartisanship was gone and many in
Congress reacted to the change in behavior with dismay.[157]

Government is all about conflict, sometimes creating it, sometimes resolving it, managing and mismanaging it, adding fuel to the fire. Conflict by itself says very little about whether governments will fail or democracy will be
overthrown. How conflict is managed is crucial.[158]

America is not immune from polarization, paranoia, or demagoguery.[159]
Despite an honored tradition of people protesting in public, mayors, sheriffs,
and presidents have filmed,[160] hosed, shot,[161] arrested, and penned peaceful demonstrators,[162] claiming fear of what the demonstrators might do. The
United States has been sufficiently moved by fear of the masses elsewhere
to intervene repeatedly against popular democratic leaders in such places as
Guatemala, Chile, and Iran.[163] That fear of others in America too threatens to
corrode our own democracy.

Paranoia and polarization are dangerous.

What Works

Opposite the power to demonize others and divide the population is the need
to break down barriers. One effort has been to change political incentives
by means of open and blanket primaries, which handed the ballot to wider
groups of voters, not just those registered in a single party. Morris Fiorina
believes it may have been a mistake for the Rehnquist Court to strike down
one such effort in California because it had the potential to reduce polarization.[164] There are potentially unintended consequences of such a change,
however, if it weakens the role of parties. As Fiorina also points out, political

vacuums are short-lived, and if parties are weakened, still narrower factions and interest groups will control politics.[165]

One would want to tread carefully on libel law but Marshall's suggestion of restricting legal damages to the actual economic cost might strengthen it constructively.[166]

Land use and discrimination law need to be rejuvenated and the American system of bringing people together needs to be revived for everyone. The American melting pot stimulated by mixing us together in the same school-rooms and military barracks[167] has support in the scientific community, where it is known as the contact hypothesis.[168] How well it works depends, among other factors,[169] on the speed of change,[170] the length of time people have to overcome their differences, support by those in authority,[171] and whether the elites of wealth and power are themselves brought together.[172]

Racial profiling at every level of the criminal process, plea bargaining under the threat of lengthy sentences, exaggeration of punitive measures, and the willingness of too many to look the other way while a portion of the population is subjected to a highly destructive system which white Americans do not apply to themselves have replaced the systematic racial violence of the KKK.[173] And that needs to end.

The social capital that Putnam described is not automatic; it did not spring magically from the grass of northern Italy; it depends on us. In a world sinking back into religious and racial violence, our unity at home is precious, and contingent on our commitment to the ideal and the practice. As Putnam eloquently put it, "the central challenge for modern, diversifying societies is to create a new, broader sense of 'we.'"[174]

8

Threat of Force

Tactics to subordinate populations have been honed in modern conflicts. Peace, law, and democracy are hard-won in an armed world.

Private Militias

Public discussion of gun ownership in the United States focuses on individual gun owners and their interest in protecting themselves from violence—murder, robbery, rape, and similar crimes. Paramilitaries have not been part of that discussion. Paramilitaries have functioned as the military arm of political movements, as revolutionaries bent on ousting government, or as gangsters seeking loot. They either fight or collaborate with the professional military, threatening democratically elected governments. In their heyday, the KKK controlled large portions of the South and several border states while the Mafia controlled America's biggest cities and through them several northern states.[1] Other locally powerful and equally violent groups also controlled portions of the country. This is not just a foreign problem.

Historical Background

The founders of the United States preferred an army of citizens to a standing army. However, from experience, they were not romantic about the safety of arming citizens. Private armies in the western lands threatened the kind of secessionist effort with which Vice President Aaron Burr was charged a few years later. Militias of riffraff threatened public order. There were rebellions in a number of states. Shays's Rebellion in Massachusetts crystallized the founders' fears. Based on significant grievances, rebels closed the courts without firing a shot. Governor Bowdoin sent state troops to put down their rebellion—troops that were much less restrained than the rebels had been. News of the rebellion spread across the new nation and added impetus to hold the Constitutional Convention in Philadelphia. Many criticized Bowdoin's economic policies and his response to the rebels. But rebels could not be allowed to take the law into their own hands.[2]

The Society of the Cincinnati, an organization of the military officers who served during the American Revolution, was much feared despite having George Washington at its head. Military power demands control. Article I of the Constitution gave Congress power to design the rules and training for all the state militias. Several years later the Second Amendment opened with its purpose to provide "a well-regulated Militia." The founders were realistic; a civilian military required regulation.[3]

The Civil War and the forces behind it gave rise to new forms of American paramilitary organizations. The infamous Colfax Massacre in Louisiana used mass murder of Republicans, black and white, to hand elections to the segregationists. In 1876, the US Supreme Court overturned the convictions of their killers, holding that federal authorities had no jurisdiction to protect African Americans trying to exercise their federally guaranteed right to vote. The shield of that and later decisions allowed the KKK and other unofficial paramilitaries to segregate and subjugate the freedmen for a century, negating most of the gains promised by the postwar Reconstruction Amendments and civil rights acts.[4] The Supreme Court's states' rights doctrine reigned largely unchanged until the Court slowly began backing up federal officials during World War II.

Since the KKK and other groups enforcing white dominance were unofficial, they did not run afoul of federal law as the Court defined federal authority. Freed of national control, they took control of the South by intimidation and violence. Their murders, lynchings, and beatings, inflicted for over a century, are now a legendary scar on the national memory of most Americans. Southern institutions could be counted on to protect the KKK, not their victims, or be too intimidated to consider taking any other action.

By the mid-twentieth century the line between unofficial organizations and public officials had almost ceased to exist. In many places, the KKK and the authorities worked in concert. Civil rights demonstrators were trained to face fire hoses, cattle prods, and beatings and to suffer without trying to fight back. For riding on unsegregated buses, Freedom Riders were beaten with bats, pipes, and chains. A bus burned while a mob tried to keep the riders inside. Others were killed while walking or driving, suspected of trying to help African Americans assert their legal and constitutional rights. Sheriffs handed prisoners to the KKK for execution. In fact, the sheriffs were often members of the KKK. The courage of the civil rights workers caused both pride and shame among many Americans: pride because Americans could persist in the face of such violence, and shame that they had to make those sacrifices. Some southern governors also called out the National Guard to defend segregation, and the media focused on the confrontations.

Eventually the demonstrators' powerful allies woke up. Presidents Eisenhower, Kennedy, and Johnson put the National Guard under national orders to defend the rights of black students to go to integrated schools, and protect both black and white civil rights workers. The national press showed the carnage to horrified readers and viewers. Presidents Kennedy and Johnson insisted FBI Director J. Edgar Hoover squelch his racism and make an effort to solve the crimes committed against the blacks and their white supporters.[5] Some courageous judges and U.S. courts of appeals came to their aid. The KKK and racists of the Old Confederacy could not have been beaten without the courage and persistence of African Americans themselves, their white allies who went South to help, and national political support.

Control by extralegal violence and intimidation is very much part of the American experience. The organized reign of terror that enforced the peculiar institutions of the segregated South was one of the most extensive examples of unofficial organized force supplanting democratic government in the history of this country; but there were other important ones, such as the goon squads attached to political machines and underworld organizations, both of which long ran large chunks of the country. Organized extralegal use of weapons has been domestic and dangerous.

Now

Hate-defined militias in the United States continue the animus of slavery, Civil War, segregation, and the KKK. National Rifle Association (NRA) President and Alabama lawyer Jim Porter told the New York Rifle and Pistol Association at their annual meeting in June 2012 that what most Americans call the Civil War, "we call . . . the 'War of Northern Aggression' down South." He went on to refer to President Obama as a "fake president" and Attorney General Eric Holder as "rabidly un-American."[6] Militiamen differentiate between whites who would have been citizens without the Fourteenth Amendment and "Fourteenth Amendment citizens," who owe their citizenship to the amendment (i.e., blacks and people of color), saying they are not "real" citizens.[7]

The Southern Poverty Law Center (SPLC) follows hate groups, private militias and vigilante organizations closely, especially those that have taken the law into their own hands, intimidating both local and federal officials from enforcing the law. They pose real local threats to democratic government and national threats of terrorism. They have affected national politics and try to take advantage of other controversies.

The SPLC identified hundreds of self-described Patriot Militias in the United States aimed at taking law into their own hands. Timothy McVeigh, the terrorist who bombed the Oklahoma City federal building in 1994, emerged from these groups. There were ninety-five "plots, conspiracies and racist rampages" between April 1995 and the end of 2012, with thirty-three people killed and more than two hundred injured in eighteen different attacks, all by homegrown terrorists.[8] Those attacks damaged or destroyed an Amtrak passenger train, Olympic and abortion facilities, a gay bar, a Jewish community center, a mosque, and a Sikh temple. The terrorists' targets included a popular black former college basketball coach, a Filipino American mailman, a Korean doctoral student, a bank security guard, police officers, a nine-year-old Latina, an IRS employee, a reporter, and random African Americans, Asians, Jews, and others whom the culture identifies as minorities and nonwhites. The attacks were committed in the name of the Sons of Gestapo, Aryan Nations, and other white supremacist and neo-Nazi groups, based on antisemitic Christian Identity theology or simply to challenge the legitimacy of the federal government. They did their damage as anti-immigrant vigilante "citizens patrols," as "sovereign citizens" who claimed the right to make their own rules, or as an anti-tax executioner. Some teach others how to avoid paying taxes, to create bogus documents and permits, and to avoid foreclosure on their property. Some steal and try to steal property for use in future attacks.[9]

Their activity declined briefly after the 9/11 attacks but mushroomed following the election of President Obama, illustrating the difference between their definitions of tyranny and the democratic choices most Americans make.

Some places in this country have become lawless as law enforcement officers dare not try to enforce the law. In many parts of the world, judges and other public officials have become vulnerable targets for violent groups seeking power by force.[10] When judges, agents, and other law enforcement personnel fear for their lives and families, a "culture of impunity" is born and some get away with anything because authorities do not dare offend them.[11] That problem has now reinfected parts of this country.

American paramilitaries share a sense of loss, believing their country has been "invaded." It is easy to dismiss them because the literature promoted at militia gatherings suggests a divorce from reality, including Holocaust denial and conspiracy theories blaming world and local affairs on "Bilderbergers," the "Trilateral Commission," international Jewry, and the belief that the United Nations is sending military units to take over the United States. However, as similarly inclined people move around to join each other, they gain in numbers locally. Not long ago, a group of armed militiamen blocked the federal government from charging Cliven Bundy the fee for grazing his cattle on federal land. Then they took their weapons to a closed federal canyon, to open it by force for use by all-terrain vehicles. They bluntly deny the authority of the federal government. To make it worse, prominent Republicans praised Bundy's refusal to pay for grazing his cattle on federal land, and the armed intervention of his militia supporters, as "patriotic."[12] As the catalog by the SPLC makes clear, these are not isolated incidents.

So-called Patriot Militia build on the right to carry guns. They tell each other they must prepare for national tyranny against a government trying to enforce rules the militias despise such as controls on guns, fees for grazing on public lands, and taxes. A common thread is the ability to take on the Bureau of Alcohol, Tobacco, and Firearms, the IRS, and the U.S. Army![13] Their language is conditional—if America is taken over by tyrants. Yet, they believe the tyrants are already here, and they need only the tanks and canon to defend themselves.

The history of the movement is not comforting. Randy Weaver moved to Ruby Ridge, Idaho, where he could be near the compound of the Aryan Nations and other American neo-Nazi, white supremacist, and anti-semitic groups. Their offshoots became terrorists; they robbed, counterfeited, and murdered their "enemies," including the Denver talk-show host Alan Berg. Weaver was arrested in 1991 on a firearms charge but failed to show up for trial. He made it clear that he would shoot anyone attempting to take him into custody and would not be taken alive. The press eventually questioned why he had not been apprehended, and the marshal tried to make the arrest. In a series of shootouts, a federal marshal as well as Weaver's wife and teenage son were killed. Ruby Ridge became a rallying cry of the white supremacist movement.[14]

The following year, the Bureau of Alcohol, Tobacco, and Firearms tried to execute search-and-arrest warrants for David Koresh in Waco, Texas, after a UPS driver discovered that he was delivering hand grenades to the Branch Davidians, and a brief investigation revealed a large cache of guns, grenades, powder, chemicals, fuses, and ammunition had been shipped via UPS. The Davidians were a religious cult preparing for God's entry into world affairs and "a cosmic struggle between good and evil; the forces of evil would be concentrated in the present center of earthly power, the government of the United States."[15] An attempt to execute the warrants resulted in two shootouts. At least four federal agents died in the initial shootout. A siege of nearly two months followed during which many people left the compound. Attorney General Janet Reno approved another effort to enforce the warrants, resulting in a shootout in which the compound caught fire. More than eighty people died inside.

The implications for enforcing federal law were clear. Many agents in several states sent their families away because of threats directed at them and their families for carrying out their assigned duties. Others simply backed off. In several cases, federal departments stopped enforcing the law for fear of creating another armed confrontation.[16]

The power of these groups reached Congress, leading the Republican majority to hold hearings on Reno's handling of these events and claims that federal officials used excessive force. Congressman Charles Schumer responded with unofficial hearings on America's private right-wing armies and the burgeoning threats against federal officials,[17] eventually driving the leadership to schedule hearings of their own. Republicans then proposed requiring federal agents to get consent from local sheriffs before executing an arrest warrant or enforcing national regulations on federal lands.[18]

These private hate-filled paramilitaries continue training across the country, with concentrations in Idaho and Montana, and stashes of weapons to defend "their" race, independence, and country against the federal government or other "enemies." Kenneth Stern points out that these groups have experience within the US Armed Forces, actively recruit within the military, and claim strong support among active-duty personnel. As Stern put it, "Timothy McVeigh was a model soldier"—at least before he bombed the Alfred P. Murrah building in Oklahoma City.

The Wide Angle of Science

Political scientists have found armed, unauthorized, and unregulated militias a significant threat to modern democracies. For that reason, as the European Commission for Democracy Through Law observed, "In numerous states . . . [there is a] general ban on the creation of para-military formations."[19] When armed militias fight, the usual outcome is autocratic rule—sometimes as a result of efforts to defeat the militias, at other times as a result of militia victory. As Juan Linz wrote, "Only those on the extremes of the political spectrum are prepared to fight or are likely to have the organizational resources to do so."[20]

Paramilitaries tempt government to abandon civil liberties. In the theatre of battle everything is "justifiable" and democracy often becomes only the memory of a luxury. Law-abiding citizens become victims to abuse by both sides. Desperate people frequently create strongmen or turn to dictators in response to the perceived failure of the central government to control violence attributed to armed paramilitaries. Sometimes they turn to the very armed groups causing the violence on the assumption they would stop attacking people, as in the infamous decision of German President Hindenburg to make Hitler chancellor. Similar processes took place in Italy, Chile, and other countries.[21] Sometimes as paramilitaries claim to act on behalf of particular racial, religious, or ethnic groups, their victims embrace hatred and prejudice in reverse, leading to a cycle of murder and devastation, all too familiar from the civil wars of the last decades. Despite rhetoric about protecting democracy and the traditions emanating from the American Revolution, paramilitaries are much more likely to threaten than to guard democracy.[22]

Even short of a successful coup or revolution, democracy loses whenever private paramilitary militias have the power to replace the ballot with lethal weapons, or declare what government may and may not do, as they have in parts of the western United States. Guns can trump other forms of influence on the political system,[23] and guns are political regarding issues from abortion to taxes.[24]

Conversely, if everyone is armed, no one is in charge. Every disagreement has the potential of becoming lethal, of drowning the country in its own blood. Gangs, private paramilitaries, warlords, and similar groups threaten chaos or tyranny, making places like Iraq and Afghanistan almost ungovernable. Abundant arms also encourage an arms race for self-protection.

Hobbes argued the public had to give up the right to self-defense.[25] The founders stressed regulation.[26] Max Weber, a major figure in the evolution of modern social science, described the state as having a monopoly on the legitimate use of force.[27] Whatever one's starting point, the separation of weapons from accountability, oversight, and regulation is dangerous for democracy.

The weak restrictions of the 1993 Brady Bill, named for the press secretary who was severely injured in an attack on President Reagan, encouraged a large increase in the membership of the Patriot Militias because of the belief that the Brady Bill created a threat to gun ownership. The militias believed, therefore, that they would have to take on the feds over the right to bear arms.

Scholars suggest that some older white groups feel a lack of respect from a government that seemed to toy with their livelihoods via farm policy, taxes, and efforts on behalf of minorities. They argue that we need to respond to those grievances that are legitimate and fuel the desire to take up arms, but in return for control over the possession of arsenals of weapons and the enforcement of law.[28]

Internationally, studies show a worldwide rise in armed conflict of about 2 percent per year since 1950. We could contrast instances abroad from the militia, gang, criminal, KKK, and other organized violence in this country.

But the patterns do not tell us whether or when it will change. Studies of civil wars and insurgencies around the globe reveal that the major causes of armed conflict are the factors that make them possible—the "technology of military conflict," places to hide, sources of support, and traffic in arms—because those inclined toward violence will take advantage of whatever they can.[29] Factors that make armed conflict possible include how weapons, owners, and organizations are accountable and "well regulated" in the words of the Second Amendment.

The NRA argues that people, not weapons, kill, but most often it is a combination of both. Internationally, the United States does not willingly arm its enemies and pushes for nuclear nonproliferation because nuclear weapons have the potential to make conflict more devastating, and because we see the advantage of multiple strategies for dealing with the people *and* the weapons.

Government-Supported Paramilitaries

Division between unauthorized and government-supported militias is fluid, a continuum of power. The KKK began as unofficial opposition to Union Army protection of the freedmen and their supporters after the Civil War. With violence, influence, assassination, coups, and voter intimidation, the KKK drove the freedmen out of government and stopped government from protecting them. Later, the KKK often dominated the state and local governments it had put in place.[30]

The use of private armies in other contexts is nothing new in the United States. Corporations hired armies of guards and used them to break up unions, leading to considerable violence until the National Labor Relations Act helped cool things down at the end of the Great Depression.[31]

The U.S. government has increasingly used private mercenaries and military organizations,[32] with appropriations in the military budget.[33] At least in theory, private companies provide economies,[34] minimize political opposition,[35] and allow the government to act by indirection;[36] the use of military contractors also allows high-profile officials or departments to deny responsibility for human rights violations.[37] The Constitution gives Congress power to control the privatization of warfare.[38] Both the law and the Constitution prohibit the violation of protected freedoms by anyone the government uses to accomplish it.[39] Deniability undermines those prohibitions. Congress tried to limit the government's involvement in violence[40] and domestic spying[41] after the Church Committee Report on covert activities by government agencies.[42] However, every new threat undermines limitations on the weapons used against alleged enemies or criminals.[43] Inevitably, violence against alleged perpetrators sweeps too broadly, regardless of intentions, and undermines personal security and trust in the protection of government.

The dangers are considerable.[44] Working in concert with the authorities, so-called death squads disappeared people in Argentina, Chile, Guatemala, and El Salvador[45] and facilitated the Rwandan genocide, among others.[46] Paramilitaries have become a worldwide threat.[47] Death threats to judges sometimes come from independent crime syndicates, extremists, or rebels, but they also come from paramilitary organizations with ties to local armies or parts of the government, often threatening a culture of impunity.[48]

Police

Americans perceive police in stark terms as the good guys chasing the bad guys. Lawyers see enough wrongdoing that they are less prone to romanticize people by job title or uniform. Police are like most groups of people. When they are good they are very good, and when they are bad, they can do a lot more damage than most of us. Given that disconnect between nuanced and unromantic views of scholars and attorneys on the one hand, and many laymen on the other, it is important to develop a realistic view of police departments and of police as individuals, and then put the problem of the use of force in context.

Do Americans Have a Police Problem?

Some of the problems involve deliberate misbehavior. Following the infamous Ramparts scandal, the Los Angeles Police Department's Board of Inquiry wrote a report, and the president of the Los Angeles Police Protective League asked the well-known law professor, now dean, Erwin Chemerinsky to analyze the report.[49] In his introduction, Chemerinsky wrote:

> Police officers framed innocent individuals by planting evidence and committing perjury to gain convictions. . . . Innocent men and women pleaded guilty to crimes they did not commit and were convicted by juries because of the fabricated cases against them. Many individuals were subjected to excessive police force and suffered very serious injuries as a result. As Los Angeles County Supervisor Zev Yaroslavsky noted, Rampart's danger far exceeds police abuse—it "is a dagger aimed at the heart of constitutional democracy."[50]

The scope of the problem was substantial. By September 8, 2000, some 100 convictions were overturned, five officers were arrested on criminal charges and seventy faced disciplinary proceedings. Chemerinsky reported that an "estimated . . . 3,000 cases need to be reviewed."[51]

One could look at the motives of the officers in detail, but Chemerinsky concluded that focusing on the individual officers minimized the scope of the problem: "[T]he report for all of its length and detail ignores the real problems in the Department and therefore fails to provide meaningful solutions. . . . Not a single recommendation of the 108 listed calls for any structural changes in the Department or its management. The Board of Inquiry [recommendations] . . . would not bring about the needed systemic reforms of the Department."[52] That's actually why the police union asked for Chemerinsky's involvement—rather than denying the problem, they understood that it was systemic and wanted the cleanup to involve the upper echelons as well.

The problem is not in any respect limited to the LAPD.[53] Framing innocent people takes place in rural as well as urban areas;[54] this problem has been repeatedly documented all over the country. [55]

Some people are framed to cover up police misbehavior; the use of charges for resisting arrest and similar crimes to cover beatings, for example, has long been documented.[56] Some percentage of government agents become involved in criminal enterprises or are otherwise corrupted on the force. And some percentage of police killings of innocent people have been the result of impulsive shootings by terrified officers—terrified not because anything illegal had happened but because they were in a minority neighborhood. When a young foreign man with limited English reached for his keys, terrified officers killed him in a hail of bullets.[57] They were acquitted. Around the same time, a bystander to a fight was sodomized with a broom handle by officers in a police station. One was convicted.[58] In 2014, widespread demonstrations took place after police officers killed unarmed men in Ferguson, Missouri, and New York City and a twelve-year-old boy with a toy gun in Cleveland, Ohio.

Police are taught that it is too late to draw a pistol, or even to try to fire one in your hand, after you realize someone else is about to shoot. Human beings cannot react fast enough. In a society where guns are ubiquitous, it seems police are very edgy: Amadou Diallo was killed for trying to put his key in his door; Gidone Busch was killed for holding a hammer; a young unarmed teen taking a shortcut was killed because his presence startled the officer; and twelve- and thirteen-year-olds were killed for playing with toy guns.[59] Killing of innocent people is likely wherever police are on edge about their own safety.

Shootings and beatings can appear to be isolated events and the source of disruption in people's lives, but they may also be understood as implying a threat, causing people to submit, flee, or strike back. That behavior has deeper consequences for the entire society. Understanding the scope of the problem, therefore, requires some background and context.

Since the Warren Court decided *Terry v. Ohio*,[60] police have been permitted to stop people for questioning without reason to believe they committed or had knowledge of any crime. Police now routinely stop people in high-crime areas, or when their racial appearance makes it seem unlikely to the officer that they belong where they are. Police find some evidence of crime and make arrests in less than 5 percent of the stops.

Most of us have probably been stopped in our cars regarding traffic laws. Many of the officers are polite and respectful; some are brusque and nasty. It is not an experience anyone looks forward to. I was once stopped twice within a few minutes; my car must have fit a description because the second officer, minutes after the first stop, asked me to open the trunk. The first officer was exceedingly polite; the second equally impolite. Unlike the rarity of my experience, some people are stopped frequently. For them, it's more than just annoying—the officer never asks if you're in a hurry (unless you were speeding and he is being sarcastic). And a patdown involves other indignities.

When the authorities are watching a particular group of people, they do not just look for direct evidence of a specific crime; they look for any transgressions. They find things they otherwise might not bother with because even minor charges act as "warnings" or push people to squeal about others. All of a sudden people are more likely to do jail time just because the police are there, looking.

The authorities also run stings to test and see if someone is inclined to evil behavior. Stings often use someone who is facing jail time because officials can offer the individual a valuable incentive to cooperate. A panel of the Tenth Circuit of the U.S. Court of Appeals once called those favors "bribes," but courts continue to allow prosecutors and law enforcement officers to offer "favors" such as not bringing charges, or reduced jail time.[61] I helped out in a minor way in defense of a Muslim cleric, who was caught in a sting by a real felon. The felon was asking the Imam to be a witness so that a financial transaction would be enforceable within the Muslim community. The transaction was supposed to involve the sale of a powerful weapon to be used against an embassy. But on the single crucial occasion where this felon was laying out the nature of the financial transaction, he forgot the recording machine in the car so there was no recording. Forgive me if as a lawyer I am very skeptical of what felons forget. In the atmosphere of terror in which that trial took place, the religious leader of that Mosque was convicted and sent to prison. I still believe he got the shaft.

What I am trying to convey is how vulnerable we are if the police want to get you. From time to time there is discussion about whether to let law enforcement officers spend time in our places of worship, looking for terrorists. Once officers or federal agents walk in, they are looking for weaknesses, for people they can arrest and turn into informers, accusing others. And with a witness who now has reasons to lie, innocent people are at risk, particularly when the witness has reasons to understand how dangerous authorities can be.

That has several consequences. Arrest rates in different communities correlate with official stereotypes, and those stereotypes cannot be validated because former arrests were based on the same stereotypes and become a circular and self-fulfilling prophecy. Moreover groups change over time, including our own ancestors. Even if they were originally accurate, stereotypes quickly become misleading. The inefficiency of profiling has been demonstrated in large-scale statistical studies.[62] Allowing police to act on their suspicions does not contribute to making communities safer.

Racial profiling, however, does a great deal of harm. If you are neither poor, an immigrant, nor a person of color, you have probably not experienced the problem. Perhaps you have assumed that the outcries about abusive policing in the black and Hispanic communities are all nonsense. In fact, those problems are well documented by generations of scholars.

For young African American men and other minorities, disrespectful stops are a constant fact of life that has corroded their relationships with the authorities. They are likely to be treated just as badly by the courts. A couple of weeks after representing a pair of African American men, a judge stopped me in the courthouse to tell me he believed the testimony of one of my clients. So I asked, "Why didn't you acquit him?" He responded, "I couldn't do that to the police."

Police chiefs will tell you there is as much drug crime in the white suburbs as there is in the black ghettos, but they focus on the crime in the ghettos. At every stage in the process—from the initial charge to the decision to send a kid back to his parents or off to jail, the likelihood of conviction, and the length of sentences—the numbers always turn harshly against African Americans, so they constitute a vastly disproportionate percent of inmates in American prisons. That different outcome reverberates in the community. In the white community, errant young white men and children are taken in hand and steered by law-abiding families. In the prisons, young black men are taken in hand and steered by other prisoners. They come out hardened for a life of crime, and leave behind many single-parent families coping without them. After they are released, their records keep them from the jobs that could eventually guarantee a decent livelihood. Our society nurtures white children and casts aside black lives. In the end, we all pay a price for the mistreatment of the African American and other minority communities.[63]

One price we pay is political. Inmates often cannot vote. Or they count as part of the population where the jails are, often exaggerating the electoral power of rural counties. Ex-convicts are often barred from voting which, in turn, permanently changes the politics of their communities, making sure that the resources that might help alleviate the conditions that lead too many into lives of crime never go to the communities where they are needed most to repair the damage.

This fraught relationship between the police and the black community means that police shootings and abuse can never be treated as isolated, accidental, or innocent instances; for minority communities it is a pattern that the police departments refuse to break. This fraught relationship means that police shootings and abuse always convey the message that blacks should live in continual fear of the police, and therefore reinforce the mutual hostility that facilitates abuse.

We all have a stake in these problems; they anger and miseducate young men in prison, waste police time, coarsen the police in the process, and waste tax dollars. We also have a stake in exercising the moral responsibility to stop it.

Guns add to the problem and the danger for both citizens and the police. Asked to address a class of policemen at a local college, I drew them out about one of my cases. But they wanted to explain to me that the officers enforced nonexistent gun control laws. In that state, laws prohibited concealed carriage of firearms but not open carry of hunting rifles. Never mind. Find a rifle, especially on a black man or a white "punk," and they would be arrested for violation of the rule against concealed carriage of weapons. They knew it was illegal but they lied to make the convictions stick. Weapons were a concern and the officers intended to control them.

Liberals support police calls for gun control. Conservatives object to the enforcement of firearms as well as tax and environmental laws by federal and state agents and inspectors. Yet they want an unregulated police force, free to act on hunches. Unregulated police tend to go after people who "look" dangerous: teenagers, especially in groups, and people of color. Conservatives want "respectable" people around and they support the police. Political scientists describe local government as largely involved with the question of exclusion—who can live where, on what acreage; who can have what zoning variances to work there; and who can walk or drive there without being harassed by the local police.[64] Liberals support the diversity that irritates conservatives, and they are not comfortable with arbitrary power. So the liberal angst is the opposite of the conservative angst—about arbitrariness more than the specific rules the police enforce.

In effect liberals and conservatives attack the police from both sides. Conservatives defend the guns. Liberals insist on standards. Politics decrees that police face guns, and citizens face largely unregulated police whose main object is to stay in control and to command obedience. The result is greater power not only to apprehend criminals, but also to act on stereotypes or prejudice. The result also escalates conflict which may be putting the police in more rather than less danger.

The Warren Court designed rules to deal with repeated coercion of confessions and other serious abuses that had been coming to the Court for decades. Nevertheless, misbehavior often goes without effective remedy. As James Madison put it in 1788: "If men were angels, no government would be necessary. . . . In framing a government which is to be administered by men over men . . . you must first enable the government to control the governed; and in the next place oblige it to control itself."[65] Support for the police should be support for good police work or it puts us all in danger. In simple language the founders would have applauded, power needs to be accountable, monitored, and controlled.

Legal Rules Are Only Part of the Answer

Steven Pinker, in THE BETTER ANGELS OF OUR NATURE, demonstrates that the likelihood of suffering a violent death from all causes has been decreasing over the centuries to a small fraction of what it used to be—depending on where we start, to as little as one-tenth or one-hundredth of earlier rates. He explains that the largest single factor reducing violent deaths has been the monopolization of force by government over the last several centuries. As Pinker puts it, "a referee hovering over" our personal struggles "can ramp down the cycle of belligerence."[66] America is running contrary to that trend. George Zimmerman's disregard of police instructions not to follow Trayvon Martin, resulting in a confrontation in which Zimmerman shot and killed Martin, illustrates the growing impotence of authorities in some parts of the country to resolve confrontations without violence.[67] Arming the public is a dangerous strategy; tolerance for powerful weapons threatens democratic institutions.

In the language of loyalty oaths that many Americans have signed, guns are crucial to any effort to "overturn" the government "by force, violence or any unlawful means."[68] That is true for firearms put in the hands of armies, paramilitaries, secret police, or, in some contexts, local authorities. It is also true in the case of revolutions or coups d'état which terrify or intimidate populations into submission. Guns also allow dominant groups to destroy democracy from the bottom up by excluding portions of the population from democratic processes. Guns are dangerous—to individuals and to democracy. To the extent that we do not live in a peaceful world, guns are also sometimes necessary. That leaves us with the problem of controlling their use and abuse.[69]

In this context, the military needs to be considered. Coups that disrupt the democratic process generally involve the army, sometimes joining the executive or the legislature to oust the other, and sometimes standing aside and blessing a takeover.[70] Provisions for civilian control of the military do not explain why they work. The fundamental democratic ideology behind those provisions may be a stronger explanation. Shared ideology makes plotting a coup dangerous and defending the existing order safer. Military leaders in modern liberal democracies tend to reflect and respect strong, clear, and consistent public views about self-government and civilian control, and find it hard to unite in opposition.[71] At vulnerable moments, we rely on our shared democratic culture and a shared sense of community, and their spread throughout the military, to protect democracy, although as we have noted above, public opinion polls do not accurately predict democratic government.

Nevertheless, we know that private and government-supported paramilitary organizations maintain ties with the armed forces; they are often composed of former soldiers and they recruit among them. We also have to expect that ideological divisions in society will be reflected in the service, albeit not necessarily in proportion to population, because soldiers are not a representative sample of the U.S. population.

The draft had built-in protections. Draftees were temporary, although draftees did not represent a cross section of America either, as their numbers were skewed by educational deferments. Nevertheless, they were more representative than a volunteer army where membership is connected to local traditions of military service. Beginning in World War I, the military integrated people from all over the country, ending the era of locally recruited commands, like Theodore Roosevelt's Rough Riders. Controversy over the war in Vietnam ended the draft, professionalized the military, and separated the internal culture of the professionalized military from civilian culture. That has new risks. Groups within the military claim they are prepared to attack civilian government.[72] In many parts of the world, armies have been poisoned by ethnic, religious, and class divisions, much like slavery divided the army into loyal and disloyal, Union and Confederate, in the run-up to the Civil War.[73] Armies become more dangerous when we look at each other with suspicion and contempt.

Part of the military ethic, and by extension the American ethic as well, has to be *e pluribus unum*. Part of dealing with guns is nation-building, or nation-repairing, among ourselves.

PART III

At the Court

9

Breakdown by Court Order

The Bill of Rights in the Roberts Court

Unlike the larger legal and political science communities, the Roberts Court does not appear to treat the safeguards of the Bill of Rights for criminal prosecutions as important protections for democratic government. The Court leaves Americans dependent on the good will and intelligence of public officials, even in cases where it is clearly lacking.

Some cases on the Court's docket are about the deliberate misuse of the criminal justice process to put and keep people in prison regardless of their innocence. The California Supreme Court described Thomas Goldstein in 1979 as "an engineering student and Marine Corps veteran with no criminal history."[1] But in 1980 he was convicted of a murder he did not commit, largely based on the testimony of a jailhouse informant after Goldstein was arrested. He was released in 2004, when his innocence became clear, after spending nearly a quarter century in prison.

Goldstein's attorneys explained: "[The] informant falsely testified that Mr. Goldstein confessed the crime to him and falsely swore that the District Attorney's Office had promised him nothing in return for his testimony. The trial deputy [district attorney] did not know, and therefore could not disclose to the defense, that this was a lie."[2] Petitioners John Van de Kamp and Curt Livesay ran the district attorney's office, and vetoed collecting any information about what favors informants received from his office for providing incriminating testimony. Because there was no file or database to check, deputies rarely knew about promises to informants made by others in the office. In Goldstein's case, the deputy apparently did not know what had happened before he received the file. Goldstein was convicted on the testimony of a jailhouse informant named Eddie Fink. The U.S. Supreme Court commented that Fink "had previously received reduced sentences for providing prosecutors with favorable testimony in other cases" so it was reasonable to infer that he was trying to get similarly favorable treatment for testifying against Goldstein.[3] In Goldstein's case, the district attorney's office promised "to slash Fink's sentence on a pending theft charge from 16 months to less than two months" in return for his testimony.[4]

Deals with witnesses work like bribes.[5] Prosecutors promise to drop charges in other cases, urge judges to release or reduce a witness's jail time, or give him or her other forms of leniency.[6] Those are powerful inducements to testify. Such promises affect witnesses' credibility and their motives to testify to please the prosecutor. Long before Goldstein was arrested, the U.S. Supreme Court decided in *Brady v. Maryland* that the prosecutor had to give the defense counsel that information, and, in *Giglio v. United States,* that the office had to turn the information over even though the prosecutor handling the trial did not know what the witness had been promised.[7] It would have helped the defense counsel and the jury evaluate whether the witness lied. Failure to disclose the promises to Fink clearly violated those and other U.S. Supreme Court rulings to turn over exculpatory information, specifically including deals with prosecution witnesses.

The story gets worse. A scandal broke a decade after Goldstein's trial and a grand jury investigated the prosecutor's office's handling of jailhouse informants. In its 1990 report the grand jury found that the "Los Angeles County District Attorney's Office failed to fulfill the ethical responsibilities required of a public prosecutor by its deliberate and informed declination to take the action necessary to curtail the misuse of jail house informant testimony."[8] The report detailed how jailhouse informants fabricate confessions from people the authorities were interested in prosecuting, often with official help in creating the confessions they claimed to have heard.[9] Although the Supreme Court did not mention it, Goldstein's counsel informed the Court that the grand jury report found the abuse of jailhouse informant testimony "began well before Mr. Goldstein's arrest . . . and continued over the course of the ensuing decade."[10] The report examined at length the decision of the district attorney's office not to keep records on the testimony and the promises made to jailhouse informants. One reason they decided not to keep those records was precisely that they would have to turn the information over to defense counsel. The report identified both their constitutional and moral duty to provide that information, so that defense counsel and juries could evaluate the witnesses' truthfulness. But the district attorney's office declined.[11]

Based on the prosecutors' deliberate efforts to prevent defense counsel from getting the information that they were entitled to and that the jury should have seen, counsel sought damages for Goldstein's twenty-four years in prison. The case came to the U.S. Supreme Court as *Van de Kamp v. Goldstein.*[12]

The Roberts Court responded by expanding the shield protecting prosecutors from any liability for their behavior. Citing the decisions which defined the constitutional obligation of prosecutors to disclose promises made to witnesses, and recognizing "that sometimes such immunity deprives a plaintiff of compensation that he undoubtedly merits,"[13] the Court nevertheless held prosecutors completely immune from liability for failing to keep records that would make disclosure possible because lawsuits would inconvenience prosecutors and might interfere with the proper performance of their jobs.[14] The Court did not specify any incentives for prosecutors to honor their obligations, prevent such miscarriages of justice in the future, and compensate Tom Goldstein for the loss of twenty-four years of his life.

Following the *Van de Kamp* decision, another man convicted of a crime he did not commit also tried to convince the Court to protect the public from abusive prosecutors. In *Connick v. Thompson*, Justice Thomas,[15] writing for the Court, described the prosecutors' behavior as "flagrant—and quite possibly intentional—misconduct."[16] Justice Ginsburg's dissent amplified what had happened. In what has been all too common misbehavior: "Throughout the pretrial and trial proceedings against [John] Thompson, the team of four [who were] engaged in prosecuting him for armed robbery and murder hid from the defense and the court exculpatory information Thompson requested and had a constitutional right to receive. The prosecutors did so despite multiple opportunities, spanning nearly two decades, to set the record straight."

Nevertheless, the Court once again protected the prosecutor and denied relief. Ginsburg commented in dissent, that "the trial record . . . reveals [that] the conceded, long-concealed prosecutorial transgressions were neither isolated nor atypical." And she concluded that "a fact trier could reasonably conclude that inattention to Brady was standard operating procedure at the District Attorney's Office."[17] For the Court, this "single" instance was insufficient basis for relief. Thompson spent eighteen years in prison, fourteen of which on death row, for a crime he did not commit. The prosecutors' only contribution, in violation of well-known constitutional obligations, was to conceal the evidence that would have acquitted him. But they were excused by the Court, 5–4.

In *Ashcroft v. Iqbal*,[18] Javaid Iqbal alleged a wide-scale discriminatory policy regarding conditions of confinement of Muslim men without evidence that they had participated in any terrorist activity. Justice Souter's dissent described the allegations more fully than the majority:

Iqbal alleges that after the September 11 attacks the FBI "arrested and detained thousands of Arab Muslim men" . . . that many of these men were designated by high-ranking FBI officials as being "of high interest" . . . and that in many cases, including Iqbal's, this designation was made "because of the race, religion, and national origin of the detainees, and not because of any evidence of the detainees' involvement in supporting terrorist activity." . . . The complaint further alleges that Ashcroft was the "principal architect of the policies and practices challenged" . . . and that Mueller "was instrumental in the adoption, promulgation, and implementation of the policies and practices challenged." . . . According to the complaint, Ashcroft and Mueller "knew of, condoned, and willfully and maliciously agreed to subject [Iqbal] to these conditions of confinement as a matter of policy, solely on account of [his] religion, race, and/or national origin and for no legitimate penological interest." . . . The complaint thus alleges, at a bare minimum, that Ashcroft and Mueller knew of and condoned the discriminatory policy their subordinates carried out. Actually, the complaint goes further in alleging that Ashcroft and Mueller affirmatively acted to create the discriminatory detention policy. If these factual allegations are true, Ashcroft and Mueller were, at the very least, aware of the discriminatory policy being implemented and deliberately indifferent to it.[19]

Iqbal's complaint was one of many brought by major civil liberties organizations challenging the discrimination toward Muslims without any basis in factual information about them.[20] But the Court's treatment of Iqbal's complaint made it difficult to hold federal officials responsible.

Rule 8 of the Federal Rules of Civil Procedure requires only that a complaint include "a short and plain statement of the claim showing that the pleader is entitled to relief." It was adopted to eliminate the need to elaborate specific facts and legal theories in the complaint and to head off lengthy technical battles about what the complaint should have said.[21] But the Court required the complaint to state the facts in some detail, continuing a redefinition of Rule 8.

Second, the Court eliminated liability for knowingly acquiescing in, or deliberate indifference to, the misbehavior of subordinates, even though counsel for Ashcroft and Meuller conceded that was the correct standard, and the issue had been neither briefed nor argued.[22]

Third, the majority treated Iqbal's allegations of misbehavior as "conclusory" and "formulaic," including allegations about who created and implemented what policy of discrimination.[23]

Fourth, having concluded that Iqbal's allegations should be treated as conclusions rather than as facts, the majority concluded that Iqbal's claims about Ashcroft and Mueller were implausible inferences from the existence of different treatment given Muslim men.[24] Although the Court denied that it was making a judgment about what Ashcroft and Mueller actually did,[25] its judgment about what counted as a factual allegation and its assessment of the implications of proof of discrimination reflected long-standing blind spots of the Court, and a lengthy battle between Congress and the Court about the evidence required to prove discrimination.[26]

Plausibility is a troubling standard because it invites judges to evaluate claims subjectively, based on their respect for the individuals, political ideologies, and exposure to the kinds of problems addressed in the complaints. One might compare the Court's solicitude for the competing public obligations of President Clinton—when the Court refused to stay a private and legally implausible lawsuit that was later dismissed[27]—with its solicitude for the competing obligations of Attorney General Ashcroft in *Iqbal* and various prosecuting attorneys in *Van de Kamp v. Goldstein* and *Connick v. Thompson* in evaluating how reliably courts might assess other subjective standards like plausibility in the early stages of litigation.[28] The system of notice pleading, abrogated only recently by the Roberts Court,[29] is much more likely to produce reliable results.[30]

Following the *Iqbal* decision, my colleague Raymond Brescia examined the impact of both *Iqbal* and a prior ruling on which the *Iqbal* decision was based.[31] Brescia concluded that *Iqbal* left courts much more likely to dismiss discrimination claims.[32] The Court's action fits a long pattern of making it difficult, if not impossible, to prove discrimination.[33]

In *Ashcroft v. al-Kidd*,[34] the Court decided Attorney General Ashcroft and others involved were immune from responsibility for abusing the power to arrest and detain material witnesses by using it against people without any intention to put them on the stand. Neither Ashcroft's nor the government's motives mattered to the Court. The Court had condoned a maliciously motivated arrest in a prior decision.[35] Now they allowed prosecutors to mislead magistrates when seeking a warrant. Concern that "a pretextual warrant . . . 'gut[s] the substantive protections of the Fourth Amendmen[t]' and allows the State 'to arrest upon the executive's mere suspicion'" escaped the Court.[36]

Abdullah al-Kidd was a native-born American citizen, neither called as a witness nor charged with a crime. He had been meeting and cooperating with federal investigators regarding an investigation of Sami Omar al-Hussayen, a terrorism suspect, but federal officials presented a magistrate with an affidavit that misrepresented al-Kidd's availability to testify at the trial of al-Hussayen fourteen months later. Before it was determined that it was sufficient to release him subject to a travel restriction for most of the fourteen months, al-Kidd was detained "in high-security cells lit 24 hours a day, strip-searched and subjected to body-cavity inspections on more than one occasion, and handcuffed and shackled about his wrists, legs, and waist."[37]

In each of those cases, the Court refused to interpret the Bill of Rights to protect the public from the abuse of power, a fundamental purpose of the founders' work.

Judicially crafted immunities protect most law enforcement personnel if they act in "good faith" and not in violation of "clearly established law."[38] *Van de Kamp* and *Connick* ignored the clearly established law and provided absolute immunity for prosecutors, while *Iqbal* ignored good faith, holding the officials' motives were irrelevant. Despite the Bill of Rights, innocent people abused by officials with guns and badges have few remedies, courtesy of the Roberts Court.[39]

Law, to the Court's conservatives, is rarely about accurate fact-finding or procedures. Instead, it is a system to control the public without regard to catching the right defendant.

The Roberts Court resists even providing reliable procedures. It took years, over sustained objections from the Court's conservatives, to decide that detainees on Guantanamo had the right to petition the courts for a writ of habeas corpus.[40] It struggled to allow the right to have attorneys who could have access and respond to government hearsay evidence.[41] It overruled two lower federal courts which had ordered Alaska to make DNA evidence available for testing, deciding that prisoners have no right to evidence that could prove their innocence.[42] Even when evidence discovered after conviction shows that a prisoner is innocent, when the evidence that led to conviction turns out to have been false and misleading, the Court has been deeply split and unable to find that alone justifies any relief.[43] Four justices have resisted every attempt at freedom, while Justice Kennedy just calls it "an open question" whether a "'federal constitutional right to be released upon proof of 'actual innocence'" exists. Kennedy noted, "We have struggled with it over the years," but he remains unwilling to decide.[44]

In these decisions, the Roberts Court repeatedly told prosecutors they are free to hide evidence, lie and let witnesses lie, and keep innocent people in prison. The Court's stance makes liberty more tenuous and conflicts with the views of the Bill of Rights' authors,[45] as well as the conclusion of modern political scientists, that fair and accurate procedures matter for the survival of democratic government.[46] Autocrats from Putin to Pinochet disregard due process as they consolidate power, illustrating the risks the Court imposes on America.

Self-Government in the Roberts Court

The Right to Vote

While *Citizens United* was percolating through the courts,[47] the Roberts Court compiled a record limiting political rights that exceeds the chutzpah and damage of that infamous decision.

Unlike courts abroad, the Roberts Court does not treat the inclusion of the public in the mechanisms of democracy as crucial to defining democratic government, nor does it consider popular control of government as a virtue to be defended. The political science community finds the inclusiveness of the democratic system strongly affects whether the system spirals into autocracy and kleptocracy or whether the democratic system strengthens in the service of the general public. In most contexts, the Roberts Court supports entrenched power over citizen control.

Justice Thomas, in an opinion joined by Justice Scalia, told us in 1994 that he does not believe that there is a fair definition of democracy that can be used to decide cases.[48] That rejection of principles of democratic choice implicates cases involving the apportionment of seats, the drawing of district lines, the registration of voters, and the protection of minority voters, among others. Constitutional structure affects the Court's reading of federalism but not its treatment of democratic institutions. Thus there is nothing subtle about the treatment of democracy by Thomas and Scalia; they head it off at the pass and attack with guns blazing.

In *Rutan v. Republican Party*, a 1990 decision about patronage practices in Illinois, the Court had to decide whether personnel decisions "involving low-level public employees may be constitutionally based on party affiliation and support."[49] In dissent, Scalia stressed the importance of "the link between patronage and party discipline, and between that and party success."[50] As Scalia recognized, patronage gives preference to loyalty over other skills. Strong "disciplined" parties are somewhat immune from the rank and file supervision. Theirs is control of, not by, their members.

Beginning in 1996, the Court adopted Scalia's position in cases about drawing district lines for legislative seats, holding that otherwise unconstitutional districting can be justified when it protects incumbents.[51] States can allocate voters for the benefit of leaders, and that trumps inequalities. Politics is a game of kings, or at least bosses, not people.

Four of the Roberts Court's conservatives have not approved an attack on the entrenchment of elected officials, and the fifth did so only rarely.

In *League of United Latin Am. Citizens v. Perry*, the Court refused to address the scientific measure of gerrymandering, known either as symmetry or neutrality. The four "liberal" members of the early Roberts Court argued, in dissent, that the definition and test for gerrymandering used by the political scientists should be employed. The four more conservative members of the Court rejected it.[52]

Chief Justice Roberts and Justice Alito wrote that "appellants have not provided 'a reliable standard for identifying unconstitutional political gerrymanders.'" They also commented that whether partisan gerrymandering presents a "case or controversy" that the Court is allowed to resolve had not been decided.[53] If gerrymandering presents no case or controversy, then—no matter how badly the districts are gerrymandered to insure victory for one party—their opponents have no right to complain.

Justices Scalia and Thomas concluded that "claims of unconstitutional partisan gerrymandering do not present a justiciable case or controversy" so the Court had no business even hearing it and the party fenced out of legislative seats had no right to complain. The political scientists' brief notwithstanding, they also concluded, "no party or judge has put forth a judicially discernible standard by which to evaluate them." They would "simply dismiss appellants' claims as nonjusticiable."[54]

Justice Kennedy was more interested in the neutrality standard: "A brief for one of the amici proposes a symmetry standard that would measure partisan bias by 'compar[ing] how both parties would fare hypothetically if they each (in turn) had received a given percentage of the vote.' . . . Under that standard the measure of a map's bias is the extent to which a majority party would fare better than the minority party, should their respective shares of the vote reverse." Still he was not satisfied: "Amici's proposed standard does not compensate for appellants' failure to provide a reliable measure of fairness." Kennedy was concerned that the model might not predict accurately whether the change would be smooth across the state or would be concentrated in certain areas. And he was skeptical of statistical predictions: "we are wary of adopting a constitutional standard that invalidates a map based on unfair results that would occur in a hypothetical state of affairs." Nevertheless Kennedy appears to have left a door open to use the symmetry standard in some yet undefined combination with other elements: "Without altogether discounting its utility in redistricting planning and litigation, I would conclude asymmetry alone is not a reliable measure of unconstitutional partisanship."[55] Given Thomas's and Scalia's rejections of neutrality and the skepticisms of Roberts and Alito, it appears that door is open only to Kennedy among the conservative justices.

The majority also rejected most objections to Texas's districting plan under section 2 of the Voting Rights Act.[56] Nevertheless, Justice Kennedy and the four justices to his left reversed the lower court's decision with respect to the redrawing of the lines of one district allocating the Hispanic community a smaller portion of southern and western Texas. Section 2(b) of the Voting Rights Act requires that nominations and election procedures should be "equally open to participation" without regard to race or language without any right to have representatives "elected in numbers equal to their proportion in the population."[57]

Gerrymandering to strengthen Republican prospects at the polls meant splintering the Democratic-leaning minority community among several surrounding districts. Roberts and Alito said Texas had done enough for the Hispanic community to satisfy its constitutional obligations, noting that the Hispanic share of Texas districts was "roughly proportional" to their share of the population.[58] Their data revealed, however, that the non-Hispanic community would have been more than proportionately represented even if another district had been designed with a Hispanic majority.

Scalia and Thomas supported splintering of the Hispanic community. They required the state to show a tremendously important justification before it could aid minority voters, which they treated as a racial preference. "In my view," Scalia wrote, "when a legislature intentionally creates a majority-minority district, race is necessarily its predominant motivation and strict scrutiny is therefore triggered."[59] But they did not object to weakening minority voting strength because they did not think favoring majority white voters was racially motivated.[60] In that circumstance, "[a]lthough a State will almost always be aware of racial demographics when it redistricts, it does not follow" that advantaging white voters would be racially motivated.[61] That contrast in standards is astonishing from a member of the Supreme Court but clearly expressed. For them, the principle of equal protection designed to protect the freed slaves and their descendants now largely protects only the descendants of their former masters and those with similar pigment and European origins. Equal protection, as they understand it, is not racially neutral–it favors whites.

So with the exception of one district, *LULAC* sustained the Republican effort to maximize control of Texas's congressional delegation by gerrymandering the state and splintering, or "cracking," the Democratic population to reduce its share of the Texas congressional delegation.

Two years later, in 2008, the Roberts Court decided five cases involving the entrenchment of political leaders. Perhaps most surprising was the unanimous result in the 2008 New York judicial nomination decision, *New York State Bd. Of Elections v. López Torres*.[62] New York, by law, holds party conventions only for judicial nominations. Voters select delegates to the nominating conventions, but not the judicial candidates themselves. After the conventions there is a limited opportunity for independent candidates to collect signatures to try to get on the general election ballot.[63] And party leaders are free to arrange cross-endorsements for candidates of the other major parties, so that the parties do not compete at the general election. Two results stand out. First, New York puts party nominations for judicial offices largely in the control of the political bosses. Second, a large proportion of judicial elections are uncontested.[64]

No one on the Court saw any problem with statutory support for political party boss control over judicial nominations. They held the provisions acceptable because party members could have adopted it. Justice Scalia wrote: "Party conventions, with their attendant 'smoke-filled rooms' and domination by party leaders, have long been an accepted manner of selecting party candidates."[65] Therefore, according to the Court, it was perfectly acceptable for the state to impose smoke-filled rooms on the nominating process by state statute.

Two months later, the Supreme Court decided parties could not control who could identify him- or herself as party candidates on the primary and general election ballots.[66] Washington adopted a run-off system in which candidates identified their party preference on the primary ballot. All candidates competed in the same primary, an *open* primary because it is open to candidates and voters of all parties. The top two vote-getters, regardless of whether they belong to the same or different parties, compete in the general election. Over the objections of Justices Scalia and Kennedy, the court upheld the Washington primary and general election system.

Washington's open primary system was an extension of Washington voters' electoral populism. The New York system reflected a preference for smoke-filled rooms. But both cases preferred government control over how parties nominate candidates. Two decades earlier, in *Tashjian v. Republican Party*, the Court had upheld—paraphrasing Barry Goldwater's famous slogan—"a choice" or "an echo." In *Tashjian*, Connecticut Republicans wanted to open their primary to independent voters to nominate the most broadly acceptable statewide candidates. Connecticut law restricted party primaries to registered party voters, but the Court blocked the state from overriding the party's choice. Previous cases similarly blocked states from requiring open primaries when the parties chose closed ones.[67] Those cases affirmed the parties' right to organize to best present their message, whether a choice or an echo.

The Supreme Court's approval of both the New York and Washington systems can, in different ways, protect the status quo. New York can protect existing officeholders by encouraging self-dealing between bosses. Washington can drown voices for policy change and drive all candidates to the center by making them appeal to the same voters so that the winning candidates will echo each other's policy preferences.[68]

In the third major election decision of 2008, *Crawford v. Marion County Election Bd.*,[69] the Court sustained Indiana's new requirement that voters produce government-issued photo identification in order to vote. The card itself was free, in deference to an old U.S. Supreme Court decision,[70] but the cost of producing the documents required to get one could be substantial. Applicants had to present a birth or naturalization certificate, a veteran's or military photo ID card, or a U.S. passport. Each document has a price tag, which varied from three to one hundred dollars, depending on which state or agency it would have to come from. And voters might have to make repeated trips to state offices to get the required photo ID card before the election, or after the election to complete the process of using a "provisional ballot" by executing an affidavit. Those trips could cost hours of lost income plus the price of transportation. Indiana did little to make it easier for voters to get the necessary photo identification, much less than other states did to make it easier to vote. All that would discourage poor or handicapped citizens from voting. The potential political consequences were obvious—as Justice Souter put it, "the interest in combating voter fraud has too often served as a cover for unnecessarily restrictive electoral rules."[71] Absentee ballots have been much easier to abuse on a much larger scale, but Indiana took no comparable measures to prevent absentee ballot fraud. Interestingly Judge Posner, who wrote the court of appeals's opinion, and Justice Stevens, who wrote the Supreme Court's opinion, have both publicly admitted they were wrong in *Crawford.*[72]

Then, in June 2008, the Court struck the so-called millionaire's amendment from federal election finance law.[73] The Bipartisan Campaign Reform Act of 2002 tried to even the odds between wealthy candidates and those with more ordinary means. The Court overturned it saying candidates have an unlimited First Amendment right to spend their own funds on their campaigns.

The Court sidestepped another 2008 election case. Ohio Republicans tried to force Secretary of State Jennifer Brunner to purge the voter lists where they were inconsistent with motor vehicle records.[74] A U.S. district judge directed Brunner to purge the records. Brunner resisted because matching lists put together at different times for different purposes would exclude more people erroneously who should be allowed to vote. The similarity of names of different people, differences in spelling, use of diminutives, and changes of address, are among the many innocent sources for inconsistencies between records. The Supreme Court, in a one-paragraph unsigned order without argument vacated the injunction on the ground that it seemed unlikely that Congress had authorized private parties to litigate the issue under the Help America Vote Act.

Thus, in its first three terms, the Court had backed the statutory entrenchment of judicial nominations by political bosses in New York, rejected science that would have subjected gerrymandering to a mathematical standard for treating voters equally without regard to party, authorized splintering minority communities to reduce their representation in Congress, and began to unravel campaign finance rules. It treated the vote not as the condition and justification for democratic government, but as a privilege, which might or might not be allowed if people did not satisfy the standards set by the governing party as sufficient to qualify.

In 2009 the Court continued emasculating the Voting Rights Act. In *Bartlett v. Strickland*,[75] the Court held that African American communities comprising less than half of a legislative district were not entitled to consideration in the way the districts were drawn. Then, near the end of the term, the Court left the constitutionality of the Voting Rights Act hanging by a thread in *Northwest Austin Municipal Utility District v. Holder*,[76] waiting to be cut down in 2013.[77]

The Voting Rights Act of 1965 came after a century of failure. The Fourteenth and Fifteenth Amendments both addressed voting. But by the time President Eisenhower took office, virtually no blacks had been allowed to vote in the states of the Confederacy. Congress passed statutes authorizing the attorney general to enforce voting rights and authorizing federal officials to register voters, during the Eisenhower administration, in 1957 and again in 1960.[78] Those, too, worked poorly.[79]

The Voting Rights Act of 1965 finally made a difference with the help of an army of civil rights volunteers and lawyers, both African Americans and white supporters, some of whom gave their lives in the effort. Section 2 prohibits voting rules that abridge or discriminate among voters because of race, color, or native language.[80] Sections 4 and 5 together bar places with histories of discrimination, including the former Confederacy, from adopting any voting rule that will weaken the voting strength of racial or language minority groups.[81] Section 5 is usually described as barring retrogression in voting rules that affect minorities, making their situation worse.[82] It added teeth by requiring those jurisdictions to submit changes in voting rules to the U.S. Attorney General for pre-clearance before they can go into effect.[83] In *Northwest Austin*, Chief Justice Roberts cited "the historic accomplishments of the Voting Rights Act," the one piece of civil rights legislation that the Court had allowed to have a significant effect on the states over the past two decades.

Before it was last renewed, Congress held hearings to find out whether minority voting rights were still threatened in the old Confederacy and other places covered by the Voting Rights Act. Congress wanted to know whether the statute had done its work and could be retired. Witnesses described constant efforts to move voting places, change district lines, reorganize the forms of government and otherwise exclude African Americans from political power. But because the Voting Rights Act gave the U.S. attorney general the authority to reject changes that attempted to turn the clock back, most of those efforts failed. The witnesses' testimony made clear that efforts to undo electoral integration continues almost unabated, however, and would come roaring back if allowed. Pamela Karlan, a well-known and highly respected professor and associate dean at Stanford Law School, told the committee at the hearings:

> [I]f you have a really bad infection and you go to the doctor, they give you a bunch of pills, and they tell you, "Do not stop taking these pills the minute you feel better. Go through the entire course of treatment because, otherwise, the disease will come back in a more resistant form." And the Voting Rights Act is strong medicine, but it needs to finish its course of treatment, and that has not yet happened for reasons that you have heard from other witnesses.

City of Boerne v. Flores,[84] decided in 1997, had a warning. Justice Kennedy compared the strong record of abuse and disenfranchisement, which justified the Voting Rights Act of 1965, to what he considered the weaker record of religious discrimination behind the Religious Freedom Restoration Act. On that basis he wrote the Court's opinion that the Religious Freedom Restoration Act unconstitutionally burdened state government. *Boerne* implied that subsequent extensions of the Voting Rights Act might be tested against a contemporary record of racial discrimination in voting and election laws.

The trend was against enforcement of the Civil Rights Acts. The Rehnquist Court had gradually narrowed the meaning of the Bill of Rights and the Fourteenth Amendment. The Rehnquist Court in *Boerne* made it clear that it would extend Congress little leeway in legislating under section 5 of the Fourteenth Amendment. If the Court would not act, Congress usually cannot.

In *Shelby County*, the Court swung the axe. The Court imported a principle of equal state rights into the Constitution.[85] To Roberts and his colleagues in the majority, that means the states of the old Confederacy have the same right to discriminate against African Americans and other minorities that all the other states do. The Court could not claim that any state has a right to discriminate;[86] that's forbidden by the Constitution in very clear language—"no state shall . . . deny to any person within its jurisdiction the equal protection of the laws."[87] But Roberts and company did not want to deprive the old Confederacy of the opportunity to try to evade that prohibition just like anyone else. The original record of discrimination was compiled before the Voting Rights Act did its work, and the Voting Rights Act did its work very well. Therefore, despite constant state requests for permission to take actions that would discriminate against African Americans and other minorities, there was no longer any reason to impose on the states covered by section 5—the very reading against which Pamela Karlan eloquently warned.[88]

With the *Shelby County* decision, the Court has largely closed the legal chapter of the civil rights movement with respect to minorities, while still treating the equal protection clause of the Fourteenth Amendment as requiring powerful remedies on behalf of the descendents of European immigrants against the descendants of African immigrants. Equality is a one-way ratchet that George Orwell would have understood—it makes some people "more equal" than others.[89]

The Court drove that point home in consistent hostility to attempts to "democratize" the political process by leveling the playing field, especially by campaign funding rules. It found limitations on the size of contributions too severe,[90] and overturned the so-called millionaires amendments that buttressed public funding programs where competitors exceeded what candidates who accepted public funding received.[91] In *Citizens United*,[92] the Court overturned the prohibition on direct spending from corporate and union treasuries that had been part of American politics for a century.[93]

The flow of money is complex and has been an area of intense study by political scientists. Before *Citizens United*, political scientists had been arguing that campaign funding should focus on "floors, not ceilings," put public money into election campaigns but do not limit what can be raised or spent except voluntarily, as candidates do if they accept public funding of presidential campaigns. Public funding could promote fair, competitive races if funds are sufficient for both candidates to get their messages across. The mantra of political scientists has long been competition.[94] Depressing available funds lessens competition, especially by challengers against incumbents. Unseating incumbents is expensive because they start with large advantages. Therefore, limiting what challengers can raise has a disproportionate effect on them and leaves leadership more entrenched. Plus, campaigns seeking votes in working-class or impoverished constituencies need financial angels. In other words, limitations on campaign contributions can also squeeze out candidates trying to represent the interests of ordinary Americans. Much of the research, however, was conducted when Democrats had long-term control of Congress, so the flow of money was strongly affected by the need to curry favor with them. That kind of protection money may have swung to support GOP candidates.

It will be a while before we have a clear understanding of the impact of the *Citizens United* decision. So far political spending still seems reasonably balanced across the political aisle. But that may not measure the impact of corporate spending. Money may shift power and ideology as much within as between the parties. That is essentially Ralph Nader's position, and he may be right. Corporate political activity directed toward lobbying for legislation tends to align their overall impact with more conservative causes.[95] And the rightward tilt of the wealthiest may be magnified by corporate governance mechanisms—minorities on corporate boards are not likely to be reflected in political spending by board majorities. Until the evidence is in and analyzed, there are good reasons to believe that the more money is allowed the more that money controls and moves politics in a counter-populist direction, although the details of the channels involved remain to be understood.

Regardless of the complexities of the flow of money that political scientists have studied, it seems likely that the Supreme Court, like most Americans, believed their decisions against campaign finance rules would give an edge to those with the money to control the process—another example of the Roberts Court's support for the entrenched political power.[96] Of the conservatives, only Justice Kennedy found a problem with the influence of money and only in the case of a West Virginia judge sitting on the case in which a three-million-dollar contributor was a party.[97]

The future of democracy, according to contemporary political science, requires universal adult suffrage, fairly and equally counted votes, nonpartisan handling of electoral mechanics, and a nonpartisan Court.[98] Those also are elements of the moral claim of democracy to govern. The conservatives currently in the majority on the Roberts Court block the path to fair elections. The Court offers no relief for malapportionment, no relief for gerrymandering, no relief for exclusion from the polls, no relief for minorities under the Voting Rights Act, and in *Bush v. Gore*, conservatives on the Rehnquist Court, most of whom continue to serve on the Roberts Court, blocked a manual recount to audit the electoral machinery. Instead, the Court offers support for statutes that lock in boss control over party nominations (especially of judges) and make it more difficult and expensive to register and vote. The Court overruled a series of efforts to democratize campaign finance and dismantled the most effective remedy of the Voting Rights Act. There are no democratic rights—no rights to vote—that this Court respects.

The New Deal and Warren Courts ended the white primaries in the South, protected black voters, and required "one person, one vote." The Roberts

Court has refused to maintain that effort at every turn. The consistency of its rulings reflects the hostile attitude toward democracy that Scalia and Thomas expressed. With the occasional exception of Justice Kennedy, none of the conservative justices have accepted any attempt to open or democratize the election process.

Voters also need a free marketplace of ideas but there is no need here to review relatively settled areas of free speech doctrine. The restructuring of the information media by the Internet and the devolution of the Internet trunk lines from public to corporate hands have the potential to present major issues of government complicity in monopolization.[99] We will not know for some time how the Court will handle those issues, although there certainly are decisions suggesting it will support both corporate and governmental control.[100]

Separation of Powers

Madison explained in the Federalist that the purpose of the separation of powers was not merely to assign different tasks to different branches, but to create mutual dependence so that the branches would check each other.[101] By requiring the operation of more than one branch for many tasks, the separation of powers limits the possibility of abuse or dictatorship and can protect freedom.

The signature separation of powers cases in the Roberts years arose from the prisoners the United States took in Iraq and Afghanistan. The conservatives—notably Roberts, Scalia, Thomas and Alito—stressed the independence of the branches, particularly the presidency, and the importance of not interfering in what the president sought to do, so that conservative references to the separation of powers did little work protecting freedom.[102] Their approach emphasized power, another major goal of the separation of powers. If the president set up military commissions, it was the Court's job to see that he got what he wanted. And if the executive acquired and reviewed phone or e-mail records, those four conservatives treated the separation of powers as reason not to consider the issues plaintiffs raised.[103] Of the conservatives, only Justice Kennedy thought that the separation of powers was to enable judicial oversight of incarceration by the executive.[104]

The conservative justices also used the separation of powers as a reason not to interfere in President Bush's faith-based initiatives or Arizona's funding of religious schools. Their position was that the Court would be intruding if it examined the actions of either the legislature or the executive on such religious matters.[105] In that way, they used the separation of powers, not to restrain government, but to protect its decisions.

The Supreme Court's conservatives have, however, been skeptical of agency action in cases dealing with corporate, environmental, and financial behaviors.[106] The result has been separation of powers doctrine which is applied to ideologically defined categories of government action, but which is unreliable to protect against abuses of power that pose serious threats to democratic government.

Turning the Melting Pot Off

American tradition, courts abroad, and political scientists studying democracy all treat building a united national community as important. Integration had been applied over two centuries to class, immigration, language, religion, ethnicity, gender, and, and finally, to race. But not by the Roberts Court.

The Roberts Court and Race

In the Roberts Court's race cases, advocates on both sides claim to take a unifying view, and blame the other for taking a divisive stand. The Roberts-led majority argues that any mention of race is divisive.[107] For its critics, the Roberts-led majority entrenches the status quo and offers no path to incorporate African Americans into the mainstream of American life.[108]

In *Parents Involved in Community Schools v. Seattle School Dist. No. 1*[109]—a pair of cases coming to the Court from Louisville, Kentucky, and Seattle, Washington—the Roberts Court confronted the racial "melting pot" and the "contact hypothesis" that contact will improve interracial relations.

Beginning in the late 1930s the U.S. Supreme Court accepted both the ideology and the impact of the melting pot and the contact hypothesis. Starting with graduate education, the Court repeatedly held that there was no substitute for seating students in the same classrooms without barriers between them.[110] The Court wrote: "[T]he State, in administering the facilities it affords for professional and graduate study, sets McLaurin apart from the other students. The result is that appellant is handicapped in his pursuit of effective graduate instruction. Such restrictions impair and inhibit his ability to study, to engage in discussions and exchange views with other students, and, in general, to learn his profession."[111] Anything less would deny African American students the chance to interact with people who would play a big part in their future professions. For lawyers, segregated professional schooling blocked their opportunities to interact with future lawyers, judges, and legislators who would affect their careers, and the benefit of conversation with them while working on their degrees. The Court did not write about changing attitudes;

but it protected the opportunity for contact. And in 1948, the Court held in *Shelley v. Kramer* that judges could not enforce racially restrictive covenants—agreements among homeowners not to sell to people of a different race.[112] Finally, in *Brown*, the Court wrote that "segregation is inherently unequal" in public elementary and secondary schools,[113] an inescapable result from those prior decisions, a conclusion the justices almost certainly realized they would reach years before *Brown* was argued.

The Warren Court did not elaborate on the implications of *Brown* for public schooling, but for a single decision shortly before Warren retired. In that decision the Court held that it was not sufficient for formerly segregated school districts simply to remove the segregation language from its laws and let parents send their children wherever they chose. The Court had been down that route with the White Primary beginning in the 1920s.[114] Instead, the justices maintained: "School boards . . . [were] clearly charged with the affirmative duty to take whatever steps might be necessary to convert to a unitary system in which racial discrimination would be eliminated root and branch."[115] By 1968 Congress committed significant federal dollars to give segregated schools an incentive to integrate. It was left to the Burger Court to enforce the obligation to eliminate the vestiges of segregation, "root and branch." And in a lengthy series of decisions the Court maintained that goal.[116]

By 2005, when the Louisville and Seattle cases came to the Court, many American school districts were still clinging, voluntarily, to the goal of bringing us together through education. Segregated neighborhoods in both cities meant that neighborhood schools would be largely segregated. Both cities created complex plans to create integrated schools with minimal reference to race. They relied on a combination of lotteries and parental choice. Only in well-defined marginal circumstances would anyone's race matter. In *Parents Involved in Community Schools*, the Roberts Court found that marginal use of race unconstitutional.[117]

Housing patterns in cities like Seattle and Louisville tend to be described as "de facto" segregation. Calling it "de facto" makes it sound like government had no responsibility. All members of the Supreme Court have agreed that the Constitution requires a remedy for official discrimination. So de facto discrimination absolves government of responsibility and eliminates the one accepted reason for affirmative action—official government discrimination. Unfortunately, documents reveal FHA officials refusing to insure loans to blacks seeking to buy suburban homes. And the FHA discouraged banks from lending to blacks seeking to purchase or renovate homes in black communities. At stake were federal guarantees of home mortgages made by lending banks. This FHA action virtually mandated the segregation of white and black communities as well as disinvestment and deterioration of black neighborhoods.[118] The practice of refusing to make loans in African American communities has been described as "redlining." For years those working in the communities involved thought the problems were the work of brokers, agents, homeowners, developers, and bankers. Official federal involvement was slow to come to light. It has now been clearly documented.[119]

Had it been raised in the litigation over school districts, the Court might have shrugged it off because the documents are about federal behavior; the school districts were all state entities. In *Milliken v. Bradley,* decided in 1974, constitutional violations at all levels of government created racial segregation in Detroit, Michigan. But the Burger Court held that the suburbs surrounding Detroit were not complicit and could not be made to participate in remedying Detroit's problem.[120] Extending that logic, it is not clear what it would accomplish to acknowledge federal culpability for Seattle, Louisville, or other areas where segregation might be traced back to federal action, because federal discrimination does not establish municipal culpability. That probably leaves no remedy against either the federal government, which bore much of the responsibility, or any obligation on the part of the white suburbs created by federal racial discrimination, whether or not those suburbs felt themselves "benefitted." No racial remedy is permitted by governmental bodies unless they have intentionally discriminated.[121] Some cities still tried to provide integrated schools for their students. The Roberts Court, in *Parents Involved,* closed off what may prove to have been the only remedy left by blocking a remedy the cities chose voluntarily.[122]

Writing for the Court, Roberts suggested that affirmative action is divisive.[123] In contemporary America, all choices are somewhat divisive. Leaving groups apart accommodates white racism, and leaves African Americans deeply isolated and bitter, so that inaction is also divisive. Bringing people together requires mixing. In moderation, groups can be brought together with minimal acrimony.[124] The Roberts Court and part of the communities regard that as divisive and unpleasant. The Seattle and Louisville schools both pointed out that few students were affected and it was acceptable to most of the voting population.[125] The Court suggested no solution it would consider constitutional. The Roberts-led stance therefore creates one form of divisiveness coupled with continued separation in order to avoid a different form of divisiveness coupled with more complete integration.

It's questionable how divisive the Louisville and Seattle plans were. Both had been adopted by local educational authorities, not imposed in a distant capital.[126] And both had been designed to bring races together. Neither plan favored any race, but merely brought them into contact in the time-honored American tradition of the coeducational public school system. That system was divisive when introduced and when each new group was brought in, but the divisions were temporary and all but forgotten except by scholars examining American educational history.[127]

How deeply does racial division affect America? The combination of financial redlining, movement of employment opportunities to the suburbs, and isolation of poor black children in minority schools, has made their communities, and even the cities in which they live, seem much more alien to the surrounding culture. Reactions to issues like affirmative action that have a racial impact are not simply code language for the racial divide. And disinterest in the plight of others has a variety of roots. But it would be equally dense to miss the contribution made by racial isolation. Continued segregation helps divide and corrode our democratic system.

The Roberts Court and Religious Establishment

The Court's Establishment Clause decisions show the same indifference to building community across faiths. It does that largely by closing the courthouse door so that it becomes impossible to challenge some forms of government support for religious activity.

Hein v. Freedom from Religion Found.[128] challenged spending federal money specifically to help faith-based organizations get federal funds. President Bush set the program up by executive order and appointed Jay Hein director of the White House Office of Faith-Based and Community Initiatives to coordinate the effort.

When government spends money, there may be no one who has a sufficient direct injury to challenge the expense in court, under Article III of the Constitution. So, for several decades, the Court accepted the "standing" of taxpayers to challenge government expenditures that might violate the constitutional ban on establishment of religion.

The Freedom from Religion Foundation sued. The Court did not decide whether the program or anything done by Hein or his office violated the Establishment Clause. Instead it held that plaintiffs had no standing to sue. In general, that means a "plaintiff must allege personal injury fairly traceable to the defendant's allegedly unlawful conduct and likely to be redressed by the requested relief."[129] Scalia and Thomas would have eliminated taxpayer standing altogether. Alito (writing also for Roberts and Kennedy) announced that taxpayers have no standing to sue for presidential actions unless they have been authorized by Congress, because the precedent for taxpayer standing referred to congressional actions and this case had nothing to do with Congress. In plain English, since most presidential authority is based on congressional grants of power,[130] the less authority the president has, the less he can be called to account. The combination of Scalia's opinion and Alito's—although they reasoned in very different ways—meant that the suit was thrown out. It also means that the president has a great deal of leeway to act on his, or her, own with regard to funding religious groups, because it will be hard to find ways to challenge it.

In *Ariz. Christian Sch. Tuition Org. v. Winn*,[131] the court threw out a challenge to tuition tax credits also on the ground that taxpayers lacked standing to object. Kathleen Winn and other Arizona taxpayers challenged Arizona "tax credits for contributions to school tuition organizations . . . [which] provide scholarships to students attending private schools, many of which are religious."[132] The Arizona plan was constitutional given decisions of the Rehnquist court a few years earlier. But denying taxpayer standing resolves a large class of issues by simply closing the courthouse. A five-member majority held that taxpayers have no standing to object to tax credits because the plaintiffs' taxes did not pay for the school tuition. Therefore there is no injury to the taxpayers sufficient to justify standing to sue. Economists and tax experts have long been describing tax credits as tax expenditures, but the majority held there was a constitutional difference.[133]

The original objection which the establishment clause was intended to address was the funding of clergy by the government.[134] The Court's decisions make it difficult to enlist the Court in preventing or stopping such funding. Justice Kagan, writing for the four dissenters, pointed out:

> Distinction [between taxes and tax credits] threatens to eliminate all occasions for a taxpayer to contest the government's monetary support of religion. Precisely because appropriations and tax breaks can achieve identical objectives, the government can easily substitute one for the other. Today's opinion thus enables the government to end-run *Flast*'s guarantee of access to the Judiciary. From now on, the government need follow just one simple rule—subsidize through the tax system—to preclude taxpayer challenges to state funding of religion.[135]

The *Hein* and *Ariz. Christian School Tuition Org.* cases facilitate funding religious schools. To understand the significance of these decisions we have to look back at the legal and political context in which they arose.

The Vinson Court erected the so-called wall of separation between church and state based on documents from this country's founding, a time when states were beginning to disestablish their churches. The wall was designed to protect individual freedom of conscience and also to protect religious institutions from government meddling.

The Rehnquist Court knocked the wall down by substituting the position that government should be neutral between faith-based and secular groups seeking to use school facilities.[136] It remained to be decided what is neutral. In *Zelman v. Simmons-Harris*,[137] the Rehnquist Court held that states could give parents vouchers for private or parochial education so long as the parents chose the school and the legislation covered individuals and schools without reference to religion. Many of the private secular schools were ineligible because their tuition exceeded the statutory maximum. Other secular schools participated in the program but admitted only a few students. Therefore the bulk of funds went to religious schools. But the Court denied that the program favored religious schools because, according to the court, parents had choices.

Zelman changed the legal meaning of neutrality. For most of the twentieth century, a secular education was neutral; the public schools gave its students a floor of knowledge in secular subjects. Public schools brought children of all faiths together and provided education without reference to religious belief. People could add the schooling of their own faiths outside of school, on any matters they thought appropriate, but at their own expense. For most Americans, Sunday school or after-school classes provided faith-based education. The wall of separation and a vibrant American religious culture flourished alongside one another, as the Court enforced both the nonestablishment and free exercise clauses of the First Amendment. The Court's interpretation of the wall of separation never barred courses in the history of religion or in comparative religion.[138] What it did bar was the use of public funds and public schools for education or indoctrination in the tenets of a single faith. Indeed, in some respects the Court was more ready to support religious expression before the Rehnquist Court substituted the rule of official neutrality.[139]

Some religious groups charged that the public schools are teaching secular humanism as a substitute for religion. On that view, if secular subjects are not taught in the form of admiration for a divine being, then they are contrary to religion, that is, not neutral at all. In the cases concluding with *Zelman*, the idea of secular subjects seemed to have changed from neutral to unequal in the Rehnquist Court's mind. If so, all that remained was to decide that vouchers were not merely permissible, they were required.

Zelman led several religious foundations and law firms to argue that official neutrality required government support for religious education.[140] That would remake American education, dividing more children by faith from the time they enter school. It would segregate American education on the model of Europe, India, and other countries where government supports religious education. In Israel, Jews, Muslims, and Christians are all educated separately, leading one to wonder how they ever expect to be able to settle their differences.

The Rehnquist Court, however, stayed its hand in *Locke v. Davey*.[141] The State of Washington funded studying at colleges and universities that met state standards, including religious schools, but not religious instruction. The state was prepared to fund students studying religion "from an historical and scholarly point of view"[142] but it refused to fund Joshua Davey's devotional program of study, which would prepare him for the ministry.

Justices Scalia and Thomas concluded in dissent that Washington had discriminated against religion. Scalia wrote: "When the State makes a public benefit generally available, that benefit becomes part of the baseline against which burdens on religion are measured; and when the State withholds that benefit from some individuals solely on the basis of religion, it violates the Free Exercise Clause no less than if it had imposed a special tax."[143] Scalia and Thomas made the crucial jump from a neutral common baseline of secular education to an obligation to fund religious education. Having made public education available, Scalia and Thomas concluded that Washington had to make religious education available on the same terms.

For prior courts adhering to the wall of separation, there was no breach of neutrality. The state provided everything secular, neutrally, to everyone, including fire, police, water, and sanitation departments. There is no antireligious bias in not providing separate faith-based services. Similarly, providing secular education did not favor or discriminate against anyone's faith or faith in general. People were free to pursue what faith they chose without interference by the government. And the government did not affect power within the churches by deciding whom to fund. In providing secular education, it was offering a public service on neutral grounds without interference with religion.

Rehnquist, joined by the rest of the Court, refused to make the leap that Scalia and Thomas did. Rehnquist, writing for the Court, maintained that this "case involves that 'play in the joints'" between the Free Exercise and Establishment Clauses of the First Amendment. In other words there is a mild nonneutrality but the state must be permitted to stay out of the funding of religion in its effort to avoid the establishment of religion that would violate the Constitution.[144] Or to put it another way, the Rehnquist Court's approach to religion stopped short of logical and doctrinal consistency, at a compromise between the wall and religious equality to public secular education.

The proliferation of schools addressed to separate segments of like-minded parents is being accomplished in a variety of ways—particularly by charter schools, which are publicly funded but run by separately chartered groups, as well as by vouchers and tax credits. *Hein* and *Ariz. Christian School Tuition Org.* expand the opportunities for separate segregated religious schooling.

Eleven o'clock on Sunday mornings has been described as the most racially segregated hour in America. It is also the most religiously, and to some extent also ethnically, segregated hour in America. Grouping ourselves by faith for religious purposes in houses of worship of our own choosing is an essential part of the free exercise of religion, to which Americans are entitled. But publicly supported religious schooling threatens to extend the separatism of Sunday mornings to the entire school week. It is hard to miss the potential contribution of religious isolation.

The Roberts Court and the Melting Pot

The Roberts Court's treatment of race and religion challenge the melting pot. The problem posed by the Court is not defined by its disdain for any specific remedy, whether affirmative action, a unified school system, or the separation of church and state. The implications are cumulative. It remains to be seen whether American traditions behind the melting pot are strong enough to survive the Court's antagonism.

What *General Welfare* Means

Political science has put financial issues at the core of stable democratic systems. Where the split between the wealthy few and impoverished mass is too great, it puts a great strain on democracy and is often the prelude to coups, violence, or other forms of breakdown of democratic government.

The Court normally works at the margins of economic change and redistribution, because legislation normally has a greater impact than the financial issues submitted to the Court. Nevertheless, the Court can ameliorate or exacerbate the problem by reinterpreting legislation or declaring it unconstitutional. And as "national storyteller" it can alter perceptions of the justness of financial power grabs. The Roberts Court has been a cheerleader for the increasing concentration of wealth, encouraging both the ideology and the support of an army of lawyers and staffers who press the Court for still greater shares of the financial pie.

Five members of the Roberts Court were members of the preceding Rehnquist Court, and three—Scalia, Kennedy, and Thomas—were part of an effort to use the so-called takings clause to limit government's ability to deal with the environment or assist the poor. It's worth spending a moment on those cases for what they reveal about the Roberts Court.

The takings clause requires government to make "just compensation" whenever it takes private property for public use. When ratified in 1791, the takings clause was understood as applicable when government took title to private property to convert it to a public use. And it was interpreted with a liberality befitting the founders' attachment to public good over private gain. However, in his 1985 book, TAKINGS: PRIVATE PROPERTY AND THE POWER OF EMINENT DOMAIN, Richard Epstein argued that even taxes were a taking unless they were used for taxpayers themselves. His approach would flatly ban public assistance to the poor or indeed anyone.

Epstein's proposal is the only imaginable explanation for a bizarre pair of cases that attempted to use the just compensation clause to deprive legal services programs for the poor of funding through the Interest on Lawyers Trust Accounts systems, known as IOLTA plans. The IOLTA plans created large unified state bank accounts out of funds that pass through attorney's hands but only funds so small, or held so briefly, that the banks would pay no interest at all for the deposits. Unified, however, the accounts generate significant interest. Realizing that, all fifty states created unified funds and used the interest they generated to fund lawyers for people who cannot afford them. Lawyers, as even conservative leaders of the American Bar Association like the then future Justice Lewis Powell understood, were crucial for people to be able to resist efforts to defraud and deprive them of what little they have.

Two cases challenging IOLTA plans reached the Court. Plaintiffs claimed state use of interest on their money violated the takings clause of the Constitution. What made the cases bizarre was that there were no damages, no harm to any individual for which just compensation could be measured and paid. Any deposit large enough to throw off interest separately had to be rejected and would be returned if deposited. Nevertheless, Rehnquist, O'Connor, Scalia, Kennedy, and Thomas agreed that the constitution was violated and remanded the first case to the lower court to assess damages. When a second case raising the issue reached the Court, Justice O'Connor agreed with the liberals that there was no violation because there were no damages.[145] That there were no damages, and therefore no constitutional violation of a duty to pay compensation, made clear the underlying ideological instinct. The votes of Scalia, Kennedy, and Thomas—now on the Roberts Court—that the IOLTA plans had to pay constitutionally required "just compensation" even though there were no damages, made clear that they were fighting against legal efforts to reduce the split between the wealthy few and impoverished many.

Reverse Robin Hood

In addition to Epstein's argument that we have no constitutional right to use government to help each other, it also helps to explore traditionally legal approaches to injury before examining the Roberts Court's conservative economic response.

Tort law, which includes the law of accidents, is an example. Tort law is a legal tool to make people and businesses pay for the damage they do. If a business or anyone else can avoid paying for the damage it does, its balance sheet is very different from the social balance sheet, because the latter includes the injuries and costs. When business can impose costs on others, their profits are larger, and larger profits encourage businesses to do the things that hurt others. When the business balance sheet includes the damage it does, business is more likely to adjust its behavior. Economists call the harm to others externalities—they are external to the business and not taken account of in its transactions. Injuries that escape business balance sheets make goods and services more expensive to society than their price. Economists seek to internalize them. Tort law provides a way to do that by making businesses accept liability and pay for any damage they cause. There are inaccuracies and imperfections, of course, sometimes favoring business and sometimes favoring the injured. On the whole, however, tort law seeks to internalize costs rather than impose them on other people, whether a pedestrian hit by a vehicle, or people whose asthma, allergies, and cleaning costs are affected by pollution. Sometimes tort law is inadequate and other regulatory tools are used. Either way, putting the cost on the people or businesses that can avoid it is one of the major purposes of many of our legal tools.[146]

Externalizing costs changes the distribution of wealth. It allows "sharp practices" to become sources of great wealth at the expense of people behaving in ordinary and responsible ways. It also changes the business climate for everybody because any means of making money encourages others to copy, and companies that successfully externalize their costs can force competitors to match them. Some may be able to resist when selling to special audiences and markets, but consumers are most able to discriminate by price, less able to discriminate on safety, and to an even lesser extent motivated or able to calculate the costs to society as a whole.

Tort law affects those incentives by adjudicating responsibility, instance by instance, so that some of the external costs are brought, piecemeal, into the financial calculus. As companies recalculate their profits in light of their potential liability, they also have incentives to improve their products and practices.

That is one way court decisions affect the extent to which the wealthy reap a larger share of national wealth while leaving the poor less. By supporting or blocking those rules, the Supreme Court affects how much unscrupulous business can dominate our lives like the infamous robber barons of the late nineteenth century.

Courts and the law are, by nature, distributive. People have a notion that markets can be "unregulated" in the sense that law is absent, but that is a misconception. Law answers disputes, favoring one of the parties and abandoning the other. The so-called absence of rules defining obligations is a legal statement that a party is immune from responsibility and can externalize the cost of the damages it does. In consumer matters, that is often the rule of caveat emptor. It is not the absence of law but rather that the law says the buyer is unprotected. Whatever the rules of the market, regardless of whom they favor and whom they abandon, those rules control and distribute the benefits and the burdens of the transactions.

Ronald Coase was a Nobel Prize–winning economist at the University of Chicago. He was admired by all economists, but conservatives think he was one of their own. In a pathbreaking piece, Coase wrote that sometimes the economy will produce the same goods regardless of how the law structures preexisting rights.[147] If it was cheaper for the railroads to put spark catchers on the old steam locomotives than for each farmer along the rails to find ways to deal with fires, then either contracts or lawsuits would eventually lead to spark catchers on engine smokestacks—provided that there are good ways to settle the dispute among all the parties. Coase was quite clear, however, that law controls the distributive consequences by defining preexisting rights and responsibilities. If the railroad had the right to emit sparks and no responsibility for the damage, farmers would have to unite to convince the company to agree to put spark catchers on the engines; but the farmers would probably have to pay the cost to the railroads to convince them to act. If the farmers had the right to be free of sparks from the train engines, they would be able to sue and the railroad would bear the costs. The party without the initial right will end up paying more or suffering injury. Distributive consequences are intrinsic to law.

Courts constantly decide who bears costs or gets benefits and thereby cause big shifts in wealth among the people. At his nomination hearing, Roberts compared judges to umpires calling balls and strikes, but the Roberts Court has reversed numerous distributive decisions of federal and state governments. Where legislation tried to protect the general public, including the poorest and most vulnerable, the Roberts Court has redistributed wealth to the strongest and wealthiest, as we are about to explore.

Monopoly's Minions

One area where the Court has been redistributing wealth is antitrust law. The market fails us where competitors agree among themselves, thereby substituting agreement for competition. Antitrust laws were created to deal with that type of market failure. But the Roberts Court, relying on the market for efficient solutions to social needs, has undercut the antitrust laws, and in doing so, undercuts the market it claims to support.

The Court made its policy preferences clear in 2007. In *Bell Atl. Corp. v. Twombly*,[148] the Court addressed proof of a conspiracy to set prices. Because price fixing is illegal, companies do not say when they've set prices. So plaintiffs start with circumstantial evidence of parallel behavior, and then use legal tools—called "discovery"—to get more information. Judges and juries are usually allowed to infer intentions from behavior. Identical moves close in time suggest an intent to work in concert, in violation of antitrust law. Similar rules permit judges and juries to infer intentions from suspicious behavior in criminal cases, statutory discrimination cases, and many others. Parallel conduct can be ambiguous, but it suggests the companies collaborated. The Court, however, decided that parallel conduct allegations were no longer enough in antitrust complaints. The Court demanded factual allegations that go beyond the inference from circumstantial evidence. Without facts "suggesting agreement, as distinct from identical, independent action [w]e hold that such a complaint should be dismissed." Without inside knowledge, plaintiffs see only external behavior suggestive of a combination. But the Court threw the case out, blocking further factual discovery. The ruling makes it much harder to bring antitrust litigation. Although the case was about what plaintiffs had to say in the complaint, the ruling implies that parallel conduct alone will neither generate an inference nor require that defendants show other reasons for their behavior, arguably making it much easier for industry to fix markets.

The decision reversed decades of decisions interpreting the Federal Rules of Civil Preocedure and the antitrust laws. The Court made its policy concern clear: "it is one thing to be cautious before dismissing an antitrust complaint in advance of discovery"; that would block the plaintiffs from going to trial. But it is "quite another to forget that proceeding to antitrust discovery can be expensive [to the defendants]."[149] As Souter explained:

> That potential expense is obvious enough in the present case: plaintiffs represent a putative class of at least 90 percent of all subscribers to local telephone or high-speed Internet service in the continental United States, in an action

against America's largest telecommunications firms (with many thousands of employees generating reams and gigabytes of business records) for unspecified (if any) instances of antitrust violations that allegedly occurred over a period of seven years.

The new rule would be cheaper for the dominant companies at the expense of weaker competitors. Stevens articulated the distributive consequence: "The transparent policy concern that drives the decision is the interest in protecting antitrust defendants—who in this case are some of the wealthiest corporations in our economy—from the burdens of pretrial discovery."[150]

A month later, the Court delivered its opinion in *Leegin Creative Leather Prods. v. PSKS, Inc.*[151] Since 1911 the rule had been that it was "*per se* illegal under § 1 of the Sherman Act, for a manufacturer to agree with its distributor to set the minimum price the distributor can charge for the manufacturer's goods."[152] Companies could not tell dealers what to charge. That's why we have the "manufacturers' suggested retail prices" label. But the Court decided the per se rule would no longer apply and the "rule of reason" would take its place. Under that rule, the issue is whether the manufacturer has good business grounds to require a specific resale price. If they do, dealers cannot compete to drive the price down, and corporations can come closer to monopoly pricing. Under the "rule of reason," courts would be asked to make individual judgments about whether such restraints are pro- or anticompetitive.

Justice Breyer responded, speaking also for Justices Stevens, Souter, and Ginsburg: "The upshot is, as many economists suggest, sometimes resale price maintenance can prove harmful; sometimes it can bring benefits. . . . But before concluding that courts should consequently apply a rule of reason, I would ask such questions as, how often are harms or benefits likely to occur? How easy is it to separate the beneficial sheep from the antitrust goats?"[153] Breyer responded to his own question, "My own answer is, *not very easily.*"[154]

If Breyer is right, the Court's "rule of reason" will make it much harder and more expensive to stop anticompetitive behavior in court and undermine the antitrust assumption that free competition makes for a better market. Essentially, the "rule of reason" is the Court's device for gutting the antitrust laws—a vague standard that masks significant economic choices behind a veneer of legal language.

No Responsibility While This Court Sits

Preemption is legal language for holdings that federal law leaves no room for state law even though there is no specific conflict. Preemption can leave those injured without any remedy if the courts hold that federal law preempts state law that would impose responsibility on manufacturers and others for the foreseeable effects of their products and practices. The Court has waxed eloquent about the importance of deferring to the states—unless there is an opportunity to throttle state regulation in order to protect large corporations.

A federal statute enacted in 1976 gave the FDA authority to regulate medical devices and barred inconsistent state law.[155] The Supreme Court and lower federal courts had harmonized state and federal law.[156] In 1996, the Rehnquist Court held federal law did not block the application of generic state tort law to the negligent design, manufacturing, and labeling of medical devices.[157] State regulation "with respect to a device" regulated by federal law would be preempted, but generic state law requirements would not be. As the Court put it in 1996, "it is impossible to ignore [Congress's] overarching concern that pre-emption occur only where a particular state requirement threatens to interfere with a specific federal interest."[158] The 1996 decision found it "implausible" that Congress had intended to preempt state law remedies for those injured by defective devices.[159] And the FDA agreed: "FDA product approval and state tort liability usually operate independently, each providing a significant, yet distinct, layer of consumer protection. . . . Preemption of all such claims would result in the loss of a significant layer of consumer protection."[160] The statute was designed to provide additional remedies, not to eliminate them.

The FDA, however, changed its view during the Bush administration,[161] and the Roberts Court's 2008 decision in *Riegel v. Medtronic, Inc.* almost entirely excluded state liability for negligence. The Court decided that the medical device statute excluded not only state law specifically aimed at medical devices but also state common law tort claims that stated a general standard of care broadly applicable to the behavior of almost everyone without regard to the kind of activity.

The Court's opinion was written by Justice Scalia. Consistent with his aversion to legislative history, the opinion states that "the only indication available [to understand congressional motives is] the text of the statute."[162] But the Court wrote that if it were to "speculate," the "text of the statute [] suggests that the solicitude for those injured by FDA-approved devices, which the dissent finds controlling, was overcome in Congress's estimation by solicitude for those who would suffer without new medical devices if juries were allowed to apply the tort law of 50 States to all innovations."[163] In *Riegel*, the Court found the company was not responsible when a Medtronic catheter ruptured in Charles Riegel's coronary artery during heart surgery—it was not the company's problem.

Again in *Bruesewitz v. Wyeth*,[164] the Court eliminated liability for design defects of vaccines by holding that state tort remedies for negligence were preempted by the National Childhood Vaccine Injury Act of 1986. The Act provides: "No vaccine manufacturer shall be liable in a civil action for damages arising from a vaccine-related injury or death associated with the administration of a vaccine . . . if the injury or death resulted from side effects that were unavoidable even though the vaccine was properly prepared and was accompanied by proper directions and warnings."[165] The problem was the word *unavoidable*. The majority said they were unavoidable if they were the unavoidable consequence of the specific design of the vaccine.[166] The dissenting justices argued that injuries were avoidable if a better design had become available.[167] Again the result placed the burden on individual victims and protected the companies.

And in *Pliva v. Mensing*,[168] the Court exempted makers of generic drugs, which account for 75 percent of prescriptions dispensed nationwide, from state law for failing to warn customers about risks associated with their products.

Each of these cases changed existing law in favor of the companies and left those injured to bear the costs of manufacturer error. In each case, the Court's explanation focused narrowly on ambiguous statutory language and treated Congress as trying to protect the companies, not the victims. None of those statutes were adopted at a time when congressional indifference to victims was a likely intention, on the part of either national party.

The Court also cut off liability by those who aid and abet securities fraud. Securities law requires a set of disclosures to purchasers of stocks and other securities. Those who aid and abet securities fraud take actions that make it possible for the corporate issuer to make the misstatements that mislead investors. In a famous opinion early in the twentieth century, when a similar problem arose in tort litigation, then Judge Cardozo held: "If to the element of danger there is added knowledge that the thing will be used by persons other than the purchaser, and used without new tests, then, irrespective of contract, the manufacturer of this thing of danger is under a duty to make it carefully. . . . If he is negligent, where danger is to be foreseen, a liability will follow."[169] The rule he stated in *MacPherson v. Buick,* has been fundamental to American law since. But not, the Roberts Court holds, to securities law.[170] Stoneridge Investment Partners bought Charter Communications stock. Charter, to keep up the price of its stock value, engaged in sham transactions with defendants Scientific-Atlanta and Motorola. But the investors could not sue those companies for participating in sham transactions, the Court announced, because they did not say anything to the buyers of the stock. In an internal battle within the Bush administration, the Treasury Department succeeded in preventing the Securities and Exchange Commission from submitting a brief to the Court. The Court's decision then overruled the SEC.[171]

In 2011, the Court went further, holding that, no matter how extensive their role in producing the false statements, investment advisors and managers cannot be sued for fraud by misled investors because only "the person or entity with ultimate authority over the statement" is the "maker" of the statement and responsible under rule 10b-5. Once again a narrow technical reading of a remedial statute left it toothless.[172] Once again, the Court simply discounted congressional concern for the victims of those manipulations.

Early in the twentieth century, before the securities legislation passed in the 1930s, the financial market was a kind of Wild West. As schemes have become more sophisticated, the Roberts Court has supported those who make such manipulations possible. Stoneridge may have been able to sustain the loss. But the principle extends to all investors.

Kosher Collusion

In mid-June 2007, *Credit Suisse Sec. (USA) LLC v. Billing* responded to a challenge to the way initial public offerings are sold, that is the sale of stocks not previously available to the public. In a decision by Justice Breyer, the Court concluded that sales by teams of underwriters working together made sense. The Court protected them by deciding that the securities laws supersede the antitrust rules, thus blessing collusion among dealers.[173] Only Justice Thomas dissented, arguing that there was no need to "decide whether the securities laws implicitly preclude application of the antitrust laws."[174] Justice Stevens suggested that the challenged practices probably made no difference and would not run afoul of the antitrust laws; and he too thought the collaboration among dealers productive. Thus eight of the justices apparently believed that the seller is entitled to a price that would be ruined by competition—a somewhat odd conclusion for anyone who actually listens to reports of market swings. Stevens objected only to the Court's approach of creating a pass around antitrust considerations.[175]

Why Comply?

In other cases, the Court removed corporate incentives to comply with the law, including the obligation not to be reckless toward others.[176] Justices Scalia, Thomas, and Ginsburg had dissented from decisions holding that the due process clause imposed narrow limits on punitive damages.[177] Punitive damages traditionally took the profits out of—and discouraged people and corporations from—particularly bad behavior. The jury thought such damages well deserved in the case of the infamous Exxon Valdez spill of millions of gallons of crude oil into Prince William Sound after it ran aground on a reef. The Roberts Court decided that a much smaller smack on the hand was all that due process would allow. It restricted punitive damages for the Exxon Valez to no more than the damages awarded to compensate victims for their physical, personal, and financial injuries. In the future, corporations would be able to calculate the cost of ignoring their responsibility to the people around. As the Court put it, the "real problem, it seems, is the stark unpredictability of punitive awards," even though the Court noted that, according to the evidence, juries "show an overall restraint."[178]

The Rest of Us Beware

Consumers beware. Antitrust litigation is fought by business against business. Arbitration law affects everyone. Many of the agreements we are required to sign—for consumer purchases, credit cards, even employment agreements—specify arbitration and provide for the forum and the arbitrators that the seller, charge card company, or employer have chosen. Nominally the agreement binds both sides. But by the choice of forum and decision makers, the likelihood that a contract can be mutually binding can be shifted radically. That is a major reason we are required to sign so many of those agreements. By keeping the cases out of the courts and making it very difficult and prohibitively expensive to hold corporations liable, we end up with rights without remedies, and encourage corporations to thumb their noses at the law.[179]

The Federal Arbitration Act makes arbitration agreements "valid, irrevocable, and enforceable, save upon such grounds as exist at law or in equity for the revocation of any contract."[180] It was passed in 1925 but the decisions of the Roberts Court have given it new and unexpected life. The Court sends all issues in all contracts with an arbitration clause to the arbitrator unless the issue relates solely to the making of the arbitration clause itself. That interpretation largely reads the savings clause out of the statute. The Roberts Court has used it to take abuses, which would otherwise have invalidated contracts, out of the hands of state and federal courts.

In *Buckeye Check Cashing, Inc. v. Cardegna*,[181] the Court decided that if contracts violate state usury laws but also contain an arbitration clause, state courts cannot hold the contracts unenforceable but must send them to arbitration. Although the usury laws applied to any and all contracts, they did not get the benefit of the statutory savings clause. Speaking through Justice

Scalia, the Court held that "the contract's validity is . . . [for] the arbitrator in the first instance."[182] Except to the limited extent that arbitration awards may be subject to review, the decision permits corporations to make an end-run around state restrictions in contracts of adhesion. No doubt arbitration is cheaper in many instances than litigation through the courts, but it also limits the force of state rules in ways that may make the transactions far more oppressive. This is particularly true with respect to contracts of adhesion, that is, standard form contracts of the kind that most people are constantly told to sign for the goods and services they want. Judicial judgments about the terms of such contracts change what corporate lawyers write into standard contracts, so that their companies can evade statutory requirements and shift risks from companies to consumers, or, in the language of economists, externalize the costs of company behavior. *Buckeye* may have added to wealth at the top of the social pyramid, but at the cost of fairness to everyone else. One cannot help but wonder whether recent judicial opinions that weakened state usury laws contributed to the downturn in credit markets because too many borrowers were unable to maintain payments at usurious rates.[183]

The court tightened the rules for class actions and made it easier for companies to do away with class actions entirely by using form contracts in cases involving the nation's largest private employer, Wal-Mart, and its second-largest cell phone company, AT&T Mobility.

In *AT&T Mobility LLC v. Concepcion*,[184] the Court decided that a form waiver defeated California law, which made provisions barring class actions illegal in most consumer contracts involving small sums of money. California had found them *unconscionable*, a legal term for fundamentally unfair. Unconscionable contracts are unenforceable in California as in most states.[185] But the Roberts Court did not give California the benefit of the savings clause. "[Justice Breyer's] dissent claims that class proceedings are necessary to prosecute small-dollar claims that might otherwise slip through the legal system." The Court decided that whether or not class actions are a "desirable" option is "unrelated" to its conclusion that class actions are "a procedure that is inconsistent with the FAA."[186]

Two months after the AT&T case, the Court held that a gender discrimination suit could not be prosecuted against Wal-Mart.[187] The Court decided that differences among the class members did not permit their suing together even though the discrimination they attacked was common to all the women employees. The issue underlying the Court's 5–4 split was how to prove discrimination. The Court has insisted on proof of intent since 1976 in constitutional cases, has interpreted or blocked other statutory methods whenever possible, and has been almost completely unreceptive to statistical, circumstantial, or, indeed, any other proof of discrimination.[188] Showing intentional discrimination in a company with alert legal counsel will prove almost impossible without the statistical evidence that the Court disdains. Since the Wal-Mart case was statutory, the Court could not insist on proof of intention but did the next best thing by effectively demanding individual proof, finding the Wal-Mart claims too different to justify putting them together in a class action. The same solicitude for the corporate employer that shows itself in the arbitration cases reinforced the result in *Wal-Mart*. The decision forces plaintiffs into costly and duplicative individual litigation without the ability to pool resources. Once again the Roberts Court shut the courthouse door in favor of major corporate defendants.

Workers beware. In *14 Penn Plaza*,[189] the Court decided that a union can waive employees' right to sue under antidiscrimination statutes. Employees sue individually when their unions have refused to represent them and may have adverse interests. Indeed the discrimination statutes, which are much more recent than the Federal Arbitration Act, authorize suits against unions.[190] Thus the fact that the arbitration is controlled by the union and the employer presents the employee alleging a statutory discrimination claim, with an arbitration chosen by a judge interested only in the defendants. In earlier decisions, the Supreme Court had concluded that employees could not be compelled to take their discrimination complaints to arbitrators but had a right to the statutory judicial forum.[191] The statute remained unchanged but the Court abandoned those earlier rulings and adopted a policy preference for arbitration. In *14 Penn Plaza* the majority referred to "our current strong endorsement of the federal statutes favoring this method of resolving disputes."[192] As Stevens noted in dissent, "The Court's derision of th[e] 'policy concern' [favoring individual rights] is particularly disingenuous given its subversion of . . . [a prior] holding in the service of an extratextual policy favoring arbitration."[193]

The arbitration cases by themselves do considerable damage to ordinary Americans. But the Court does not stop there. In *Ledbetter v. Goodyear Tire & Rubber Co.*,[194] a 5–4 decision, the Court overruled the "paycheck accrual rule" in discrimination cases. Prior to Lilly Ledbetter's suit, failure to pay women what men were paid for the same work was treated as a continuing violation. Ledbetter asserted that some years prior she was given a smaller raise for an increase of responsibilities than men got. Subsequent raises were based on a percentage of salary. So the original discrimination was multiplied in subsequent raises. None of this was revealed to her, of course. When, years after this had begun, she found out what had happened, she brought suit. But the Court said it was too late. The discriminatory decision was too old to litigate and the subsequent raises were not discriminatory. So Ledbetter had no cause of action. In effect, the majority required people who have been discriminated against in the wages they are paid to sue within half a year of the initial discriminatory paycheck. Justice Ginsburg had experience in discrimination litigation and wrote, in dissent, that it is rare for a plaintiff even to be aware of discrimination at this stage. The result of this reinterpretation of the statute therefore prevents most litigation over pay differentials. Once again the Court sacrificed fairness for a rule that protects employers against litigation. The corporation would benefit but the employees would not until Congress amended the statute.[195]

Barely two weeks later, the Court decided *Long Island Care at Home, Ltd. v. Coke*,[196] a unanimous decision written by Justice Breyer. The decision excluded employees of home health care agencies from coverage under the Fair Labor Standards Act, including minimum wages and overtime. The statute excluded people "employed in domestic service employment to provide companionship services for individuals . . . unable to care for themselves" from coverage.[197] At issue was whether the exclusion of "domestic service" extended to employees employed by third parties, that is, agencies that contracted to provide the services needed. The Court held that the Department of Labor was authorized to exclude this class of workers. It should be noted that the exclusion of domestic service and agricultural labor in the original 1938 statute before the amendment at issue in *Long Island Care at Home* meant that blacks were largely outside the protections of social security, the minimum wage, overtime, and other provisions of the Fair Labor Standards Act, an exclusion that has only partially been remedied over the years since.[198] Despite the unanimity of the Court, the distributive consequences are clear.

The following year, the Court decided in favor of a Chamber of Commerce challenge to a California statute that prohibited state contractors from using state funds "to assist, promote, or deter union organizing."[199] Restrictions on the use of public funds by private organizations are not uncommon. But the Court held that sixty-year-old provisions of the National Labor Relations Act generically protecting the speech rights of labor and management preempted California's effort.

Whistleblowers need to beware of government promises. The Court discouraged people who see that the government is being defrauded from getting that money back for the government. In *Schindler Elevator Corp. v. United States ex rel. Kirk*,[200] the Court refused to let a private litigator reap the reward for helping the government get its due under the False Claims Act. Daniel Kirk had worked for Schindler and had been alert to false claims by the company. To check on his intuition and document the abuse, the Kirks made Freedom of

Information Act (FOIA) requests for documents that should have been filed by the defendant. The absence of the documents they sought for some years and their scarcity in other years, revealed the defendant's failure to provide required opportunities for veterans. Kirk sued on behalf of the government for the value of the noncompliance. The Roberts Court decided that the government FOIA response regarding what documents were on file amounted to a government report. Private litigants are not permitted to claim a share of the amount collected on behalf of the government based on government reports. The Court interpreted the statutory term *report* to include a response to a FOIA request. Because he was relying on the government report, namely, the answers to the FOIA requests, Kirk could not collect a share. Dissenters pointed out in vain that this was Kirk's work, not a report that would have been generated without his effort. Having used a discovery device to back up his belief, he was disqualified. From now on, the government may have to do without the services of private litigants who investigate their claims in official records before filing suit.

* * *

Markets are defined by law. Economists tell us that the benefits of a market economy depend on true competition, protections for participants, effective remedies for breach of contracts, reasonably available information, and a floor of requirements so that the product of the market is not more damaging than beneficial to the community, third parties, and the participants. Law can turn markets into engines of theft or human happiness.

Decisions like *Long Island Care, Ledbetter,* and other class action, antitrust, product liability, and arbitration cases change the way the market works; they also shift resources from ordinary wage-earning individuals to corporate enterprises, and risks toward individuals. All these decisions change the floor on which ordinary people are compensated and the value of their income. Minimum wages, conditions of employment, and consumer protections represent social judgments about the proper distribution of resources. The basic concept is traditionally republican—that resources have to be distributed for republican government to survive and function properly. It is both about the fortunes of those at the minimum and the fortunes of the rest of society, because the economy, like the law, is a seamless web and the bell, inevitably, "tolls for thee."[201] As with the objections that slavery depressed everyone's wages, so also, whatever floor society puts under employment and commercial relations affects everyone, and affects the distribution of resources. For the same reason there is no "natural" level for wages or well-being.

Decisions like *Stoneridge Partners* and *Credit Suisse* assist the movement of profits into finance from other parts of the economy by reducing liability and making it legally easier and potentially more lucrative to sell securities that embody large risks both to the unwary and to society caught in the financial whirlwinds. They contribute to the hollowing out of the American economy by protecting speculation over production and services.[202]

These decisions appear less damaging when looked at individually. In combination, the Roberts Court's rewriting of the rules of the market make it difficult to hold financial and other corporations accountable. The Court claims its decisions were required by clear statutory language. Dissenters saw other meanings closer to congressional intentions. More important, these cases in combination shift the distribution of American wealth further from the people at large as employees and consumers.

Since Lipset's groundbreaking work more than half a century ago, political scientists have been warning us that growing disparity that makes dictatorship more likely and stacks the deck against democracy.[203] As the Court rewrites the rules of the economy, it increases the risks. As its decisions make more people desperate, more people become available for dangerous, nefarious and violent enterprises.[204] As fewer people become more powerful, it becomes easier for the elected branches to ignore the populace in favor of a smaller group of powerful supporters whose loyalty can be bought—the classic opportunity for dictators to shape kleptocratic states for their own and their friends' benefits.[205] As the Court's decisions concentrate wealth they increase the stakes for rich and poor alike, ultimately threatening a showdown over democracy.[206]

Guns and the Roberts Court

In a dramatic pair of rulings, the Roberts Court reversed the Court's prior Second Amendment jurisprudence. The initial decision, addressed regulation by the federal government and the District of Columbia. In *District of Columbia v. Heller*,[207] it upheld an "individual-rights interpretation of the Amendment," to which it gave clear but not unlimited support. It held that the Second Amendment protects weapons "typically possessed by law-abiding citizens for lawful purposes," including "handgun possession in the home" kept "operable for the purpose of immediate self-defense."[208] Addressing public safety, the Court preserved an unspecified "variety of tools for combating" "handgun violence in this country." The second ruling, *McDonald v. City of Chicago*,[209] held "the Second Amendment right is fully applicable to the States."[210]

Although the Court touched on it only briefly, it confirmed the public right to prohibit "private paramilitary organizations,"[211] "bodies of men

[who] associate together as military organizations, or to drill or parade with arms in cities and towns unless authorized by law."[212] Historians and political scientists see great risks for democratic governments in arming their peoples, especially in paramilitary organizations. Public ability to ban and control "private paramilitary organizations" was a significant issue when the Fourteenth Amendment was adopted and for several decades thereafter because of groups like the KKK which preyed on the freedmen for various purposes.[213] And the Court's distinction of the individual rights at issue in *Heller* from the legitimate prohibition of private paramilitary organizations is significant, although the impact may be hard to separate.[214] The Court's decisions seem to have unleashed considerable gun and ammunition purchases, as well as saber rattling at political and other events that go well beyond what the Court protected and seems to have intimidated legislators and government agents.[215]

The Court's focus was individual, on the ability to defend oneself and one's home and family. Battles over the service of warrants at Ruby Ridge and Waco, over rules for use of federal land, bombings like Oklahoma City, and stockpiles of weapons amassed by some of the groups involved, raise the question what those groups, *militias*, and their members, individually and collectively, are entitled to have. Surely they will take advantage of whatever the rest of us are entitled to have. Warrants at Waco were about weapons violations. Keeping the peace is a much more complex problem than telling everyone to defend themselves. Indeed, if Steven Pinker is correct, we owe our longevity to the surrender of arms and interposition of neutral arbiters.[216]

It's not clear whether the Court's Second Amendment decisions have any impact yet on America except ideologically. On the other hand, ideology is not chopped liver. Obviously, the story is to be continued.

The Roberts Court and Federalism

Lawyers and scholars like to talk about whether the Court prefers the states or the nation, is for federalism or against it. The Court itself talks about federalism in only a small portion of the cases in which it has to choose. This Court preempts a great deal of state law which makes it seem nationalistic. But the question here is not whether these nine justices like federalism. We are concerned with their impact on our democracy.

Protecting the Democratic Bargain

What political scientists call a "pacted" constitution, one that embodies an agreement between powerful opponents to submit their futures to a common government,[217] requires a court to stick closely to the language and specific intentions of those who participated in the agreement. Any other reading could jeopardize national unity and democratic government. That need fades as the constitution ages because the specific bargains begin to lose their relevance and new problems arise.

The American Constitution was originally a pacted Constitution, involving significant and necessary bargains between the slave and free sections of the country, among other bargains. As the Civil War approached, the effort to honor the original bargain, or do even more for the proslavery states, turned out to be as ineffective as it was inhumane.[218] The original bargain, particularly those elements affected by the existence of slavery, had no real relevance after the Civil War and the Reconstruction Amendments. And therefore, from the perspective of political science, tight focus on eighteenth century specifics contributes little to the stability of contemporary democracy or unity. If anything, honoring that proslave past may encourage more contemporary violence.

Federalism would have had an important role in keeping the country together under a democratic government in the early years of the Republic. The current conservative majority works from close textual readings of the language as they believe it would originally have been understood two centuries ago, as applied to eighteenth century problems, and then makes analogies to contemporary issues.[219] From the perspective of protecting democratic government, the need to interpret the Constitution that way had waned and other issues and influences became more important by the time of the nationalistic heyday of the Marshall Court.[220]

A Well-Oiled Machine

Federalism can contribute to democracy by making it more efficient. There was a period in the nineteenth century when the Court looked at problems to see whether they could best be resolved at federal, state, or local levels and sent them to the level of government that appeared best able to handle them.[221] From that perspective it could be helpful to understand the division of powers in light of the purpose communicated to the Committee of Detail, to give Congress power to deal with issues beyond the capacity of the states or where the states came into conflict. That perspective on original history has been clearest in dissent on the Roberts Court.[222]

Mutually exclusive authority can make problems unsolvable.[223] They can be structurally unsolvable because state jurisdiction stops at state borders. So, for example, in the Obamacare case, Massachusetts could not keep uninsured patients from other states out of Massachusetts's hospitals.[224] And problems can be politically unsolvable because what even strong majorities want to do at either national or state levels can be impossible at the other. The Roberts Court's approach to the allocation of governmental powers, however, has been textual and conceptual rather than pragmatic. It addresses which level of government has the power without consideration of whether they are or should be frustrating majorities of state or nation. Its version of federalism, therefore, is not about governmental efficiency.

Checks and Balances

Federalism as a check and balance can empower the federal government to limit abusive behavior by the states or local government. The Roberts Court certainly overrules state laws and decisions with some frequency; its role has been to protect corporations from state efforts to curb abuses.[225] Federalism could be employed to empower the states as a staging ground for opposition to federal action.[226] But the unnecessary designation of mutually exclusive authority weakens the states as staging ground for opposition. The Roberts Court preempts state law even when state law supplements national statutes, and had previously been read as consistent with federal law. So, contrary to the history of federal statutes in the medical field, which were written to fill gaps left by the states, the Court concluded that state law treated corporations too harshly and preempted it.[227] The Court bars federal power even when the states argue in favor of the national government. Thus for example, the Court insulated private individuals from federal regulation in *Rapanos* despite state lack of objection.[228] In fact state officials told one of the private developers to cease and desist, objected to the proposal by the other petitioners, and joined thirty-two other states in urging affirmance in favor of federal regulation.[229] Roberts Court federalism certainly functions as a limitation but not as national-state checks and balances.

Local Self-Government

Federalism could maximize local self-government, thereby allowing the people of several states to reach their own solutions. Other than where it conflicts with the needs and desires of a national majority or violates individual rights, local self-government allows people to feel more in control and to tailor policy to their own preferences. But the Roberts Court does not seem to support that goal. It overrode state statutes that made contracts illegal, so that corporate lawyers could block state and federal judges from passing on their companies' illegal, sometimes criminal, practices, and give those cases to company-selected arbitration programs.[230] It decided that states could not stop companies from putting language in ordinary consumer contracts that excluded class actions in the courts, and the Roberts Court then blocked states from requiring the availability of class arbitration in any contract for arbitration.[231] None of those decisions were in support of local government in an area of law that had been governed by state law since the beginning of the republic.

Calming Troubled Waters

The major concern of political scientists with respect to federalism is the possibility that federal boundaries will spark sectional divisions that can tear nations apart.

Federalism can undermine democratic government by geographically intensifying differences, turn them into animosities and provide the basis of separatist movements and civil wars which do a great deal of damage. Conversely, federalism can help consolidate and protect democratic government by working as an escape hatch for tensions that would otherwise destroy the government or the country. It can allow people to come together with a promise of local rule, and often does. As political scientists look at federalism, the problem is that it can easily do either.

It's not clear whether the Court should consider the general fear of sectional antagonisms discussed in the political science literature or attempt to cool down public reaction to its decisions. Disagreement is part of democracy, and for a court to respond to concern about public reactions means, almost by definition, to consider rejecting human rights. Fear of the consequences could just give the courts an excuse to protect fewer rights than they do now. The difference between using federalism as a safety hatch and applying the Bill of Rights—and being more careful about the ways that businesses try to take advantage of the powerless—is that the safety hatch idea is vague, unclear, and largely perverse. Allowing the states to act as escape hatches for the strong feelings on contentious issues could have been used as an argument that federal courts should have declined to get into any of the social issues of the last half century. The most prominent exercise of the effort to use Supreme Court decisions to cool tempers in disputes among the states were the proslavery decisions of the pre–Civil War Supreme Court—hardly an example to be followed.

Nevertheless, as will become clear, the Court does look at the effect of decisions on public tempers and the possibility of violence, at some times more intelligently than others. And one of the quirks of our political system, is that deciding in favor of the states, which would seem to relieve pressure on the nation, makes organizing easier, and thus decisions in favor of state power can actually heat up an issue instead of cooling it down. Social issues are the major area in which passions rise high. The Court addressed both segregation and abortion long before the Roberts Court. Both presented strong moral issues. Plainly federalism and sectional antagonisms are not the only considerations for judicial action.

In the case of segregation, cooling tempers should not have changed the result both because it was morally right and for reasons of national unity. The issue was festering; neglecting this issue made it worse, encouraging violence and considerable sectional strife. Foreign diplomats, visitors, and many Americans avoided the segregated states for both personal and business trips. Despite continuing political divisions between the formerly segregated states and much of the rest of the country, there is good reason to believe that the nation is much more integrated than when the southern states were allowed to maintain their "peculiar institutions."[232]

Even so, the deal struck between Chief Justice Warren and Justice Reed that the Court, in *Brown*, would not require immediate desegregation of the schools, was about inflaming tempers in the North and South and the likelihood of violence. The segregated states were not democracies, most prominently because a large portion of their population was excluded from every aspect of democratic governance. Passions over the issue of race led to Civil War a century earlier. Both the Court and the NAACP did think about the reaction. The NAACP thought about it in planning the lengthy legal campaign that led to *Brown*, and in their internal discussions about whether it was too soon to try to overturn *Plessy*. The Court thought about it in its resistance to overturning *Plessy* until the right time, defined internally by unanimity on the Court and externally by the change in American culture in the years before and after World War II.[232]

As dramatic as *Brown* was, it came at the end of a series of decisions over a period of decades, and the delay before mandating desegregation not only gave the defenders of segregation a chance to organize but also provided the rest of the country with the opportunity, through demonstrations and media coverage, to stare into the heart of racism and unite in determination to fulfill the command of *Brown*.[233] Warren knew what he was doing, although it took the heroics and sacrifice of many to fulfill that part of the dream.

In the contemporary world, the Roberts Court's continuing battle against any deliberate effort to mix students across racial lines cools no serious threat to democracy or national unity. Prohibiting local, voluntary community-wide efforts, as it did in Seattle and Louisville, seems an unlikely path to managing conflict. Conversely, prohibiting efforts to mix the populations preserves the problem, the issue, and the heat in intergroup relations.[234]

The abortion issue is somewhat different. Although it was a hot issue before *Roe v. Wade*, and will continue to be, *Roe* made what had been handled locally into a national issue. Justice Ginsburg has famously argued that the Burger Court should have decided *Roe* much more modestly, just declaring the extreme statute before the Court unconstitutional, and not imposing the three-trimester system that it did. That would have allowed a more liberal system in New York than in Texas, may have resulted in less tension over federal judicial power, and might well have led to the development of more liberal abortion law across the nation.[235]

Justice Ginsburg's suggestion that *Roe* should have been handled in a more minimal way is happening in reverse—the Court announced the right and has been retreating in the way she thought it should advance. Despite criticism of the Warren Court's activism, the Burger Court did not appear to think about how boldly to announce its direction in *Roe v. Wade*.

While *Roe* has remained a national flashpoint, the Rehnquist and Roberts Courts backed the states in most of their efforts to limit abortions. When the Supreme Court rejected a state effort to prohibit an abortion procedure, the federal Partial-Birth Abortion Ban Act of 2003 was enacted to reverse that decision. In *Gonzales v. Carhart*, the Roberts Court backed up Congress's decision. Thus the abortion issue has remained a national one though the states have retained considerable freedom to allow or control abortions.[236]

The changes in the constitutional status of women's rights and sexual orientation took place gradually, more on the model of racial equality. That's not to say that race, sex, and sexual orientation have reached full equality, but there have been significant strides. *Bowers v. Hardwick*, which rejected gay rights, spawned a great deal of national discussion. *Romer v. Evans*, a decade later, addressed only the extremity of not just barring behavior but barring all rights and protections. By the time of *Lawrence v. Texas*, nearly two decades after *Bowers*, the nation had time to prepare itself mentally and philosophically for the change. Marriage remained a flash point but the Court did not address it for another decade while Congress took a conservative position in the Defense of Marriage Act, setting a rule for recognizing marriage with respect to federal benefits and programs.[237]

In *United States v. Windsor*,[238] nearly three decades after *Bowers*, the Court decided that it was unconstitutional to refuse to recognize marriages that were valid under state law. Following that decision, the federal government would honor same-sex marriages that were legal in states where they took place. The

Windsor decision left part of the issue to the states, retaining only the federal implications of state marriages. It's not clear that any resolution would have been either more or less inflammatory, but the involvement of the Court and Congress focused some intersectional anger. That may have contributed to a resolution—there are now national social standards regarding same-sex marriage, just as the nationalization of the issue of segregation in the media, the courts and Congress ultimately led to some national standards regarding race.

One should add that many issues have sectional dimensions, including economic, environmental, and regulatory ones. The Court nationalized the issue of decency several decades ago in pornography decisions that remind the right wing to this day that, from its perspective, the world went mad. The seesaw of decisions about the Establishment Clause also nationalized the role of religion and helped energize the so-called religious right. Conversely, the Roberts Court's deference to the states on the funding of religious education, while important on other grounds, neither raises nor cools any serious anger.

The question is whether any of this matters. By themselves none of these issues raise the kind of threat that political scientists worry about coming from federalism gone awry. None will significantly roil the fabric of the republic. Still, the social issues examined here do tear at the heart of the country, significantly changing our way of life today from the way our parents lived and creating a great deal of heat. Those antagonisms do track geographic divisions, red and blue states, urban and rural, etc. These issues have repeatedly challenged the quality of our democracy, yet we continue to stumble on. Previous chapters explored the trends toward greater inequality, cracks to the melting pot, decline in the social capital it prepares, and the strong hatred and ideology now rallying around the Second Amendment. If these trends continue, the geographic organization of these issues can magnify the risks of rupture.

The Court Matters to the Future of Democracy in America

In each area that political scientists, historians, jurists, and legal scholars, both in the United States and abroad, have identified as crucial to the survival of democracy, the Roberts Court has been leading in the opposite direction. No one decision destroyed democracy the way *Dred Scott* contributed to the Civil War and damaged or destroyed the lives of the generation who fought in that struggle. But collectively, the Court is an influential institution, driving American institutions when those institutions are themselves unable to act.

Alexander Bickel argued that the Court may sometimes produce a better result by avoiding than facing an issue. He argued that the Court should cultivate "passive virtues," that is, ways of avoiding intractable issues.[239] The statute which gave the Court the ability to control its own docket made that somewhat easier since 1925.[240] Bickel did not argue that the Court could never resolve an issue or act to protect democracy. He was clerk to Supreme Court Justice Frankfurter during the Court's deliberations on *Brown v. Board of Education* and wrote a famous study of the intention of the draftsmen of the Fourteenth Amendment, concluding that the amendment did not exclude decisions like *Brown*.[241] In Bickel's view, the appropriateness of exercising judicial power needs to be addressed separately on each issue.

Some like Gerald Rosenberg have gone further than Bickel by questioning the power of the Court to change American life.[242] That claim is global, as the title of his book implies, expectations that the courts can make a large difference is a "HOLLOW HOPE." Rosenberg took on some of the major controversies in which the Court had been involved and argued that none worked. His evidence is that Congress and the Johnson administration did the crucial work. Because of their work, Rosenberg concluded that the courts did not matter.

Rosenberg overstated his case.[243] Because little or nothing happened to desegregate the schools for a decade after *Brown*,[244] when things did change, he argued it was because Congress and the president acted, not the Court. Historians and political scientists who try to quantify the impact of different institutions would certainly treat the actions of the executive and legislative branches as extremely important to what ultimately was achieved. But lawyers and most scholars would also ask a different question: would any of that have happened without the Court?

Rosenberg's allocation of responsibility to the political branches alone treats politics as wholly independent of the Court.[245] Those who lived through the era when the schools were desegregated, however, understood that the Court had changed the debate, the agenda, and the options.[246] What some had treated as the South's problem became illegal, thus adding impetus to the movement to end segregation—swaying some because the Court had declared the law—and making segregation a national problem. Congress was very much affected by the Court's decision.[247]

When Presidents Eisenhower and Kennedy met resistance to the entrance of African Americans in Southern schools and colleges, the country rallied behind enforcing "the law" and ending the mistreatment they now watched on television. President Lyndon Johnson pushed for civil rights legislation in the wake of confrontations over the enforcement of Supreme Court decisions and those of lower courts carrying out its mandates. Court decisions and their enforcement are theater and the drama they put in play added to national readiness to end segregation. The fact that the Court mattered is also evident in the long conservative effort to take over the courts. Rosenberg's specific skepticism about the importance of *Brown* looks wrong as is the general conclusion that courts cannot spawn important changes in society. Rosenberg was certainly correct that the actions of three presidents and Congress were all important—indeed necessary to the extensive desegregation that took place—but their importance does not eliminate the necessity of the Court's actions as well as the importance of the lower federal courts, which acted in reliance on the Supreme Court's directions in *Brown* and subsequent cases.

The impact of *Brown* and desegregation on society is a much more complex issue. There have been major reactions and pushback. It appears that large parts of the country are resegregating.[248] And, as Michelle Alexander demonstrates in her book THE NEW JIM CROW, the criminal process has been abused to profile, discriminate, and incarcerate much of the African American male population grossly out of proportion to their participation in criminal activity as well as out of proportion to the ways white males are treated in similar situations. One result is that a large proportion of black males have been neutered in the competition for jobs, rebalancing opportunities in favor of white Americans and against those who would have been newly empowered African Americans but for the abuse of the criminal system.[249] Alexander is by no means suggesting that *Brown* should have been decided in favor of upholding the old separate but equal doctrine of the 1896 *Plessy* decision. The end of Reconstruction in the courts and the withdrawal of the military from the defeated Confederacy empowered the KKK and other southern racists to terrorize and intimidate the African American population for a century.[250] Black life before *Brown* was no picnic. Nevertheless, she demonstrates that a far larger proportion of the African American community has been incarcerated nationally after *Brown* than before it.[251] That has been a disaster of enormous proportions, diverting some of what should have been the gains of the African American community into prison building, jobs for prison guards, and a large African American underclass.

Efforts to quantify the impact of courts on society in other areas are ongoing. The information available confirms both that courts, like other institutions, sometimes fail to handle situations well and that they frequently have a great deal of influence.[252]

The importance of many of the lines of decisions in areas related to democracy have been repeatedly confirmed even though the long-run impact is always subject to events and evidence yet to be unearthed. Courts have been involved in the issues crucial to American democracy since virtually the founding of the republic.[253] Election issues have constantly made their way into the courts, and decisions about how to count votes have determined elections.[254] Only the possibility that courts might decide those issues in favor of inclusion and equality makes some people question the appropriateness of judicial power.

The Supreme Court voting rights and white primary decisions played a crucial role in improving the quality of American democracy, although later civil rights legislation certainly did much to make those decisions more effective. The Court required and got reapportionment on the one person one vote standard.[255] Many others were involved but Court decisions were crucial in creating the opportunity for the work done by attorneys in the Department of Justice and for the many volunteer civil rights attorneys. The work of the Court was crucial for the organizers who went to courts to enforce the Supreme Court's mandates, and who could encourage others to act by promising that lawyers dedicated to civil rights would back them up in court.

Reapportionment was a failure of state legislatures. Those legislatures had strong political motives not to make changes unless forced because change would imperil the party in power in the state legislatures and the representation of their party's interests in Congress. Since the founding of the republic, reapportionment was sporadic, delayed, grudging, and incomplete. It is impossible to imagine the regular reapportionment after each decennial census that has become customary after the work of the Warren Court without the intervention of the courts.

The courts have always been deeply involved in defining rights to the American economy, and their decisions have been implicated in such major economic events as the housing bubble and the deep recession that began in 2008.[256] The importance of the courts and legal rules in permitting development[257] and sustaining robust markets is assumed in business contexts.[258] The very ordinariness of the Court's economic decisions obscures its impact on the shape of the economy. Litigants spend large sums to get the decisions they want and, as Marc Galanter explained in a classic article, the very fact that large corporations are repeatedly in court allows them to invest in fighting for precedents that have greater value than any individual case.[259] Steering the rewards of the economy away from ordinary Americans and toward those who control large commercial and financial institutions increases the latter's power as well as the stakes.

A common objection is that courts cannot successfully and properly deal with distributive justice, in light of the powerful control by other political actors over distributive issues. Nevertheless, courts matter even with respect to distributive justice.[260] In fact, the role of the courts in shaping the economy has a large impact. They provide one of the important "forms of government regulation, the judicially fashioned common law and state regulatory practices."[261] State and federal courts have helped to shape public discussion of economic issues in their respective jurisdictions by their interpretation of state and federal statutes and constitutions.[262] Courts have an impact by what they forbid or discourage,[263] by what they embolden and legitimate,[264] and by the extremes they allow or encourage.[265] In effect the courts are an important cultural and political institution; although they do not control culture or politics they nevertheless are a powerful force in shaping both.

The Court raises the stakes with its divisive approach to race, schooling, and support for gun rights, which also increases the likelihood of conflict taking a violent turn. All are areas in which longstanding judicial decisions are at the root of current controversies.[266] The Roberts Court's rejection of many of the principles of the Bill of Rights, the Reconstruction Amendments and the structural principles of the Constitution leaves democracy without the safeguards most Americans assume. The internal evidence in each of these areas suggests judicial power: litigants fighting over decisions as if a great deal depends on them; subsequent cases arriving at all levels of the court system addressing the meaning of Supreme Court decisions; and the decisions themselves about the ways that important institutions, public and private, function. And externally we can track levels of compliance and noncompliance in many of these areas, like apportionment and desegregation. Support for the Court's work and compliance with it varies geographically, by segments of the population and the economy and over time. The Court is not omnipotent, but neither is it pathetic in impotence.

To the extent that the Court makes a difference, the Roberts Court's rejection of democratic values is a serious problem. Like many human dynamics, movements can be self-reinforcing, or they may be met by opponents. But clashes over fundamental democratic values are dangerous. Ultimately, the fear of the political scientists and historians who have studied the breakdown of democratic institutions is that as the stakes get too large, people's willingness to stand down peacefully shrinks. The Roberts Court is heading in the wrong direction.

10

Judicial Interpretation for Democracy

The Roberts Court counters what democratic government needs to survive, and counters the American majority, not only by overturning the decisions of the democratically elected branches, but also by obstructing the ways that a democratic people can throw out governments they do not like, entrenching existing officeholders, maximizing government power to control election outcomes, and boosting incentives to overturn democracy by aggravating the gulf between the fortunate few and the powerless many. There are available American traditions and scientific conclusions about how to protect democracy. Roberts, Scalia, Kennedy, Thomas, and Alito consistently treat protecting and promoting democracy as "not my job."

Justices Ginsburg, Breyer, Sotomayor, and Kagan often dissent in these cases, with Justice Breyer writing extensively to argue that it is their job.[1] Other top national courts, explored in chapter 4, have signaled that they take democracy, that is, its perfection and survival, quite seriously. This chapter explores the question whether the U.S. Supreme Court should as well.

In its famous *Carolene Products* footnote, the Supreme Court under Chief Justice Charles Evans Hughes sketched the constitutional importance of democratic process, and the conflict between democracy and discrimination. While the specific formulas in the footnote can be refined and improved, those fundamental insights are crucial to the survival of self-government. The Court under Chief Justices Hughes, Stone, Vinson, and Warren protected rights to speak, worship and vote and treated discrimination as a major scourge on the operation and future of democratic government. They saw violations of due process victimize the same people who suffered discrimination, imprisoning innocent people for the wrong skin, faith, or politics. The Burger Court, somewhat inconsistently, continued their work.

Increasingly, conservatives argued that neither the specific formulas nor the democratic philosophy of *Carolene Products* are implied by the Constitution, or the founders' words, and are not part of American law. The Court rejected the implications of paragraph two in the voting rights, apportionment and gerrymandering decisions described in chapter 9.[2] And it rejected paragraph three in cases regarding race.[3] The Court rejected lines of decision driven by the philosophy of the *Carolene Products* footnote—protections for

BOOK HOUSE
of STUYVESANT PLAZA
(518) 489-4761 // WWW.BHNY.COM

<<>> <<>> <<>> <<>> <<>>

FIERCELY INDEPENDENT SINCE 1975
Use our Bonus Card & earn a 10% discount

```
   513972 Reg 1 7:05 pm 03/24/16
S UNFIT FOR DEMOCRA   1 @  55.00      55.00
SUBTOTAL                              55.00
SALES TAX - 8%                         4.40
TOTAL                                 59.40
VISA PAYMENT                          59.40
Account# XXXXXXXXXXXX7203 Exp Date 0119
Authorization# 01778C
```

I agree to pay the above total amount
according to the card issuer agreement.

Return for refund or store credit within
30 days in new condition with receipt.
Exceptions include special orders, test
   prep, bargain books, sales items,
        magazines & food.

I agree to pay the above total amount
according to the card issuer agreement.

Return for refund or store credit within
30 days in new condition with receipt.
Exceptions include special orders, test
prep, bargain books, sales items,

voters,[4] racial minorities,[5] the wall of separation between church and state,[6] and protections in the criminal process.[7] Conservatives argued the Warren Court imported its own values into the Constitution in those areas.[8] They made the same objection to the Burger Court's *Roe v. Wade*.[9] Liberals respond that judges of all persuasions incorporate their own values into their understanding of the Constitution,[10] and cannot avoid it.[11]

Ultimately the argument is about values. Conservatives argued the Warren Court was too liberal, "coddled" criminals (as if they loved killers and thieves), ignored the needs of law enforcement and the rights of victims. Some specifics look different in retrospect as many conservatives support downsizing prisons, understanding that convicting the innocent is a double problem because it leaves the guilty at large while ruining innocent lives. Nevertheless, conservatives refused to find the values that the Warren Court found in the Constitution, especially the values inherited from *Carolene Products*.[12]

In response to political scientists' descriptions of threats to the future of self-government, conservatives on and off the Supreme Court are poised to answer in the language of a trial: "Objection; irrelevant, immaterial and prejudicial." They approach constitutional interpretation based on what words meant in the eighteenth or nineteenth century when the provisions of the Constitution and Reconstruction Amendments were adopted. Later developments in the science of government—which the draftsmen and ratifiers did not know and could not have had in mind—cannot count.

Contrary to conservative objections, virtually all the interpretive work of American courts, including the Roberts Court, and among American commentators, including conservatives, is driven by the claim that we are and should handle our legal duties as a democracy.[13] In other words, the conservative objection, from inside and outside the Court, is self-contradictory oratory designed to justify decisions motivated by conservative policy views, with a tenuous connection to the document.

The fact that everyone's theory of interpretation is based on democracy implies that courts should protect democracy. To do less is inconsistent and incoherent. That conclusion has enormous implications. The knowledge gained in the past century about the survival and breakdown of democratic government is both relevant and crucial because many areas of law matter for the future survival of American democracy.[14]

That split between democratic rationalizations and the real consequences of the work of the Roberts Court is what drives our examination of constitutional interpretation and indeed the entire book.[15]

Looking at the real world consequences of judicial opinions would have seemed quite natural to Holmes, Brandeis, Cardozo, and lawyers trained in their shadow. The Court has long considered evidence drawn from the social sciences.[16] The controversial issue is the purpose of using that information. Central to what those great justices tried to teach us was to use whatever science helped us accomplish the founders' goals. Primary among those was to protect the democratic republic they bequeathed us.

But after the Warren Court, some on both left and right converged on theories of legal positivism. The left, especially in Congress, looked for justices who would "follow the law," especially the law according to the Warren Court. That bequeathed us the bizarre charade of John Roberts claiming that justices are merely umpires calling balls and strikes. (Growing up in Brooklyn we had little respect for the quality of umps' eyes, criticism now borne out by television cameras.) The positivism of the right came from its attack on the Warren Court's insistence on racial and political equality, respect for religious obligations without governmental interference, and riding herd on the abuses of the system of justice.

The positivism either of precedent or the founders' intentions leaves little room for the insights of other disciplines. Such positivism obscures any need to self-consciously protect American democracy. For most Americans, democracy is defined by the Constitution, a complex, if familiar blend of majority rule with checks and balances, federalism, separation of powers among the branches of government, and the Bill of Rights. All courts need to do is to follow the Constitution and *ipso facto* they will be protecting democracy—but arguments about how to interpret the Constitution reopen the meaning of democracy. Suddenly it is less obvious and quite contested what democracy is or ought to be and how to protect it.

Members of the U.S. Supreme Court are our storytellers in chief. Their story that their conclusions are delivered to them in the Temple of Justice straight from the Constitution is as fabricated as Mark Twain's short story, "The Celebrated Jumping Frog of Calaveras County." But unlike Twain's story, the Court's story seems indispensable to the respect it seeks. Clearly the Constitution and its creators intended the Court to play a significant role. Although modern eyes find it inexplicit, giving the Court jurisdiction for cases "arising under the Constitution" told eighteenth-century readers that this Court would check legislation for constitutionality.[17] So if the important role the founders envisioned for the Court depends on the myth that its opinions come straight from the document, then perhaps the justices have to perpetuate it and the fiction that our law is independent of the study of risks to self-government—in the same spirit that we tell our children stories about Santa Claus and fairy godmothers.

Universal Premise: Democracy Is Central to All Forms of Constitutional Reasoning

According to James McHenry, a Maryland delegate to the Constitutional Convention, "Mrs. Powel [*sic*] of Philadelphia" asked Dr. Franklin whether "we got a republic or a monarchy—A republic, replied the Doctor, if you can keep it."[18] Franklin's challenge is fundamental to constitutional reasoning and interpretation. Can any theory of constitutional reasoning and interpretation that does not take account of our ability to maintain a republican form of government be valid or coherent?[19]

Beginning late in the nineteenth-century, judges and scholars argued about the extent to which courts should defer to Congress. Gradually debate shifted to arguments about how to interpret the Constitution. Judges and scholars have justified their conclusions about what the Constitution means by examining its text, history, structure, precedent, or the consequences of decisions, among other forms of argument. Inevitably they disputed which method was better or more legitimate. Several Supreme Court justices made the issue central to their arguments.[20] Phillip Bobbitt, at the University of Texas, became a principal scholar of the competing approaches to constitutional interpretation. He provided an entertaining overview of who used what methods, and the arguments for and against each. Scholars continue to elaborate and improve on the well-worn ways of thinking about constitutional argument that Bobbitt described. This chapter is built on the justifications for those different forms of constitutional argument, claims about why they are legitimate ways to understand the Constitution. I will canvass, in turn, the arguments Bobbitt described, and some others, for the light they shed on Dr. Franklin's challenge.[21]

All forms of constitutional discourse presuppose that competing methods differ, and that the justification for each do not also justify the other competing methods. That assumption cannot withstand analysis. The same justifications underlie the competing hypotheses.[22] Proper operation of each method requires insights from the others. No method of constitutional discourse can stand alone. All acceptable choices rest on theories of democracy.

Textualism

All interpretation starts with the language of the Constitution. Rehnquist, Scalia, and a legion of conservative scholars have argued that nothing counts except the text and original history.[23] As some liberal writers delved into constitutional history, conservatives took it as a sign of victory and are waxing triumphant, claiming we're all textualists.[24] Of course, trying to understand the text is common ground. The real dispute is about how much the text answers without being supplemented by other methods of analysis.[25] As textualists and their critics all understand, the power of textualism depends on the determinacy of the language of the Constitution, whether we can identify underlying assumptions about how it would be understood, and the inferences we are willing to make from the language.[26]

However, what is the source of our obligation to obey a two-century-old text, let alone nothing but the text? There are very few circumstances in which we are required to honor contracts we did not sign or otherwise agree to, entered into hundreds of years before we were born. Americans are not obligated to support the British Crown regardless of what colonists might have signed. One of the many reasons why slavery was such an abomination was that contracts of purchase and sale among white men supposedly obligated other people and their descendants to serve them in perpetuity. Writings do not legitimate themselves.

The "rule of law" might seem to support obedience to constitutional text, but if that were enough, we would be obligated to serve the Queen, slaves to serve their masters, and to honor contracts that we have learned to reject. The dry legalism of following any contract as written does not reflect the way Americans actually address obedience to constitutional text.[27]

American theories of obedience to constitutional text are rooted in theories of popular sovereignty and democratic government.[28] There is no unanimous way of making that connection.[29] But textual models in this country find their way home to some conception of democracy. The conservatives themselves make that point.[30] We are all shaped by the language of the consent of the governed in the Declaration of Independence, so it is easy for many to jump to a contractual theory of constitutional law in which consent was supplied in the ratification process.

That contractual theory points to the real bite of the textual argument about the proper way to read the text. If the Constitution was a contract among people in 1788, then popular sovereignty combined with the contract theory suggests the words should mean what they did then, if that is possible and we can agree on what counts to define the founders' meaning. Text functions as the agent of democracy when it is followed. Anything else would vary the constitutional text. Historical meaning embodies an original agreement. Such historical approaches to text therefore join "originalism" to textualism— the text should be understood historically. That leads to the discussion of the role of history and original meaning in the next section. The two ideas, textualism and originalism, are closely tied in modern practice.

They are not, however, enough to explain why such "original" consent to the document by a portion of the population in 1788 binds us now. Women and slaves were excluded from the voting population so that even in 1788 the document spoke for considerably less than a majority of the population.[31] There is no clear way that the consent of contemporary Americans can be expressed other than by assumption.[32]

The legitimacy of the Constitution is better based on contemporary justice, a conclusion shared by scholars on both sides of the political spectrum.[33] It could not have withstood that standard before the Reconstruction Amendments eliminated slavery and made provision for the vote of black men and the Nineteenth Amendment made provision for the vote of women. Reality often falls short of constitutional standards but the Constitution now protects fundamental human rights, protections emulated around the globe. One essential part of justice is self-government.[34] Insofar as the Constitution creates a democratic government, it is a legitimate text.

Starting from popular sovereignty, however, supports a different kind of textualism, based on present rather than ancient meaning. That way of thinking makes the people judges of the meaning of the document.[35] Thus political philosophy links textualism and democracy in these two different ways—as proper because it is democratic, and as the expression of popular sovereignty, even though those ideas can lead down different forks of meaning.

Language has consequences for democratic government. Clear and specific provisions are more likely to bind judges to the people's constitutional commands, certainly a plus in drafting.[36] That research supports Justice Scalia's concern that interpretation of nonspecific language in constitutions is hard, contestable, and contested. Those who see in constitutional language a warrant for change are also right, even though their approach is on a collision course with his. Flexibility requires less specific provisions but promotes constitutional endurance, which is also something draftsmen of a democratic constitution should, and did, consider.[37] Justice Scalia's attempt to squeeze the flexibility out of general language is as contestable and contested as the interpretations he opposes. It cannot be otherwise. As he has repeatedly made clear, his own approach is based on his belief that his method constrains judges, rather than on the language itself.[38] Democracy is, after all, a method for reaching conclusions in the face of disagreement. It is important to add that those arguments—about the effects of specificity, flexibility, and constraining judges—are all arguments based on the consequences for democratic government.

Notice the surprising result—textualism does not exist in a vacuum but actually depends on other ways of thinking: democracy, popular sovereignty, and consequentialism.

Historic or Original

Historical methods for understanding the Constitution are also rooted in democracy, popular sovereignty, and ownership of the Constitution.[39] James Madison based his understanding on the compact among the people and with their new government. Madison suggested the ratification process would be the most authoritative source for the original meaning of the Constitution. It was an agreement among the sovereign people; this was their constitution.[40] Discussion leading to ratification reflected some of the people's voices— although numerous voices argued at cross-purposes. Nevertheless, to the extent that it can be compiled and understood, historical meaning is consistent with democratic principles, and can help to settle the meaning of the document.[41]

Originalists differentiate between the intent of those who participated in the drafting and the public meaning of the document to the man in the street in 1788, if indeed the mass of readers actually had specific understandings of the clauses they read that could be ascertained.[42] Either works; fidelity to both intentional and public meaning versions of historicism in constitutional law are based on democratic principles.[43]

Difficulties with historical methodology are not significant to the argument of this chapter or the book, but worth noting. Records of legislative history were not kept before the Philadelphia Convention.[44] At best people sometimes had a generalized awareness of whatever problem led to legislation. Nevertheless, from the first Congress, participants drew on their conflicting memories of why provisions were included or excluded. Madison was still preparing his Notes, our primary record of the Convention, when he died just short of the fiftieth anniversary of his great work—they were first printed soon after. THE FEDERALIST PAPERS, whose authors were personally involved, are brilliant and unique in their thorough exposition. The authors published THE FEDERALIST PAPERS as arguments to encourage ratification, but their eighteenth-century influence, either on people's preferences or their understanding, is questionable. Period dictionaries were rudimentary, written across the Atlantic, or yet to be constructed.[45] In fast-moving discussions, dictionaries are almost necessarily incomplete and lag behind the times.[46] Treatment of the Constitution in the founding generation reflected a multitude of methods. And they certainly did not show the consensus on which so many originalists have built their theories. Plain meaning was one of the competing traditions about how to read legal texts.[47] Original history is enlightening and often persuasive, but it is questionable that it alone can be dispositive.

Popular sovereignty did not cease in 1791. When Madison found that the people disagreed with him about the meaning of the Constitution, even though he participated in writing and ratifying the document, he relented, pointing to the people's right to interpret the document as they chose.[48] Madison thought the first Bank of the United States unconstitutional when proposed in 1791, but as president he signed the bill in 1816 for the Second Bank of the United States. It was the people's constitution, whatever the language may have meant in 1787.

Putting aside flaws in originalist methodology, the central point here is that turning to original history is fundamentally about popular sovereignty, about democracy.

Doctrinal

Precedent is judge-made law and neither liberals nor conservatives have much respect for law made by judicial foes. They attack each other's doctrinal innovations, while justifying their own decisions by citing the other judges they profess to admire. So, in practice, doctrine is a method for interpreting the Constitution, but it is usually under fire.

The modern argument about the legitimacy of judicial review stems from the work of Alexander Bickel, who had been a law clerk to Justice Frankfurter when *Brown v. Board* was under consideration. Bickel became a prominent professor at Yale Law School. In THE LEAST DANGEROUS BRANCH, an influential study of the Supreme Court, Bickel wrote about the "counter-majoritarian difficulty," created by the fact that when courts declare something unconstitutional, they are reversing the work of the elected branches of government.[49] Federal judges and a large portion of the state judiciary are appointed. So when they find something unconstitutional, they are saying no to the people's representatives. That, for Bickel and many of his followers, is undemocratic.

Bickel's argument is influential on both sides of the aisle. Liberals and conservatives differ in their views about how and when the courts should defer to the elected branches. Neither, however, is prepared to do away with judges—this country's first administrative officials—or with judicial review.

Just as Bickel's argument is based on a conception of democracy, the argument about the proper exercise of judicial review also rests on democracy.[50]

An appropriately restrained judiciary is rooted in this concern that it is the people's will, not the Court's, which ultimately should control.[51] Indeed that point was echoed in the Convention when James Wilson spoke of the degree of unconstitutionality which would lead the Court to refuse to support the other branches.[52]

The response of the "judicial process" school of thought is that doctrine reflects a process for accomplishing constitutional intentions. Process controls the independent will of the judges and organizes them in realizing the principles of the document. Reasoning from precedent gives priority to the past over change.[53] That is a strength because judicial process can steer the legal vehicle toward what the Constitution was designed to do. If it does, the judicial process serves as the people's agent.[54]

The judiciary also draws legitimacy from its constitutional charge, which is rooted in popular sovereignty and democracy.[55] Federal judges are removed from direct accountability to the people by the appointment process. But Madison and others continually pointed to the republican principle as the necessary basis of the appointment process.[56] They argued that we could have institutions resting on the shoulders of other institutions if they ultimately rested on the people. As it is, presidents, who nominate, and senators, who confirm judges, are popularly elected.

This argument is not logically reversible. Judicial review is authorized by the Constitutional Convention and the Constitution and thus by democracy. But what the Court does with judicial review is not necessarily consistent with democracy or popular will, hence the counter-majoritarian difficulty. Once again, reaching conclusions about the requirements of the Constitution goes back to democracy, regardless of which side one is on.

Structural

By the structure of the Constitution, American lawyers and jurists mean the *separation of powers* among the president, the Congress, and the courts; *federalism*, the division of powers between the federal and state governments; and *democracy*, the provisions for the election of the executive and legislative branches of government. Philip Bobbitt defined structural arguments as "inferences from the existence of constitutional structures and the relationships that the Constitution ordains among the structures of government."[57]

We make such inferences all the time. In 1819, for one example among legions, Chief Justice John Marshall famously extrapolated from the very fact that the Court was interpreting a Constitution to the latitude of congressional powers: "we must never forget, that it is a constitution we are expounding . . .

a constitution intended to endure for ages to come, and, consequently, to be adapted to the various crises of human affairs."[58] In another famous example, the Court, in 1867, extrapolated from our federal system that we have a right to travel.[59] In 1983, the Burger Court extrapolated from the separation of powers to specific allocations of executive and legislative power.[60] The Rehnquist Court used the fairly limited protections given to the states by the language of the Tenth and Eleventh Amendments to buttress its conception of federalism and a much more expansive notion of states' rights.[61] And, as Justice Breyer put it, democracy "resonates throughout the Constitution."[62]

Structural interpretation benefits from the same insight: it enforces the popular will as expressed in the Constitution. The people created and adopted the Constitution, and the Constitution they adopted includes provisions which structure the ways that government is to work. The Court can do no less than to respect the work and the thinking embodied in those provisions.

Alexander Bickel and Philip Bobbitt have criticized structural argument to the extent that it does not embody permanent protections that are immune to human and judicial will.[63] Structural argument is a weak protection for the popular will expressed in the Constitution. No doctrine, of course, is practically immune to human will. More important here, their criticism reinforces the point that structural arguments are efforts to implement the people's Constitution; they seek to realize and protect it. Once again, the Constitution and arguments about its meaning stand on the back of democracy.

Consequential, Prudential, or Functional

From its earliest days, the Constitution has been understood in light of its presumed purposes, whether national power in *Gibbons*,[64] democratic authority in *McCulloch*,[65] economic progress in *Charles River Bridge*,[66] or, unfortunately, slavery in *Prigg v. Pennsylvania*.[67]

"Compelling government interests" are about consequences dangerous to our country and our democratic society—fighting crime, protecting national security, and similarly important purposes together with the inevitable vacuous interlopers.[68] The Court "balances" constitutional rights against presumably bad consequences. It announces that the government has a "compelling government interest" to avoid that bad consequence. That becomes its explanation for not carrying out constitutional language to the full extent of its logical consequences. Justice Scalia dislikes that approach because of a consequence he claims to find still more devastating, that balancing is vague enough to free the judiciary to act as it pleases.[69] But there has never been a period in the history of the Court in which it has not been concerned with the consequence of its decisions.

Sometimes, instead of the language of balancing, the Court simply defines constitutional language to avoid the problem or ostensibly bases its decisions on the text. But textual decisions incorporate consequences sub rosa. The Court avoids what it does not like, whether through the language of compelling interests or through definitions that miraculously skirt what the justices believe bad. By burying consequences in lexical argument the justices appear to stand against means-ends thought. But any trip to hear an argument at the Court makes plain the obvious—that they are deeply interested in the consequences. The Court's explanation of its decision in *Circuit City v. Adams*, for example, elaborately defined the word *commerce* in two sections of a 1925 statute so that they had opposite meanings and reached a result precisely contrary to the original relation of the two sections of the statute. It makes no sense, of course, until one identifies the majority's purpose to encourage, indeed require, arbitration to the maximum extent possible. The justices buried their purposes behind cascades of language as they often do. They seldom blind themselves, however, to their own purposes.[70]

Instrumental constitutional reasoning flows smoothly from democracy. Consequences can threaten the republic, its democratic system, or any of the people's purposes expressed in their Constitution. Ignoring consequences puts all that at risk. As the Court wrote in a 1963 decision, affirming power to enact a draft and enforce military service, the Constitution "is not a suicide pact."[71] The Court's concern with consequences was based at least in part on protecting American democracy.

Judicial restraint is also based on the consequences of judicial activism for democracy. James Bradley Thayer, a famous nineteenth-century Harvard Law professor, prominent Supreme Court justices, and Alexander Bickel, who provided its most prominent modern statement—all argued the Court should avoid finding legislation unconstitutional because doing so would be undemocratic, or counter-majoritarian.[72] The Constitution says nothing about restraint.[73] The theory of restraint is based, instead, on the consequences of activism, on the risks to the Court and to popular constitutionalism. Consequentialism joins judicial restraint in the pragmatism of Judge Richard Posner, and he too is explicit about their basis in democratic thinking.[74]

Thus both with respect to protecting democracy and to shaping notions of the judicial role, consequentialism in constitutional law often expresses democratic principles and is questionable if it does not.[75]

Ethical or Philosophical

Perhaps the most contentious method of constitutional discourse is ethical or philosophical argument. Many commentators argue that such ideas are unavoidable to make sense of the document.[76] Examining which judges turn to their ethical beliefs is chimerical—they all do. Examining whether they should is equally chimerical—judges cannot help it. More helpful would be criticism directed toward their choice of arguments.

Opponents insist that there are adequate and appropriate methods of constitutional discourse that do not invite moral argument. They express horror at the possible directions moral argument might take, whether to Marxian communism or a Nietzschean superman.[77] Of course most observe the use of moral arguments only in opponents and never in themselves, reflecting a common human lack of self-awareness.

In fact the Constitution is built on the philosophical views current in eighteenth-century America. Democracy remains part of American political philosophy and liberty remains a core American value.[78] Both are proclaimed in the Declaration of Independence, protected in the Bill of Rights, and celebrated by justices on all sides of the spectrum.[79] Of the liberties that mattered to the nation's founding generation, none were as important as self-government.[80] Self-government in turn is central to liberty, equality, and human dignity; it is a part of what has come to be known as *human rights*. Without self-government, the people are subordinated to their masters.[81] To understand our Constitution without democracy as a core component is neither ethical nor coherent. It leaves us insisting on the implications while burying the premise. And it risks a core value of the American way of life.

Even the opponents of ethical or philosophical arguments concede the legitimacy of examining those that influenced the founders, although some, like Justice Scalia, prefer to avoid even that much.[82] Beyond that boundary, other than occasional resort to religious texts, American recourse to ethical and philosophical values has been consistently focused on equality and self-government.[83] Democratic philosophy is part of the Constitution, part of American values, and should have a large place in American law.

Regardless of whether the use of ethical and philosophical models is proper,[84] the crucial point for the argument in this book is that the use of those ideas in the United States draws from democracy. Whatever the merits of the "noninterpretivist" position, or the accuracy of the noninterpretivist label, human rights and any legitimate ethical traditions in this country have democratic underpinnings. They point in the same democratic direction as all the other approaches to constitutional reasoning in use in this country.

Traditional

It should not be a surprise that American traditions are democratic. This is as true among conservatives among whom approved ethics are absorbed into traditions, as among liberals among whom approved traditions are absorbed into ethics. Traditionalism was at the center of much of the work of the Burger Court.[85] For the most part, traditionalism has not been in favor on the Rehnquist and Roberts Courts.[86] Nevertheless members of the Rehnquist Court sometimes defined state rights and state action in terms of traditions of what states do,[87] and Justice Scalia has defined due process as traditional governmental behavior.[88]

Traditionalism does not immediately call popular sovereignty to mind. Tradition could just be efficient, a justification for stare decisis, or respect for what has already been done. But as a practice of constitutional interpretation, as interpreted by Justices Harlan, Powell, and other members of the Court, traditions we should respect are popular, not elite, notions about what the people want to do with their own legal systems, as evidenced by what they have been doing.[89] Like everybody else, traditionalists justify their approach by democratic values, telling us we should respect the popular will as reflected in their traditions.

Ask a democratic people for their traditions and get a democratic response.

Coherence

Philip Bobbitt wrote in 1980: "[N]o sane judge or law professor can be committed solely to one approach. Because there are many facets to a single constitutional problem and . . . many functions performed by a single opinion, the jurist or commentator uses different approaches as a carpenter uses different tools, and often many tools, in a single project."[90] The only argument is among those who would exclude some methods or insist on the absolute priority of others. Conversely decisions are stronger when different methods point in the same direction.

In all forms, the legitimacy of constitutional argument rests on democracy. Democracy drives theories of constitutional reasoning.[91] They are linked by their common justification. Where original historical materials are sufficiently clear or understandable, they are surely appropriate. Structure is the pattern of the text. Doctrine is authorized by its language. Ethical reasoning is unavoidable where the text calls for forms of fairness or justice or the meaning is otherwise tied to ethics. It is unavoidable for the continued legitimacy of the Constitution for a people who did not write and ratify it. To an extent then each method implies the others. There are separate arguments about technique, sources, and appropriate inferences. But arguments about the legitimacy of any of the common practices of constitutional reasoning likely implicate the others, if not all.

This brings us to the major point of this review of the practices of constitutional reasoning—that to argue for one or more methods without arguing for the democratic premise is both incoherent and unjustified, since all are implications of the same ethical source, the imperative of self-government. All sides of the argument about constitutional reasoning treat at least some of the implications of democracy for constitutional argument as true. The implications are treated as true because the premise, democracy, is treated as true. That premise, democracy, is common ground, recognized as morally valid and valuable. For all sides, democracy is a fundamental constitutional value, unless of course some sides are merely feigning attachment. But even that yields an important result, that this country is committed to democracy and its role in constitutional reasoning, regardless of the vagaries of particular commentators.

If judges impose their will on the law, as Justice Scalia and Professor Bickel recognized, then there may be good reason to cabin their discretion, as Justice Scalia constantly demands, but in a democratic direction.

Analogy to Other Structural Protections

So far we have been arguing that democracy is a premise of every approach to constitutional reasoning. It is incoherent to argue for the conclusions while denying the authority of the democratic premise. This section comes at the issue in reverse, from one conclusion to another by parity of reasoning, by analogy. Courts and commentators make structural inferences from constitutional provisions regarding the three branches of the federal government and the relations between the federal and state governments. Constitutional language describing the electoral system should be the basis for democratic implications by parity of reasoning. In both ways, democracy deserves protection.[92]

Federalism is an inference from the existence of different levels of government—national, state and local—and the provision for those relationships in the Constitution itself. Article I, section 8 sets out the powers of the national government. Article I, section 10 restricts state governments. Article IV is known as the states-relations article because it provides some of the rules for the interrelations of states, the admission of new states, and the requirement of republican government. The Tenth Amendment is, as Rehnquist has remarked, literally a truism, and the Eleventh Amendment language is only about federal courts and diversity jurisdiction, but the Court has read them well beyond their language as stating "the spirit" of federalism. These provisions create a set of parallel governments with different responsibilities and limitations. There are no constitutional provisions that define federalism apart from the specifics. The Court infers federalism from all these sources, and then uses and protects it. Whether any or all of the court's inferences are appropriate is not the point; the point is that federalism is an inference from the structure of government set up by the Constitution.[93]

Similarly, the separation of powers is an inference from provisions for Congress in Article I, the executive in Article II, and the Courts in Article III. The Constitution nowhere mentions the separation of powers or provides a rule of construction apart from the specifics.[94] Nevertheless, the Court has concluded that the separation of powers provides a set of principles to be applied in constitutional disputes.[95]

By parity of reasoning, the same should be true for democracy. One of the structures of the Constitution is its democratic character and the electoral process it carefully maps. The Constitution provides how representatives shall be chosen in Article I,[96] how senators will be selected in the Seventeenth Amendment, and the election of the president in Article II[97] and the Twelfth Amendment. It prohibits denying the vote by race, sex, or age for those eighteen or more, and prohibits making the right to vote contingent on paying a poll tax.[98]

Examining the democratic character of the Constitution, Charles Black, in a book well known to professors of constitutional law, explained that principles we treat as flowing from the First Amendment would flow as well from that fundamental democratic structure of the Constitution.[99] Justice Hugo Black insisted that the one-person-per-vote requirement was dictated by the democratic structure of Article I.[100] The Court had generalized the point in *United States v. Carolene Products*.[101]

There is no warrant for honoring the spirit of federalism or the structure of the separation of powers while ignoring the democratic structure of the Constitution. Democracy is a fundamental structure in the text, and, by parity of reasoning, deserves to be treated as such.[102]

Consequentialism and Democracy

To protect democracy requires a look at the consequences of our decisions. I examined consequential interpretation briefly above to make clear that that approach too expresses democratic values. Having found democratic values throughout the interpretive armory, it is time to examine whether consequential interpretation poses special problems. To consider consequences requires us to do more than read the language in the document. There are serious issues to study and judge. Evaluative choices are more obvious when we have to balance constitutional language with its consequences, though all forms of interpretation are riddled with the assumptions judges make that conceal their many choices.[103]

Some positivists and originalists see their mission as avoiding choices. They prefer to see choices as having been made for them so that they can assume the stance of umpires behind the plate, saying, "Don't blame me; I just call 'em as I see 'em." But by ignoring democracy, justices effectively reject it. That is not a moral choice.

Seeing the choices as having all been made has other strange consequences as well. The founders worked hard to develop "government of the people, by the people, and for the people" that "shall not perish from the earth."[104] The founding generation was familiar with the concept, and its use in court, that necessity might require courts to adjust the rules.[105] Alexander Hamilton wrote, "Necessity is admitted in all moral reasonings as an exception to general rules."[106] The founders were students of the science of politics; they expected it to improve, and they expected later generations would better understand the principles of government they were trying to build into the Constitution than they did. To read the language of the Constitution as if all that were excluded, to read it as a frozen text, imputes assumptions to the founders that demeans and would have been anathema to them.[107]

That points to the larger problem. Positivists who look only at the implications of their words, as if their meanings were unchanged over the centuries, have to interpret the law amorally. Positivism does not get around moral choices. That form of positivism means judges choose to act amorally—they are making the choice that they "should" apply rules regardless of the consequences. That is a choice, nonetheless, an unfortunate choice, about moral values.

Neither judges nor commentators actually avoid choices among values. Positivism and originalism has been a veil obscuring the real choices justices make. Kathleen Sullivan made clear long ago that judges claim their arguments opportunistically.[108] At bottom are their values. Whatever their methodological claims, we can discern their values.[109] Values and the consequences they rank are inescapable, as even Chief Justice Rehnquist and Justice Scalia admitted in more candid moments.[110]

The real choice is whether values are frankly discussed and their application subject to direct criticism or hidden behind false claims of modesty.

Other legal cultures are more frank about applicable values. The constitutional courts of countries like Germany and South Africa take it as an obligation to carry the values of their constitutions into their adjudication of other issues, including their development of private law.[111] Some legal cultures describe as "transformative constitutionalism" their use of constitutional values beyond the four corners of the provisions in which they may be explicit or implicit "to [transform] a country's political and social institutions and power relationships in a democratic, participatory, and egalitarian direction."[112]

That said, democratic consequentialism sometimes has surprising conclusions. In new democracies, such as the United States before the Civil War, rigid adherence to text may be justified if it avoids war or a coup.[113] On the other hand, the bold decisions of the John Marshall Court were much more successful at holding the country together than the Taney Court's dedication to the proslavery aspects of the original bargain.[114] Rigidity can do a great deal of damage where the Court sets dynamics in motion that can tear the fibers of democracy.

The Roberts Court has plenty of latitude to protect democracy when and if it chooses to do so. The Supreme Court of the United States is not in the perilous position of the early Court. Chief Justice John Marshall held a federal statute unconstitutional only once, in *Marbury v. Madison*. He had a good political sense of the limits of power. Chief Justice Taney also held a federal statute unconstitutional only once, in *Dred Scott*. The reaction to that decision demonstrated both the error and the weakness of the Court.

But the modern Supreme Court has no such problem in dealing with the requirements of democracy. The Warren Court's reapportionment decisions, for all the lingering objections of Justices Scalia and Thomas, have become a normal part of the political system. The Court's power in the area of campaign finance is manifest. This is not the pre–Civil War Court which had to see whether anyone would obey its dictates regarding the rules of democracy; although there certainly are areas where Court decisions are undoubtedly honored "in the breach," like strictures against government participation in some religious activities.[115]

Judges and justices will be poor scientists, historians, humanists, and interpreters. Perhaps no one is truly neutral. Judges certainly are not. No doubt they will abuse the best guides. They have been doing that for most of the Court's history. But missing the crucial questions will not help.

To put it another way, since we cannot sidestep the question of the values to choose, democracy has a strong claim on us. The country was born proclaiming the right of self-government. The Preamble to the Constitution proclaims the "blessings of liberty" of which the principal one, the revolution-aries claimed, was the franchise.[116] The fundamental value—at the root of all the practices and at the root of the originalists' moral claim—is democracy. There is no excuse for ignoring the consequences for democratic government.

Application of democratic values cannot make the Court less true to the original meaning, purpose, or intent of the Constitution than the Roberts Court's conservative constitutional straitjacket. At bottom, the Roberts Court's call for a jurisprudence of crumbled language amounts to a call to ignore the very values on which this government is founded.

The Meaning of Democracy

There are, however, different versions of democratic theory. On some issues it is not sufficient to say that the Constitution is founded on democratic principles, the modern version of the "republican principle" about which the founders wrote and spoke. That is the expressed view of Justices Thomas, Scalia, and the late Justice Harlan.[117] It will be necessary to resolve, or battle over, what democracy means and how to achieve it.

That may be less of a problem than it first appears. Logic may push the different versions toward a common core, or different versions may appear to be flawed approaches to a central meaning. Pure majoritarianism may not be a contender if it is no more sustainable in fact than it is coherent in theory.[118] And the conflicting definitions of democracy may be less of a problem be-cause the evidence and the sources of breakdown political scientists have un-covered converge toward common conclusions. That has been the case with much of the history of the breakdown of democratic regimes. That has been the argument of this book – that history and modern scientific scholarship push us toward some central understandings of what is necessary to preserve self-government.

Democracy can be understood on continuums from least to most inclusive of the population, and from least to most competitive.[119] A dictatorship is neither inclusive nor competitive. The United States in 1800 was competitive, but women, slaves, and many propertyless whites did not have the franchise. One could therefore define democracy by the objectives of inclusion and competition. Breyer has offered a relatively inclusive and participatory ap-proach to democracy,[120] from which Thomas and Scalia demur, arguing that democracy is too imprecise to be used as a standard for judicial decision mak-ing.[121] Judge Posner, avoiding both positions, has suggested an inclusive but otherwise relatively minimalist definition of democracy based on the work of Joseph Schumpeter.[122]

I have tried to respond to their skepticism by seeking to ascertain what is necessary to keep even a minimalist system of elective government alive.[123] As described in chapter 6, many political scientists would collapse the continuum because less inclusive democracies are fragile and easily succumb to autocracy. Therefore, as described in chapters 1-8, prescriptions to keep elective government alive require a democracy that is based on principles of equality and universality, one that is inclusive and competitive. Keeping elective government alive requires procedural protections for the mechanisms of democracy and for the safety of the people, and it requires a wide distribution of resources among the population, a democracy whose character is shaped by "a broader sense of 'we,'" and one which controls the use of force. These propositions bring us close to the assumptions and efforts of the founding generation of the United States about what it would take to keep their experiment alive.

Some confuse democracy with pure majoritarianism. The original Pennsylvania Constitution of 1776 was a purely majoritarian government; it had virtually no checks or balances at all, lodging all governmental power and authority in a unicameral legislature. But pure majoritarianism collapses easily. The seizure of the Egyptian government by the Muslim Brotherhood demonstrates how easily pure majoritarianism destroys itself—the Brotherhood was elected by a majority and then claimed all the power, including the ability to define the shape of future elections to protect their hold on power. The Egyptian experience also reinforces the conclusion that democracy depends on inclusion; exclusion breeds a reaction to take or hold power or, as in Egypt, both. At the time of writing, the Egyptian military was moving to exclude the Muslim Brotherhood entirely, effectively teaching them that peaceful electoral participation does not work either. That is likely to restore autocracy and enlarge support for violence both in Egypt and, sympathetically, in much of the Muslim world.

Democracy is better understood as including the requisites of ongoing democracy so that no temporal majority can exclude the possibility of being replaced by a different coalition or amalgam of voters.[124] That is the version Americans are intended to have, indeed the version of democracy the founders worked hard to create. It includes protections of the vote, speech, press, assembly, petition, association, and all manner of protections against the abuse of the powers of government for the purpose of terrifying and controlling the population. Logically and functionally that version of democracy is most coherent and durable. It receives the most support from political science and fits well with both American and international traditions of democracy. Just as clearly it excludes mechanisms to weight the votes of some and devalue the votes of others in order to hold on to power.

For those reasons, contrary to the position of Thomas and Scalia, and contrary to the decisions of the Roberts Court, there is a lot in democratic theory and in the science of protecting elective government that have clear implications for which legal rules are consistent with the survival of elective and democratic government.

Majoritarian democracies, minority rule, and minority-respecting democracies cannot always be distinguished in practice because of the power of political shenanigans to shift a small percentage of voters and thus shift the balance of power from a majority to a minority.[125] This was perhaps most obvious in the presidential elections of 1876 and 2000. In 1876 the election was thrown in doubt by allegations of election fraud in Louisiana, although fraud was probably a problem in other states as well. The presidential election for the entire nation depended on the accuracy of the vote totals in Louisiana. Similarly, the 2000 presidential election depended on the accuracy of the vote totals in Florida. Gore had won the popular vote regardless of the Florida totals but a few votes in Florida determined the national presidential election. And if the winning party could then entrench its position with more exclusionary or vote-shifting tactics, future majorities could be effectively disenfranchised. There have been efforts to translate the 2000 presidential election victory into Republican dominance via the exclusion of some voters in subsequent elections.[126] Thus the distinction between majority or minority rule and minority-respecting democracy blurs in actual electoral politics. And courts determine just how much, as they have in the recent series of voting rights decisions.[127] Thus judicial adherence to democratic principles is crucial to the survival of self-government.

The Question of Evidence

Frederick Schauer, a prolific and widely admired constitutional scholar, has argued that whether the judiciary should be involved is separate from the question what the shape of democracy should be.[128] Even if all theories of constitutional reasoning depend on the idea of democracy, it could still be that the courts are lousy interpreters of the democratic spirit of the Constitution, and indeed the evidence in this book and elsewhere certainly supports that claim much of the time.

It is only a partial—and not very satisfactory—response to point out that courts also do poorly as historians, including constitutional historians, and that the courts constantly misunderstand the law as well.[129] The Supreme Court, by constitutional design, is a generalist institution and has all the strengths and weaknesses of generalists. It can take a broad view and see many aspects of problems. But it does not have a specialist's knowledge of most fields, including most areas of law.

It is not clear, however, that Schauer's question about judicial competence presents a realistic option. Courts in the United States have always been involved in and are continuously impacting who can be elected in the United States.[130] Were that question to be considered, it is not clear that there is any way to extract the courts—the line between issues on which the courts should and should not become involved would remain not only as a typical problem of legal line drawing but as outcome determinative between competing factions.

Realistically, the question becomes whether courts would resolve issues that affect democracy better if they ignored democracy or took it seriously. Taking democracy seriously meant, most prominently, ending whites-only political primaries, requiring one-person-one-vote reapportionment so that voters are equally represented in legislatures, and securing the right of African Americans and other racial minorities to vote. My own judgment is that the only period in which the Supreme Court did reasonably well in deciding those issues is the period in which the justices took democracy seriously.

Although the political systems and cultures in countries like Canada, Germany, India, and South Africa differ from American systems and cultures, these countries are broadly democratic; and even though U.S. courts might well reach different answers on particular issues, evidence from the courts in Canada, Germany, India, South Africa, and the European Union suggests that explicit consideration of the future of democracy can usefully inform decisions. Canada, Germany, South Africa, and the European Union have constitutional language that requires courts to look at the consequences for democracy of at least some of their rulings. And each of those courts takes the future of democracy seriously.

A related question is the form in which the courts might consider the evidence. Obviously, where the political science is well established and the conclusions widely shared, this problem is easier to handle. Where the political science is contested, the relevance of political science to law is much more doubtful.

Frye v. United States set the rule dominant from 1923 to 1993, that scientific evidence would be admitted only if "the thing from which the deduction is made ... [is] sufficiently established to have gained general acceptance in the particular field in which it belongs."[131] That changed for the federal courts in 1993 when the Supreme Court decided in *Daubert v. Merrell Dow Pharmaceuticals* that:

[T]he trial judge must determine . . . whether the expert is proposing to testify to (1) scientific knowledge that (2) will assist the trier of fact to understand or determine a fact in issue. This entails a preliminary assessment of whether the reasoning or methodology underlying the testimony is scientifically valid and of whether that reasoning or methodology properly can be applied to the facts in issue.[132]

Under the *Frye* rule the question was general acceptance by people in the field whether or not their judgment had a sound scientific basis. That would make it difficult to introduce material if there were disagreements in the relevant field. Under *Daubert*, general acceptance is no longer required but scientific validity and proper application to the facts are required, although the Court admitted that acceptance might be relevant.[133] *Daubert* implies that courts will deal with contested science but will use rules of science to decide what should be trusted.

David Faigman comments that in *Daubert* the "scientific revolution finally had reached the law."[134] But that is not to say that the information will prove understandable, or usable, by courts. Scientific information is and will continue to be difficult for courts to evaluate.[135]

Part of the problem is judicial unfamiliarity with science. *Daubert* assumed the use of trial testimony to help the courts. John Monahan and Laurens Walker propose that written briefs discussing written papers would be a better substitute: "Courts should place confidence in social science research to the extent that the research (a) has survived the critical review of the scientific community, (b) has used valid research methods, (c) is generalizable to the legal question at issue, and (d) is supported by a body of other research. Finally . . . appellate courts should also not be bound by trial courts' conclusions about empirical research."[136] The Monahan and Walker formulation has the virtue of directing attention to the body of social scientific literature in more carefully stated and well-organized presentations than the testimony of expert witnesses.[137]

A second and less tractable difficulty flows from the preconceptions and lack of preparation of jurists. The current Supreme Court has values that are somewhat inconsistent with where the science presented here would take it. Such dissonance always makes it difficult to communicate accurately.

Despite both difficulties, knowledge should produce better answers than ignorance. Obviously it does not always work. But in general, John Stuart Mill still seems right, that over time, the opportunity to learn leads to better answers.[138]

The Constitution Should Be Interpreted Democratically

A democratic constitution should be interpreted in a democratic way. Voting, civil, political, and equal rights flow directly from a democratic interpretation of the Constitution. The language is there. The actions of the government are at issue. We merely need to interpret it to protect the future of the American republic. And that path has been cleared before.

Social scientists have been pointing the way toward important steps to preserve and protect democratic self-government. The Supreme Court's handling of the economic questions explored in chapter 9, disputes between private parties about their obligations under state or federal law, runs counter to the warnings from social science and was not reasonably required by statute or precedent. The Court simply used its interpretive muscle to suit its patrons. That is a misuse of the constitutional authority of a court in a democracy. Democratic values should inform its conclusions about government behavior, about its own behavior, and about the regulation of private behavior.

Courts in much of the free world treat their constitutions as creating values that should bear on law regulating private transactions. This is known as the direct horizontal effect of the constitution.[139] Those courts treat it as part of their responsibility. In the United States, the Supreme Court has sometimes understood that responsibility, conforming the law of libel to First Amendment values, the law of private remedies to due process values, and the law of property and the law of private political associations to equal protection values.[140] Examples could be multiplied. The issue, as stated in *Shelley v. Kraemer* is the responsibility of the courts. Where the values are important, the court has the responsibility to shape law by those values, balancing private rights and needs as appropriate without losing sight of the courts' democratic responsibilities. It does this not because the private parties are governmental, but because it is government in its judicial authority that prescribes the rules. The Court should handle economic rules in light of constitutional values because it is important to the future of self-government. The Supreme Court is not free to foul the democratic future of the United States to feed the thieves at its feast.

* * *

The major positive development has been gay rights, in which the Court has been part of the national change of heart.[141] The emergence of gay men and lesbian women, as well as of transgendered and bisexual individuals, has made it possible for them to come out of the closet and take active roles in politics. The ability to advocate is a necessary step to make voting power effective. Justice Kennedy has made possible one bright spot on an otherwise exclusionary landscape.

The Court's recent decision overturning parts of the Defense of Marriage Act,[142] however, came one day after the court's decision ending the most effective form of federal supervision of voting rights in the states of the former Confederacy. Based on the evidence at the hearings, the Court likely traded one form of inclusion for another.[143]

* * *

Interpretive methods based on claims of deference to democracy—without a method for protecting democracy—generate law without logic, mind, or soul and reveal the partisanship of the Court. The approach defined in the 1938 *Carolene Products* footnote and elaborated over a half century from the Hughes Court through the early Burger Court is far more positive than the lip service that the Rehnquist and Roberts Courts have paid to democracy while undercutting its foundations.

To protect democracy, constitutional law needs to be able to absorb the insights of science. Failing that, the Court is "counter-majoritarian" in the most fundamental sense—it leaves us defenseless against the enemy within.

NOTES

CHAPTER 1. LEGACIES

1 3 THE RECORDS OF THE FEDERAL CONVENTION OF 1787, at 85 (Yale Univ. Press, Max Farrand, ed. 1966) (hereinafter Farrand).

2 LEONARD L. RICHARDS, SHAYS'S REBELLION: THE AMERICAN REVOLUTION'S FINAL BATTLE 130–32 (Univ. of Pennsylvania Press 2002); Michael Lienesch, *Reinterpreting Rebellion: The Influence of Shays's Rebellion on American Political Thought, in* IN DEBT TO SHAYS: THE BICENTENNIAL OF AN AGRARIAN REBELLION 161 (Univ. Press of Virginia, Robert A. Gross, ed. 1993).

3 CLINTON ROSSITER, SEEDTIME OF THE REPUBLIC: THE ORIGIN OF THE AMERICAN TRADITION OF POLITICAL LIBERTY 41, 44–45 & 122–24 (Harcourt, Brace 1953) (on the mutual impact of faith, commerce and college affiliation); GORDON S. WOOD, CREATION OF THE AMERICAN REPUBLIC, 1776–1787 (Univ. of No. Carolina Press 1969) (on "republican" praise of homogeneity and "federalist" praise for diversity); DONALD S. LUTZ, POPULAR CONSENT AND POPULAR CONTROL: WHIG POLITICAL THEORY IN THE EARLY STATE CONSTITUTIONS (Louisiana State Univ. Press 1980) (same).

4 German, Dutch, French, Spanish, and Native American languages were all locally dominant or exclusive.

5 1 Farrand, *supra* note 1, at 72 (Hamilton, June 1, 1787); *id.* at 134–36 (Madison, June 6, 1787); *id.* at 143; *and see* THE FEDERALIST NO. 10, at 77 (Madison) (New American Library, Clinton Rossiter, ed. 1961).

6 U.S. CONST. art. IV, sec. 2 (on protected citizens); U.S. CONST. art. I, sec. 8, and art. III, sec. 2 (on supported commerce).

7 *See* H. D. FORBES, ETHNIC CONFLICT: COMMERCE, CULTURE, AND THE CONTACT HYPOTHESIS 2 (Yale Univ. Press 1997) (quoting MONTESQUIEU, THE SPIRIT OF THE LAWS [1748]).

8 On the Enlightenment, free will, and religious views, *see* VINCENT BLASI, MILTON'S AREOPAGITICA AND THE MODERN FIRST AMENDMENT 13–19 (Yale Law School occasional papers 1995); Timothy L. Hall, *Roger Williams and the Foundations of Religious Liberty,* 71 B.U. L. REV. 455, 490–91 (1991); JOHN LOCKE, *A Letter Concerning Toleration, in* TREATISE OF CIVIL GOVERNMENT AND A LETTER CONCERNING TOLERATION 173 & 192 (Appleton, Charles L. Sherman, ed. 1965).

On the theology of religious choice, *see* Charles Teague, *Freedom of Religion: The Freedom to Draw Circles, in* RELIGIOUS TRADITIONS AND THE LIMITS OF

TOLERANCE 18 (Anima Books, Louis J. Hammann and Harry M. Buck, eds. 1988); Scott W. Gustafson, *The Scandal of Particularity and the Universality of Grace, in id.* at 28; ROSSITER, *supra* note 3, at 40 & 54; Midrash Rabbah–Leviticus III:2 and particularly footnote 8; Babylonian Talmud, Sanhedrin 56a; *and see* Ali S. Asani, *On Pluralism, Intolerance, and the Quran,* 71 THE AMERICAN SCHOLAR 52–60 (2002), http://www.twf.org/Library/Pluralism.html.

9 7 Alexander Hamilton, *Report on the Bank, in* THE PAPERS OF ALEXANDER HAMILTON, 1790–1791, at 340–41 (Columbia Univ. Press, Harold C. Syrett, ed. 1963).

10 *Id.* For belief in import of "stake" in society, *see id.* at 68–69; 1 Farrand, *supra* note 1, at 138 (June 6, 1787, Madison).

11 U.S. CONST. art. I, sec. 2, cl. 1. On congressional control of the president, *see* U.S. CONST., art. I, sec. 7, sec. 8 cl. 18, sec. 9, cl. 6; art. II, sec. 2, cl. 2, sec. 3. On the judicial power, *see* U.S. CONST., art. III, sec. 2, par. 1. On the stakes of the bargain for a bicameral Congress, *see* Staughton Lynd, *The Compromise of 1787,* 81 POL. SCI. Q. 225–50 (1966) (though specific hypothesized meeting probably did not happen). *See also* Calvin C. Jillson, *The Representation Question in the Federal Convention of 1787: Madison's Virginia Plan and its Opponents,* 8 CONGRESSIONAL STUDIES 21 (1981). Washington grew to oppose slavery and freed his slaves in his will.

12 *See* THE FEDERALIST NO. 10, *supra* note 5, at 80–81 (James Madison).

13 *Id.,* NO. 51 (Madison).

14 CHARLES L. BLACK, STRUCTURE AND RELATIONSHIP IN CONSTITUTIONAL LAW (1969) (Ox Bow Press 2000). Wesberry v. Sanders, 376 U.S. 1 (1964) (per Justice Black); Bolling v. Sharpe, 347 U.S. 497 (1954) (equal protection principle to the federal government). On need for more than mere "parchment barriers," *see* THE FEDERALIST NO. 25, *supra* note 5 at 167 (Hamilton); THE FEDERALIST NO. 48, *id.* at 308 (James Madison); 2 Farrand, *supra* note 1, at 77 (Madison, July 21, 1787). The definition of democracy is addressed above and in chapters three, four and five; see also an influential definition in "Methodology Fact Sheet" for "Freedom in the World 2014" (Freedom House annual report, 41st ed.), http://www.freedomhouse.org/report/methodology-fact-sheet#.UusGwJoo4qQ.

15 WOOD, *supra* note 3.

16 *Compare* Chavez v. Martinez, 538 U.S. 760, 766–767 (2003) (Thomas, J., plurality opinion) with *id.* at 779–80 (Souter, J., in this portion for the Court), *Id.* at 783 (Stevens, J., dissenting in part), *id.* at 789 (Kennedy, J., dissenting in part), and *id.* at 799 (Ginsburg, J., dissenting in part).

17 WOOD, *supra* note 3, 538–543; ROSSITER, *supra* note 3.

18 AKHIL REED AMAR, THE BILL OF RIGHTS: CREATION AND RECONSTRUCTION xii (Yale Univ. Press 1998).

19 *But see* Stephen E. Gottlieb, *The Dilemma of Election Campaign Finance Reform,* 18 HOFSTRA L. REV. 213 (1989).

20 *See* JACK P. GREENE, PERIPHERIES AND CENTER: CONSTITUTIONAL DEVELOPMENT IN THE EXTENDED POLITIES OF THE BRITISH EMPIRE AND

THE UNITED STATES, 1607–1788, at 8, 10, 23 and *passim* (Univ. of Georgia Press 1986) (on the problem of distance under the British Crown).

21 2 Farrand, *supra* note 1, at 131–32.

22 *See id.,* vol. 1, at 346 (Mason, June 20, 1787); *id.* at 414 and 417 (Ellsworth, June 25, 1787); *id.,* vol. 2, at 326 (Mason, Aug. 18, 1787); *id.* at 388 (Madison, Aug. 23, 1787); *id.* at 329 (Gerry, Aug. 18, 1787); *id.* at 509 (Gerry, Sept. 5, 1787); *id.* at 563 (Randolph, Sept. 10, 1787); *id.* at 616–17 (Mason, Madison, Morris, Pinkney and Bedford, Sept. 14, 1787); *id.* at 640 (Mason); *Id.,* vol. 3, at 129 (Charles Pinkney); *id.* at 157, 158 (Luther Martin, Nov. 29, 1787); Luther Martin's "Letter to the Citizens of Maryland", Mar. 25, 1788, in *id.* at 295; *id.* at 319 (Madison and Randolph, June 14, 1788); Gouverneur Morris to Moss Kent, Jan. 12, 1815, *in id.* at 421; *id.* at 453 (Madison, 1821); SUPPLEMENT TO MAX FARRAND'S THE RECORDS OF THE FEDERAL CONVENTION OF 1787, at 92 (Yale Univ. Press, James Hutson, ed. 1987) (hereinafter Hutson) (Hamilton, June 18, 1787).

23 2 Farrand, *supra* note 1, at 329; Hutson, *supra* note 22, at 229.

24 Art. I, secs. 8 & 11. *See also* Lugar v. Edmondson Oil Co., 457 U.S. 922 (1982) Norwood v. Harrison, 413 U.S. 455, 465 (1973) (government may not encourage private parties to do what it cannot, unconstitutional action).

25 Samuel Adams, *Excerpt from Governor Samuel Adams's Farewell Address, 1797, in* THE MILITARY IN AMERICA FROM THE COLONIAL ERA TO THE PRESENT 107–08 (Free Press, Peter Karsten, ed., rev. ed. 1986); *see also* RUSSELL F. WEIGLEY, HISTORY OF THE UNITED STATES ARMY 3–12 (Macmillan 1967).

26 William B. Skelton, *Officers and Politicians: The Origins of Army Politics in the United States before the Civil War,* in MILITARY IN AMERICA, *supra* note 25, at 113. On exceptions to the Army's apolitical role, *See, e.g.,* Richard H. Kohn, *The Inside History of the Newburgh Conspiracy: American and the Coup d'Etat, in id.* at 79; Harold M. Hyman, *Johnson, Stanton, and Grant: A Reconsideration of the Army's Role in the Events Leading to Impeachment, in id.* at 177; Mary R. Dearing, *The Role of the G.A.R. in the Constitutional Crisis of 1867–1868, in id.* at 191.

27 2 Farrand, *supra* note 1, at 202–03 (Aug. 7, 1787).

28 Property qualifications would now tilt politics toward wealth, *see* Quinn v. Millsap, 491 U.S. 95, 104 (1989); Phoenix v. Kolodziejski, 399 U.S. 204 (1970); Kramer v. Union Free School Dist., 395 U.S. 621 (1969); *but see* Ball v. James, 451 U.S. 355 (1981); Salyer Land Co. v. Tulare Lake Basin Water Storage Dist., 410 U.S. 719 (1973). But in the eighteenth century, property qualifications protected voters' independence and were often used to democratize the vote, *see* THOMAS JEFFERSON, NOTES ON THE STATE OF VIRGINIA 164–65 & 292 (Univ. of North Carolina Press, William Peden, ed. 1955) (1787); *see also* Linda A. Malone, *Reflections on the Jeffersonian Ideal of an Agrarian Democracy and the Emergence of an Agricultural and Environmental Ethic in the 1990 Farm Bill,* 12 STAN. ENVTL. L.J. 3, at 5 (1995); LANCE BANNING, JEFFERSON AND MADISON: THREE CONVERSATIONS FROM THE FOUNDING 43–44 (Madison House Publishers 1995).

29 James Madison, National Gazette, Jan. 23, 1792, quoted in 3 IRVING BRANT, JAMES MADISON: FATHER OF THE CONSTITUTION, 1787–1800, at 175 (Bobbs-Merrill 1950).

30 *See* BRANT, *supra* note 29, at 174–76; William M. Treanor, *The Original Understanding of the Takings Clause and the Political Process*, 95 COLUM. L. REV. 782, 844–48 (1995); THE FEDERALIST NO. 47, *supra* note 5, at 301 (Madison).

31 PETER ONUF, STATEHOOD AND UNION: A HISTORY OF THE NORTHWEST ORDINANCE 33 (Indiana Univ. Press 1987). Peter S. Onuf, *Liberty, Development, and Union: Visions of the West in the 1780s*, 43 WM. & M. Q. 179, 190 (1986). Elizabeth V. Mensch, *The Colonial Origins of Liberal Property Rights*, 31 BUFF. L. REV. 635, 636, 641–60, 671–78 (1983). JAMES HARRINGTON, JAMES HARRINGTON'S OCEANA 15, 16 (1656) (Hyperion Press, S. B. Liljegren, ed. 1979) (*italics* in original), urged broad land distribution so that "no one man, or number of men, within the compasse of the *Few* or *Aristocracy*, overbalance them."

32 Madison, National Gazette, *supra* note 29; *and see, e.g.*, U.S. CONST., art. I, sec. 2, par. 3; art. I, sec. 9, par. 2–4, par. 8; art. IV, sec. 2, par. 1; art. IV, sec. 4.

33 Act of Aug. 7, 1789, ch. 8, 1 Stat. 50 (reenacting the Northwest Territory Ordinance of 1787), collected in 1 SOURCES AND DOCUMENTS OF UNITED STATES CONSTITUTIONS, 2d ser. 385 (Oceana Publications, William F. Swindler, ed. 1982).

34 2 Farrand, *supra* note 1, 344; *and see* WOOD, *supra* note 3, 107–24 (on aversion to British officeholders' pomp as a source of the Revolution).

35 Steven Boyd, *The Contract Clause and the Evolution of American Federalism, 1789–1815*, 44 WM. & M. Q. 529–48 (1987).

36 U.S. CONST., art. I, sec. 9, cl. 8 (prohibiting titles of nobility); *Id.* cl. 1 (slave trade); art. I, sec. 8, cl. 8 (limited duration of patents and copyrights); *Id.* sec. 8, cl. 1 and sec. 9, cls. 4, 6 (same treatment of states); sec. 9, cl. 2–4 (protections for individuals); *and see* sec. 10, cl. 1. On changes in the common law, *see* WILLIAM EDWARD NELSON, AMERICANIZATION OF THE COMMON LAW: THE IMPACT OF LEGAL CHANGE ON MASSACHUSETTS SOCIETY, 1760–1830, at 48 (Harvard Univ. Press 1975); LAWRENCE M. FRIEDMAN, A HISTORY OF AMERICAN LAW 205–15 (Simon & Shuster 1973); Mensch, *supra* note 31.

37 Homestead Act, 12 Stat. 392 (1862). For a brief description see PAUL W. GATES, HISTORY OF PUBLIC LAND LAW DEVELOPMENT 393–94 (Arno Press 1979).

38 CHILTON WILLIAMSON, AMERICAN SUFFRAGE: FROM PROPERTY TO DEMOCRACY, 1760–1860 (Princeton Univ. Press 1960), the classic study looking behind the rules at actual practices. For more recent work, *see* ROBERT J. DINKIN, VOTING IN REVOLUTIONARY AMERICA: A STUDY OF ELECTIONS IN THE ORIGINAL THIRTEEN STATES, 1776–1789, at 30–43 (Greenwood Press 1982); Alexander Keyssar, THE RIGHT TO VOTE: THE CONTESTED HISTORY OF DEMOCRACY IN THE UNITED STATES 24 (Basic Books 2000); and RICHARD R. BEEMAN, THE VARIETIES OF POLITICAL EXPERIENCE IN EIGHTEENTH CENTURY AMERICA *passim* (U. Penn. Press 2004) and *id.* at 281 (disappearance of property qualifications).

39 *See* DAVID BICKNELL TRUMAN, THE GOVERNMENTAL PROCESS: POLITICAL INTERESTS AND PUBLIC OPINION (Knopf 1951); ROBERT A. DAHL, A PREFACE TO DEMOCRATIC THEORY (Univ. of Chicago Press 1956), and ROBERT A. DAHL, WHO GOVERNS (Yale Univ. Press 1961).

40 WOOD, *supra* note 3, at 61–64.

41 On frequent reference to "genius of the people" as preference, culture, or talent, *see, e.g.,* 1 Farrand, *supra* note 1, at 66 (Randolph, June 1, 1787). Delegates reserved the term *democratic* for direct democracy, excluding representative government. Conforming to modern usage, *democracy* is used here for representative democracy.

42 Peter S. Onuf, *State Politics and Republican Virtue: Religion, Education, and Morality in Early American Federalism, in* TOWARD A USABLE PAST: LIBERTY UNDER STATE CONSTITUTIONS 91–116 (Univ. of Georgia Press, Paul Finkelman and Stephen E. Gottlieb, eds. 1991); *see also* James A. Henretta, *The Rise and Decline of "Democratic-Republicanism": Political Rights in New York and the Several States, 1800–1915, in Id.* at 50–90.

43 *See* Onuf, *supra* note 42, at 91–111; Thomas James, *Rights of Conscience and State School Systems in Nineteenth-Century America, in* TOWARD A USABLE PAST, *supra* note 42, at 122.

44 *See* LAWRENCE A. CREMIN, AMERICAN EDUCATION; THE COLONIAL EXPERIENCE, 1607–1783, at 102–04 (Harper & Row 1970).

45 For a brief description, *see* Stephen E. Gottlieb, Brown v. Board of Education *and the Application of American Tradition to Racial Division* 34 SUFFOLK U. L. REV. 281, 292–96 (2001); for more extensive treatment *see* STEPHEN MEYER III, THE FIVE-DOLLAR DAY: LABOR MANAGEMENT AND SOCIAL CONTROL IN THE FORD MOTOR COMPANY, 1908–1921, at 156 (State Univ. of New York Press 1981); Gary Gerstle, *Liberty, Coercion, and the Making of Americans* 84 J. AMER. HIST. 524 (1997); Bruce White, *The American Military and the Melting Pot in World War I, in* MILITARY IN AMERICA, *supra* note 25, at 317–23.

46 On public school texts, *see* FRANCES FITZGERALD, AMERICA REVISED: HISTORY SCHOOLBOOKS IN THE TWENTIETH CENTURY (Little, Brown 1979). *See also* LAWRENCE A. CREMIN, TRANSFORMATION OF THE SCHOOL: PROGRESSIVISM IN AMERICAN EDUCATION 1876–1957 (Vintage Books 1961); MEYER, *supra* note 45; DAVID TYACK AND ELISABETH HANSOT, LEARNING TOGETHER: A HISTORY OF COEDUCATION IN AMERICAN SCHOOLS (Yale Univ. Press 1990); Gerstle, *supra* note 45. On "Americanization" and integration of class, gender, ethnic groups, and race, *see* Gottlieb, *supra* note 45.

47 ALEXIS DE TOCQUEVILLE, DEMOCRACY IN AMERICA (Knopf 1945, Phillips Bradley ed., Henry Reeve trans., Francis Bowen rev. 1836).

48 *See* TATU VANHANEN, THE EMERGENCE OF DEMOCRACY: A COMPARATIVE STUDY OF 119 STATES, 1850–1979, at 35 (Finnish Society of Sciences and Letters [Societas Scientiarum Fennica], 1984), citing 1 TOCQUEVILLE, *supra* note 47, 46–54, 288–298, *and see id.* vol. 2, bk. 4, ch. 1, at 287–88; *see also* ROBERT A. DAHL, A PREFACE TO ECONOMIC DEMOCRACY 10 (Univ. of California Press 1985).

49 Discussed in DAHL, PREFACE TO DEMOCRATIC THEORY, *supra* note 39, at 10 & 45–49.

50 THOMAS JEFFERSON, *Notes on the Letter of Christoph Daniel Ebeling* [after Oct. 15, 1795], *in* 28 THE PAPERS OF THOMAS JEFFERSON 509 (Princeton Univ. Press, John Catanzariti, ed. 2000).

51 On nineteenth-century parties and elections, *see* Stephen E. Gottlieb, *Rebuilding the Right of Association: The Right to Hold a Convention as a Test Case*, 11 HOFSTRA L. REV. 191, 196–203, 221–30 & 238–43 (1983).

52 *See* Nigel Anthony Summers, *Treasonous Tenant Farmers and Seditious Share Croppers: The 1917 Green Corn Rebellion Trials*, 27 OKLA. CITY U. L. REV. 1097, 1105–06 (2002); Thomas J. Humphrey, *Conflicting Independence: Land Tenancy and the American Revolution*, 28 J. EARLY REPUBLIC 159 (2008); STAUGHTON LYND, CLASS CONFLICT, SLAVERY, AND THE CONSTITUTION 25–77 (Bobbs-Merrill 1967) was the groundbreaking study.

53 Quoted in DAHL, PREFACE TO ECONOMIC DEMOCRACY, *supra* note 48 at 66.

54 PAUL FINKELMAN, DEFENDING SLAVERY: PROSLAVERY THOUGHT IN THE OLD SOUTH: A BRIEF HISTORY WITH DOCUMENTS 28 (Bedford/St. Martin's 2003); Fisher's Negroes v. Dabbs, 14 Tenn. 119 (1834); *and see* THOMAS R. R. COBB, AN INQUIRY INTO THE LAW OF NEGRO SLAVERY IN THE UNITED STATES OF AMERICA TO WHICH IS PREFIXED AN HISTORICAL SKETCH OF SLAVERY ccxvii–ccxviii (1858) (Univ. of Georgia Press, Paul Finkelman, ed. 1999).

55 *See* Gottlieb, *supra* note 45, at 288–89.

56 *See* WILLIAM E. NELSON, *MARBURY V. MADISON*: THE ORIGINS AND LEGACY OF JUDICIAL REVIEW (Univ. Press of Kansas 2000).

57 JAMES W. CEASER, PRESIDENTIAL SELECTION: THEORY AND DEVELOPMENT 123–69 (Princeton Univ. Press 1979).

58 MANCUR OLSON, THE LOGIC OF COLLECTIVE ACTION: PUBLIC GOODS AND THE THEORY OF GROUPS (Harvard Univ. Press 1965). THE FEDERALIST NO. 51, *supra* note 5 (Madison). On parties, *see* ALFRED STEINBERG, THE BOSSES (New York, Macmillan 1972); JOSEPH PRATT HARRIS, ELECTION ADMINISTRATION IN THE UNITED STATES (Brookings Institution 1934); FREDERICK WILLIAM DALLINGER, NOMINATIONS FOR ELECTIVE OFFICE IN THE UNITED STATES (Arno Press 1974) (1897); and *see* Gottlieb, *supra* note 51, at 225–27 (1982).

59 MARK TWAIN AND CHARLES DUDLEY WARNER, THE GILDED AGE: A TALE OF TODAY (American Pub. Co. 1873) named the era. HARRY CAUDILL, NIGHT COMES TO THE CUMBERLANDS (Little, Brown 1964).

60 ROBERT M. BASTRESS, THE WEST VIRGINIA STATE CONSTITUTION: A REFERENCE GUIDE 23 & 114 (Greenwood Press 1995).

61 Child Labor Tax Case [Bailey v. Drexel Furniture Company], 259 U.S. 20 (1922); Hammer v. Dagenhart, 247 U.S. 251 (1918). Marquette Nat'l Bank v. First of Omaha Service Corp., 439 U.S. 299 (1978) is a modern example of cross-border barriers to enforcement of state policy.

62 Sherman Act, 15 U.S.C. 1 as amended; originally enacted July 2, 1890, 51 Cong. ch. 647; 26 Stat. 209, codified at 15 U.S.C. secs. 1–7 as amended (2000). *See also* Clayton Act, Act of Oct. 15, 1914, 63 P.L. 212, 63 Cong. ch 323, 38 Stat. 730 codified at 15 U.S.C. 12–27 as amended; Brown v. Pro Football, 518 U.S. 231, 253 (1996) (Stevens, J., dissenting).

63 *See, e.g.,* LOUIS DEMBITZ BRANDEIS, THE CURSE OF BIGNESS; MISCELLANEOUS PAPERS OF LOUIS D. BRANDEIS (Kennikat Press, Osmond K. Fraenkel, ed. 1965) (1934); LOUIS DEMBITZ BRANDEIS, OTHER PEOPLE'S MONEY, AND HOW THE BANKERS USE IT (Martino Pub. 2009) (1914).

64 RICHARD HOFSTADTER, *What Happened to the Antitrust Movement?, in* THE PARANOID STYLE IN AMERICAN POLITICS AND OTHER ESSAYS 188–273 (1964) (Harvard Univ. Press 1996); THE AUTOBIOGRAPHY OF THEODORE ROOSEVELT, CONDENSED FROM THE ORIGINAL EDITION, SUPPLEMENTED BY LETTERS, SPEECHES, AND OTHER WRITINGS 246–27 (Charles Scribner's Sons, Wayne Andrews, ed. 1958) (1913), *available at* http://www.presidentialrhetoric.com/historic-speeches/roosevelt_theodore/muckrake.html; THEODORE ROOSEVELT, THEODORE ROOSEVELT: AN AUTOBIOGRAPHY 449–60 (Charles Scribner's Sons 1925); Letter from Theodore Roosevelt to Jacob August Riis (Apr. 18, 1906), *in* 5 THEODORE ROOSEVELT, THE LETTERS OF THEODORE ROOSEVELT 212–13 (Harvard Univ. Press, Elting E. Morison, ed. 1952); Letter from Theodore Roosevelt to William Plumer Potter (Apr. 23, 1906) and to Lyman Abbott (Apr. 23, 1906), *in id.* at 216–219.

65 *Cf.* pre- and post-1937 decisions: Adkins v. Children's Hospital, 261 U.S. 525 (1923); Bailey v. Drexel Furniture Co., 259 U.S. 20 (1922); Schechter Poultry Corp. v. United States, 295 U.S. 495 (1935); United States v. Butler, 297 U.S. 1 (1936); Carter v. Carter Coal Co., 298 U.S. 238 (1936); West Coast Hotel v. Parrish, 300 U.S. 379 (1937); Steward Machine Co. v. Davis, 301 U.S. 548 (1937); National Labor Relations Board v. Jones & Laughlin Steel Corporation, 301 U.S. 1 (1937); Wickard v. Filburn, 317 U.S. 111 (1942).

66 *See* MARTY STRANGE, FAMILY FARMING: A NEW ECONOMIC VISION 127–65 (Univ. of Nebraska Press 1988).

67 PA Const. of 1776, sec. 32. Bradley A. Smith, *Campaign Finance Reform: The General Landscape: The Sirens' Song: Campaign Finance Regulation and the First Amendment,"* 6 J.L. & POL'Y 1, 20, 21 (1997); ROBERT E. MUTCH, CAMPAIGNS, CONGRESSES, AND COURTS: THE MAKING OF FEDERAL CAMPAIGN FINANCE LAW 6 (Praeger 1988).

68 McConnell v. F.E.C., 540 U.S. 93 (2003).

69 Citizens United v. F.E.C., 130 S. Ct. 876 (2010).

70 This section draws heavily on Gottlieb, *supra* note 45.

71 1 Farrand, *supra* note 1, 72 (Hamilton, June 1, 1787); *id.* at 134–36 (Madison, June 6, 1787); *see also id.* at 143; THE FEDERALIST NO. 10, *supra* note 5 (James Madison).

72 WOOD, *supra* note 3 (comparing republicans, praising homogeneity, with Federalists, praising diversity); LUTZ, *supra* note 3 (same); ROSSITER, *supra* note 3, at 41, 44–45 & 122–24 (1953) (on interrelations among faiths, commerce and colleges).

73 *See generally*, HECTOR ST. JOHN DE CREVECOEUR, LETTERS FROM AN AMERICAN FARMER (E. P. Dutton, John Doe, ed. 1957) (1782); *see also* ISRAEL ZANGWILL, THE MELTING POT: DRAMA IN FOUR ACTS (Arno Press, John Doe, ed. 1975) (1909); Gerstle, *supra* note 45.

74 *See* Cremin, *supra* note 46, at 10.

75 NATHAN GLAZER, AFFIRMATIVE DISCRIMINATION: ETHNIC INEQUALITY AND PUBLIC POLICY, 8–9, 22–25 & 29–30 (Harvard Univ. Press 1975); DIVIDED NATIONS IN A DIVIDED WORLD 447–50 (D. McKay Co., Gregory Henderson, Richard Ned Lebow, and John George Stoessinger, eds. 1974); MAX L. MARGOLIES AND ALEXANDER MARX, A HISTORY OF THE JEWISH PEOPLE 532–40 (Atheneum 1972).

76 RICHARD KLUGER, SIMPLE JUSTICE: THE HISTORY OF BROWN V. BOARD OF EDUCATION AND BLACK AMERICA'S STRUGGLE FOR EQUALITY 488 (Knopf 1976).

77 *See generally* TYACK AND HANSOT, *supra* note 46.

78 *Id.* at 114–16, 131 & 137.

79 *Id.* at 94.

80 *Id.* at 74.

81 *Id.* at 17, 91, 94, 99–100 & 102–04.

82 *Id.* at 92, 134, 138 & 142–43.

83 *Id.* at 89.

84 Quoted in *id.* at 92.

85 *Id.* at 112.

86 *Id.* at 117–18.

87 *Id.* at 146–64.

88 MEYER, *supra* note 45 at 156.

89 *Id.* at 160–61.

90 Gerstle, *supra* note 45, at 524, 530–31 & 540 (describing both continuing influence of and problems with Crevecoeur's thought).

91 WEIGLEY, *supra* note 25, at 3–12; *see also* MILITARY IN AMERICA, *supra* note 25, at 1–78, 92–103 & 137–41.

92 Gerald Linderman, *The Spanish-American War and the Small-Town Community*, *in* MILITARY IN AMERICA, *supra* note 25 at 275–86.

93 John Whiteclay Chambers, II, *Conscripting for Colossus: The Progressive Era and the Origin of the Modern Military Draft in the United States in World War I*, *in id.* at 300–01.

94 *Id.* at 302.

95 *Id.* at 306.

96 *Id.* at 306.

97 Bruce White, *The American Military and the Melting Pot in World War I*, *in id.* at 317–18.

98 *Id.* at 322–23.

99 *Id.* at 320.

100 *Id.* at 320–21.

101 *Id.* at 321.

102 *Id.* at 323–27.

103 *Social Research and the Desegregation of the U.S. Army: Two Original 1951 Field Reports*, 176 (Leo Bogart, ed. 1969), reprinted in MILITARY IN AMERICA, *supra* note 25, at 375.

104 Paul Finkelman, *Introduction: "Let Justice Be Done, Though the Heavens May Fall": The Law of Freedom*, 70 CHI. KENT L. REV. 325, 339–42 (1994).

105 Roberts v. Boston, 59 Mass. (1 Cush.) 198, 206 (1850) and compare with Brown v. Bd. of Educ., 347 U.S. 483 (1954).

106 Mass. Acts 1855, C. 256; JAMES OLIVER HORTON AND LOIS E. HORTON, BLACK BOSTONIANS: FAMILY LIFE AND COMMUNITY STRUGGLE IN THE ANTEBELLUM NORTH 70–75 (Holmes & Meier 1979) (discussing Boston schooling for black children before the Civil War). On Shaw and race, *see* ROBERT M. COVER, JUSTICE ACCUSED: ANTISLAVERY AND THE JUDICIAL PROCESS 249–52 & 265–67 (Yale Univ. Press 1975).

107 *See* WYN CRAIG WADE, THE FIERY CROSS: THE KU KLUX KLAN IN AMERICA, 324–25 (Oxford Univ. Press 1987).

108 *See* FLORIDA BOARD OF REGENTS WITH MAXINE D. JONES, LARRY E. RIVERS, DAVID R. COLBURN, R. TOM DYE, AND WILLIAM R. ROGERS, A DOCUMENTED HISTORY OF THE INCIDENT WHICH OCCURRED AT ROSEWOOD, FLORIDA IN JANUARY, 1923 (Florida Board of Regents 1993), *available at* http://www.displaysforschools.com/rosewoodrp.html (Feb. 1, 2014); Richard Hixson (Special Master), *Rosewood Legacy Report*, SPECIAL MASTER'S FINAL REPORT TO THE HONORABLE BO JOHNSON, SPEAKER OF THE [FLORIDA] HOUSE OF REPRESENTATIVES, Mar. 24, 1994; *see* Rosewood Bibliography (Florida Dept. of State, Div. Lib. & Info. Servs.), *available at* http://dlis.dos.state.fl.us/library/bibliographies/rosewood_bib.cfm; OKLAHOMA COMMISSION TO STUDY THE RACE RIOT OF 1921, TULSA RACE RIOT (Okla. Hist. Soc'y), *available at* http://www.okhistory.org/research/forms/freport.pdf ; 1898 WILMINGTON RACE RIOT COMMISSION, 1898 WILMINGTON RACE RIOT–FINAL REPORT, May 31, 2006 (N. C. Off. of Archives & Hist.), *available at* http://www.ah.dcr.state.nc.us/1898-wrrc/report/report.htm; Elliot Jasper, *Forced out by Virtue of Race, in* ALBANY TIMES UNION, July 9, 2006, at A1.

109 *See* W.E.B. Du Bois, *Does the Negro Need Separate Schools?*, 4 J. OF NEGRO EDUC. 328 (1935) (preferring improvement of black schools).

110 Loving v. Virginia, 388 U.S. 1, 7 (1967); Alfred H. Kelly, *The School Desegregation Case, in* QUARRELS THAT HAVE SHAPED THE CONSTITUTION 254 (Harper & Row, John A. Garraty, ed. 1964); Jack Greenberg, *Litigation for Social Change: Methods, Limits and Role in Democracy, in* REC. OF THE ASS'N OF THE B. OF THE CITY OF NEW YORK 320, 357 (1974).

111 Plessy v. Ferguson, 163 U.S. 537 (1896); MARTIN BAUML DUBERMAN, PAUL ROBESON 236–38 (Knopf 1988).

112 On the half century after the Civil War, *see* C. VAN WOODWARD, THE STRANGE CAREER OF JIM CROW (Oxford Univ. Press 1955). On the background of *Brown see* KLUGER, *supra* note 76.

113 4 SAMUEL STOUFFER ET AL., STUDIES IN SOCIAL PSYCHOLOGY IN WORLD WAR II (Princeton Univ. Press, Peter Smith, ed. 1950) (on cultural and religious integration of servicemen); *see also* BRUNO BETTELHEIM AND MORRIS JANOWITZ, SOCIAL CHANGE AND PREJUDICE 4–14 (Harper & Row 1964) (on post–World War II decline in prejudice); James A. Davis, *The Log Linear Analysis of Survey Replications, in* SOCIAL INDICATOR MODELS 75, 88–101 (Russell Sage Foundation, Kenneth C. Land and Seymour Spilerman, eds. 1975) (on rising support for civil liberties between 1954 and 1972).

114 KLUGER, *supra* note 76, at 501, 502 & 504–05.

CHAPTER 2. IN THE SHADOW OF WAR

1 *See* WILLIAM J. NOVAK, INTELLECTUAL ORIGINS OF THE STATE POLICE POWER: THE COMMON LAW VISION OF A WELL-REGULATED SOCIETY (Inst. for Leg. Stud., Univ. of Wis.–Madison Law Sch. 1989); DONALD S. LUTZ, POPULAR CONSENT AND POPULAR CONTROL: WHIG POLITICAL THEORY (Louisiana State Univ. Press 1980); LOUIS HARTZ, ECONOMIC POLICY AND DEMOCRATIC THOUGHT IN PENNSYLVANIA, 1776–1860 (Harvard Univ. Press 1949); 4 CHARLES M. ANDREWS, THE COLONIAL PERIOD IN AMERICAN HISTORY (H. Milford, Oxford Univ. Press 1937). *See also* WILLIAM NOVAK, THE PEOPLE'S WELFARE: LAW AND REGULATION IN NINETEENTH-CENTURY AMERICA (Univ. of North Carolina Press 1996).

2 *See* Louis Lusky, *Minority Rights and the Public Interest*, 52 YALE L.J. 1, 14 (1942).

3 *See* Carlo Wolff, *Manufacturing Hysteria: A History of Scapegoating, Surveillance, and Secrecy in Modern America*, THE CHRISTIAN SCIENCE MONITOR, Aug. 17, 2011, http://www.csmonitor.com/Books/Book-Reviews/2011/0817/Manufacturing-Hysteria-A-History-of-Scapegoating-Surveillance-and-Secrecy-in-Modern-America (visited Sept. 28, 2012) (book review).

4 Meyer v. Neb., 262 U.S. 390 (1923); Bartels v. Iowa, 262 U.S. 404 (1923).

5 FREDERICK LEWIS ALLEN, ONLY YESTERDAY 31–53 (Bantam Books 1931).

6 Pierce v. Soc'y of Sisters, 268 U.S. 510 (1925).

7 WILLIAM MANCHESTER, THE GLORY AND THE DREAM: A NARRATIVE HISTORY OF AMERICA, 1932–1972, at 3–4 & 10–18 (Little, Brown 1975).

8 JONATHAN ALTER, THE DEFINING MOMENT: FDR'S HUNDRED DAYS AND THE TRIUMPH OF HOPE 2 (Simon and Schuster 2007).

9 MANCHESTER, *supra* note 7, at 111 (citing JONATHAN DANIELS, THE TIME BETWEEN THE WARS: ARMISTICE TO PEARL HARBOR 253 [Doubleday 1966]).

10 MANCHESTER, *supra* note 7, at 108–11 & 176; CHAS E. COUGHLIN, AM I AN ANTI-SEMITE ?: 9 ADDRESSES ON VARIOUS "ISMS" ANSWERING THE QUESTION 36–37 (The Condon Printing Co. 1939); SHELDON MARCUS, FATHER

COUGHLIN; THE TUMULTUOUS LIFE OF THE PRIEST OF THE LITTLE FLOWER 169–70 (Little, Brown 1973); DONALD WARREN, RADIO PRIEST: CHARLES COUGHLIN, THE FATHER OF HATE RADIO 94 & 192 (Free Press 1996); CHARLES J. TULL, FATHER COUGHLIN AND THE NEW DEAL 197–98 (Syracuse Univ. Press 1965).

11 Grosjean v. American Press Co., 297 U.S. 233 (1936).

12 MANCHESTER, *supra* note 7, at 113–15; ALAN BRINKLEY, VOICES OF PROTEST: HUEY LONG, FATHER COUGHLIN, AND THE GREAT DEPRESSION 9 (Knopf 1982); T. HARRY WILLIAMS, HUEY LONG 751 (Knopf 1969); HARNETT KANE, HUEY LONG'S LOUISIANA HAYRIDE: THE AMERICAN REHEARSAL FOR DICTATORSHIP: 1928–1940, at 3–4 (Pelican Pub. 1971) (1941); RAYMOND SWING, FORERUNNERS OF AMERICAN FASCISM 70 & 106–07 (J. Messner, Inc. 1935).

13 The following account draws heavily on NANCY BERMEO, ORDINARY PEOPLE IN EXTRAORDINARY TIMES: THE CITIZENRY AND THE BREAKDOWN OF DEMOCRACY 22–52 (Princeton Univ. Press 2003), as well as THE BREAKDOWN OF DEMOCRATIC REGIMES (Johns Hopkins Univ. Press, Juan J. Linz and Alfred Stepan, eds. 1984), which includes separate volumes on Europe, Latin America, and Chile.

14 BERMEO, *supra* note 13, at 48.

15 Perkins v. Elg, 307 U.S. 325 (1939); Guaranty Trust Co. v. Henwood, 307 U.S. 247 (1939); Cummings v. Deutsche Bank und Disconto-Gesellschaft, 300 U.S. 115 (1937); Schoenamsgruber v. Hamburg American Line, 294 U.S. 454 (1935); Norman v. Baltimore & O.R. Co., 294 U.S. 240 (1935); Woodson v. Deutsche Gold und Silber Scheideanstalt Vormals Roessler, 292 U.S. 449 (1934); FTC v. R. F. Keppel & Bro., 291 U.S. 304 (1934); Factor v. Laubenheimer, 290 U.S. 276 (1933); May v. Hamburg-Amerikanische Packetfahrt Aktiengesellschaft, 290 U.S. 333 (1933); Burnet v. Brooks, 288 U.S. 378 (1933); Norwegian Nitrogen Products Co. v. United States, 288 U.S. 294 (1933); Nashville, C. & St. L. Ry. v. Wallace, 288 U.S. 249 (1932); Cook v. United States, 288 U.S. 102 (1933); United States ex rel. Stapf v. Corsi, 287 U.S. 129 (1932); Burnet v. Chicago Portrait Co., 285 U.S. 1 (1932); Farbwerke Vormals Meister Lucius & Bruning v. Chemical Foundation, Inc., 283 U.S. 152 (1931); Russian Volunteer Fleet v. United States, 282 U.S. 481 (1931).

16 Hague v. Committee for Indus. Org., 307 U.S. 496 (1939); Kessler v. Strecker, 307 U.S. 22 (1939); Guaranty Trust Co. v. United States, 304 U.S. 126 (1938); United States v. Belmont, 301 U.S. 324 (1937); Herndon v. Lowry, 301 U.S. 242 (1937); De Jonge v. Oregon, 299 U.S. 353 (1936); United States v. Bank of New York & Trust Co., 296 U.S. 463 (1936); Herndon v. Georgia, 295 U.S. 441 (1935); Stromberg v. California, 283 U.S. 359 (1931); Russian Volunteer Fleet v. United States, 282 U.S. 481 (1931); Whitney v. Cal., 274 U.S. 357 (1927); Gitlow v. New York, 268 U.S. 652 (1925); Abrams v. United States, 250 U.S. 616 (1919).

17 West Virginia State Board of Education v. Barnette, 319 U.S. 624 (1943) and Taylor v. Mississippi, 319 U.S. 583 (1943).

18 ALPHEUS THOMAS MASON, BRANDEIS: A FREE MAN'S LIFE 429 (Viking Press 1956).

19 Testimony of Louis D. Brandeis (Jan. 23, 1915) in Final Report and Testimony of the Commission on Industrial Relations, 64th Cong., 1st Sess., S. Doc. No. 415, vol. 19, 7659–60 (1916), http://www.archive.org/details/industrialrelatio8unitrich.

20 LOUIS D. BRANDEIS, BRANDEIS ON DEMOCRACY 156, 159 & 174 (Univ. Press of Kansas, Philippa Strum, ed. 1995).

21 Allon Gal, *Brandeis, Judaism, and Zionism* in BRANDEIS AND AMERICA 71 (Univ. Press of Kentucky, Nelson L. Dawson, ed. 1989).

22 BRANDEIS, *supra* note 20, at 163.

23 *Id.* at 164.

24 *Id.* at 156 & 163.

25 *Id.* at 159.

26 *Id.* at 156.

27 *Id.* at 160.

28 Brandeis to Elizabeth Brandeis Raushenbush (Nov. 19, 1933), *in* BRANDEIS, *supra* note 20, at 194.

29 Louis Brandeis to Rabbi Stephen Wise, June 13, 1934, in 5 LETTERS OF LOUIS D. BRANDEIS 541 (State Univ. of New York Press, Melvin I. Urofsky and David W. Levy, eds. 1978).

30 *Id.* at 562.

31 288 U.S. 591 (1933).

32 Morrison v. California, 291 U.S. 82, 89–90 (1934).

33 Letter to Felix Frankfurter (Mar. 30, 1933), quoted in ANDREW L. KAUFMAN, CARDOZO 156 (Harvard Univ. Press 1998).

34 Letter to Felix Frankfurter (Jan. 31, 1936), quoted in KAUFMAN, *supra* note 33, at 488–89.

35 Letter to Irving Lehman (Apr. 26, 1938), quoted in ALPHEUS THOMAS MASON, HARLAN FISKE STONE: PILLAR OF THE LAW 515 (Viking Press 1956).

36 Letter to Irving Brant (Oct. 29, 1937), quoted in MASON, *supra* note 35, at 544.

37 MASON, *supra* note 35, at 518 & 544–47.

38 LOUIS LUSKY, BY WHAT RIGHT: A COMMENTARY ON THE SUPREME COURT'S POWER TO REVISE THE CONSTITUTION 113 (Michie Co. 1975).

39 Hebert v. Louisiana, 272 U.S. 312, 316 (1926).

40 Snyder v. Massachusetts, 291 U.S. 97, 105 (1934). Chief Justice Hughes quoted that language in Brown v. Mississippi, 297 U.S. 278, 285 (1936).

41 Palko v. Connecticut, 302 U.S. 319, 326, 327 (1937).

42 Richard Polenberg, *Cardozo and the Criminal Law: Palko v. Connecticut Reconsidered*, 2 J. SUP. CT. HIST. 92, 93 (1996).

43 Palko at 326–327.

44 Palko at 328 (quoting Hebert v. Louisiana, 272 U.S. 312, 316 [1926]).

45 *See* Codispoti v. Pennsylvania, 418 U.S. 506, 534 (1974) (Rehnquist, J., dissenting); STEPHEN E. GOTTLIEB, MORALITY IMPOSED: THE REHNQUIST COURT AND LIBERTY IN AMERICA 225–227 (New York Univ. Press 2000).

46 United States v. Carolene Products Co., 304 U.S. 144, 155 (1938) (Black, J., concurring in part).

47 Poe v. Ullman, 367 U.S. 497, 541–45 (1961) (Harlan, J., dissenting).

48 *See* Schneider v. New Jersey, 308 U.S. 147 (1939); Lovell v. Griffin, 303 U.S. 444 (1938); De Jonge v. Oregon, 299 U.S. 353 (1937); Grosjean v. American Press Co., 297 U.S. 233 (1936); Near v. Minnesota, 283 U.S. 697 (1931).

49 United States v. Classic, 313 U.S. 299 (1941).

50 Nixon v. Condon, 286 U.S. 73 (1932); *and see* Nixon v. Herndon, 273 U.S. 536 (1927); *but see* Grovey v. Townsend, 295 U.S. 45 (1935).

51 *See* Chambers v. Florida, 309 U.S. 227 (1940); Powell v. Alabama, 287 U.S. 45 (1932).

52 304 U.S. 144 (1938).

53 Letter to Irving Lehman (Apr. 26, 1938), quoted in MASON, *supra* note 35, at 515.

54 United States v. Carolene Products Co., 304 U.S. at 152 n. 4; Mason, *supra* note 35, at 512–17; Louis Lusky, *Footnote Redux: A Carolene Products Reminiscence*, 82 COLUM. L. REV. 1093 (1982); H. JEFFERSON POWELL, THE MORAL TRADITION OF AMERICAN CONSTITUTIONALISM: A THEOLOGICAL INTERPRETATION 159–65 (Duke Univ. Press 1993).

55 *See* Robert F. Nagel, *"Unfocused" Governmental Interests, in* PUBLIC VALUES IN CONSTITUTIONAL LAW 61–62 (Univ. of Michigan Press, Stephen E. Gottlieb, ed. 1993).

56 *See* Missouri ex rel. Gaines v. Canada, 305 U.S. 337 (1938); Coleman v. Miller, 307 U.S. 433, 448–50 (1939). Walter Dellinger described the background and connection of these cases in a talk at the 2012 Annual Meeting of the Association of American Law Schools; I look forward to seeing his description in print.

57 LUSKY, *supra* note 38, at 109.

58 Hugo L. Black to Mr. Justice Stone (Apr. 21, 1938), reprinted in Lusky, *supra* note 54, 82 COLUM. L. REV. at 1105.

59 *See* Buchanan v. Warley, 245 U.S. 60, 73 (1917); Yick Wo v. Hopkins, 118 U.S. 356 (1886).

60 *See* Chambers v. Florida, 309 U.S. 227 (1940); Powell v. Alabama, 287 U.S. 45 (1932); CHARLES LANE, THE DAY FREEDOM DIED: THE COLFAX MASSACRE, THE SUPREME COURT, AND THE BETRAYAL OF RECONSTRUCTION (: Henry Holt and Co. 2008); *see generally* RICHARD KLUGER, SIMPLE JUSTICE: THE HISTORY OF BROWN V. BOARD OF EDUCATION AND BLACK AMERICA'S STRUGGLE FOR EQUALITY 3–26 (Knopf 1976).

61 *See* note 45 *supra*.

CHAPTER 3. EXPORT

1 *Compare* Chambers v. Florida, 309 U.S. 227, 241 (1940) *with* Chavez v. Martinez, 538 U.S. 760 (2003).

2 Minersville School Dist. v. Gobitis, 310 U.S. 586, 591–2 (1940).

3 Harlan Fiske Stone, *The Conscientious Objector*, COLUM. UNIV. Q., Oct. 1919 at 270; ALPHEUS T. MASON, HARLAN FISKE STONE: PILLAR OF THE LAW 525–34 (Viking Press 1956).

4 W. Va. State Bd. of Educ. v. Barnette, 319 U.S. 624, 630 (1943).

5 319 U.S. 624 (1943).

6 *Id.* at 642.

7 *Id.* at 8–9.

8 Everson v. Bd. of Educ., 330 U.S. 1, 16 (1947).

9 Illinois ex rel. McCollum v. Bd. of Educ., 333 U.S. 203 (1948).

10 *See* Everson v. Bd. of Educ.; Lemon v. Kurtzman, 403 U.S. 602 (1971). *But see* Zelman v. Simmons-Harris, 536 U.S. 639, 650 (2002).

11 Korematsu v. United States, 323 U.S. 214 (1944); Hirabayashi v. United States, 320 U.S. 81 (1943); DeFunis v. Odegaard, 416 U.S. 312, 349 (1974) (Douglas, dissenting from the denial of certiorari).

12 Hirabayashi v. United States, 828 F.2d 591, 608 (9th Cir. 1987) *and* Korematsu v. United States, 584 F. Supp. 1406, 1416–18 (N.D. Cal. 1984); Susan Kiyomi Serrano, *Dale Minami, Korematsu v. United States: A "Constant Caution" in a Time of Crisis*, 10 ASIAN L.J. 37, 42–44 (2003); JUSTICE DELAYED: THE RECORD OF THE JAPANESE AMERICAN INTERNMENT CASES 221 (Wesleyan Univ. Press, Peter Irons, ed. 1989).

13 Skinner v. Oklahoma, 316 U.S. 535, 541 (1942) (on Okla. Habitual Criminal Sterilization Act).

14 Nixon v. Herndon, 273 U.S. 536 (1927); Nixon v. Condon, 286 U.S. 73 (1932).

15 Grovey v. Townsend, 295 U.S. 45 (1935).

16 *See* Smith v. Allwright, 321 U.S. 649 (1944); Terry v. Adams, 345 U.S. 461 (1953); *and see* Oregon v. Mitchell, 400 U.S. 112, 203 (1970) (Harlan, J., concurring and dissenting).

17 334 U.S. 1 (1948).

18 Missouri *ex rel.* Gaines v. Canada, 305 U.S. 337 (1938); Sipuel v. Oklahoma, 332 U.S. 631 (1948); Sweatt v. Painter, 339 U.S. 629 (1950); McLaurin v. Oklahoma State Regents, 339 U.S. 637 (1950); *and see* Brown v. Bd. of Educ., 347 U.S. 483, 491–92 (1954).

19 Brown v. Bd. of Educ., 347 U.S. at 495.

20 Colegrove v. Green, 328 U.S. 549, 556 (1946) (plurality opinion by Frankfurter, J.).

21 Adamson v. California, 332 U.S. 46, 57–8 (1947).

22 HORACE EDGAR FLACK, THE ADOPTION OF THE FOURTEENTH AMENDMENT (Johns Hopkins Univ. Press 1908).

23 Adamson v. California, 332 U.S. at 72–76, 92–123 (Black, J., dissenting).

24 *Id.* at 52–3. *See also* Saenz v. Roe, 526 U.S. 489 (1999).

25 *See* Malloy v. Hogan, 378 U.S. 1, 10–11 (1964) (overruling *Adamson* on self-incrimination).

26 JOHANNES MORSINK, THE UNIVERSAL DECLARATION OF HUMAN RIGHTS: ORIGINS, DRAFTING & INTENT 36–50 (Univ. Penn. Press 1999).

27 Corfield v. Coryell, 6 F. Cas. 546, 549–52, 555 (1823); The Antelope, 23 U.S. 66 (1825).

28 G.A. Res 217(III), art. 7.

29 Morsink, *supra* note 26, at 44.

30 *Cf.* Art. IV to U.S. CONST., Amend. 13.

31 *Cf.* Art. V to U.S. CONST., Amend. 8.

32 *Cf.* Art. XII with U.S. CONST., Amend. 4.

33 *Cf.* Article 13 with Saenz v. Roe, 526 U.S. 489 (1999).

34 *Cf.* Article 17 with U.S. CONST. art. I, sec. 9; *Id.* Amends. 5 and 14.

35 Articles 14 and 15.

36 G.A. Res. 217(III) at arts. 23–24.

37 G.A. Res. 217(III) at art. 21, par. 1, 3.

38 *See* Terry v. Adams, 345 U.S. 461 (1953); Smith v. Allwright, 321 U.S. 649 (1943).

39 Shelley v. Kramer, 334 U.S. 1 (1948).

40 *See* cases cited *supra* note 18.

41 G.A. Res. 217 (III), at art. 19.

42 *Id.* at art. 20.

43 *Id.* at art. 21, par. 2.

44 *Id.* at art. 7.

45 *See* Act of Mar. 3, 1917, ch. 159, Title II, 39 Stat. 1000; Act of Oct. 3, 1917, ch. 63, Title II, 40 Stat. 302; Act of Feb. 24, 1919, ch. 18, Title III, 40 Stat. 1088; Act of Nov. 23, 1921, ch. 136, Title III, 42 Stat. 271; Act of Oct. 8, 1940, ch. 757, Title II, 54 Stat. 974; Act. of Jan. 3, 1951, ch. 1199, Title I, 64 Stat. 1137.

46 ULYSSES LEE, UNITED STATES ARMY IN WORLD WAR II: SPECIAL STUDIES–THE EMPLOYMENT OF NEGRO TROOPS 688–705 (U.S. Government Printing Office for the Center of Military History, United States Army 1966), http://www.history.army.mil/books/wwii/11-4/chapter22.htm (visited Oct. 13, 2012).

47 Samuel Stouffer et al., *Measurement and Prediction*, in 4 STUDIES IN SOCIAL PSYCHOLOGY IN WORLD WAR II (Princeton Univ. Press 1950) (on effect of cultural and religious integration on servicemen).

48 Leo Bogart, *Troops in Segregated and in Integrated Units Answer a Question about Race Relations, 1951, in* THE MILITARY IN AMERICA FROM THE COLONIAL ERA TO THE PRESENT 375 (Free Press, Peter Karsten, ed., rev. ed. 1986).

49 Act of June 22, 1944, ch. 268, 58 Stat. 284, codified at 38 U.S.C. 1801 *et seq* as amended.

50 *See* Daniel P. McMurrer, Mark Condon, and Isabel V. Sawhill, *Intergenerational Mobility in the United States: A Companion Piece to "The Declining Importance of Class"* (Urban Institute: Opportunity in America Series May 1997), http://www.urban.org/publications/406796.html (visited July 17, 2013).

51 Florence Wagman Roisman, *The Lessons of American Apartheid: The Necessity and Means of Promoting Residential Racial Integration*, 81 IOWA L. REV. 479, 486 (1995) (reviewing DOUGLAS S. MASSEY AND NANCY A. DENTON, AMERICAN APARTHEID); CHARLES ABRAMS, FORBIDDEN NEIGHBORS: A STUDY OF PREJUDICE IN HOUSING 229–37 (Harper 1955); KENNETH T. JACKSON, CRABGRASS FRONTIER: THE SUBURBANIZATION OF THE UNITED STATES 203–15 (Oxford Univ. Press 1985); DOUGLAS S. MASSEY AND NANCY A. DENTON,

AMERICAN APARTHEID: SEGREGATION AND THE MAKING OF THE UNDERCLASS 54–55 (Harvard Univ. Press 1993); MELVIN L. OLIVER AND THOMAS M. SHAPIRO, BLACK WEALTH/WHITE WEALTH: A NEW PERSPECTIVE ON RACIAL INEQUALITY 17–18, 51–52, 150 & 174 (Routledge 1995); *see also* NATIONAL COMMISSION ON URBAN PROBLEMS, BUILDING THE AMERICAN CITY: REPORT OF THE NATIONAL COMMISSION ON URBAN PROBLEMS TO THE CONGRESS AND TO THE PRESIDENT OF THE UNITED STATES generally and at 101 (U.S. Govt. Print. Off. 1969).

52 *See, e.g.,* WILLIAM L. RIORDON, PLUNKITT OF TAMMANY HALL (Signet Classic 1996); FRANK S. ROBINSON, MACHINE POLITICS: A STUDY OF ALBANY'S O'CONNELLS (Transaction Books 1977); ALFRED STEINBERG, THE BOSSES (Macmillan 1972); T. HARRY WILLIAMS, HUEY LONG, 753–59 (Knopf 1969); Edward C. Banfield, *Corruption as a Feature of Governmental Organization*, 18 J. L. & ECON. 587, 588–91 (1975); Stephen E. Gottlieb, *Rebuilding the Right of Association: The Right to Hold a Convention as a Test Case*, 11 HOFSTRA L. REV. 191, 221–27 & 238–43 (1982); *and see* DAVID A. DILLDINE ET AL., A BIBLIOGRAPHY OF CASE STUDIES OF BOSSES AND MACHINES (Vance Bibliographies 1978).

53 *See* HARRY M. CAUDILL, THE WATCHES OF THE NIGHT 217–18 (Little, Brown 1976); HOWARD R. PENNIMAN, SAIT'S AMERICAN PARTIES AND ELECTIONS 338–41 (Appleton-Century-Crofts, Inc., 5th ed. 1952).

54 David Ziskind, *Labor Provisions in Constitutions of Europe*, 6 COMP. LAB. L. & POL'Y J. 311, 316n (1984).

55 *Id.*

56 Weimar Constitution, 1922 translation by Howard Lee McBain and Lindsay Rogers, *available at* http://en.wikisource.org/wiki/Weimar_constitution.

57 Arts. 109–34 & 142–65.

58 Ir. Const., 1937, art. 45. Foreign constitutions are available in translations on national websites, at https://www.constituteproject.org/#/search or at http://www.constitution.org/cons/natlcons.htm.

59 *See* Stephen Gardbaum, *The Myth and the Reality of American Constitutional Exceptionalism*, 107 MICH. L. REV. 391, 447 (2008).

60 Williams v. Department of Human Services, 116 N.J. 102, 109, 561 A.2d 244 (NJ 1989) quoting Roe v. Kervick, 42 N.J. 191, 212–13 (1964). *See also* Michele Landis Dauber, *"Overtaken by a Great Calamity": Disaster Relief and the Origins of the American Welfare State: The Sympathetic State*, 23 LAW & HIST. REV. 387 (2005).

61 N.Y. Const., art. 11, sec. 1 & art. 17, sec. 1. *See* Gardbaum, *American Constitutional Exceptionalism*, 107 MICH. L. REV. 453.

62 Dai Nihon Teikoku [Meiji Kenpo] [Constitution] (1889), English translation from the Japanese National Diet Library at http://www.ndl.go.jp/constitution/e/etc/c02.html#s3.

63 RAY A. MOORE AND DONALD L. ROBINSON, PARTNERS FOR DEMOCRACY: CRAFTING THE NEW JAPANESE STATE UNDER MACARTHUR 11 (Oxford Univ. Press 2002).

64 Nihonkoku Kenpo [Constitution] arts. 79, 81. English translation at http://www. servat.unibe.ch/icl/jaooooo_.html. For history and background, *see* MOORE AND ROBINSON, *supra* note 63, at 50–78, 301–02 & 331–35.

65 Kenpo, arts. 1–7.

66 Kenpo, arts. 11–29 & 31–40.

67 On Japanese views, *see* MOORE AND ROBINSON, *supra* note 63, at 299.

68 Kenpo arts. 22 & 27–28.

69 Kenpo art. 24. *See* MOORE AND ROBINSON, *supra* note 63, at 131 & 223–27.

70 Kenpo arts. 26–27.

71 Kenpo art. 29.

72 On Japanese sources of this article, *see* MOORE AND ROBINSON, *supra* note 63, at 271 & 277–78.

73 *See* Asahi v. Japan, 21 Minshũ 5 at 1043 (Supreme Court of Japan 1967), excerpted in VICKI C. JACKSON AND MARK TUSHNET, COMPARATIVE CONSTITUTIONAL LAW, 1665–67 (2d ed. 2006).

74 Costituzione [Cost.] (It.) art. 3 [common translations vary slightly].

75 *Id.* art. 4.

76 *Id.* art. 32.

77 *Id.* art. 36.

78 *Id.* art. 38.

79 Charles J. Friedrich, *Rebuilding the German Constitution, I*, 43 AM. POL. SCI. REV. 461, 465 (1949), *available at* http://www.ibiblio.org/pha/policy/1945/450802a.html.

80 *Id.*

81 *Id.* at 467.

82 English translations available at http://en.wikisource.org/wiki/Weimar_constitution, or at http://www.zum.de/psm/weimar/weimar_vve.php. On fundamental rights and duties, *see* arts. 109–165. On individual rights, *see* arts. 109–118; on religion, *see* arts. 135–141. On the executive, *see* arts. 41–49. *Cf.* Friedrich, *supra* note 79, at 463.

83 Robert G. Neumann, *New Constitution in Germany*, 42 AM. POL. SCI. REV. 448, 451 (1948).

84 Art. 131, secs. 1 and 2, quoted in Neuman, *supra* note 83, at 450n.

85 Bavarian Verf. Bay, Art. 106, sec. 1, and 166, sec. 2, quoted in Neuman, *supra* note 83, at 450n.

86 Neuman, *supra* note 83, at 465.

87 *Id.* at 455.

88 *Id.* at 467.

89 *Id.* at 454.

90 *Id.* at 457–58.

91 *See* Grundgesetz für die Bundesrepublik Deutschland [Grundgesetz] [GG] [Basic Law], May 23, 1949, BGBl. I (Ger.) art. 4, 140 (regarding religious denominations). Translations by Christian Tomuschat and David P. Currie, *available at* https://www. btg-bestellservice.de/pdf/80201000.pdf. The original unamended 1949 Basic Law is at http://www.cvce.eu/obj/The_Basic_Law_of_the_FRG_23_May_1949-en-7fa618bb-

604e-4980-b667–76bf0cdodd9b.html. References are to the original 1949 Basic Law. Versions and amendments to the Basic Law can be tracked with Axel Tschentscher, *The Basic Law (Grundgesetz): The Constitution of the Federal Republic of Germany* (May 23, 1949), SSRN Working Paper Edition Mar. 2011 (latest revision at http://ssrn.com/abstract=1501131). Notes below use the Tschentsher paper to identify changes from the original.

92 Grundgesetz, art. 20, par. 2, 20(1).

93 Grundgesetz, art. 20, par. 2.

94 Grundgesetz, art. 38; *see* Tschentscher, *supra* note 91, at note 52.

95 Grundgesetz, art. 36[1], 54[3]; and Gesetz zur Anderung des Grundgesetzes [Law Amending Basic Law], 1968, BGBl. I (Ger.) art. 53a[1].

96 Grundgesetz, art. 51; the 1949 Basic Law was expanded with unification in 1990, *see* Tschentscher, *supra* note 91 at note 68.

97 Grundgesetz, art. 5.

98 Grundgesetz, arts. 8, 9, 17 & 21. Arts. 9 & 21 amended in other respects, *see* Tschentscher, *supra* note 91 at notes 15 and 36.

99 Grundgesetz, art. 39, details of timing amended in 1976 and 1998, *see* Tschentscher, *supra* note 91, at nn. 52–58.

100 Grundgesetz, arts. 54 & 63.

101 Grundgesetz, art. 21, par. 2.

102 Language quoted from art. 10 but similar language runs through the section on rights, *see* Tschentscher, *supra* note 91, at n. 17.

103 Grundgesetz, art. 18 ("democratic order"). *See also* arts. 10 & 11 as amended. Arts. 2 & 9 ("constitutional order"); art. 5 ("allegiance to the constitution"); art. 20 ("social federal state"); *and see* Tschentscher, *supra* note 91, at nn. 15 & 33.

104 Grundgesetz, art.18, otherwise amended in 1993, *see* Tschentscher, *supra* note 91, at n. 31.

105 Grundgesetz, art. 19, par. 2.

106 Grundgesetz, arts. 1, 6, 9, 12. The language of arts. 1, 9, and 12 otherwise amended, *see* Tschentscher, *supra* note 91, at n.12, 15, 21–22. *And see* Peter E. Quint, *The Constitutional Guarantees of Social Welfare in the Process of German Unification*, 47 AM. J. COMPARATIVE L. 303, 305–08 (1999); MARY ANN GLENDON, A WORLD MADE NEW: ELEANOR ROOSEVELT AND THE UNIVERSAL DECLARATION OF HUMAN RIGHTS xvii (Random House 2002).

107 Grundgesetz, art.7.

108 Grundgesetz, art. 14, par. 2.

109 Grundgesetz, arts. 14–15.

110 Grundgesetz, art. 28, otherwise amended in 1993, *see* Tschentscher, *supra* note 91, at n.42.

111 Grundgesetz, art. 74, par. 1, otherwise amended, *see* Tschentscher, *supra* note 91, at notes 96, 99.

112 Grundgesetz, art. 87, par. 2, otherwise amended, *see* Tschentscher, *supra* note 91, at n. 139.

113 Grundgesetz, art.2.

114 Grundgesetz, arts. 4; 10, par. 1; 11, par. 1.

115 Grundgesetz, arts. 1–19. Art. 1, "executive" substituted for "administration" in 1956, *see* Tschentscher, *supra* note 91, at n. 12.

116 Grundgesetz, art. 3.

117 Grundgesetz, art. 13, supplemented regarding technical means of surveillance in 1998, *see* Tschentscher, *supra* note 91, at n. 25; arts. 101–04.

118 Kesavananda Bharati Sripadagalvaru and Ors. v. State of Kerala and Anr., 1973 AIR 1461 [566] (India Supreme Court 1973) (opinion of Shelat and Grover, JJ.).

119 Akhil Amar in a 1990 phone conversation with the author focused the author's attention on the importance of that delayed shift.

120 *Cf.* GUISEPPE DI PALMA, TO CRAFT DEMOCRACIES: AN ESSAY ON DEMOCRATIC TRANSITIONS (Univ. of California Press 1990); Jack N. Rakove, *The Great Compromise: Ideas, Interests, and the Politics of Constitution Making*, 44 WM. & M. Q. 424 (3d Ser. 1987).

121 On Rau, *see* H. R. KHANNA, MAKING OF INDIA'S CONSTITUTION 9–10 (Eastern Book Co., n.d., the Sulakhani Devi Mahajan Memorial Lectures at the Indian Law Institute, New Delhi, Mar. 23–25, 1981).

122 *See id.* at 38 & 40–43.

123 *Id.* at 36–37.

124 *Id.* at 21.

125 India Const. pmbl. [capitalization in the original].

126 Art. 14 and *see* KHANNA, *supra* note 121, at 27.

127 KHANNA, *supra* note 121, at 29.

128 On equality, see arts. 14–18, 25–30, 80–81, 326 & 329–42.

129 India Const. arts. 36–51.

130 KHANNA, *supra* note 121, at 57–58.

131 *Id.* at 58–60.

132 SURESH MANE, THE MAN WHO CODIFIED INDIAN INDEPENDENCE, n.p. (Bahujanvartha Publications 2010).

133 *Smt. Indira Nehru Gandhi vs Shri Raj Narain And Anr.*, A.I.R. 1975 S.C. 2299, pars. 159–254 (opinion of Khanna, J.); *Kesavananda Bharati's* case (1973) 4 S.C.C. 225 and see the dissenting opinion of Justice Khanna in the habeas corpus case, Additional District Magistrate, Jabalpur v. S. S. Shukla Etc., A.I.R. 1976 S.C.1207, 1976 Suppl. S.C.R. 172, 1976 S.C.C. 521, *available at* http://supremecourtofindia.nic.in/.

134 KHANNA, *supra* note 121, at 55–56.

135 Convention for the Protection of Human Rights and Fundamental Freedoms, Nov. 4, 1950, Europ.T.S. No. 5; 213 U.N.T.S. 221.

136 *Cf. id.*, art. VI.

137 The Constitution Act, adopted Mar. 29, 1982; The Canada Act, 1982, c. 11 (U.K.) [Mar. 29, 1982].

138 Canadian Charter of Rights and Freedoms, Part I of the Constitution Act, 1982, Schedule B to the Canada Act, 1982 c. 11 sec. 2 (U.K.) [hereinafter Canadian Charter of Rights and Freedoms].

139 Canadian Charter of Rights and Freedoms, sec. 3.

140 *Id.* sec. 15, *and see id.* secs. 16–22, 25, 27, 28 & 29.

141 *Id.* sec. 36.

142 *Id.* sec. 1.

143 *Id.* sec. 7.

144 *Id.* sec. 19(3).

145 *Id.* secs. 16–18.

146 *Id.* sec. 46.

147 *Id.* sec. 9; *see also id.* secs. 6, 13, 30–31.

148 *Id.* secs. 22–29.

149 *Id.* sec. 36(1).

150 *See id.* secs. 79, 80, 144 & 166–167, among others.

151 *See* sect. 57 (1b) & (2b), 61(2), 70 (1b) & (2b&c), 116 (1b) & 2(b), 152 (1a), 160 (8b), 181 (1), 195 (1), 234 & 236.

CHAPTER 4. FOREIGN COURTS

1 Many foreign courts number paragraphs. We use those markings where available.

2 Gregory H. Fox and Georg Nolte, *Intolerant Democracies*, 36 HARV. INT'L L. J. 1, 16 & 69 (1995).

3 For the 1787 Convention, *see* 1 THE RECORDS OF THE FEDERAL CONVENTION OF 1787, at 19 (Yale Univ. Press, Max Farrand, ed. 1966) (Randolph, May 29, 1787); *id.* at 315, 479, vol. 2 at 93 (Madison, June 19, June 29 and July 23, 1787); *id.*, vol. 2 at 74 (Ellsworth, July 21, 1787). *See also* U.S. CONST., art. I, sec. 8, -par. 10. *See also,* Ogden v. Saunders, 25 U.S. 213, 259 (1827); *The Antelope*, 23 U.S. 66, 115 (1825); *id.* at 117–18; Murray v. The Schooner Charming Betsy, 6 U.S. 64, 118 (1804); Pennoyer v. Neff, 95 U.S. 714, 722–23, 729–33 (1878); Andrew L. Strauss, *Beyond National Law: The Neglected Role of the International Law of Personal Jurisdiction in Domestic Courts*, 36 HARV. INT'L L. J. 373, 394–96 (1995); Patrick J. Borchers, *The Death of the Constitutional Law of Personal Jurisdiction: From Pennoyer to Burnham and Back Again*, 24 U.C. DAVIS L. REV. 19, 25 (1990).

4 Roper v. Simmons, 543 U.S. 551, 575–78 (2005); *id.* at 604–05 (O'Connor, dissenting); Atkins v. Virginia, 536 U.S. 304, 316 n. (2002); Thompson v. Okla., 487 U.S. 815, 830 (1988) (plurality opinion); *id.* at 847, 857 (O'Connor, J., concurring in the judgment); Enmund v. Fla., 458 U.S. 782, 796 n. (1982); Coker v. Ga., 433 U.S. 584, 596 n. 10 (1977); *and see* Trop v. Dulles, 356 U.S. 86, 101 (1958) (plurality opinion). *See also* Graham v. Florida, 130 S. Ct. 2011, 2033–34 (2010).

5 Lawrence v. Texas, 539 U.S. 558, 572–73, 576 (2003). *See also* Nicholas Bamforth, *New Natural Law, Religion, and Same-Sex Marriage: Current Constitutional Issues*, 1 WAKE FOREST J. L. & POL'Y 207, 266 (2011). Lawrence v. Texas, 539 U.S. 558, 564 (2003) cited Griswold v. Connecticut, 381 U.S. 479, 503–04 (1965) *but see id.* at 485; Skinner v. Oklahoma, 316 U.S. 535, 541 (1942).

6 Foster v. Florida, 537 U.S. 990 (2002) (Thomas, J., concurring in denial of certiorari).

7 Lawrence v. Texas, 539 U.S. at 598 (Scalia, J., dissenting).

8 Roper v. Simmons, 543 U.S. at 608 (2005) (Scalia, J., dissenting).

9 *Id.* at 608 (Scalia, J., dissenting); *see also id.* at 626. *See also* A. Christopher Bryant, *Foreign Law as Legislative Fact in Constitutional Cases*, 2011 B.Y.U. L. REV. 1005, 1025–26, 1030 & 1035–40 (2011).

10 Graham v. Florida, 130 S. Ct. 2011, 2033–34 (2010); McDonald v. City of Chicago, 130 S. Ct. 3020, 3055–56 (2010) (Scalia, J., concurring); Christian Legal Soc'y Chapter of the Univ. of Cal. v. Martinez, 130 S. Ct. 2971, 3020 (2010) (Alito, J., dissenting). *But see* McDonald v. City of Chicago, 130 S. Ct. 3020, 3026 (2010).

11 *See, e.g.*, SCOTT DOUGLAS GERBER, FIRST PRINCIPLES: THE JURISPRUDENCE OF CLARENCE THOMAS (New York Univ. Press 2002); Antonin Scalia, *Originalism: The Lesser Evil*, 57 U. CIN. L. REV. 849, 864 (1989). *See also* McDonald v. City of Chicago, 130 S. Ct. 3020, 3028–31 (2010); *Id.* at 3059 (Thomas, J., concurring in part).

12 *See* H. Jefferson Powell, *The Original Understanding of Original Intent*, 98 HARV. L. REV. 885 (1985).

13 Zachary Elkins, Tom Ginsburg, and Beth Simmons, *Getting to Rights: Treaty Ratification, Constitutional Convergence, and Human Rights Practice*, 54 HARV. INT'L L. J. 61 (2013).

14 *See* Toby James, *Voter ID in Britain? A Note of Caution from Academic Research*, Jan. 7, 2014 (School of Political, Social and International Studies, Univ. of East Anglia), *available at* http://www.ueapolitics.org/2014/01/07/voter-id-in-britain/.

15 Where available I have used translations from DONALD P. KOMMERS, THE CONSTITUTIONAL JURISPRUDENCE OF THE FEDERAL REPUBLIC OF GERMANY (Duke Univ. Press, 2d ed. 1997). At the time of writing, a third edition was published; although I consulted the 3d edition, references to KOMMERS are to the second edition, except where noted. All translations of German language material not otherwise identified other than the Basic Law are by Anne Jelliff, my assistant who grew up in Germany. Case names are supplied by KOMMERS, Anne Jelliff, or myself.

16 Southwest State Case, BVerfGE 1, 14, at 32 (1951). Internal quote from the Bavarian Constitutional Court. Translation from KOMMERS, *supra* note 15, at 63.

17 Lüth Case, BVerfGE 7, 198 at 207 (1958), translation from KOMMERS, *supra* note 15, at 364–65; Der Spiegel, BVerfGE 20, 162, at 174 (1966), translation from KOMMERS, *supra* note 15, at 398; Deutschland Magazine Case, BVerfGE 42, 143 (1976); the case is briefly described in KOMMERS, *supra* note 15, at 377–78; Lüth Case, BVerfGE 7, 198 (1958), translation from KOMMERS, *supra* note 15, at 365; quoted in The Schmid-Spiegel Case, BVerfGE 12, 113, at 124–25 (1961), translation from KOMMERS, *supra* note 15, at 370.

18 Publication of Convict Personal Information Case, BVerfGE 35, 202 (1972), pars. 51–52. On criminal records, *see* Publication of Convict Personal Information Case, BVerfGE 35, 202 (1972). On misrepresentation, *see* Eppler Case, BVerfGE 54, 148 (1980), *and see* KOMMERS, *supra* note 15, at 320–23. For the census, *see* Census Act Case, BVerfGE 65, 1 (1983), discussed in KOMMERS, *supra* note 15, at 322–26. On dignity, see

Neomi Rao, *On the Use and Abuse of Dignity in Constitutional Law*, 14 COLUM. J. EUR. L. 201, 210, 254–55 (2008); Rex D. Glensy, *The Right to Dignity*, 43 COLUM. HUM. RTS. L. REV. 65 (2011). And see Campaign Slur Case, BVerfGE 61, 1, at 13 (1982), translation from KOMMERS, *supra* note 15, at 380.

19 *See e.g.*, Ruti Teitel, *Militating Democracy: Comparative Constitutional Perspectives*, 29 MICH. J. INT'L L. 49 (2007); Ronald J. Krotoszynski, Jr., *A Comparative Perspective on the First Amendment: Free Speech, Militant Democracy, and the Primacy of Dignity as a Preferred Constitutional Value in Germany*, 78 TUL. L. REV. 1549 (2004).

20 Extremists Decision, BVerfGE 39, 334, at 367–69 (1975), translation from KOMMERS, *supra* note 15 at 232. *See also* Fox and Nolte, *supra* note 2, 36 HARV. INT'L L.J. 32–34.

21 Socialist Reich Party Case, BVerfGE 2, 1, at 12 (1952), translation from KOMMERS, *supra* note 15, at 220. *See* Samuel Issacharoff, *Fragile Democracies*, 120 HARV. L. REV. 1405, 1433–34, 1462–63 (2007).

22 Gregory H. Fox and Georg Nolte, *Intolerant Democracies*, 36 HARV. INT'L L.J. 1, 32–34 (1995).

23 Issacharoff, *supra* note 21, 120 HARV. L. REV. 1434.

24 Official Propaganda Case, BVerfGE 44, 125, at 138 (1977), translation from KOMMERS, *supra* note 15, at 178.

25 BVerfGE 1, 14, at 33, translation from KOMMERS, *supra* note 15, at 63.

26 BVerfGE 44, 125, at 141, 142, translation from KOMMERS, *supra* note 15, at 179.

27 Voting Rights of Resident Aliens in Schleswig-Holstein, BVerfGE 83, 37, at 50 (1990), translation from KOMMERS, *supra* note 15, at 198.

28 *See* Basic Law, art. 28, *and see* the Maastrict Treaty Cases, 89 BVerfGE 155 (1993). For foreign constitutions, *see* https://www.constituteproject.org/#/search, http://www. constitution.org/cons/natlcons.htm, and relevant national websites. For a partial translation of the decision *see* NORMAN DORSEN, MICHEL ROSENFELD, ANDRÁS SAJÓ, AND SUSANNE BAER, COMPARATIVE CONSTITUTIONALISM: CASES AND MATERIALS 59–62 (West Group 2003). On guest workers, *see* Ronald J. Krotoszynski, Jr., *A Comparative Perspective on the First Amendment: Free Speech, Militant Democracy, and the Primacy of Dignity as a Preferred Constitutional Value in Germany*, 78 TUL. L. REV. 1549, 1599–1601 (2004).

29 Rights of Independent Party Representatives (AKA Wüppesahl Case), BVerfGE 80, 188, at 218 (1989), translation from KOMMERS, *supra* note 15, at 175.

30 National Unity Election Case, BVerfGE 82, 322 (1990), translation from KOMMERS, *supra* note 15, at 187.

31 National Unity Election Case, translation from KOMMERS, *supra* note 15, at 188. Kommers discusses the Court's action and the legislative response at 191.

32 Investigation Committee of the Schleswig-Holstein Parliament, BVerfGE 49, 70, at 85 (1978), translation from KOMMERS, *supra* note 15, at 167.

33 *Id.* BVerfGE 49, 70, at 86, translation from KOMMERS, *supra* note 15, at 169. *Cf.* Green Party Access to Intelligence Budget, BVerfGE 70, 324, at 366 (1986), translation

from KOMMERS, *supra* note 15, at 172; Rights of Independent Party Representatives (AKA Wüppesahl Case), BVerfGE 80, 188, at 218 (1989), translation from KOMMERS, *supra* note 15, at 175; Wüppesahl Case, BVerfGE 80, 188, at 218, translation from KOMMERS, *supra* note 15, at 175–76.

34 *See* DONALD P. KOMMERS AND RUSSELL A. MILLER, THE CONSTITUTIONAL JURISPRUDENCE OF THE FEDERAL REPUBLIC OF GERMANY 600, 601 & 622–24 (Duke Univ. Press, 3d ed. rev. & exp. 2012). Peter E. Quint, *Free Speech and Private Law in German Constitutional Theory*, 48 MD. L. REV. 247, 345–47 (1989); Family Burden Compensation Case, 99 BVerfGE 216 (1998), partial translation available in Dorsen *et al.*, *supra* note 28, at 1219–23. *Compare* Susanne Baer, *Constitutional Equality: Equality: The Jurisprudence of the German Constitutional Court*, 5 COLUM. J. EUR. L. 249, 273, 279 (1999) *with* Edward J. Eberle, *Equality in Germany and the United States*, 10 SAN DIEGO INT'L L. J. 63 (2008).

35 *See* cases collected in KOMMERS, *supra* note 15, at 461–486.

36 School Head-Scarf Case, 2 BvR 1436/02, Sept. 24, 2003, at par. 41, *available at* http://www.bverfg.de/entscheidungen/rs20030924_2bvr143602.html.

37 School Head-Scarf Case, 2 BvR 1436/02, at par. 41.

38 Ruben Seth Fogel, *Headscarves in German Public Schools: Religious Minorities are Welcome in Germany, Unless–God Forbid–They are Religious*, 51 N.Y. L. SCH. L. REV. 618, 620–24 (2006). *See also* Edward J. Eberle, *Free Exercise of Religion in Germany and the United States*, 78 TUL. L. REV. 1023, 1086–87 (2004).

39 DAVID P. CURRIE, THE CONSTITUTION OF THE FEDERAL REPUBLIC OF GERMANY 152 (Univ. of Chicago Press 1994).

40 BASIC LAW, art. 72; Daniel Halberstam and Roderick M. Hills, Jr., *State Autonomy in Germany and the United States*, 574 ANNALS OF THE AM. ACAD. OF POL. & SOC. SCI.: THE SUPREME COURT'S FEDERALISM: REAL OR IMAGINED? 173, 176–77 (Mar. 2001), *available at* http://www.jstor.org/stable/1049063.

41 Southwest State Case, BVerfGE 1, 14, 23, 44, translation from KOMMERS, *supra* note 15, at 62 & 66.

42 Foreign Voters I Case, BVerfGE 83, 37 (1990), translation from KOMMERS, *supra* note 15, at 199.

43 *See* VICKI JACKSON AND MARK TUSHNET, COMPARATIVE CONSTITUTIONAL LAW 1638–61 (Foundation Press, 2d ed. 2006). *See, e.g., Lüth Case*, BVerfGE 7, 198, at 208 (1958), translation from KOMMERS, *supra* note 15, at 365. The translation in KOMMERS AND MILLER, 3d ed. rev. and expanded, *supra* note 34, at 445–46, is slightly different but to the same effect. *See* Peter E. Quint, *Free Speech and Private Law in German Constitutional Theory*, 48 MD. L. REV. 247 (1989).

44 On state action doctrine, see N.C. State Bd. of Dental Exam'rs v. FTC, 135 S. Ct. 1101 (U.S. 2015); Civil Rights Cases, 109 U.S. 3 (1883). For exceptions extending constitutional obligations to primaries and libel suits, see Terry v. Adams, 345 U.S. 461 (1953); New York Times v. Sullivan, 376 U.S. 254 (1964). For denial of federal power over private action which facilitated a century of political violence, see United States v. Cruikshank, 92 U.S. 542, 553–55 (1876). Compare with U.S. CONST., Amend. XIII.

45 *See* Jim Yardley, *Panic Seizes India as a Region's Strife Radiates*, N.Y. TIMES, Aug. 18, 2012.

46 *See* ASHUTOSH VARSHNEY, ETHNIC CONFLICT AND CIVIC LIFE: HINDUS AND MUSLIMS IN INDIA (Yale Univ. Press 2002).

47 Ismail Faruqui v. Union of India (1995) A.I.R. 605 (Sup. Ct., India, 24 Oct. 1994), par. 1. Judgments available on Supreme Court of India official website at http://judis. nic.in/supremecourt/chejudis.asp.

48 *Id.* at par. 33.

49 *Id.* at par. 38.

50 *Id. See also* Bukhari v. Mehra (Sup. Ct., India 1975) A.I.R. 1778 (2 Sup. Ct., India, Apr. 5, 1975); Issacharoff, *supra* note 21, 120 HARV. L. REV. 1423–29.

51 Aruna Roy v. Union of India (2002) (3) L.R.I. 643 (emphasis in original).

52 *Id.* at par. 36 (judgment of Dharmadhikari, J.); *and see id.* at par. 32 (judgment of Shah, J.).

53 *Id.* at par. 38.

54 *Id.* at par. 39 (judgment of Shah, J.).

55 *Id.* at par. 36 (Judgment of Shah, J.).

56 *Id.* at par. 1 (Judgment of Dharmadhikari, J.).

57 Epperson v. Arkansas, 393 U.S. 97, 106 (1968).

58 INDIA CONST. (1950) art. 19, secs. 1–2.

59 INDIA CONST. (1950) art. 19, secs. 1, 3–5.

60 Dr. Ramesh Yeshwant Prabhoo v. Shri Prabhakar Kashinath Kunte (1996) A.I.R. 1113 (Sup. Ct., India, Dec. 11, 1995).

61 Kesavananda Bharati Sripadagalvaru v. State of Kerala (1973) (72) A.I.R. 1461(Sup. Ct., India) (Apr. 24, 1973).

62 *Id.* at par. 1480. *See also id.* at par. 506 (Sikri, C.J.); *id.* at par. 620 (*per* Shelat and Grover, JJ.); *Id.* at par. 787 (K. S. Hegde and A.K. Mukherjea, JJ.); *id.* at par. 1260 (P. Jaganmohan Reddy, J.).

63 *Id.* at par. 1476.

64 *Id.* at par. 2013) (opinion of S. N. Dwivedi, J.). *See also id.* at par. 1285) (opinion of D.G. Palekar, J.).

65 *Id.* at par. 1227) (opinion of P. Jaganmohan Reddy, J).

66 *Id.* at par. 72 (S. M. Sikri, C.J.).

67 *Id.* at par. 569 (opinion of J. M. Shelat and A. N. Grover, JJ.).

68 *Id.* at par. 324 (*per* S. M. Sikri, C.J.).

69 *Id.* at par. 1208) (opinion of P. Jaganmohan Reddy, J).

70 *Id.* at 685.

71 *Id.* at par. 1208) (opinion of P. Jaganmohan Reddy, J).

72 *Id.* at par. 620 (*per* Shelat and Grover, JJ.).

73 Kesavananda Bharati Sripadagalvaru v. State of Kerala (1973) (72) A.I.R. 1461(Sup. Ct., India,) (Apr. 24, 1973) at par. 521 (*per* Shelat and Grover, JJ.).

74 Smt. Indira Nehru Gandhi v. Shri Raj Narain and Anr. (1975) A.I.R. SC 2299 (Sup. Ct., India, Nov. 7, 1975) par. 1, *available at* http://indiankanoon.org/doc/936707/.

75 *See id.* at par. 21.

76 *See id.* opinion of Ray, C.J., pars. 1–158; Khanna, J., pars. 159–254; Mathew, J. pars. 255–388; Beg, J., pars. 389–637; Chandrachud, J., pars. 638–697; Vivek Krishnamurthy, *Colonial Cousins: Explaining India and Canada's Unwritten Constitutional Principles*, 34 YALE J. INT'L L. 207, 228–29 (2009).

77 Sankaran Krishna, *Constitutionalism, Democracy and Political Culture in India*, in POLITICAL CULTURE AND CONSTITUTIONALISM 168 (Daniel P. Franklin and Michael J. Baun, eds. 1994).

78 *See* Minerva Mills v. Union of India (Sup. Ct., India 1980) 2 S.C.C. 591; discussed in Krishnamurthy, *Colonial Cousins: Explaining India and Canada's Unwritten Constitutional Principles*, 34 YALE J. INT'L L. at 229 (2009).

79 Sr Chaudhuri v. State of Punjab (Sup. Ct., India 2001) A.I.R. 2707, at par. 33.

80 Union of India v. Association for Democratic Reforms (Sup. Ct., India 2002) A.I.R. 2112 (2002) (2) LRI 305 par. 22.

81 *Id.* at par. 25, *quoting* Mohinder Singh Gill v Chief Election Commissioner (Sup. Ct., India 1978) S.C.R. 272, 291 par.23.

82 People's Union of Civil Liberties (PUCL) v. Union of India (Sup. Ct., India 2003) (2) LRI 13 par. 17 at 15 (pagination internal to document) (opinion of Shah, J.).

83 Union of India v Ass'n for Democratic Reforms at pars. 41 & 43 (quoting Secretary, Ministry of Information and Broadcasting, Government of India v. Cricket Association of Bengal (Sup. Ct., India 1995) 2 S.C.C. 161 par. 82).

84 *Id.* at par. 53.

85 *Id.*; *see also People's Union of Civil Liberties (PUCL)* at par. 17 ("For having unpolluted healthy democracy, citizens-voters should be well-informed.").

86 Dr. Subramanian Swamy v. Election Commission of India, Civil Appeal No. 9093 OF 2013 (Sup. Ct., India Oct. 8, 2013), pars. 29–31.

87 Sr Chaudhuri v. State of Punjab (Sup. Ct., India 2001) 2707 A.I.R. (2001) (3) L.R.I. 1094 par. 20.

88 *Id.* at par. 33.

89 *Arundhati Roy, Re* (Sup. Ct., India 2002) (1) L.R.I. 497 par. 25, quoting Dr.D.C. Saxena v. Hon'ble the Chief Justice of India (Sup. Ct., India 1996) 5 S.C.C. 216.

90 *Id.* at par. 36 quoting P.N. Duda v. P. Shiv Shanker (Sup. Ct., India 1988) 3 S.C.C. 167.

91 *Arundhati Roy, Re* (Sup. Ct., India 2002) (1) L.R.I. 497 par. 25, quoting Dr.D.C. Saxena v. Hon'ble the Chief Justice of India (Sup. Ct., India 1996) 5 S.C.C. 216.

92 *Id.* at par. 36 quoting P.N. Duda v. P. Shiv Shanker (Sup. Ct., India 1988) 3 S.C.C. 167.

93 Sunil Fulchand Shah v. Union of India and other appeals (Sup. Ct., India 2000) 2 L.R.I. 724 par. 7.

94 Fox and Nolte, *supra* note 2, 36 HARV. INT'L L.J. at 1, *and see* State of Madras v. V. G. Row (Sup. Ct., India 1952) S.C.R. 597, 607–08, *quoted* in Fox and Nolte, *supra* note 2, 36 HARV. INT'L L.J. at 31–32.

95 Lalita Kumari v. Govt. of U.P., Writ Petition (Criminal) No. 68 of 2008 (Sup. Ct., India Nov. 12, 2013).

96 *See* Kesavananda Bharati Sripadagalvaru v. State of Kerala (1973) (72) A.I.R. 1461(Sup. Ct., India,) (Apr. 24, 1973) at par. 316 (opinion of Sikri, J.).

97 *Id.* at par. 568 (opinion of Shelat and Grover, JJ.).

98 *Id.* at pars. 2193–94 (opinion of Chandrachud, J.).

99 *Id.* at par. 352 (opinion of Sikri, J.); pars. 515 & 517 (opinion of Shelat and Grover, JJ.); *Id.* at pars. 954, 1036 (opinion of Ray, J.).

100 For varying assessments of the Court's work, *see* S. P. Sathe, *Judicial Activism: The Indian Experience,* 6 WASH. U. J. L. & POL'Y 29 (2001); Carl Baar, *Social Action Litigation in India: The Operation and Limits of the World's Most Active Judiciary,* in COMPARATIVE JUDICIAL REVIEW AND PUBLIC POLICY (Praeger, Donald W. Jackson and C. Neal Tate, eds. 1992); Jamie Cassels, *Judicial Activism and Public Interest Litigation in India: Attempting the Impossible?* 37 AM. J. COMP. L. 495 (1989).

101 R. v. Oakes [1986] 1 S.C.R. 103, 1986 S.C.R. Lexis 953, 1986 N.R. LEXIS 2848, at 15, 5, pars. 3 & 64.

102 R. v. Keegstra, 1990 N.R. LEXIS 959 at 66, par. 45, quoting *Oakes,* 1 S.C.R., at 136.

103 *Id.* at 98–104, pars. 74–79.

104 *Id.* at 115, par. 90.

105 R. v. Keegstra [1990] 3 S.C.R. 697, 1990 N.R. LEXIS 959, at 26–27, pars. 2–3.

106 *Id.*at 836, 855 & 859–60 (McLachlin, J., dissenting).

107 Taylor and Western Guard Party v. Canadian Human Rights Comm'n, 117 N.R. 191, 216, par. 41 (N.R. 1990), quoted in Fox and Nolte, 36 HARV. INT'L L.J. 1, 27.

108 Reference Re Secession of Quebec [1998] 2 S.C.R. 217, 1998 N.R. LEXIS 472, par. 2.

109 *Id.* at 39–40, par. 32.

110 *Id.* at 54 par. 51.

111 *Id.* at 52, par. 49.

112 On federalism, *See, e.g.,* Alden v. Maine, 527 U.S. 706 (1999); Fla. Prepaid Postsecondary Educ. Expense Bd. v. College Sav. Bank, 527 U.S. 627 (1999); College Sav. Bank v. Fla. Prepaidpostsecondary Ed. Expense Bd., 527 U.S. 666 (1999). On separation of powers, *See, e.g.,* Youngstown Sheet & Tube Co. v. Sawyer, 343 U.S. 579 (1952). On the First Amendment, *see* Griswold v. Connecticut, 381 U.S. 479, 483 (1965); CHARLES L. BLACK, JR., STRUCTURE AND RELATIONSHIP IN CONSTITUTIONAL LAW (Louisiana State Univ. Press 1969).

113 *Id.* at 64, par. 63, quoting Reference re Provincial Electoral Boundaries (Sask.), [1991] 2 S.C.R. 158, at 186.

114 *Id.* at 65–66, par. 65.

115 *Id.* at 66, par. 65.

116 *Id.* at 66, par. 65, and Canadian Charter of Rights and Freedoms, sec. 33.

117 *Id.* at 64, par. 64.

118 *Id.* at 65, par. 64, quoting *Oakes,* 1 S.C.R. at 136.

119 *Id.* at 68, pars. 63 & 67–68.

120 *Id.* at 42–46, 69, 76, pars. 38–42, 69 & 79.

121 *Id.* at 42, 130–31, pars. 45 & 149.

122 *Id.* at 102–29, pars. 109–46.

123 *Id.* at 117–23, pars. 131–39.

124 Sauvé v. Canada (Chief Electoral Officer), [2002] 3 S.C.R. 519; 2002 SCC 68; 2002 S.C.R. LEXIS 591.

125 Canada Elections Act, R.S.C. 1985, c. E-2 section 51(e).

126 *Sauvé v. Canada,* par. 9, *and see* par. 19.

127 *Id.* at pars. 38 & 41.

128 *Id.* at par. 31.

129 *Id.* at par. 31.

130 *Id.* at par. 31.

131 *Id.* at par. 31.

132 *Id.* at par. 41.

133 *Id.* at par. 44.

134 Multani v. Commission scolaire Marguerite-Bourgeoys, 2006 Can. Sup. Ct. LEXIS 6; 2006 SCC 6; [2006] S.C.J. No. 6, pars. 3–4, 26, 76, & 78, quoting R. v. M. (M.R.), [1998] 3 S.C.R. 393, par. 3.

135 *Id.* at par. 78.

136 *Id.* at pars. 76.

137 *See In re:* Certification of the Constitution of the Republic of South Africa, *1996,* 1996 (10) BCLR 1253 (CC) 1996 SACLR LEXIS 79 (CC), pars. 13–17. See also Certification of the Amended Text of the Constitution of the Republic of South Africa, 1996 (CCT37/96) [1996] ZACC 24; 1997 (1) BCLR 1; 1997 (2) SA 97 (4 Dec. 1996).

138 S. Afr. Interim Constitution, 1993, Schedule 4, principles I, VIII, XIV & XVII.

139 *Certification of the Constitution of the Republic of South Africa*, pars. 13–17.

140 *Id.* at par. 483.

141 *Id.* at par. 45.

142 *Id.* at par. 180.

143 *Id.* at par. 48.

144 *Id.* at par. 50.

145 *Id.* at par. 51.

146 *Id.* at par. 90.

147 *Id.* at par. 189, nn. 137–38.

148 *Id.* at par. 195.

149 *Id.* at par. 196.

150 *Id.* at par. 195.

151 *Id.* at par. 195.

152 *Id.* at pars. 224, 225 & 227.

153 *Id.* at par. 180.

154 *Id.* at pars. 183 & 185–86.

155 *Id.* at par. 184.

156 *Id.* at par. 108–09.

157 *Id.* at par. 111.

158 *Id.* at par. 482.

159 Soobramoney v. Minster of Health (Kwazulu-Natal) (SC 1997), 1997 (12) BCLR 1696 (CC); 1997 SACLR LEXIS 41 (CC), par. 9 (*per* Chaskalson, President).

160 *Id.* at par. 7.

161 *Id.* at par. 8.

162 *Id.* at par. 9.

163 *Id.* at par. 42.

164 *Id.* at par. 52.

165 *Id.* at par. 53.

166 *Id.* at par. 54.

167 Gov't v. Grootboom, 2000 (11) BCLR 1169 (CC), 2000 SACLR LEXIS 126 (CC).

168 *Id.* at par. 7.

169 *Id.* at par. 4.

170 *Id.* at par. 23.

171 *Id.* at par. 2.

172 *Id.* at par. 96; Constitution of South Africa, sec. 26(2).

173 *See* Theunis Roux, ch. 10, *Democracy* in STU WOOLMAN, ET AL CONSTITUTIONAL LAW OF SOUTH AFRICA (Juta & Co, Original Service, 2d ed. 2006), sec. 10.4(c).

174 *Minister of Health and Others v Treatment Action Campaign and Others*, CCT8/02, 2002 (10) BCLR 1033 (CC), 2002 SACLR LEXIS 26, May 7, 2002 and see S. Afr. Const. sec. 27(a).

175 *Id.* at par. 135(3)(a).

176 *August v Electoral Commission*, 1999 (3) SA 1 (CC); 1999 (4) BCLR 363 (CC).

177 *Minister of Home Affairs v National Institute for Crime Prevention and the Re-integration of Offenders (NICRO)*, 2005 (3) SA 280 (CC), 2004 (5) BCLR 445 (CC). On obligation to provide for exercise of the right, *see* par. 28.

178 *See id.* at par. 33.

179 *Id.* at par. 28, quoting *August*, par. 16.

180 *Id.* at par. 47 (Chaskalson, CJ, for the majority, consisting of nine of the eleven justices).

181 *See* Michelle Alexander, THE NEW JIM CROW: MASS INCARCERATION IN THE AGE OF COLORBLINDNESS (The New Press 2010); *compare* United States v. Armstrong, 517 U.S. 456 (1996).

182 *NICRO* at par. 65.

183 *Id.* at par. 22, quoting *August v Electoral Commission*, 1999 (3) SA 1 (CC); 1999 (4) BCLR 363 (CC), at par. 17.

184 *African Christian Democratic Party v The Electoral Commission and Others*, CCT10/06, 2006 (5) BCLR 579 (CC), 2006 SACLR LEXIS 5 (2006).

185 *Id.* at par. 23.

186 Matatiele Municipality and Others v President of the Republic of South Africa and Others, 2006 (5) BCLR 622, Feb. 27, 2006, par. 41, quoting Executive Council, Western Capre v. Minister of Provincial Affairs, 2000 (1) SA 661 (CC), 1999 (12) BCLR 1360 (CC) at par. 50.

187 Matatiele Municipality and Others v President of the Republic of South Africa and Others, Aug. 18, 2006, CCT73/05, 2007 (1) BCLR 47 (CC), 2006 SACLR LEXIS 20 (2006).

188 *Id.* at par. 55, quoting the S. Afr. Const., sec. 116(1)(b). *See also, Id.* at pars. 63, 65 & 66 *and* par. 40, quoting Doctors for Life International v. The Speaker of the National Assembly, CCT 12/05, 17 Aug. 2006, 2006 (12) BCLR 1399 (CC), at par. 121.

189 *United Democratic Movement v President of the Republic of South Africa and Others* (African Christian Democratic Party and Others Intervening ; Institute for Democracy in South Africa and Another as Amici Curiae) (No 2) (CCT23/02) [2002] ZACC 21; 2003 (1) SA 495; 2002 (11) BCLR 1179 (Oct. 4, 2002), http://www.saflii.org/za/cases/ZACC/2002/21.html.

190 *Id.* at par. 17.

191 *Id.* at par. 34.

192 *Id.* at par. 35.

193 *Id.* at par. 53. *See also* par. 76.

194 *Id.* at par. 47.

195 *Id.* at par. 74.

196 *Id.* at par. 55; *and see id.* at par. 66.

197 *Id.* at pars. 113–14.

198 *Democratic Alliance and Another v Masondo NO and Another* (2002) (CCT29/02) [2002] ZACC 28; 2003 (2) BCLR 128 ; 2003 (2) SA 413 (CC) (Dec. 12, 2002), http://www.saflii.org/za/cases/ZACC/2002/28.html.

199 *See Democratic Alliance*, pars. 8–9 (Langa, J., for the Court); *Id.* at par. 60 (O'Regan, J., dissenting).

200 S. Afr. Const. sec. 160(8).

201 *Id.* at par. 22 (Langa, J., for the Court); *Id.* at par. 40 (Sachs, J., concurring).

202 *See* S. Afr. Const. sec. 152, and *Democratic Alliance*, par. 17 (Langa, J., for the Court); *Id.* at par. 22.

203 *Id.* at par. 72 (O'Regan, J., dissenting).

204 *Id.* at par. 38 (Sachs, J., concurring).

205 *Id.* at par. 42 (Sachs, J., concurring).

206 Doctors for Life International v. The Speaker of the National Assembly, CCT 12/05, 17 Aug. 2006, 2006 (12) BCLR 1399 (CC), par. 121.

207 *Id.* at 37.

208 *Id.* at 35 & 57.

209 *Id.* at 98.

210 *Id.* at 98–99.

211 *Id.* at 99.

212 *Id.* at 100.

213 *Id.* at 109.

214 *S v Mamabolo* (E TV, Business Day and the Freedom of Expression Institute Intervening), CCT44/00, 2001 (5) BCLR 449 (CC), 2001 SACLR LEXIS 24 (Apr. 11, 2001), par. 5.

215 *Id.*

216 *Id.* at par. 10.

217 *Id.* at pars. 11–12 & 64.

218 *Id.* at par. 65.

219 *Id.* at par. 15.

220 *Id.* at par. 30.

221 *Id.* at par. 37.

222 *Id.* at par. 37.

223 *Id.* at pars. 16–17.

224 *Id.* at par. 38.

225 *Id.* at par. 38.

226 S. Afr. Const. 165(4).

227 *S v Mamabolo*, CCT44/00, 2001 (5) BCLR 449 (CC), 2001 SACLR LEXIS 24 (Apr. 11, 2001), at par. 38.

228 *Id.* at par. 78.

229 *Islamic Unity Convention v Independent Broadcasting Authority and Others*, CCT 36/01, 2002 (5) BCLR 433 (CC); 2002 SACLR LEXIS 2 (Nov. 4, 2002), at pars. 1–2 & 22.

230 *Id.* at par. 21.

231 *Id.* at par. 26, quoting South African National Defence Union v Minister of Defence and Another 1999 (6) BCLR 615 (CC); 1999 (4) SA 469 (CC), at sec. 8.

232 *Islamic Unity Convention*, at par. 26, quoting *South African National Defence Union*, at par. 7.

233 *Id.* at par. 26, quoting *S v Mamabolo* (E TV, Business Day and the Freedom of Expression Institute Intervening), CCT44/00, 2001 (5) BCLR 449 (CC), 2001 SACLR LEXIS 24 (Apr. 11, 2001), at 4 par. 37.

234 *Id.* at par. 29.

235 *Id.* at pars. 35–36, 43–44, 51.

236 Roux, *supra* note 173, at sec. 10.5.

237 Roux, *supra* note 173, at sec. 10.2(b).

238 *See* Teitel, *supra* note 19, at 62 & 65.

239 Olgun Akbulut, *Criteria Developed by the European Court of Human Rights on the Dissolution of Political Parties*, 34 FORDHAM INT'L L. J. 46, 75 (2010).

240 *Vogt v Germany* (1996) 21 EHRR 205, [1995] ECHR 17851/91 [GC] (Sept. 26, 1995) par. 59.

241 *Id.*

242 Luzius Wildhaber, *The European Court of Human Rights: The Past, the Present, the Future*, 22 AM. U. INT'L L. REV. 521, 534 (2007).

243 International Covenant on Civil and Political Rights, art. 25. *See also* Fox and Nolte, *supra* note 2, 36 HARV. INT'L L.J. at 3, 61 & 69.

244 Wildhaber, *supra* note 242, at 532–33.

245 Hirst v. The United Kingdom (No. 2), [2005] ECHR 74025/01 [GC] (6 Oct. 2005), at par. 36.

246 Leyla Şahin v. Turkey, [2005] ECHR 44774/98 [GC] (10 Nov. 2005), at par. 113.

247 *Hirst v. The United Kingdom,* par. 36. followed, Firth and others v. The United Kingdom [2014] ECHR 47784/09 [4th section] (12 Aug. 2014). ECHR cases are available at http://hudoc.echr.coe.int.

248 *Id.* at par. 21.

249 *Id.* at pars. 12–13, 20 & 52.

250 *Id.* at pars. 9 & 55.

251 *Id.* at pars. 33 & 81.

252 *Id.* at pars. 81–83.

253 *Id.* at par. 36.

254 *Id.* at par. 36.

255 *Id.* at par. 36.

256 *Id.* at par. 38.

257 *Id.* at par. 39.

258 *Id.* at par. 58.

259 *Id.* at par. 59.

260 *Id.* at par. 61.

261 *Id.* at par. 62.

262 *Id.* at par. 62.

263 *Id.* at par. 62.

264 *Id.* at par. 69.

265 *Id.* at par. 82.

266 *Id.* at par. 82.

267 Wildhaber, *supra* note 242 at 529 citing United Communist Party of Turkey v. Turkey, 1998-I Eur. Ct. H.R. 1.

268 G. BINGHAM POWELL, CONTEMPORARY DEMOCRACIES: PARTICIPATION, STABILITY, AND VIOLENCE (Harvard Univ. Press 1982).

269 Tănase v. Moldova, [2010] ECHR 7/08 [GC] (27 Apr. 2010).

270 *Id.* at par. 42; *id.* at par. 3 of the Court's order; *id.* at par. 178, *and see* par. 158, quoting Aziz v. Cyprus, no. 69949/01, sec. 28, ECHR 2004-V.

271 *Id.* at par. 167.

272 *Id.* at par. 167.

273 *Id.* at par. 175.

274 Yumak & Sadak v. Turkey [2008] ECHR 10226/03 [GC] (July 8, 2008).

275 *Id.* at par. 110.

276 *Id.* at par. 109 (iv).

277 *Id.* at par. 106.

278 *Id.* at par. 107.

279 *Id.* at par. 136.

280 *Id.* at par. 109 (iv).

281 *Id.* at par. 109(i).

282 *Id.* at par. 147.

283 *Id.* at par. 109.

284 *Id.* at par. 109.

285 *Id.* at par. 109.

286 *Id.* at par. 110.

287 *Id.* at par. 131.

288 *Id.* at par. 131.

289 *Id.* at pars. 112 & 137.

290 *Id.* at par. 137.

291 *Id.* at par. 122.

292 *Id.* at par. 125.

293 European Commission for Democracy Through Law (Venice Commission), GUIDELINES ON PROHIBITION AND DISSOLUTION OF POLITICAL PARTIES AND ANALOGOUS MEASURES, adopted by the Venice Commission at its 41st plenary session (Venice, 10–11 Dec. 1999), *available at* http://www.venice.coe.int/docs/2000/ CDL-INF(2000)001-e.pdf, revised and incorporated in CODE OF GOOD PRACTICE IN THE FIELD OF POLITICAL PARTIES adopted by the Venice Commission at its 77th Plenary Session (Venice, 12–13 Dec. 2008) and Explanatory Report adopted by the Venice Commission at its 78th Plenary Session (Venice, 13–14 Mar. 2009) 2008, *available at* http://www.venice.coe.int/docs/2009/CDL-AD(2009)002-e.asp.

294 *Id.*

295 CODE, *supra* note 293, *available at* http://www.venice.coe.int/docs/2009/ CDL-AD(2009)021-e.asp#_ftnref23.

296 Yumak & Sadak v. Turkey [2008] ECHR 10226/03 [GC] (July 8, 2008), pars. 106, 109, 110.

297 *See* CHARLES L. BLACK, JR., STRUCTURE AND RELATIONSHIP IN CONSTITUTIONAL LAW (Louisiana State Univ. Press 1969).

298 Akbulut, *supra* note 239, 34 FORDHAM INT'L L.J. at 46 & 48.

299 *Id.* at 54.

300 United Communist Party of Turkey v. Turkey (1998) 26 EHRR 121, [1998] ECHR 19392/92 [GC], par. 10.

301 *Id.* at par. 55.

302 Issacharoff, *supra* note 21, 120 HARV. L. REV. at 1446–47.

303 *See* http://www.ihd.org.tr/images/pdf/IHD_1999_2008_Comparative_Balance_ Sheet.pdf.

304 *United Communist Party of Turkey v. Turkey*, at par. 25.

305 *Id.* at par. 27.

306 *Id.* at par. 57.

307 *Id.* at par. 52.

308 Akbulut, *supra* note 239, 34 FORDHAM INT'L L.J. at 54–55.

309 Refah Partisi (The Welfare Party) and others v. Turkey, [2003] ECHR 41340/98 [GC] (13 Feb. 2003), at par. 119.

310 Leyla Şahin v. Turkey, [2005] ECHR 44774/98 [GC] (10 Nov. 2005), at par. 113.

311 Wildhaber, *supra* note 271, at 529–30.

312 *Refah Partisi*, at par. 119.

313 Azizah al-Hibri, in an e- mail to the author, Apr. 4, 2012; I am indebted to her for comments on the language in an earlier draft.

314 *Refah Partisi*, at par. 123.

315 *Id*. at par. 123.

316 *See* Akbulut, *supra* note 239, 34 FORDHAM INT'L L.J. at 60–61.

317 *Refah Partisi*, at par. 123.

318 *Id*. at par. 123.

319 *See* MICHAEL WALZER, ON TOLERATION (Yale Univ. Press 1997).

320 See the discussion in Akbulut, *supra* note 239, 34 FORDHAM INT'L L.J. at 66–70. Compare Holder v. Humanitarian Law Project, 130 S. Ct. 2705, 2713 (2010); Arnett v. Kennedy, 416 U.S. 134, 182 (1974); Brandenburg v. Ohio, 395 U.S. 444 (1969); Ibrahim v. Dep't of Homeland Sec., 669 F.3d 983, 988–90 (9th Cir. Cal. 2012); Carl A. Auerbach, *The Communist Control Act of 1954: A Proposed Legal-Political Theory of Free Speech*, 23 U. CHI. L. REV. 173, 188 (1956); Fox and Nolte, *supra* note 3, 36 HARV. INT'L L.J. at 68; and *see* Hans A. Linde, *"Clear and Present Danger" Reexamined: Dissonance in the Brandenburg Concerto*, 22 STAN. L. REV. 1163, 1183 (1970).

321 *Id*. at 66–69.

322 *Vogt v Germany* (1996) 21 EHRR 205, [1995] ECHR 17851/91 [GC] (Sept. 26, 1995), at pars. 59 & 61.

323 See Yahoo! Inc. v. La Ligue Contre Le Racisme et L'antisemitisme, and L'union Des Etudiants Juifs De France, 433 F.3d 1199 (9th Cir. 2006).

324 Lehideux and Isorni v. France, 5 BHRC 540 [GC] (23 SEPT. 1998), at par. 55.

325 *Id*.

326 *Id*.

327 *Id*. *See also* Nilsen and Johnsen v. Norway, [1999] ECHR 23118/93[GC] (25 NOV. 1999) par. 43.

328 Explanatory Report, incorporated as part III of GUIDELINES ON PROHIBITION AND DISSOLUTION OF POLITICAL PARTIES, note 361 above, at par. 11, available at http://www.venice.coe.int/docs/2000/CDL-INF(2000)001-e.pdf.

329 *Id*. at pars. 11, 38 & 34.

330 Hasan And Chaush v. Bulgaria, [2000] ECHR 30985/96 [GC] (26 Oct. 2000), at pars. 60 & 78.

331 Teitel, *supra* note 19, at 45.

332 *Id*. at 56.

333 *See id*. at 58–62.

334 *Id*. at 57–62.

335 *See id*. at 67–69.

336 Leyla Şahin v. Turkey, [2005] ECHR 44774/98 [GC] (10 Nov. 2005), pars. 47, 113.

337 *Id*., pars. 30–51, 119–20.

338 *Id*., par. 106; Convention Art. IX, par. 2.

339 Leyla Şahin, par. 111.

340 *Id*., par. 113.

341 *See id.*, par. 111.

342 *Id.*, par. 109.

343 *Compare* Employment Div. v. Smith, 494 U.S. 872, 886 (1990); and contrast *Id.* at 901 (O'Connor, J., concurring).

344 *Leyla Şahin v. Turkey, supra* note 336, par. 113.

345 *Id.*, par. 165.

346 *Id.*, pars. 115–16.

347 *Id.*, par. 113.

348 *Id.*, par. 114.

349 *Id.*, par. 104.

350 *Id.*, pars. 105–06.

351 *Id.*, par. 107.

352 *Id.*, par. 108.

353 *Id.*, par. 108.

354 *Id.*, par. 110.

355 *Id.*, par. 4 (dissenting opinion of Judge Tulkens).

356 *Id.*, par. 5 (dissenting opinion of Judge Tulkens).

357 Hasan And Chaush v. Bulgaria, [2000] ECHR 30985/96 [GC] (26 Oct. 2000), at par. 87.

358 *Id.* at par. 87.

359 Segerstedt-Wiberg and Others v. Sweden, [2006] ECHR 62332/00 (6 June 2006).

360 *Id.* at par. 76 and *see generally*, Kim Lane Scheppele, *When the Law Doesn't Count: The 2000 Election and the Failure of the Rule of Law*, 149 U. PA. L. REV. 1361, 1370–95 (2001).

361 *Segerstedt-Wiberg*, at par. 76.

362 *Id.* at par. 76.

363 *Id.* at par. 76.

364 *Id.* at par. 76.

365 *Id.* at par. 79.

366 *Id.* at par. 73.

367 *Id.* at par. 88.

368 Wildhaber, *supra* note 242, at 529–31.

369 *Id.* at 535.

370 *Id.* at 536.

371 *Id.* at 535.

372 *See* Judgment, C-402/05 P and C-415/05 P *Yassin Abdullah Kadi and Al Barakaat Int'l. Found. v Council of the European Union and Com'n of the European Communities* (Sept. 3, 2008), *available at* http://curia.europa.eu/jcms/jcms/j_6; Opinion, Advocate Gen. Poiares Maduro, in *Id.* delivered on Jan. 23, 2008; Kim Lane Scheppele, *The International State of Emergency: Challenges to Constitutionalism after September 11*, http://digitalcommons.law.umaryland.edu/cgi/viewcontent.cgi?article=1048&context=schmooze_papers.

373 Wildhaber, *supra* note 242, at 536.

374 *Id.* at 537.

375 *Id.*

376 *Id.* at 536.

377 Carlos Bernal Pulido, *There Are Still Judges in Berlin: On the Proposal to Amend the Ecuadorian Constitution to Allow Indefinite Presidential Reelection*, INT'L J. CONST. L. (blog), Sept. 10, 2014, http://www.iconnectblog.com/2014/09/there-are-still-judges-in-berlin-on-the-proposal-to-amend-the-ecuadorian-constitution-to-allow-indefinite-presidential-reelection/.

CHAPTER 5. RULES OF DEMOCRACY

1 *See* Niels Petersen, *The Principle of Democratic Teleology in International Law*, 34 BROOKLYN J. INT'L L. 33, 37–40 (2008); *and see* ROBERT A. DAHL, POLYARCHY: PARTICIPATION AND OPPOSITION 3–4 (Yale Univ. Press 1971).

2 Gerardo L. Munck and Jay Verkuilen, *Conceptualizing and Measuring Democracy: Evaluating Alternative Indices*, 35:1 COMP. POL. STUD. 5, 29–30 (Feb. 2002); updated in GERARDO L. MUNCK, MEASURING DEMOCRACY: A BRIDGE BETWEEN SCHOLARSHIP & POLITICS 13–37 (Johns Hopkins Univ. Press 2009).

3 U.S. CONST., art. I, secs. 9–10, art. III, sec. 3, art. IV, sec. 2, par. 1; *Id.* sec. 4; Amends. 2–6, 8, *and see generally*, IRVING BRANT, THE BILL OF RIGHTS: ITS ORIGIN AND MEANING (Bobbs-Merrill 1965).

4 U.S. CONST., Amends. 1, 14, 15, 17, 19, 23, 24, & 26.

5 1 ANNALS OF CONG. 454 (U.S. H. Rep., 1st Cong., 1st Sess., June 8, 1789).

6 U.S. CONST., Amends. 13–15, 19, 24 & 26.

7 THE FEDERALIST NO. 25, at 167 (Alexander Hamilton) (New American Library, Clinton Rossiter, ed. 1961); *The Federalist No. 48, in id.* at 308 (Madison); *The Federalist No. 49, in id.* at 317 (Madison); *The Federalist No. 73, in id.* at 442 (Hamilton).

8 CULLEN MURPHY, ARE WE ROME: THE FALL OF AN EMPIRE AND THE FATE OF AMERICA (Houghton Mifflin 2007).

9 PAUL KENNEDY, THE RISE AND FALL OF THE GREAT POWERS (Random House 1987).

10 KEVIN PHILLIPS, WEALTH AND DEMOCRACY: A POLITICAL HISTORY OF THE AMERICAN RICH 171–200 (Broadway Books 2002).

11 Eric Lichtblau, *F.B.I. Scrutinizes Antiwar Rallies*, N.Y. TIMES, Nov. 23, 2003, sec. 1, at 1.

12 Quoted in James Bamford, *The Agency That Could Be Big Brother*, N.Y. TIMES, Dec. 25, 2005.

13 *See* Scott Shane, *Election Spurred A Move to Codify U.S. Drone Policy*, N.Y. TIMES, Nov. 25, 2012, at A1; Ethan Bronner, *With Longer Reach, Rockets Bolster Hamas Arsenal*, N.Y. TIMES, Nov. 18, 2012, at A1; Jonathan Masters, *Targeted Killings* (Council on Foreign Relations), May 23, 2013, http://www.cfr.org/intelligence/targeted-killings/p9627; Peter W. Singer, *Do Drones Undermine Democracy?*, N.Y. TIMES, Jan. 22, 2012, at SR5; International Covenant on Civil and Political Rights, art. 6, 999 U.N.T.S. 171. The ACLU also follows this issue on its website under the heading "targeted killings."

14 Hedges v. Obama, 2012 U.S. Dist. Lexis 130354 (S.D.N.Y. 2012).

15 Hedges v. Obama, 2013 U.S. App. LEXIS 14417 (2d Cir. July 17, 2013).

16 Ctr. for Nat'l Sec. Studies v. United States DOJ, 215 F. Supp. 2d 94 (D.D.C. 2002), rev'd, 331 F.3d 918 (D.C. Cir. 2003), cert. den. 540 U.S. 1104 (2004); Id. at 937 (Tatel, J., dissenting). See also Eunice Moscoso, Secret Detention of Suspects Upheld; Federal Judges Say That Disclosure Could Tip Terrorists to U.S. Investigations, Security Efforts, ATLANTA JOURNAL-CONSTITUTION, June 18, 2003, at 1A; Michael Kirkland, On Law: "Secret Arrests" and Liberty (United Press International), June 20, 2003, http://www.upi.com/Business_News/Security-Industry/2003/06/20/On-Law-Secret-arrests-and-liberty/UPI-93511056132863/.

17 DWIGHT LOWELL DUMOND, ANTISLAVERY ORIGINS OF THE CIVIL WAR 13 & 32–34 (U. of Michigan Press 1959).

18 LEEANNA KEITH, THE COLFAX MASSACRE: THE UNTOLD STORY OF BLACK POWER, WHITE TERROR, AND THE DEATH OF RECONSTRUCTION (Oxford Univ. Press 2008); CHARLES LANE, THE DAY FREEDOM DIED: THE COLFAX MASSACRE, THE SUPREME COURT, AND THE BETRAYAL OF RECONSTRUCTION (Henry Holt & Company 2008); C. VANN WOODWARD, THE STRANGE CAREER OF JIM CROW, 65–91 (Oxford Univ. Press 1957).

19 See WYN CRAIG WADE, THE FIERY CROSS: THE KU KLUX KLAN IN AMERICA 324–25 (Oxford Univ. Press 1987).

20 See WILLIAM L. RIORDON, PLUNKITT OF TAMMANY HALL (Signet Classic 1996); FRANK S. ROBINSON, MACHINE POLITICS: A STUDY OF ALBANY'S O'CONNELLS (Transaction Books 1977); ALFRED STEINBERG, THE BOSSES (Macmillan 1972); Darryl McGrath, Albany Is Us, METROLAND, Apr. 28, 2005, http://www.metroland.net/back_issues/vol28_no17/features.html. See also Stephen E. Gottlieb, Rebuilding the Right of Association: The Right to Hold a Convention as a Test Case, 11 HOFSTRA L. REV. 191, 221–27, 238–43 (1982).

21 See Theola S. Labbe, Federal Intervention a Rare Move, ALBANY TIMES UNION, Apr. 26, 2001, at B11; Marv Cermak, Officials Discuss Police Plan with Feds, ALBANY TIMES UNION, Mar. 5, 2002, at B5; Kim Martineau, Prosecutor Recuses Self from Review of Police, ALBANY TIMES UNION, Mar. 5, 2002, at A1.

22 COMM'N TO INVESTIGATE ALLEGATIONS OF POLICE CORRUPTION AND THE ANTI-CORRUPTION PROCEDURES OF THE POLICE DEP'T, CITY OF NEW YORK (THE "MOLLEN COMM'N"), COMM'N REPORT (1994), available at http://www.parc.info/clientfiles/Special%20Reports/4%20-%20Mollen%20Commission%20-%20NYPD.pdf.

23 See Erwin Chemerinsky, An Independent Analysis of the Los Angeles Police Department's Board of Inquiry Report on the Rampart Scandal, 34 LOY. L.A. L. REV. 545 (2001).

24 Richard Perez-Pena, Supervision of Troopers Faulted in Evidence-Tampering Scandal, N.Y. TIMES, Feb. 4, 1997, at B1; Ronald Sullivan, Trooper's 2d Tampering Charge, N.Y. TIMES, Jan. 6, 1994, at B9.

25 *See* DA's Office v. Osborne, 557 U.S. 52, 82 (2009) (Alito, J., concurring) and citing Erin Murphy, *The New Forensics: Criminal Justice, False Certainty, and the Second Generation of Scientific Evidence*, 95 CAL. L. REV. 721, 772–773 (2007) (collecting examples).

26 Van de Kamp v. Goldstein, 555 U.S. 335 (2009); Connick v. Thompson, 131 S. Ct. 1350 (2011); *Id.* at 1371–75 (Ginsburg, J., dissenting).

27 *See* Colbert I. King, *Whose Rights Will They Come for Next?*, ALBANY TIMES UNION, June 13, 2002, at A13; Eric Lichtblau, *F.B.I. Scrutinizes Antiwar Rallies*, N.Y. TIMES, Nov. 23, 2003, A1; *and see* ATHAN THEOHARIS, FROM THE SECRET FILES OF J. EDGAR HOOVER (I.R. Dee 1991); DOUGLAS M. CHARLES, J. EDGAR HOOVER AND THE ANTI-INTERVENTIONISTS: FBI POLITICAL SURVEILLANCE AND THE RISE OF THE DOMESTIC SECURITY STATE, 1939–1945 (Ohio State Univ. Press 2007); WILLIAM W. KELLER, THE LIBERALS AND J. EDGAR HOOVER: RISE AND FALL OF A DOMESTIC INTELLIGENCE STATE (Princeton Univ. Press 1989); OVID DEMARIS, THE DIRECTOR: AN ORAL BIOGRAPHY OF J. EDGAR HOOVER 96 (Harper's Magazine Press 1975); Alan Brinkley, *Black Sites* (review of JANE MAYER, THE DARK SIDE), N.Y. TIMES BOOK REVIEW, Aug. 3, 2008; Matt Taibbi, *The Hunters and the Hunted* (review of SETH ROSENFELD, SUBVERSIVES: THE FBI'S WAR ON STUDENT RADICALS, AND REAGAN'S RISE TO POWER), N.Y. TIMES BOOK REVIEW, Oct. 7, 2012.

28 *See* NEW YORK CIVIL LIBERTIES UNION, TAKING TASERS SERIOUSLY: THE NEED FOR BETTER REGULATION OF STUN GUNS IN NEW YORK (2011), *available at* http://www.nyclu.org/files/publications/nyclu_TaserFinal.pdf.

29 Mike Goodwin, *Claim against Ex-Cops Rejected*, ALBANY TIMES UNION, May 26, 2005, at A1; Paul Grondahl, *Grim End to a Grim Journey*, ALBANY TIMES UNION, Apr. 4, 2010, at A1.

30 PAUL CHEVIGNY, POLICE POWER: POLICE ABUSE IN NEW YORK CITY (Pantheon 1969), *and see* Kami Chavis Simmons, *Cooperative Federalism and Police Reform: Using Congressional Spending Power to Promote Police Accountability*, 62 ALA. L. REV. 351, 362 (2011).

31 Labbe, *supra* note 21; MICHELLE ALEXANDER, THE NEW JIM CROW: MASS INCARCERATION IN THE AGE OF COLOR-BLINDNESS (New Press 2012).

32 William J. Stuntz, *Local Policing After the Terror*, 111 YALE L.J. 2137 (2002); JEFFREY IAN ROSS, THE DYNAMICS OF POLITICAL CRIME 100 (Sage Publications 2003); Lincoln Caplan, *William Stuntz*, N.Y. TIMES, Mar. 24, 2011, at A30.

33 Simmons, *supra* note 30, 62 ALA. L. REV. at 353–54 & 360–66.

34 *See* ALEXANDER, *supra* note 31.

35 Simmons, *supra* note 30, 62 ALA. L. REV. at 354.

36 *Id.* at 362.

37 *Id.* at 355.

38 NATIONAL COMM'N ON LAW OBSERVANCE AND ENFORCEMENT (THE "WICKERSHAM COMM'N"), REPORT ON LAWLESSNESS IN LAW ENFORCEMENT 5 (GPO 1931), *and see* Miranda v. Ariz., 384 U.S. 436, 447 (1966).

39 MOLLEN COMM'N REPORT, *supra* note 22.

40 INDEPENDENT COMM'N ON THE LOS ANGELES POLICE DEPARTMENT (THE "CHRISTOPHER COMM'N"), REPORT (1991), *available at* http://www.parc. info/client_files/Special%20Reports/1%20-%20Chistopher%20Commision.pdf.

41 H.R. Doc. No. 102–242(I), at 136–138 tit. Omnibus Crime Control Act of 1991 (Oct. 7, 1991), 1991 WL 206794, *available at* http://web2.westlaw.com/find/default.wl?cit e=1991+WL+206794&rs=WLW13.04&vr=2.0&rp=%2ffind%2fdefault. wl&sv=Full&fn=_top&mt=208.

42 CHEVIGNY, *supra* note 30.

43 ALEXANDER, *supra* note 31.

44 DAHL, POLYARCHY, *supra* note 1, at 3; PAUL WILKINSON, TERRORISM VERSUS DEMOCRACY: THE LIBERAL STATE RESPONSE 75–100 & 194–95 (Routledge, 3d ed. 2011); JENNIFER S. HOLMES, TERRORISM AND DEMOCRATIC STABILITY (Manchester Univ. Press 2001).

45 Raymond D. Gastil, *The Comparative Survey of Freedom: Experiences and Suggestions, in* ON MEASURING DEMOCRACY: ITS CONSEQUENCES AND CON-COMITANTS 21–46 (Transaction, Alex Inkeles, ed. 1991); Ted Robert Gurr, Keith Jaggers and Will H. Moore, *The Transformation of the Western State: The Growth of Democracy, Autocracy, and State Power since 1800, in id.* at 69–104; Joseph E. Ryan, *Survey Methodology,* 25:1 FREEDOM REVIEW 9–13 (1994).

46 *See* DAHL, POLYARCHY, *supra* note 1, at 3 & 17–32.

47 *See generally* HOLMES, *supra* note 44. *See also* WILKINSON, *supra* note 44, at 79–85 & 203.

48 WILKINSON, *supra* note 44, at 199–200 & 203.

49 *Id.* at 207; HOLMES, *supra* note 44.

50 ALEXANDER, *supra* note 31.

51 BRUCE BUENO DE MESQUITA AND ALASTAIR SMITH, THE DICTATOR'S HANDBOOK: WHY BAD BEHAVIOR IS ALMOST ALWAYS GOOD POLITICS (Public Affairs 2011).

52 COMMEMORATIVE BIOGRAPHICAL ENCYCLOPEDIA OF DAUPHIN COUNTY, PENNSYLVANIA: CONTAINING SKETCHES OF PROMINENT AND REPRESENTATIVE CITIZENS AND MANY OF THE EARLY SCOTCH-IRISH AND GERMAN SETTLERS 37–38 (J.M. Runk & Co. 1896), *available at* http:// archive.org/stream/commemorativebiooojmru#page/n53/mode/2up/search/buckshot; THOMAS FREDERICK WOODLEY, THADDEUS STEVENS 114–41 (The Telegraph Press 1934), *available at* http://babel.hathitrust.org/cgi/pt?id=wu.89096842679;view= 1up;seq=148.

53 Nigel Anthony Summers, *Treasonous Tenant Farmers and Seditious Share Croppers: The 1917 Green Corn Rebellion Trials,* 27 OKLA. CITY U. L. REV. 1097, 1105–06 (2002).

54 On intimidation with an open ballot, *see* ROBERT M. BASTRESS, THE WEST VIRGINIA STATE CONSTITUTION: A REFERENCE GUIDE 114 (Greenwood Press 1995). On white control over black votes *See, e.g.,* Susan Pace Hamill, *The Book That*

Could Change Alabama, 56 ALA. L. REV. 219 (2004) (reviewing HARVEY H. JACKSON III, INSIDE ALABAMA: A PERSONAL HISTORY OF MY STATE); GUNNAR MYRDAL, AN AMERICAN DILEMMA: THE NEGRO PROBLEM AND MODERN DEMOCRACY 480 (Harper & Brothers 1944). *And see* Brian K. Landsberg, *Sumter County, Alabama and the Origins of the Voting Rights Act*, 54 ALA. L. REV. 877 (2003). On intimidation of blacks, *see* RICHARD KLUGER, SIMPLE JUSTICE: THE HISTORY OF BROWN V. BOARD OF EDUCATION AND BLACK AMERICA'S STRUGGLE FOR EQUALITY 3, 10, 23–25, 222–24, 303 & 229–31 (Knopf 2004); *and see* Virginia v. Black, 538 U.S. 343, 354–357, 363 (2003); NAACP v. Alabama, 357 U.S. 449, 462–67 (1958); WYN CRAIG WADE, THE FIERY CROSS: THE KU KLUX KLAN IN AMERICA 324–25 (Oxford Univ. Press 1987). On intimidation in the former Confederate states, *see* Maj. Gen. Carl Schurz, Report on the Condition of the South, Ex. Doc. No. 2, U.S. Sen, 39th Cong., 1st Session, at 17–21, 30–34, 36–38 & 50–51 (1865).

55 Shelby County v. Holder, 133 S. Ct. 2612, 2636 (2013) (Ginsburg, J., dissenting); Statement of Pamela S. Karlan, in THE CONTINUING NEED FOR SECTION 5 PRE-CLEARANCE, Hearing Before the Committee on the Judiciary, United States Senate, 109th Cong., 2d Sess., May 16, 2006, Serial No. J–109–77, at 5–7.

56 *See* sources cited, *supra* note 20.

57 *See* ANDREW GUMBEL, STEAL THIS VOTE 113 (Nation Books 2005).

58 JOSEPH P. HARRIS, ELECTION ADMINISTRATION IN THE UNITED STATES 15–17, 150–54 & 315–22 (Brookings Inst. 1934), *available at* http://www.nist.gov/itl/vote/josephharrisrpt.cfm; STEINBERG, *supra* note 20.

59 *See* Philip Converse *Change in the American Electorate, in* THE HUMAN MEANING OF SOCIAL CHANGE, 282 & 286–288 (Russell Sage Foundation, Angus Campbell and Philip E. Converse, eds. 1972).

60 *See* HARRY M. CAUDILL, THE WATCHES OF THE NIGHT (Little, Brown 1976).

61 *Id.* at 217–18; HOWARD R. PENNIMAN, SAIT'S AMERICAN PARTIES AND ELECTIONS 338–41 (Appleton-Century-Crofts, Inc., 5th ed. 1952).

62 *See* Jaikumar Vijayan, *Election Watchdogs Keep Wary Eye on Paperless E-Voting Systems*, COMPUTERWORLD, Oct. 30, 2012, http://www.computerworld.com/s/article/9233058/Election_watchdogs_keep_wary_eye_on_paperless_e_voting_systems.

63 Bob Sullivan, *New Jersey's Email Voting Suffers Major Glitches, Deadline Extended to Friday*, NBCNEWS.COM, Nov. 6, 2012, http://usnews.nbcnews.com/_news/2012/11/06/14974588-new-jerseys-email-voting-suffers-major-glitches-deadline-extended-to-friday?lite; Jaikumar Vijayan, *Use of E-voting Machines Unaltered Despite Power Outages Caused by Hurricane Sandy*, COMPUTERWORLD, Nov. 2, 2012, http://www.computerworld.com/s/article/9233196/Use_of_e_voting_machines_unaltered_despite_power_outages_caused_by_Hurricane_Sandy?taxonomyId=13.

64 John M. Broder, *In Case of a Recount, a Long Wait for Ohio*, N.Y. TIMES, Nov. 6, 2012, at A10; Lizette Alvarez, *Obama Win Is Confirmed in Florida*, N.Y. TIMES, Nov. 11, 2012, at A33; Editorial, *A Broken Election System*, N.Y. TIMES, Nov. 21, 2012, at A26.

65 Declan McCullagh, *Pennsylvania E-voting Machine Casts Wrong Ballot. Oops*, CNET NEWS, Nov. 6, 2012, http://news.cnet.com/8301-13578_3-57545940-38/pennsylvania-e-voting-machine-casts-wrong-ballot-oops/.

66 Kate Taylor and David W. Chen, *After a Chaotic Election, City Leaders and Watchdogs Call for a System Overhaul*, N.Y. TIMES, Nov. 8, 2012, at A16.

67 GUMBEL, *supra* note 57, and JOHN FUND, STEALING ELECTIONS: HOW VOTER FRAUD THREATENS OUR DEMOCRACY (Encounter Books 2004).

68 Alexander Keyssar, *Something Has Changed about Election Night*, N.Y. TIMES (blog) (E-Day Campaign Stops), Nov. 6, 2012, http://campaignstops.blogs.nytimes.com/2012/11/06/e-day/#Keyssar.

69 David Barstow and Don Van Natta, Jr., *How Bush Took Florida: Mining the Overseas Absentee Vote*, N.Y. TIMES, July 15, 2001, sec. 1, at 1.

70 *See* the findings on "Disenfranchised Voters" in U.S. COMM'N. ON CIVIL RIGHTS, VOTING IRREGULARITIES IN FLORIDA DURING THE 2000 PRESIDENTIAL ELECTION (June 2001), available at http://www.usccr.gov/pubs/vote2000/report/exesum.htm; Abby Goodnough, *In Florida, Wrestling Again Over Felons and Voting*, N.Y. TIMES, June 9, 2004, at A16; Katharine Q. Seelye, *Divided Civil Rights Panel Approves Election Report*, N.Y. TIMES, June 9, 2001, at A8; GREG PALAST, THE BEST DEMOCRACY MONEY CAN BUY: AN INVESTIGATIVE REPORTER EXPOSES THE TRUTH ABOUT GLOBALIZATION, CORPORATE CONS AND HIGH FINANCE FRAUDSTERS 6–43 (Pluto Press 2002).

71 Robert F. Kennedy Jr., *Was the 2004 Election Stolen?*, ROLLING STONE, June 1, 2006, *available at* http://www.rollingstone.com/news/story/10432334/was_the_2004_election_stolen.

72 *Id.*

73 *See* Becket Adams, *Fact Check: Does George Soros Own an Overseas Company That Will Count U.S. Votes?*, THE BLAZE, Sept. 13, 2012, http://www.theblaze.com/stories/fact-check-does-soros-own-an-overseas-company-that-will-count-u-s-votes/, and *SCYTL*, SNOPES.COM, Sept. 11, 2012, http://www.snopes.com/politics/ballot/scytl.asp; *Election Fraud Now Outsourced to Socialist Spain*, REDSTATE, Apr. 11, 2012, http://www.redstate.com/lastgopinillinois/2012/04/11/election-fraud-now-outsourced-to-socialist-spain/.

74 Wesberry v. Sanders, 376 U.S. 1, 10, 14–15 (1964).

75 Art. I, sec. 2, par. 3; art. II, sec. 1, par. 2.

76 *See* 1 RECORDS OF THE FEDERAL CONVENTION OF 1787, at 604 (Yale Univ. Press, Max Farrand, ed. 1966) (remarks of Gouverneur Morris, July 13, 1787); Jack Rakove, *The Great Compromise: Ideas, Interests and the Politics of Constitution Making*, 44 WM. & MARY Q. 3d ser. 424, 450 & 452 (1987); STAUGHTON LYND, CLASS CONFLICT, SLAVERY, & THE UNITED STATES CONSTITUTION 185–213 (Bobbs-Merrill 1967); CALVIN C. JILLSON, CONSTITUTION MAKING: CONFLICT AND CONSENSUS IN THE FEDERAL CONVENTION OF 1787 (Agathon Press 1988); Calvin C. Jillson, *The Representation Question in the Federal Convention of 1787; Madison's Virginia Plan and its Opponents*, 8 *Congressional Studies* no. 1, at

21–41 (1981); and Staughton Lynd, *The Compromise of 1787,* 81 POL. SCI. Q. 225–50 (1966).

77 *See* 27 Cong. Ch. 47; 5 Stat. 491 (enacted June 25, 1842).

78 *See* Baker v. Carr, 369 U.S. 186 (1962); Wesberry v. Sanders, 376 U.S. 1 (1963); Reynolds v. Sims, 377 U.S. 533 (1964); *and see* Gordon E. Baker, *The Unfinished Reapportionment Revolution,* in POLITICAL GERRYMANDERING AND THE COURTS (Agathon Press, Bernard Grofman, ed. 1990).

79 Kramer v. Union Free School Dist., 395 U.S. 621 (1969); Moore v. Ogilvie, 394 U.S. 814 (1969); Kirkpatrick v. Preisler, 394 U.S. 526 (1969); Wells v. Rockefeller, 394 U.S. 542 (1969); *and see* Baker, *Unfinished Reapportionment Revolution, supra* note 78, at 24–25.

80 GEORGE ORWELL, ANIMAL FARM ch. 10 (Harcourt, Brace & Co. 1946).

81 Brown v. Thomson, 462 U.S. 835, 839 (1983) (Brennan, J., dissenting). The numbers are confusing but the difference between most and least well-represented voters reached 2.5 and 3 to 1, *id.* at 854–55 (Brennan, J., dissenting).

82 *See also* MORALITY IMPOSED: THE REHNQUIST COURT AND LIBERTY IN AMERICA 38–48 (N. Y. Univ. Press 2000) and *The Rehnquist Court (1986–): Radical Revision of American Constitutional Law,* in THE UNITED STATES SUPREME COURT: THE PURSUIT OF JUSTICE 327, 336–40 (Houghton Mifflin with the Am. Bar Found., Christopher L. Tomlins, ed. 2005).

83 League of United Latin American Citizens [LULAC] v. Perry, 548 U.S. 399, 512 (2006) (Scalia, J., concurring in the judgment in part and dissenting in part); Holder v. Hall, 5412 U.S. 874, 896–903 (1994) (Thomas, J., concurring in the judgment).

84 Bush v. Vera, 517 U.S. 952, 965 (1996) (plurality opinion).

85 Vieth v. Jubelirer, 541 U.S. 267 (2004).

86 DE MESQUITA AND SMITH, THE DICTATOR'S HANDBOOK, *supra* note 51, at 264–68 (Public Affairs 2011).

87 See G. BINGHAM POWELL, JR., CONTEMPORARY DEMOCRACIES: PARTICIPATION, STABILITY, AND VIOLENCE 75–77 (Harvard Univ. Press 1982); M. Rainer Lepsius, *From Fragmented Party Democracy to Government by Emergency Decree and National Socialist Takeover: Germany,* in THE BREAKDOWN OF DEMOCRATIC REGIMES: EUROPE 44–45 (Johns Hopkins Univ. Press, Juan J. Linz and Alfred Stepan, eds. 1978); Juan J. Linz, *From Great Hopes to Civil War: The Breakdown of Democracy in Spain,* in *id.* at 169.

88 Stephanopoulos, Nicholas, *Our Electoral Exceptionalism,* 79 U. CHI. L. REV. 769 (2013), *available at* SSRN: http://ssrn.com/abstract=2139123.

89 See Brief Amicus Curiae of Gary King, *et al,* in support of neither party in *LULAC, supra* note 83, at 5–6; CHARLES STEWART III, ANALYZING CONGRESS 204 (W.W. Norton 2000).

90 *See* Daniel Lowenstein and Jonathan Steinberg, *The Quest for Legislative Districting in the Public Interest: Elusive or Illusory?,* 33 UCLA L. REV. 1 (1985).

91 Vieth v. Jubilirer, 541 U.S. 267, 311–12 (2004).

92 *See, e.g.,* "Supreme Court Dismisses Ojukwu's Appeal Against Yar'Adua," Africa News, Apr. 25, 2009 (Nigeria); Abraham Korir Sing'Oei, *The ICC As Arbiter in Kenya's*

Post-Electoral Violence, 19 MINN. J. INT'L L. ONLINE 5, 12–13 (Kenya); Peter W. Schroth and Ana Daniela Bostan, *International Constitutional Law and Anti-Corruption Measures in the European Union's Accession Negotiations: Romania in Comparative Perspective*, 52 AM. J. COMP. L. 625, 637n (2004); United States v. Cruikshank, 92 U.S. 542 (1875); *and see* sources cited *supra* note 18.

93 *See* CHARLES DE SECONDAT, BARON DE MONTESQUIEU, L'ESPRIT DE LOIS OR THE SPIRIT OF LAWS (G. Bell & Sons, Ltd. 1914) (1748).

94 *See* POWELL, CONTEMPORARY DEMOCRACIES *supra* note 87.

95 THE FEDERALIST, *supra* note 7.

96 *See* Gregory E. Maggs, *A Concise Guide to the Federalist Papers as a Source of the Original Meaning of the United States Constitution*, 87 B.U. L. REV. 801, 802 (2007); J. Christopher Jennings, *Note: Madison's New Audience: The Supreme Court and the Tenth Federalist Visited*, 82 B.U. L. REV. 817 (2002); Ira C. Lupu, *The Most Cited Federalist Papers*, 15 CONST. COMMENT. 403 (1998); *and see, e.g.*, Hamdan v. Rumsfeld, 548 U.S. 557, 602 (2006); *id.* at 675 (Scalia, J., dissenting); *id.* at 679 & 691 (Thomas, J., dissenting); Gonzales v. Raich, 545 U.S. 1, 57 (2005) (O'Connor, J., dissenting); *id.* at 65, 66 & 69 (Thomas, J., dissenting).

97 JUAN J. LINZ, THE BREAKDOWN OF DEMOCRATIC REGIMES: CRISIS, BREAKDOWN, & REEQUILIBRATION 72–74 (Johns Hopkins Univ. Press 1978); G. BINGHAM POWELL, JR., ELECTIONS AS INSTRUMENTS OF DEMOCRACY: MAJORITARIAN AND PROPORTIONAL VISIONS (Yale Univ. Press 2000).

98 Adam Przeworski, Michael Alvarez, José Antonio Cheibub and Fernando Limongi, *What Makes Democracies Endure?* 7 J. DEMOCRACY 39, 46 (1996).

99 *Id.*

100 *Id.* at 63–64 & 72.

101 Boumediene v. Bush, 553 U.S. 723, 742–44, 765 (2008); *Id.* at 833–34 (Scalia, J., dissenting); Hamdan v. Rumsfeld, 548 U.S. 557, 690–91 (2006) (Thomas, J., dissenting); Hamdi v. Rumsfeld, 542 U.S. 507, 535–36 (2004) (O'Connor, J., plurality opinion); Cheney v. United States Dist. Court, 542 U.S. 367 (2004); *but see* Morrison v. Olson, 487 U.S. 654 (1988).

102 *The Federalist No. 48*, *supra* note 7, at 308 (Madison); *and see*, *The Federalist No. 27*, *in id.* at 305 (Madison).

103 *See* Youngstown Sheet & Tube Co. v. Sawyer, 343 U.S. 579, 634 (1952) (Jackson, J. concurring); H. JEFFERSON POWELL, THE PRESIDENT AS COMMANDER IN CHIEF: AN ESSAY IN CONSTITUTIONAL VISION (Carolina Academic Press 2014); RAYMOND TATALOVICH AND THOMAS S. ENGEMAN, THE PRESIDENCY AND POLITICAL SCIENCE: TWO HUNDRED YEARS OF CONSTITUTIONAL DEBATE (Johns Hopkins Univ. Press 2003); FORREST MCDONALD, THE AMERICAN PRESIDENCY: AN INTELLECTUAL HISTORY (Univ. Press of Kansas 1994).

104 This section is based on Stephen E. Gottlieb, *What Federalism & Why? Science Versus Doctrine*, 35 PEPP. L. REV. 47 (2007).

105 *See* ALBERT O. HIRSCHMAN, EXIT, VOICE, AND LOYALTY: RESPONSES TO DECLINE IN FIRMS, ORGANIZATIONS, AND STATES 21 (Harvard Univ. Press 1970).

106 *Compare* New York v. United States, 505 U.S. 144, 188 (1992), *with* VICKI C. JACKSON AND MARK TUSHNET, COMPARATIVE CONSTITUTIONAL LAW 825–26 (Foundation Press 1999).

107 *See* JACKSON AND TUSHNET, *supra* note 106, at 825–43 (materials on German federalism).

108 *See* SEYMOUR MARTIN LIPSET, POLITICAL MAN: THE SOCIAL BASES OF POLITICS 64–86 (Johns Hopkins Univ. Press 1981) (1960); Graham Smith, *Mapping the Federal Condition: Ideology, Political Practice and Social Justice, in* FEDERALISM: THE MULTIETHNIC CHALLENGE 1 & 16–22 (Longman, Graham Smith, ed. 1996).

109 *See* SUSAN L. WOODWARD, BALKAN TRAGEDY: CHAOS AND DISSOLUTION AFTER THE COLD WAR 29 (Brookings Inst. 1995).

110 *See* Vesna Popovski, *Yugoslavia: Politics, Federation, Nation, in* FEDERALISM: THE MULTIETHNIC CHALLENGE, *supra* note 108, at 180 & 186–93 (discussing the history of the Yugoslav Federation).

111 *Id.* at 188.

112 *Id.* at 196–203.

113 *See, e.g.,* LIPSET, *supra* note 108; Bernard Grofman and Robert Stockwell, *Institutional Design in Plural Societies: Mitigating Ethnic Conflict and Fostering Stable Democracy* (Ctr. for the Study of Democracy) June 1, 2001, http://repositories.cdlib.org/cgi/viewcontent.cgi?article=1075&context=csd.

114 *See* WOODWARD, *supra* note 109, at 380–82.

115 *Compare* AREND LIJPHART, PATTERNS OF DEMOCRACY: GOVERNMENT FORMS AND PERFORMANCE IN THIRTY-SIX COUNTRIES (Yale Univ. Press 1999) *and* AREND LIJPHART, DEMOCRACY IN PLURAL SOCIETIES: A COMPARATIVE EXPLANATION (Yale Univ. Press 1977) *with* POWELL, CONTEMPORARY DEMOCRACIES *supra* note 87, at 212–18 & 270–71, POWELL, ELECTIONS AS INSTRUMENTS, *supra* note 97; G. Bingham Powell Jr., *Political Responsiveness and Constitutional Design, in* DEMOCRACY AND INSTITUTIONS: THE LIFE WORK OF AREND LIJPHART 9 (Univ. of Michigan Press, Markus M. L. Crepaz et al., eds. 2000); WOODWARD, *supra* note 109.

116 *See* Otto K. Kaufmann, *Swiss Federalism, in* FORGING UNITY OUT OF DIVERSITY: THE APPROACHES OF EIGHT NATIONS 206 (American Enterprise Institute, Robert A. Goldwin et al., eds. 1989); DANIEL J. ELAZAR, FEDERAL SYSTEMS OF THE WORLD: A HANDBOOK OF FEDERAL, CONFEDERAL, AND AUTONOMY ARRANGEMENTS 132 (Longman, 2d ed. 1994); Thomas O. Hueglin, *New Wine in Old Bottles? Federalism and Nation States in the Twenty-First Century: A Conceptual Overview, in* RETHINKING FEDERALISM: CITIZENS, MARKETS, AND GOVERNMENTS IN A CHANGING WORLD 203 & 205–09 (UBC Press, Karen Knop et al., eds. 1995); JACKSON AND TUSHNET, *supra* note 106, at 843–62.

117 *See* Richard Cullen, *Adaptive Federalism in Belgium*, 13 U. NEW S. WALES L. J. 346 (1990); Alexander Murphy, *Belgium's Regional Divergence: Along the Road to Federation, in* FEDERALISM: THE MULTIETHNIC CHALLENGE, *supra* note 108, at 73; JACKSON AND TUSHNET, *supra* note 106, at 925–46.

118 *See* JACKSON AND TUSHNET, *supra* note 106, at 889–925.

119 LIPSET, *supra* note 108, at 81.

120 *See* the work of LIJPHART and POWELL cited *supra* note 115.

121 *See* WOODWARD, *supra* note 109.

122 *See generally* GIUSEPPE DI PALMA, TO CRAFT DEMOCRACIES: AN ESSAY ON DEMOCRATIC TRANSITIONS (Univ. of California Press 1990); Barry R. Weingast, *The Political Foundations of Democracy and the Rule of Law*, 91 AM. POL. SCI. REV. 245 (1997); Minasse Haile, *The New Ethiopian Constitution: Its Impact upon Unity, Human Rights and Development*, 20 SUFFOLK TRANSNAT'L L. REV. 1 (1996), excerpted in JACKSON AND TUSHNET, *supra* note 106, at 949–62.

123 *See* John Bell, FRENCH CONSTITUTIONAL LAW (Oxford Univ. Press 1992), excerpted in JACKSON AND TUSHNET, *supra* note 106, at 504–05.

124 *See* Prigg v. Pennsylvania, 41 U.S. 539, 611, 624 (1842) (Story, J.).

125 Larry Diamond *et al.*, *Building and Sustaining Democratic Government in Developing Countries: Some Tentative Findings*, 150 WORLD AFFAIRS 5, 12–13 (1987); *see also* MICHAEL WALZER, ON TOLERATION 21 (Yale Univ. Press 1997).

126 The late Harry Eckstein in discussion at the 1994 meeting of the American Political Science Association.

127 *See* Garcia v. San Antonio Metro. Transit Auth., 469 U.S. 528 (1985).

128 *See* Grofman and Stockwell, *supra* note 113, at 5–6; 1 RECORDS OF THE FEDERAL CONVENTION, *supra* note 76, at 296 (remarks of Hamilton, June 18, 1787).

129 *See* WOODWARD, *supra* note 109, at 84.

130 *See* Garcia v. San Antonio Metro. Transit Auth., 469 U.S. 528, 546 (1985).

131 LIJPHART, DEMOCRACY IN PLURAL SOCIETIES, *supra* note 115, at 53–103.

132 Ian Shapiro, *Notes Toward a Conditional Theory of Rights and Obligations in Property*, *in* STEPHEN E. GOTTLIEB, BRIAN H. BIX, TIMOTHY D. LYTTON AND ROBIN L. WEST, JURISPRUDENCE CASES AND MATERIALS: AN INTRODUCTION TO THE PHILOSOPHY OF LAW AND ITS APPLICATIONS 998 & 999 (LexisNexis 2d ed. 2006).

133 LINZ, *supra* note 97, at 62.

134 ROBERT A. DAHL, DILEMMAS OF PLURALIST DEMOCRACY: AUTONOMY VS. CONTROL 102–07 (Yale Univ. Press 1982).

135 *See* William Michael Treanor, *The Original Understanding of the Takings Clause and the Political Process*, 95 COLUM. L. REV. 782, 866–67 (1995) and William A. Fischel, *Exploring the Kozinski Paradox: Why Is More Efficient Regulation a Taking of Property?* 67 CHI.-KENT L. REV. 865, 886 (1991) (empirically supporting Madison, *The Federalist No. 10*).

136 *The Federalist No. 44*, *supra* note 7 at 280 (Madison) (discussing the Necessary and Proper Clause and restrictions on the power of the states and pointing out the extent to which the states would restrain the national government);*The Federalist No. 51, in id.* at 320 & 323 (Madison) ("The different governments will control each other, at the same time that each will be controlled by itself.");*The Federalist No. 85, in id.* at 520 & 521 (Hamilton) (describing "additional securities to republican government, to

liberty, and to property . . . [from] the restraints which the preservation of the Union will impose on local factions and insurrections, and on the ambition of powerful individuals in single States, who might acquire credit and influence enough from leaders and favorites to become the despots of the people. . . .").

137 *The Federalist No. 39, supra* note 7, at 240 (Madison).

138 *SeeThe Federalist No. 48, in id.* at 308 (Madison) ("Unless these departments be so far connected and blended as to give to each a constitutional control over the others, the degree of separation which . . . [is] essential to a free government, can never in practice be duly maintained.").

139 *The Federalist No. 51, in id.* at 320 (Madison).

140 *See* Virginia Resolution (Dec. 21, 1798) repr. in 5 THE FOUNDERS' CONSTITUTION, at 135 (Liberty Fund, Philip B. Kurland and Ralph Lerner, eds. 1987), *available at* http://www.yale.edu/lawweb/avalon/virres.htm; Kentucky Resolution (Nov. 16, 1798) and Kentucky Resolution (Nov. 10, 1799), repr. in *id.* at 134, *available at* http://avalon.law.yale.edu/18th_century/kenres.asp; *and see* H. Jefferson Powell, *The Principles of '98: An Essay in Historical Retrieval*, 80 VA. L. REV. 689 (1994). On subsidiarity as a check, *see* Alex Mills, *Federalism in the European Union and the United States: Subsidiarity, Private Law, and the Conflict of Laws*, 32 U. PA. J. INT'L L. 369 (2010).

141 *See generally* POWELL, ELECTIONS AS INSTRUMENTS, *supra* note 97; Powell, *Political Responsiveness, supra* note 115.

142 *The Federalist No. 10*, in THE FEDERALIST, *supra* note 7, at 77 (Madison).

143 *See* Martha Minow, *Putting Up and Putting Down: Tolerance Reconsidered*, in COMPARATIVE CONSTITUTIONAL FEDERALISM: EUROPE AND AMERICA 77 (Greenwood, Mark Tushnet, ed. 1990).

144 "Stacking" and "cracking" are techniques of gerrymandering. Votes are wasted by stacking or packing as many voters of one political stripe into one or a small number of districts. Votes are wasted by cracking or spreading them into as many districts as possible. Gerrymandering combines both. See my *Identifying Gerrymanders*, 15 ST. LOUIS U. L.J. 540, 546–53 (1971) (explaining gerrymandering as a combination of otherwise benign procedures to produce a distorted result).

145 DAHL, DILEMMAS, *supra* note 134, at 85–107.

146 *Id.*

147 See Richard Simeon and Katherine Swinton, *Introduction: Rethinking Federalism in a Changing World*, in RETHINKING FEDERALISM, *supra* note 116, at 3.

148 *The Federalist No. 10, supra* note 7, at 77 (Madison).

149 Theodore J. Lowi, *Our Millennium: Political Science Confronts the Global Corporate Economy*, 22 INT'L POL. SCI. REV. 131, 141–42 (2001).

150 See*The Federalist No. 10, supra* note 7 at 77 (Madison); Minow, *supra* note 143.

151 See Slaughter-House Cases, 83 U.S. 36, 128–29 (1872) (Swayne, J., dissenting).

152 Coleman v. Thompson, 501 U.S. 722, 759 (1991) (Blackmun, J., dissenting); quoted in United States v. Lopez, 514 U.S. 549, 576 (1995); New York v. United States, 505 U.S. 144, 181 (1992).

153 *Coleman*, 501 U.S. at 759.

154 *Lopez*, 514 U.S. at 576.

155 *See supra* note 142 and accompanying text.

156 *See* Diamond *et al., supra* note 125.

157 *See* Powell, *Political Responsiveness, supra* note 115.

158 Garcia v. San Antonio Metropolitan Transit Authority, 469 U.S. 528, 546, 550–51 (1985).

159 *See, e.g.*, Br., States of Arizona, et al. as Amici Curiae in Support of Petitioners, United States v. Morrison, 529 U.S. 598 (1999), 1999 U.S. S. Ct. Briefs LEXIS 219.

CHAPTER 6. GENERAL WELFARE

1 Seymour Martin Lipset, *Some Social Requisites of Democracy: Economic Development and Political Legitimacy*, 53 AM. POL. SCI. REV. 69 (1959), ideas incorporated in SEYMOUR M. LIPSET, POLITICAL MAN: THE SOCIAL BASES OF POLITICS (Doubleday 1960).

2 NANCY BERMEO, ORDINARY PEOPLE IN EXTRAORDINARY TIMES: THE CITIZENRY AND THE BREAKDOWN OF DEMOCRACY 38–41 (Princeton Univ. Press 2003).

3 *See* SAMUEL P. HUNTINGTON, THE THIRD WAVE: DEMOCRATIZATION IN THE LATE TWENTIETH CENTURY (Univ. of Oklahoma Press 1991).

4 *See* JUAN J. LINZ, CRISIS, BREAKDOWN, & REEQUILIBRATION 3, 11–13 & 72–74 (Johns Hopkins Univ. Press, Juan J. Linz and Alfred Stepan, eds. 1978, THE BREAKDOWN OF DEMOCRATIC REGIMES, vol. 1).

5 The following account draws heavily on BERMEO, *supra* note 2, as well as THE BREAKDOWN OF DEMOCRATIC REGIMES (Johns Hopkins Univ. Press, Juan J. Linz and Alfred Stepan, eds. 1984), four volumes of studies of individual national histories; *see also* TRANSITIONS FROM AUTHORITARIAN RULE: COMPARATIVE PERSPECTIVES (Johns Hopkins Univ. Press, Guillermo O'Donnell, Philippe C. Schmitter, and Laurence Whitehead, eds. 1986).

6 BERMEO, *supra* note 2, at 28.

7 Juan J. Linz, *From Great Hopes to Civil War: The Breakdown of Democracy in Spain, in* THE BREAKDOWN OF DEMOCRATIC REGIMES: EUROPE 160–71 (Johns Hopkins Univ. Press, Juan J. Linz and Alfred Stepan, eds. 1978).

8 *Id.* at 48.

9 *See* DARON ACEMOGLU AND JAMES A. ROBINSON, ECONOMIC ORIGINS OF DICTATORSHIP AND DEMOCRACY (Cambridge Univ. Press 2006).

10 *See* AMY CHUA, WORLD ON FIRE: HOW EXPORTING FREE MARKET DEMOCRACY BREEDS ETHNIC HATRED AND GLOBAL INSTABILITY 1–5 & 153–57 (Doubleday 2003) for a portrait of class relations in the Philippines; Carl H. Lande, *Review of Booty Capitalism: The Politics of Banking in the Philippines. By Paul D. Hutchcroft*, 94 AMER. POL. SCI. REV. 216 (2000).

11 CHUA, *supra* note 10, at 4.

12 John D. Stephens, *The Contribution of Barrington Moore's Social Origins of Dictatorship and Democracy to the Study of the Historical Development of Democracy*, 11:1 COMP. DEMOCRATIZATION 1, 8 (Jan. 2013).

13 HUNTINGTON, *supra* note 3.

14 G. BINGHAM POWELL, JR., CONTEMPORARY DEMOCRACIES: PARTICIPATION, STABILITY, AND VIOLENCE 35–38, 71 & 72 (Harvard Univ. Press 1982).

15 *Id.* at 35–37.

16 *Id.* at 69–71.

17 ACEMOGLU AND ROBINSON, *supra* note 9; CARLES BOIX, DEMOCRACY AND REDISTRIBUTION (Cambridge Univ. Press 2003); IAN SHAPIRO, THE STATE OF DEMOCRATIC THEORY 86–93 (Princeton Univ. Press 2003); ROBERT A. DAHL, A PREFACE TO ECONOMIC DEMOCRACY 10 & 45–46 (Univ. of California Press 1985); Gary King and Langche Zeng, *Research Note: Improving Forecasts of State Failure*, 53 WORLD POLITICS 623, 637 (2001), *available at* http://gking.harvard.edu/files/civil.pdf; Larry Diamond, Seymour Martin Lipset and Juan Linz, *Building and Sustaining Democratic Government in Developing Countries: Some Tentative Findings*, 150:1 *World Affairs* 5, 12–13 (Summer 1987); *but see* Gerardo L. Munck, "Democracy Studies: Agendas, Findings, Challenges," paper prepared for the Annual Meeting of the APSA, 2001, 6n.

18 DANIEL C. ESTY ET AL., STATE FAILURE TASK FORCE REPORT: PHASE II FINDINGS 59–62 (Woodrow Wilson International Center for Scholars, Environmental Change & Security Project Report, Issue No. 5, Summer 1999); *and see* Political Instability Task Force, Consolidated State Failure Events 1955–2006, http://globalpolicy. gmu.edu/pitf/pitftabl.htm (last visited Apr. 9, 2009).

19 ESTY ET AL. *supra* note 18, at 62.

20 *Id.* at 56–57.

21 *Id.* at 62.

22 King and Zeng, *supra* note 17, 53 WORLD POL. at 648–50, 652 & 654.

23 *See* CHARLES TILLY, THE POLITICS OF COLLECTIVE VIOLENCE 26–54 & 231–32 (Cambridge Univ. Press 2003).

24 ROBERT A. DAHL, A PREFACE TO ECONOMIC DEMOCRACY 45 (Univ. of California Press 1985).

25 *Id.* at 45–46. On correlation of economic development and longevity of constitutions, *see* Tom Ginsburg, Zachary Elkins, and James Melton, *The Lifespan of Written Constitutions*, 16 (Center for the Study of Democratic Governance, Working Paper No. SES-0648288, 2007), http://jenni.uchicago.edu/WJP/Vienna 2008/Ginsburg-Lifespans-California.pdf. On correlation of preference for revolution and inequality. Robert MacCulloch, *Income Inequality and the Taste for Revolution*, 48 J. L. & ECON. 93 (2005). See also Adam Przeworski, Michael Alvarez, Jose Antonio Cheibub and Fernando Limongi, *What Makes Democracies Endure?*, 7 J. DEMOCRACY 39, 46–47 (1996).

26 See TATU VANHANEN, PROSPECTS OF DEMOCRACY: A STUDY OF 172 COUNTRIES 277–343 (Routledge 1997); *and see* TATU VANHANEN, DEMOCRATIZATION: A COMPARATIVE ANALYSIS OF 170 COUNTRIES 2 (Routledge 2003).

27 Murphy's Law, http://www.merriam-webster.com/dictionary/murphy's%20law (Merriam-Webster Dictionary) (defining Murphy's Law as, "anything that can go wrong will go wrong").

28 TATU VANHANEN, THE EMERGENCE OF DEMOCRACY: A COMPARATIVE STUDY OF 119 STATES, 1850–1979 (Finnish Society of Sciences and Letters [Societas Scientiarum Fennica], 1984); TATU VANHANEN, POWER AND THE MEANS OF POWER: A STUDY OF 119 ASIAN, EUROPEAN, AMERICAN, AND AFRICAN STATES, 1850–19 (Univ. Microfilms International 1979); TATU VANHANEN, THE PROCESS OF DEMOCRATIZATION: A COMPARATIVE STUDY OF 147 STATES, 1980–88 (Taylor & Francis 1990); VANHANEN, PROSPECTS OF DEMOCRACY, *supra* note 26; VANHANEN, DEMOCRATIZATION, *supra* note 26.

29 VANHANEN, EMERGENCE OF DEMOCRACY, *supra* note 28, at 129. *See also* VANHANEN, DEMOCRATIZATION, *supra* note 26, at 1–2, in which he introduces another hypothesis: nations tend to become democratic at about the same level of resource distribution. *Id.* at 5. I have not explored that second hypothesis because of deep flaws in his indices which have been pointed out by many scholars.

30 *See* VANHANEN, PROSPECTS FOR DEMOCRACY, *supra* note 26, at 277–343.

31 PAUL FINKELMAN, DEFENDING SLAVERY: PROSLAVERY THOUGHT IN THE OLD SOUTH: A BRIEF HISTORY WITH DOCUMENTS 28 (Bedford/St. Martin's, The Bedford Series in History and Culture 2003); Fisher's Negroes v. Dabbs, 14 Tenn. 119 (1834); THOMAS R. R. COBB, AN INQUIRY INTO THE LAW OF NEGRO SLAVERY IN THE UNITED STATES OF AMERICA TO WHICH IS PREFIXED AN HISTORICAL SKETCH OF SLAVERY ccxvii–ccxviii (Univ. of Georgia Press, Paul Finkelman, ed. 1999) (1858).

32 A finite group of firms can agree to control a market, explicitly or by following a leader, aided by publicity and extensive media coverage of rivals. Economists describe oligopoly as a market with few firms that can act more like a monopoly. Competitors who can't win by bucking the market fall into line. What signals count, and who can exercise what power is a moving target.

33 BRUCE BUENO DE MESQUITA AND ALASTAIR SMITH, THE DICTATOR'S HANDBOOK: WHY BAD BEHAVIOR IS ALMOST ALWAYS GOOD POLITICS (Public Affairs 2011); BRUCE BUENO DE MESQUITA ET AL., THE LOGIC OF POLITICAL SURVIVAL (MIT Press 2003).

34 King and Zeng, *supra* note 17, at 637; James D. Fearon and David D. Laitin, *Ethnicity, Insurgency, and Civil War*, 97 AM. POL. SCI. REV. 75, 88 (2003).

35 King and Zeng, *supra* note 17, at 637.

36 Fearon and Laitin, *supra* note 34, at 88.

37 BOIX, *supra* note 17, at 13–14.

38 ACEMOGLU AND ROBINSON, ECONOMIC ORIGINS, *supra* note 9, at 312–13; BOIX, *supra* note 17, at 10–12; Matthew D. Fails and Jonathan Krieckhaus, *Colonialism and Democratization,* 12 COMP. DEMOCRATIZATION 1, 4 (2014); Stephan Haggard, Robert Kaufman and Terence Teo, *Inequality and Regime Change: The Role of Distributive Conflict,* 11:3 COMP. DEMOCRATIZATION 1 at 6 (Oct. 2013); Carles Boix, *RMDs,* 11:3 COMP. DEMOCRATIZATION 2 at 13, 14 (Oct. 2013); Daron Acemoglu, Suresh Naidu, Pascual Restrepo, and James A. Robinson, *Democracy, Public Policy and Inequality,* in *id.* 2 at 16; Christian Houle, *Inequality, Democratization and Democratic Consolidation,* in *id.* 3 at 21, 24 (Oct. 2013).; John R. Freeman and Dennis P. Quinn, *The Economic Origins of Democracy Reconsidered,* 106 AMER. POL. SCI. REV. 58 (2012); *see also* Noam Lupu and Jonas Pontusson, *The Structure of Inequality and the Politics of Redistribution,* 105 AMER. POL. SCI. REV. 317 (2011).

39 See sources cited *supra* note 38, *and see also* Daniel Ziblatt, *Why Do We Read Barrington Moore? Some Reflections on the Survival of an Intellectual Icon,* 11:1 COMP. DEMOCRATIZATION 1, at 6 (Jan. 2013); Stephens, *supra* note 12, at 8; Michael Bernhard and Jeffrey Kopstein, *Moore as Sovietologist: The Contributions of Revolutionary Violence to Post-Communist Gradualism,* 11:1 COMP. DEMOCRATIZATION 2, at 10 (Jan. 2013); *and see* Sheri Berman, *Lessons Lost? What Social Origins of Dictatorship and Democracy Still Has to Teach Us about Political Development, Id.,* 2, at 12.

40 Houle, *supra* note 40, at 21.

41 On breakdown, *see id.* at 12, 13; Houle, *supra* note 38, at 21 & 24; on democratization, *see* Boix, *supra* note 38, at 13; Haggard, Kaufman, and Teo, *supra* note 38, at 5–6; Ben Ansell and David Samuels, *Rethinking Inequality and Democratization: How Inequality Divides Elites and Underpins Regime Change,* 11:3 COMP. DEMOCRATIZATION 1, at 8 (Oct. 2013); *but see* Houle, *supra* note 38, at 21.

42 *See* BUENO DE MESQUITA AND SMITH, *supra* note 33; BUENO DE MESQUITA ET AL., *supra* note 33.

43 CHUA, *supra* note 10, at 1–5, 11 & 153–57.

44 Tomila Lankina, *Trends in Within-Legacy and Cross-Legacy Analysis of Democracy and Development,* 12:1 COMP. DEMOCRATIZATION 1, at 8 (Mar. 2014).

45 HUNTINGTON, *supra* note 3, at 59–72; *see also* CHARLES TILLY, DURABLE INEQUALITY (Univ. of California Press 1998); Raymond H. Brescia, *The Cost of Inequality: Social Distance, Predatory Contact, and the Financial Crisis,* 66 NEW YORK U. ANN. SURV. OF AM. L. 641 (2011).

46 HUNTINGTON, *supra* note 3, at 59–72; *and see* SAMUEL P. HUNTINGTON, AMERICAN POLITICS: THE PROMISE OF DISHARMONY 144–45 (Belknap Press 1981).

47 FREDERICK WILLIAM DALLINGER, NOMINATIONS FOR ELECTIVE OFFICE IN THE UNITED STATES 96 & 99 (Arno Press 1974 [c1897]); AUSTIN RANNEY, CURING THE MISCHIEFS OF FACTION: PARTY REFORM IN AMERICA 156–57 (Univ. of California Press 1975).

48 JOHN A. WOOD, THE PANTHERS AND THE MILITIAS: BROTHERS UNDER THE SKIN 31–32 (Univ. Press of America 2002); Judd Marmor, *Psychosocial Roots of Violence, in* VIOLENCE AND RESPONSIBILITY: THE INDIVIDUAL, THE FAMILY AND SOCIETY 15 (SP Medical & Scientific Books, distributed by Halstead Press, Robert L. Sadoff, ed. 1978). *See also* A. Maslow and J. Honigman, *Synergy—Some Notes of Ruth Benedict*, 72 AMER. ANTHROPOLOGIST 320 (1970).

49 *See* HUNTINGTON, *supra* note 3, at 59–72; King and Zeng, *supra* note 17, at 637.

50 *See* DALLINGER, *supra* note 47, at 96 & 99; RALPH KORNGOLD, THADDEUS STEVENS: A BEING DARKLY WISE AND RUDELY GREAT 53–63 (Harcourt Brace 1955); RANNEY, *supra* note 47, at 156–57; EUGENE H. ROSEBOOM, A HISTORY OF PRESIDENTIAL ELECTIONS 41–42 (Macmillan 1957); ALFRED STEINBERG, THE BOSSES 3 (Macmillan 1972); Philip E. Converse, *Change in the American Electorate, in* THE HUMAN MEANING OF SOCIAL CHANGE 263, 278–96 (Russell Sage Foundation, Angus Campbell and Philip E. Converse, eds. 1972); Noble E. Cunningham, Jr., *The Jeffersonian Republican Party, in* 1 HISTORY OF UNITED STATES POLITICAL PARTIES 239, 250 (Chelsea House Publishers, Arthur M. Schlesinger, Jr., ed. 1973). On the development of patronage practices, see LEONARD D. WHITE, THE JACKSONIANS: A STUDY IN ADMINISTRATIVE HISTORY, 1829–1861, at 307–16 (Macmillan 1954); LEONARD D. WHITE, THE JEFFERSONIANS: A STUDY IN ADMINISTRATIVE HISTORY, 1801–1829, at 347–64 (Macmillan 1956). On specific machines, see HARRY M. CAUDILL, THE WATCHES OF THE NIGHT 217–18 (Little, Brown 1976); HOWARD R. PENNIMAN, SAIT'S AMERICAN PARTIES AND ELECTIONS 338–41 (Appleton-Century-Crofts, Frederic A. Ogg, ed., 5th ed. 1952); FRANK S. ROBINSON, MACHINE POLITICS: A STUDY OF ALBANY'S O'CONNELLS (Transaction Books 1977); T. HARRY WILLIAMS, HUEY LONG 753–59 (Knopf 1969); *and see* Stephen E. Gottlieb, *Rebuilding the Right of Association: The Right to Hold a Convention as a Test Case*, 11 HOFSTRA L. REV. 191, 225–30 (1982).

51 *See also* INTER-AMERICAN DIALOGUE, THE AMERICAS IN A NEW WORLD: THE 1990 REPORT OF THE INTER-AMERICAN DIALOGUE 63 (Aspen Institute 1990) quoted in Jose Nun, *Democracy and Modernization, Thirty Years Later*, 20 LATIN AMERICAN PERSPECTIVES 7 (The Struggle for Popular Participation 1993), *available at* http://www.jstor.org/stable/2633911.

52 *See, e.g.*, Dandridge v. Williams, 397 U.S. 471, *reh'g den.*, 398 U.S. 914 (1970).

53 Ayn Rand, *Man's Rights, in* CAPITALISM: THE UNKNOWN IDEAL 19 (New American Library, Ayn Rand, ed. 1967); *and see* William F. Buckley, Jr., *Our Mission Statement*, Nov. 19, 1955, NATIONAL REVIEW ONLINE, http://www.nationalreview. com/articles/223549/our-mission-statement/william-f-buckley-jr#; Mount Vernon Statement of Constitutional Conservatism, available at http://www.themountvernon-statement.com/ (issued Feb. 17, 2010) (last visited Nov. 18, 2012).

54 *See* ROBERT DEVIGNE, RECASTING CONSERVATISM: OAKESHOTT, STRAUSS, AND THE RESPONSE TO POSTMODERNISM 59–64 (Yale Univ. Press 1994); DANIEL BELL, THE CULTURAL CONTRADICTIONS OF CAPITALISM (Basic

Books 1976); James Q. Wilson, *The Rediscovery of Character: Private Virtue and Public Policy*, 81 PUB. INTEREST 1 (Fall 1985).

55 FRIEDRICH A. VON HAYEK, THE ROAD TO SERFDOM 46–47 & 77–79 (Univ. of Chicago Press 1944).

56 *See* KEVIN PHILLIPS, WEALTH AND DEMOCRACY (Random House 2002); GARDINER C. MEANS AND ADOLPH A. BERLE, THE MODERN CORPORATION AND PRIVATE PROPERTY (Macmillan 1932); LOUIS HARTZ, THE LIBERAL TRADITION IN AMERICA (Harcourt, Brace & World 1955); RICHARD HOFSTADTER, THE AGE OF REFORM: FROM BRYAN TO F.D.R. (Knopf 1955); ERIC GOLDMAN, RENDEZVOUS WITH DESTINY (Vintage Books, rev. & abridged ed. 1956).

57 *See* Marsh v. Alabama, 326 U.S. 501 (1946).

58 HARRY M. CAUDILL, NIGHT COMES TO THE CUMBERLANDS: A BIOGRAPHY OF A DEPRESSED AREA (Little, Brown 1962).

59 This conclusion is fundamental to the findings of BUENO DE MESQUITA AND SMITH, *supra* note 33; *and see* DARON ACEMOGLU AND JAMES A. ROBINSON, WHY NATIONS FAIL: THE ORIGINS OF POWER, PROSPERITY, AND POVERTY (Crown Publishers 2012).

60 Chad Stone *et al.*, *A Guide to Statistics on Historical Trends in Income Inequality* (Center on Budget and Policy Priorities) (rev. Dec. 5, 2013), http://www.cbpp.org/files/11–28–11pov.pdf, at 11–12.

61 These conclusions have been documented repeatedly. *See* Jacob S. Hacker, Suzanne Mettler and Dianne Pinderhughes, *Inequality and Public Policy* (Table 1), *in* INEQUALITY AND AMERICAN DEMOCRACY: WHAT WE KNOW AND WHAT WE NEED TO LEARN 160–62 (Russell Sage Foundation, Lawrence R. Jacobs and Theda Skocpol, eds. 2005, research reports for the APSA Task Force on Inequality and American Democracy); EDWARD N. WOLFF, TOP HEAVY: THE INCREASING INEQUALITY OF WEALTH IN AMERICA AND WHAT CAN BE DONE ABOUT IT (New Press, rev. ed. 2002, A Century Foundation Report); *see also* James B. Davies *et al.*, *Estimating the Level and Distribution of Global Household Wealth*, Research Paper No. 2007/77, United Nations Univ. World Institute for Development Economics Research, Nov. 2007, *available at* http://www.wider.unu.edu/publications/working-papers/research-papers/2007/en_GB/rp2007-77/_files/78517347310961664/default/rp2007-77.pdf (visited Apr. 30, 2008).

62 . Anders Bjorklund and Markus Jantti, *Intergenerational Income Mobility in Sweden Compared to the United States*, 87 AMER. ECON. REV. 1009, 1017 (1997); WOLFF, TOP HEAVY, *supra* note 61, at 31–36. *See also* Daniel P. McMurrer and Isabel V. Sawhill, "The Declining Importance of Class," Urban Institute, No. 4 in series "Opportunity in America," http://webarchive.urban.org/publications/307017.html, and Daniel P. McMurrer, Mark Condon, and Isabel V. Sawhill, *Intergenerational Mobility in the United States: A Companion Piece to The Declining Importance of Class*, http://webarchive.urban.org/publications/406796.html (May 1997).

63 HERBERT MCCLOSKY AND JOHN ZALLER, THE AMERICAN ETHOS: PUBLIC ATTITUDES TOWARD CAPITALISM AND DEMOCRACY 163, 174, 182 & 185 (Harvard Univ. Press, Twentieth Century Fund Report 1984); Paul M. Sniderman *et al.*, *The Fallacy of Democratic Elitism: Elite Competition and Commitment to Civil Liberties*, 21 BRIT. J. OF POL. SCI. 349 (1991); *and see* HERBERT MCCLOSKY AND ALIDA BRILL, DIMENSIONS OF TOLERANCE: WHAT AMERICANS THINK ABOUT CIVIL LIBERTIES (Russell Sage 1983).

CHAPTER 7. A SENSE OF *WE*

1 Robert D. Putnam, *E Pluribus Unum: Diversity and Community in the Twenty-First Century*, 30 SCANDINAVIAN POL. STUD. 137, 139 (2007).

2 James L. Gibson, *The Political Consequences of Intolerance: Cultural Conformity and Political Freedom*, 86 AM. POL. SCI. REV. 338 (1992); *and see* WILLIAM KORNHAUSER, THE POLITICS OF MASS SOCIETY (Free Press 1959).

3 *See* SAMUEL A. STOUFFER, COMMUNISM, CONFORMITY, AND CIVIL LIBERTIES: A CROSS-SECTION OF THE NATION SPEAKS ITS MIND (Doubleday 1955); Steven E. Finkel, Lee Sigelman, and Stan Humphries, *Democratic Values and Political Tolerance*, *in* 2 MEASURES OF POLITICAL ATTITUDES 216–19 (Academic Press, John P. Robinson, Phillip R. Sahver, and Lawrence S. Wrightsman, eds. 1999); *and see* G. BINGHAM POWELL, CONTEMPORARY DEMOCRACIES: PARTICIPATION, STABILITY, AND VIOLENCE 212–25 (1982).

4 ROBERT D. PUTNAM, MAKING DEMOCRACY WORK: CIVIC TRADITIONS IN MODERN ITALY (Princeton Univ. Press 1993).

5 Robert D. Putnam, *Bowling Alone: America's Declining Social Capital*, 6 J. OF DEMOCRACY 65 (1995); *see also* ROBERT D. PUTNAM, BOWLING ALONE: THE COLLAPSE AND REVIVAL OF AMERICAN COMMUNITY (Simon & Schuster 2000).

6 Conference on Democracy & Trust, Georgetown Univ., Nov. 7–9, 1996.

7 Putnam, *E Pluribus Unum*, *supra* note 1, at 138.

8 *See* Barry R. Weingast, *The Political Foundations of Democracy and the Rule of Law*, 91 AM. POL. SCI. REV. 245–63 (1997).

9 *See* DAVID C. MCCLELLAND, THE ACHIEVING SOCIETY (VanNostrand 1961). *See also* David C. McClelland, *National Character and Economic Growth in Turkey and Iran*, *in* COMMUNICATION AND POLITICAL DEVELOPMENT 152, 163 (Princeton Univ. Press, Lucian W. Pye, ed. 1963).

10 DAVID RIESMAN, THE LONELY CROWD: A STUDY OF THE CHANGING AMERICAN CHARACTER (Yale Univ. Press, in collaboration with Reuel Denney and Nathan Glazer 1950).

11 Thanks to Kim Lane Scheppele for reminding me of the methodological criticism in a conversation in 2007. In the 1960s and 1970s, I corresponded with McClelland regarding some of those criticisms. He referred me to his 1975 introduction to THE ACHIEVING SOCIETY and a new preface by David Atkinson to DAVID C. MCCLELLAND ET AL., THE ACHIEVEMENT MOTIVE (Irvington Publishers 1976).

12 *See* An Ordinance for the Government of the Territory of the United States north-west of the river Ohio, July 1787), *reprinted in* Act of Aug. 7, 1789, ch. 8, 1 Stat. 50, 51–53 n.(a) (Northwest Ordinance, art. III, on schools); Thomas Jefferson, *Preamble to a Bill for the More General Diffusion of Knowledge, quoted in* LAWRENCE A. CREMIN, AMERICAN EDUCATION: THE COLONIAL EXPERIENCE, 1607–1783, at 440 (Harper & Row 1970); Peter S. Onuf, *State Politics and Republican Virtue: Religion, Education, and Morality in Early American Federalism, in* TOWARD A USABLE PAST: LIBERTY UNDER STATE CONSTITUTIONS 91–111 (Univ. of Georgia Press, Paul Finkelman, and Stephen E. Gottlieb, eds. 1991); Thomas James, *Rights of Conscience and State School Systems in Nineteenth-Century America, in Id.* at 122.

13 Madison, *Federalist No. 10* responds.

14 1 ALEXIS DE TOCQUEVILLE, DEMOCRACY IN AMERICA 263 (A. A. Knopf, Francis Bowen and Phillips Bradley, eds., Henry Reeves, trans. 1945) (1835).

15 RIESMAN, *supra* note 10; KORNHAUSER, *supra* note 2.

16 *See* STOUFFER, *supra* note 3.

17 *See* Gibson, *supra* note 2, at 339 & 340–41; HERBERT MCCLOSKY AND ALIDA BRILL, DIMENSIONS OF TOLERANCE: WHAT AMERICAN BELIEVE ABOUT CIVIL LIBERTIES (Russell Sage Foundation 1983); JOHN L. SULLIVAN, JAMES PIERESON AND GEORGE E. MARCUS, POLITICAL TOLERANCE AND AMERICAN DEMOCRACY 27–49, 106–09 & 112 (Univ. of Chicago Press 1982); *see also* John T. Jost, Jack Glaser, Aric W. Kruglanski, and Frank J. Sulloway, *Political Conservatism as Motivated Social Cognition,* 129 PSYCHOL. BULL. 339, 345–46 (2003); *and see* NAT HENTOFF, FREE SPEECH FOR ME—BUT NOT FOR THEE: HOW THE AMERICAN LEFT AND RIGHT RELENTLESSLY CENSOR EACH OTHER (HarperCollins 1992).

18 On the philosophical issues, *see* TOLERATION AND ITS LIMITS: NOMOS XLVIII (New York Univ. Press, Melissa S. Williams and Jeremy Waldron, eds. 2004); ROBERT PAUL WOLFF, BARRINGTON MOORE, JR., AND HERBERT MARCUSE, A CRITIQUE OF PURE TOLERANCE (Beacon Press 1969). *See also* SANFORD LEVINSON, CONSTITUTIONAL FAITH 98 (Princeton Univ. Press 1988); Robert Post, *The Social Foundations of Defamation Law,* 74 CALIF. L. REV. 736, 736–37 (1986). For impact of waves of intolerance, *see* DAVID HALBERSTAM, THE COLDEST WINTER: AMERICA AND THE KOREAN WAR 198 & 238–47 (Hyperion 2007).

For legal fallout, *see* MARTIN H. REDISH, THE LOGIC OF PERSECUTION: FREE EXPRESSION AND THE MCCARTHY ERA 137–41 (Stanford Univ. Press 2005). *And see* SAMUEL WALKER, IN DEFENSE OF AMERICAN LIBERTIES: A HISTORY OF THE ACLU 197 (Southern Ill. Univ. Press, 2d ed. 1999). On spies and foreign agents compared to McCarthy's charges and popular fears, *see* Jacob Weisberg, *Cold War Without End,* N.Y. TIMES MAGAZINE, Nov. 28, 1999, at 116; Maurice Isserman, *They Led Two Lives,* N.Y. TIMES BOOK REV., May 9, 1999, at 34; David Oshinsky, *In the Heart of the Heart of Conspiracy,* N.Y. TIMES BOOK REV., Jan. 27, 2008, at 23; *and see* RED CHANNELS (American Business Consultants 1950) (the "blacklist").

19 *See* Adam Clymer, *No Deal; Politics and the Dead Arts of Compromise,* N.Y. TIMES, Oct. 22, 1995, sec. 4, at 1.

20 *See* STOUFFER, *supra* note 3.

21 Gibson, *supra* note 2, at 342 & 348–50.

22 Robert J. Samuelson, *Polarization Myths*, WASH. POST, Dec. 3, 2003, at A29.

23 Donna Lieberman (NYCLU Executive Director), Letter to the Editor, *NYCLU Assesses Giuliani Administration*, N.Y. TIMES, Dec. 31, 2001, *available at* http://www. nyclu.org/content/letter-nyclu-assesses-giuliani-administration.

24 *See* Stauber v. City of New York, 45 No. 03 Civ. 9162, 2004 U.S. Dist. LEXIS 13350 (S.D.N.Y. July 16, 2004), discussed in Coalition to Protest the Democratic Nat'l Convention v. City of Boston, 327 F. Supp. 2d 61, 74 (D. Mass. 2004).

25 Bush v. Gore, 531 U.S. 1046, 1047 (2000) (Scalia, J., concurring) (counting votes "threaten irreparable harm to petitioner . . . by casting a cloud upon . . . the legitimacy of his election").

26 Bush v. Gore, 531 U.S. 98 (2000). *See also* Stephen E. Gottlieb, *Bush v. Gore Typifies the Rehnquist Court's Hostility to Voters*, *in* THE U.S. SUPREME COURT AND THE ELECTORAL PROCESS 58 (Georgetown Univ. Press, David Ryden, ed., 2d ed. 2002).

27 Andrew Kohut, introduction to *The 2004 Political Landscape: Evenly Divided and Increasingly Polarized*, PEW RES. CTR. FOR THE PEOPLE & THE PRESS (Nov. 5, 2003), http://www.people-press.org/files/legacy-pdf/196.pdf.

28 *Id.* at 7.

29 John Leo, *Splitting Society, Not Hairs*, U.S. NEWS & WORLD REP., Dec. 15, 2003, at 66.

30 *Partisan Polarization Surges in Bush, Obama Years: Trends in American Values: 1987–2012*, PEW RES. CTR. FOR THE PEOPLE & THE PRESS 1, 19 & 99–102 (June 4, 2012), http://www.people-press.org/2012/06/04/ partisan-polarization-surges-in-bush-obama-years/.

31 Gary Dorrien, Book Review, CHRISTIAN CENTURY, May 24, 2000, at 618 (reviewing KYLE A. PASEWARK AND GARRETT E. PAUL, THE EMPHATIC CHRISTIAN CENTER: REFORMING AMERICAN POLITICAL PRACTICE 618 [1999]).

32 Martin Gottlieb, *Hyper-Partisanship No Illusion; Many Forces Selfishly Push Americans Apart*, DAYTON DAILY NEWS (Ohio), Jan. 14, 2004, at A6 [hereinafter Gottlieb, *Hyper-Partisanship No Illusion*].

33 Richard Tomkins, *Analysis: Climate of Hate in 2004 Contest*, UNITED PRESS INT'L (Jan. 14, 2004, 12:36 PM), http://www.upi.com/Business_News/Security-Industry/2004/01/14/Analysis-Climate-of-hate-in-2004-contest/UPI-67141074101819/.

34 Mark O'Keefe, *A Divide Forms When Politics Battles Religion*, HOUS. CHRON., Feb. 14, 2004, Religion, at 1.

35 *Id.*, quoting John Kenneth White, E Pluribus Duo: Red State vs. Blue State America: An Analysis of the O'Leary Report/Zogby International Values Poll 2 (2003) (unpublished manuscript on file with author).

36 Jean M. Twenge, *SDSU—A Corrision of Trust*, ACADEMICMINUTE.ORG, 12/9/14, http://academicminute.org/2014/12/jean-m-twenge-sdsu-a-corrision-of-trust/.

37 Robert B. Reich, *Secession of the Successful*, N.Y. TIMES MAG., Jan. 20. 1991, at 16 & 42–44; Pamela A. Popielarz, *(In)voluntary Association: A Multilevel Analysis of Gender Segregation in Voluntary Organizations*, 13 GENDER AND SOC'Y 234 (1999) (finding that women are more likely to belong to gender-segregated groups and women's groups are also likely to restrict membership to the same age, education, marital and work status).

38 Thomas C. Schelling, *On the Ecology of Micromotives*, 25 THE PUBLIC INTEREST 59 (1971).

39 *See, e.g.*, Naomi Cahn and June Carbone, *Deep Purple: Religious Shades of Family Law*, 110 W. VA. L. REV. 459, 471–73.

40 *See* THRIVENT FINANCIAL FOR LUTHERANS, https://www.thrivent.com/ (last visited Jan. 29, 2013).

41 MELVIN L. OLIVER AND THOMAS M. SHAPIRO, BLACK WEALTH/WHITE WEALTH: A NEW PERSPECTIVE ON RACIAL INEQUALITY 17–18, 51–52, 150 & 174 (Routledge 1995); DOUGLAS S. MASSEY AND NANCY A. DENTON, AMERICAN APARTHEID: SEGREGATION AND THE MAKING OF THE UNDERCLASS 54–55 (Harvard Univ. Press 1993); KENNETH T. JACKSON, CRABGRASS FRONTIER: THE SUBURBANIZATION OF THE UNITED STATES 203–15 (Oxford Univ. Press 1985); Florence Wagman Roisman, *The Lessons of American Apartheid: The Necessity and Means of Promotiong Residential Racial Integration*, 81 IOWA L. REV. 479, 486 (1995) (reviewing MASSEY AND DENTON, AMERICAN APARTHEID); *and see* NAT'L COMM'N ON URB. PROBLEMS, BUILDING THE AMERICAN CITY: REPORT OF THE NATIONAL COMMISSION ON URBAN PROBLEMS TO THE CONGRESS AND TO THE PRESIDENT OF THE UNITED STATES 101 (GPO 1969).

42 42 USCS secs. 1971 *et seq.*

43 *See* Thomas D. Boston, *Trends in Minority-Owned Businesses, in* 2 AMERICA BECOMING: RACIAL TRENDS AND THEIR CONSEQUENCES 190, 196–97 (National Academy Press, Neil J. Smelser, William Julius Wilson and Faith Mitchell, eds. 2001).

44 CHARLES C. MOSKOS AND JOHN SIBLEY BUTLER, ALL THAT WE CAN BE: BLACK LEADERSHIP AND RACIAL INTEGRATION THE ARMY WAY 66–70 (Basic Books 1996); Carl E. Brody, Jr., *A Historical Review of Affirmative Action and the Interpretation of its Legislative Intent by the Supreme Court*, 29 AKRON L. REV. 291, 301–13 (1996).

45 Erica Frankenberg, Chungmei Lee, and Gary Orfield, *A Multiracial Society with Segregated Schools: Are We Losing the Dream?*, THE CIVIL RIGHTS PROJECT, HARVARD UNIV. (Jan. 16, 2003), http://civilrightsproject.ucla.edu/research/k-12-education/integration-and-diversity/a-multiracial-society-with-segregated-schools-are-we-losing-the-dream/frankenberg-multiracial-society-losing-the-dream.pdf.

46 *See* C. VANN WOODWARD, THE STRANGE CAREER OF JIM CROW 74–83 (Oxford Univ. Press 1955).

47 Elizabeth S. Anderson, *Integration, Affirmative Action, and Strict Scrutiny*, 77 N.Y.U.L. REV. 1195 (2002) at 1199; MICHAEL O. EMERSON AND CHRISTIAN

SMITH, DIVIDED BY FAITH: EVANGELICAL RELIGION AND THE PROBLEM OF RACE IN AMERICA 80–81 (Oxford Univ. Press 2000); Richard D. Alba and John R. Logan, *Minority Proximity to Whites in Suburbs: An Individual Level Analysis of Segregation*, 98 AM. J. SOC. 1388, 1388–1427 (1993).

48 Anderson, *supra* note 47; *and see* OLIVER AND SHAPIRO, BLACK WEALTH/ WHITE WEALTH, *supra* note 41.

49 ASHUTOSH VARSHNEY, ETHNIC CONFLICT AND CIVIC LIFE: HINDUS AND MUSLIMS IN INDIA (Yale Univ. Press 2002).

50 William H. Frey and Dowell Myers, *Neighborhood Segregation in Single-Race and Multirace America: A Census 2000 Study of Cities and Metropolitan Areas*, FANNIE MAE FOUNDATION 9 (2002), http://www.censusscope.org/FreyWPFinal.pdf; *see also* U.S. Census Bureau, *Residential Segregation of African-Americans Declines; Signals Mixed for Other Groups, Analysis Shows* (Nov. 27, 2002), http://www.census.gov/ newsroom/releases/archives/census_2000/cb02cn174.html (regarding report by Iceland and Weinberg) (last visited Jan. 31, 2014).

51 Steven Greenhouse, *Suit Claims Discrimination Against Hispanics on Job*, N.Y. TIMES, Feb. 9, 2003, at 20.

52 Wards Cove Packing Co. v. Atonio, 490 U.S. 642 (1989).

53 Anderson, *supra* note 47, at 1200.

54 John Dart, *Hues in the Pews*, THE CHRISTIAN CENTURY FOUNDATION (Feb. 28, 2001), http://hirr.hartsem.edu/cong/articles_huesinthepews.html.

55 EMERSON AND SMITH, *supra* note 47, at 161.

56 *Id.* at 80–81.

57 *Table 1. Percent Born in State of Residence and Rank: 1990*, U.S. CENSUS BUREAU, https://www.census.gov/hhes/migration/files/decennial/pob-rank.txt (last visited Feb. 4, 2014). *See Geographical Mobility 1995–2000*, U.S. CENSUS BUREAU 8 TBL. 6, http://www.census.gov/prod/2003pubs/c2kbr-28.pdf.

58 Jason Schachter, *Why People Move: Exploring the March 2000 Current Population Survey*, U.S. CENSUS BUREAU (May 2001), http://www.census.gov/prod/2001pubs/ p23–204.pdf.

59 *See* Daniel P. McMurrer and Isabel V. Sawhill, *The Declining Importance of Class*, URB. INSTIT. (Apr. 1997), http://www.urban.org/UploadedPDF/opp4.pdf. *See also* Alison Aughinbaugh, *Reapplication and Extension: Intergenerational Mobility in the United States*, 7 LABOUR ECONOMICS 785 (2000) (confirming the .4 correlation).

60 H. Elizabeth Peters, *Patterns of Intergenerational Mobility in Income and Earnings*, 74 REV. OF ECON. & STAT. 456, 460–61 (1992).

61 These data are explored more fully in Daniel P. McMurrer, Mark Condon, and Isabel V. Sawhill, *Intergenerational Mobility in the United States: A Companion Piece to "The Declining Importance of Class,"* URB. INSTIT. (May 1997), http://www.urban.org/ publications/406796.html (hereinafter *A Companion Piece to "The Declining Importance of Class"*).

62 *Geographical Mobility: 1995–2000*, *supra* note 57.

63 Anders Bjorklund and Markus Jantti, *Intergenerational Income Mobility in Sweden Compared to the United States,* 87 AM. ECON. REV. 1009 (1997); *The Declining Importance of Class, supra* note 59; *see also A Companion Piece to "The Declining Importance of Class," supra* note 61.

64 Mary C. King, *Occupational Segregation by Race and Sex, 1940–88,* 115 MONTHLY LABOR REV. 30 (Apr. 1992); Anderson, *supra* note 47, at 1200; Greenhouse, *supra* note 51.

65 EMERSON AND SMITH, *supra* note 47; Dart, *supra* note 54; Elfriede Wedam, *Ethno-Racial Diversity within Religious Congregations in Indianapolis,* 2 RESEARCH NOTES (The Polis Ctr., Project on Religion and Urb. Culture), Aug. 1999, *available at* http://www.polis.iupui.edu/RUC/Newsletters/Research/vol2no4.htm.

66 1 RECORDS OF THE FEDERAL CONVENTION OF 1787, at 253 (Yale Univ. Press, Max Farrand, ed. 1966) (remarks of James Wilson, June 16, 1787).

67 *See* Raymond H. Brescia, *The Cost of Inequality: Social Distance, Predatory Conduct and the Financial Crisis,* 66 N.Y.U. ANN. SURV. AM. L. 641, 659–93 (2011) (surveying the literature and some of its consequences).

68 Comm. on Pol. Parties, Am. Pol, Sci. Ass'n, *Toward a More Responsible Two-Party System,* 44 AM. POL. SCI. REV. (1950).

69 *See* Barbara C. Neff, *Bush and God-Talk: Presidential Language Puts Off Some in Religious Community,* NAT'L CATH. REP. 4 (Feb. 21, 2003).

70 Leo, *supra* note 29.

71 O'Keefe, *supra* note 34.

72 Debra Gersh, *Promulgating Polarization,* EDITOR & PUBLISHER 30 (Oct. 10, 1992).

73 Leo, *supra* note 29; Gottlieb, *Hyper-Partisanship No Illusion, supra* note 32.

74 Gottlieb, *Hyper-Partisanship No Illusion, supra* note 32.

75 Morris P. Fiorina, *Parties, Participation, and Representation in America: Old Theories Face New Realities, in* POLITICAL SCIENCE: THE STATE OF THE DISCIPLINE, 511, at 524–26, 532, 534–35 & 537–38 (W. W. Norton and the American Political Science Assn., Ira Katznelson and Helen V. Milner, eds. 2002).

76 *See* JAMES W. CEASER, PRESIDENTIAL SELECTION: THEORY AND DEVELOPMENT 236–59 (Princeton Univ. Press 1979).

77 17 U.S.C. sec. 111(c)–(d) (2006) (compulsory licensing); Cable Television Syndicated Program Exclusivity Rules, 79 F.C.C.2d 663 (1980) (ending restrictions on cable rebroadcast of broadcast signals); DOUGLAS H. GINSBURG AND MARK D. DIRECTOR, REGULATION OF BROADCASTING: 1983 SUPPLEMENT 72–102 (1983) (describing rules change sequence).

78 *See* ERIK BARNOUW, A TOWER IN BABEL, 96–98, 121–22, 172–74, 218–19, 258–61 & 271–72 (Oxford Univ. Press, A HISTORY OF BROADCASTING IN THE UNITED STATES, vol. 1, 1966).

79 *See* CONG. RESEARCH SERV., RL32589, THE FEDERAL COMMUNICATIONS COMMISSION: CURRENT STRUCTURE AND ITS ROLE IN THE CHANGING TELECOMMUNICATIONS LANDSCAPE 2 (2013).

80 *See* LAWRENCE D. GASMAN, TELECOMPETITION: THE FREE MARKET ROAD TO THE INFORMATION HIGHWAY 74–75 (Cato Inst. 1994); ERIK BARNOUW, THE IMAGE EMPIRE 68–79 & 126 (Oxford Univ. Press, A HISTORY OF BROADCASTING IN THE UNITED STATES, V. 3, 1970).

81 STEVEN J. SIMMONS, THE FAIRNESS DOCTRINE AND THE MEDIA 34, 61–62 (Univ. of California Press 1978); Erik BARNOUW, THE GOLDEN WEB 137 (Oxford Univ. Press, A HISTORY OF BROADCASTING IN THE UNITED STATES, vol. 2, 1968).

82 Memorandum from Chip Shooshan to Subcommittee on Communications of House Committee on Interstate and Foreign Commerce, in Staff of S. Comm. on Communications, Options Papers, H.R. Doc. No. 95–13, at 45–65 (1977); Neil K. Alexander, Jr., Note, *The Local Service Objective and FCC Broadcast Allocations, in* DOUGLAS H. GINSBURG, REGULATION OF BROADCASTING: LAW AND POLICY TOWARDS RADIO, TELEVISION AND CABLE COMMUNICATIONS 163–68 (West 1979) (describing policy).

83 *See* Shooshan, *supra* note 82, at 55–60; Alexander, *supra* note 82.

84 47 U.S.C. sec. 315 (2000).

85 *See generally* BARNOUW, GOLDEN WEB, *supra* note 81, at 271–303. For legal challenges, see Comm. for the Fair Broad. of Controversial Issues, 25 F.C.C.2d 283 (1970); Bus. Executives' Move for Vietnam Peace, 25 F.C.C.2d 242 (1970). *See also* Yale Broad. Co. v. FCC, 478 F.2d 594 (D.C. Cir. 1973), *cert. den.*, 414 U.S. 914 (1973).

86 *See, e.g.*, BARNOUW, GOLDEN WEB, *supra* note 81, at 44–51 & 221–24; Brandywine-Main Line Radio, Inc. v. FCC, 473 F.2d 16, 51 (D.C. Cir. 1972).

87 *See* The Handling of Public Issues Under the Fairness Doctrine and the Pub. Interest Standards of the Communications Act, 89 F.C.C.2d 916, 919–20 (1982); for statutory support, *see* 47 U.S.C. sec. 315(a); for final withdrawal of the doctrine. *See In re* Complaint of Syracuse Peace Council 2 F.C.C.R. 5043 (1987).

88 Nat'l Broad. Co. v. FCC, 516 F.2d 1101 (D.C. Cir. 1974), *vacated*, 516 F.2d 1101 at 1180 (D.C. Cir. 1975), *cert. den. sub nom* Accuracy in Media v. Nat'l Broad. Co., 424 U.S. 910 (1976); *see also* EDWARD JAY EPSTEIN, NEWS FROM NOWHERE: TELEVISION AND THE NEWS 65–72 (Random House 1973).

89 BARNOUW, IMAGE EMPIRE, *supra* note 80, at 128 (describing the increase in news documentaries); *Id.* at 181; Scott Pelley, *"Evening News" Marks Golden Anniversary of 30-Minute Broadcast*, CBS News (Sept. 2, 2013, 7:28 p.m.), http://www.cbsnews.com/news/evening-news-marks-golden-anniversary-of-30-minute-broadcast/.

90 *See* HERBERT T. GANS, DECIDING WHAT'S NEWS: A STUDY OF CBS EVENING NEWS, NBC NIGHTLY NEWS, NEWSWEEK, AND TIME (Pantheon Books 1979).

91 *See* Michael Robinson, *Television & American Politics: 1956–76*, 48 PUB. INT. 3, 9–39 (1977).

92 *See* Cable Television Report and Order, 36 F.C.C.2d 143 (1972) (relating cable signal carriage to copyright rules).

93 *See* H.R. Rep. No. 94–1476, at 88–91 (1976), *reprinted in* 1976 U.S.C.C.A.N. 5679, 5702 (on sec. 111 of the Copyright Act of 1976 creating compulsory license).

94 Malrite T. V. of N.Y v. FCC, 652 F.2d 1140, 1143–47 (2d Cir. 1981), cert. den. *sub nom.* Nat't Football League, Inc. v. FCC, 454 U.S. 1143 (1982) (describing regulation of cable before and after Copyright Act of 1976).

95 *See* VINCENT MOSCO, BROADCASTING IN THE UNITED STATES: INNOVATIVE CHALLENGE AND ORGANIZATION CONTROL (Ablex Pub. Corp. 1979) (FCC protected three-network broadcasting oligopoly for half a century).

96 *See, e.g.,* Editorial, *The Nuclear Wedge Issue,* N.Y. TIMES, Feb. 28, 1995, at A22.

97 N.Y. Times Co. v. Sullivan, 376 U.S. 254, 258–69 (1964).

98 *See* Randall P. Bezanson, *Libel Law and the Realities of Litigation: Setting the Record Straight,* 71 IOWA L. REV. 226, 227–30 (1985). *But see* Philadelphia Newspapers v. Hepps, 475 U.S. 767 (1986).

99 *See* Rosenbloom v. Metromedia, 403 U.S. 29, 86 (1971) (Marshall, J., dissenting); John Soloski, *The Study and the Libel Plaintiff: Who Sues for Libel,* 71 IOWA L. REV. 217, 219–20 (1985).

100 Editorializing by Broad. Licensees, 13 F.C.C. 1246, 1247 (1948); Mayflower Broad. Corp., 8 F.C.C. 333, 340 (1940) (on origins of doctrine); *and see* Stephen E. Gottlieb, *In the Name of Patriotism: The Constitutionality of "Bending" History in Public Secondary Schools,* 62 N.Y.U. L. REV. 497, 553–77 (1987).

101 The Handling of Public Issues Under the Fairness Doctrine and the Public Interest Standards of the Communications Act, 58 F.C.C.2d 691, 708–11 (1976) (Robinson, Comm'r, dissenting), rev'd in part, 567 F.2d 1095 (D.C. Cir. 1977), *cert. den.,* 436 U.S. 926 (1978).

102 Nat'l Broad. Co. v. FCC, 516 F.2d 1101 (D.C. Cir. 1974), *vacated,* 516 F.2d 1101, at 1180 (D.C. Cir. 1975), *cert. den. sub nom* Accuracy in Media v. Nat'l Broad. Co., 424 U.S. 910 (1976).

103 *See* FCC v. League of Women Voters of Cal., 468 U.S. 364, 376 n.11, 378 n.12 (1984); Meredith Corp. v. FCC, 809 F.2d 863 (D.C. Cir. 1987); Syracuse Peace Council, 2 F.C.C.R. 5043 (1987).

104 Materials on licensing from 1930s–1970s collected in GINSBURG (1st ed.), *supra* note 82, at 75–334. *See also* BARNOUW, IMAGE EMPIRE, *supra* note 80; MOSCO, *supra* note 95; *and see* 47 U.S.C. sec. 309(i); 47 U.S.C. sec. 309 (j); Balanced Budget Act of 1997, Pub. L. No. 105–33, sec. 3002, 111 Stat. 258, 260; Reexamination of the Comparative Standards for Noncommercial Educ. Applicants, 15 F.C.C.R. 7386 (2000).

105 Metro Broad., Inc. v. FCC, 497 U.S. 547 (1990) *overruled by* Adarand Constructors, Inc. v. Pena, 515 U.S. 200 (1995).

106 47 U.S.C. sec. 230(c) (2000).

107 Zeran v. Am. Online, Inc., 129 F.3d 327 (4th Cir. 1997).

108 *See* Blumenthal v. Drudge, 992 F. Supp. 44, 50 (D.D.C. 1998).

109 MOSCO, *supra* note 95.

110 Memorandum, Lewis Powell to Eugene B. Sydnor, Jr., Chairman, Educ. Comm., U.S. Chamber of Commerce (Aug. 23, 1971), *available at* http://www2.

bc.edu/%7Eplater/Newpublicsite05/ 02.5.pdf; *see also* David Harvey, *Political and Economic Dimensions of Free Trade: Neobalism as Creative Destruction*, 610 ANNALS 22, 30 (2007) (describing the memo); Zygmunt J. B. Plater, *Law, Media, & Environmental Policy: A Fundamental Linkage in Sustainable Democratic Governance*, 33 B.C. ENVTL. AFF. L. REV. 511, 529–31 (2006).

111 *See, e.g.*, ERIC ALTERMAN, WHAT LIBERAL MEDIA? THE TRUTH ABOUT BIAS AND THE NEWS (Basic Books 2003) (documenting media holdings).

112 *Id.* at 225; C. EDWIN BAKER, MEDIA CONCENTRATION AND DEMOCRACY: WHY OWNERSHIP MATTERS 88–96 (Cambridge Univ. Press 2007); *see also* C. EDWIN BAKER, ADVERTISING AND A DEMOCRATIC PRESS (Princeton Univ. Press 1994); Frank Rich, *All the News That's Fit to Bully*, N.Y. TIMES, July 9, 2006, sec. 4, at 12.

113 *See* KEVIN PHILLIPS, WEALTH AND DEMOCRACY 326 (Random House 2002).

114 *See* GANS, *supra* note 90, at 116–45.

115 *Id.* at 145, 201–2.

116 *See generally* ERIK BARNOUW, THE SPONSOR: NOTES ON A MODERN POTENTATE (Oxford Univ. Press 1978).

117 *See* Gersh, *supra* note 72, at 30.

118 On history of nomination process, *see* Stephen E. Gottlieb, *Rebuilding the Right of Association: The Right to Hold a Convention as a Test Case*, 11 HOFSTRA L. REV. 191 (1983).

119 V. O. KEY, AMERICAN STATE POLITICS: AN INTRODUCTION 145–65 (Knopf 1956).

120 Delegate Selection Rules for the 1980 Democratic National Convention (1978); McGovern-Fraser Comm'n, Mandate for Reform: A Report of the Commission on Party Structure and Delegate Selection to the Democratic National Committee (Apr. 1970), *reprinted in* 117 CONG. REC. 32, 908–917 (1971); CEASER, *supra* note 76, at 260–303 (describing changes); *and see* Democratic Party of the U.S. v. Wisconsin ex rel. La Follette, 450 U.S. 107 (1981); Cousins v. Wigoda, 419 U.S. 477 (1975).

121 *See* Tashjian v. Republican Party of Conn., 479 U.S. 208 (1986).

122 *See, e.g.*, Reynolds v. Sims, 377 U.S. 533 (1964); Wesberry v. Sanders, 376 U.S. 1 (1964); Baker v. Carr, 369 U.S. 186 (1962); Vieth v. Jubelirer, 541 U.S. 267, 364 (2004) (Breyer, J., dissenting).

123 Gordon E. Baker, *The Unfinished Reapportionment Revolution*, in POLITICAL GERRYMANDERING AND THE COURTS 11, 24–25 (Agathon Press, Bernard Grofman, ed. 1990).

124 *See, e.g.*, League of United Latin Am. Citizens v. Perry, 548 U.S. 399, 471 (2006) (*LULAC*) (Stevens, J., dissenting) citing Samuel Issacharoff and Pamela S. Karlan, *Where to Draw the Line? Judicial Review of Political Gerrymanders*, 153 U. PA. L. REV. 541, 574 (2004).

125 Davis v. Bandemer, 478 U.S. 109, 130–31 (1986) (White, J., plurality); *and see* Stephen E. Gottlieb, *Fashioning a Test for Gerrymandering*, 15 J. LEGIS. 1, 7 (1988);

Stephen E. Gottlieb, *Identifying Gerrymanders*, 15 ST. LOUIS U. L. J. 540, 546–53 (1971).

126 Robert J. Samuelson, *Polarization Myths*, WASH. POST, Dec. 3, 2003, at A29.

127 *Id.*; *see also Identifying Gerrymanders, supra* note 125, at 547.

128 *LULAC*, 548 U.S. at 414, 419–20.

129 Buckley v. Valeo, 424 U.S. 1 (1976); Federal Election Campaign Act of 1971, Pub. L. No. 92–225, 86 Stat. 3 (1972) (codified at 2 U.S.C. sec. 431–55 (2006)). *See also* Fed. Election Comm'n v. Colo. Republican Fed. Campaign Comm., 533 U.S. 431, 465 (2001); Dave Levinthal, *Campaign Contribution Limits Increase for 2012 Election Cycle*, CTR. FOR RESPONSIVE POL. (Feb. 3, 2011, 5:27 PM), http://www.opensecrets.org/news/2011/02/campaign-contribution-limits-increa.html.

130 2 U.S.C. sec. 441a(a)(1)(A), 441a(c), 441a(3).

131 2 U.S.C. sec. 441a(1)-(6). *See* 2 U.S.C. sec. 441a(7); *see* Stephen E. Gottlieb, *Fleshing out the Right of Association: The Problem of the Contribution Limits of the F.E.C.A.*, 49 ALB. L. REV. 825 (1985).

132 Buckley v. Valeo, 424 U.S. 1, 39–51 (1976).

133 *See, e.g.*, LARRY J. SABATO, PAYING FOR ELECTIONS: THE CAMPAIGN FINANCE THICKET 5 (Priority Press 1989).

134 *See* Stephen E. Gottlieb, *The Dilemma of Election Campaign Finance Reform*, 18 HOFSTRA L. REV. 213, 255 (1989); Ian Ayres and Jeremy Bulow, *The Donation Booth: Mandating Donor Anonymity to Disrupt the Market for Political Influence*, 50 STAN. L. REV. 837, 838 (1998). BRUCE ACKERMAN AND IAN AYRES, VOTING WITH DOLLARS: A NEW PARADIGM FOR CAMPAIGN FINANCE (Yale Univ. Press 2004); Bruce E. Cain, *Cheap Talk Citizenship: The Democratic Implications of Voting with Dollars*, 37 U. RICH. L. REV. 959, 961 (2003).

135 *See* Richard A. Viguerie and David Franke, *The Big Winners*, WASH. POST, Oct. 24, 2004, at B1.

136 *See* Sarah Parnass, *Obama's White House Fundraising "Unseemly but Perfectly Legal,"* ABC NEWS BLOG (June 28, 2011, 1:22 PM), http://abcnews.go.com/blogs/politics/2011/06/president-obama-joins-ranks-of-predecessors-in-unseemly-but-perfectly-legal-white-house-campaign-act/; Daniel Henninger, The Democrats Have a Nominee, WALL ST. J., Apr. 24, 2008, at A11; Peter Baker, *Two of a Kind?*, WASH. POST, Mar. 10, 2008, at A13.

137 Norman J. Ornstein, *The House That Jack Built*, N.Y. TIMES, Jan. 14, 2007, sec. 7, at 25 (reviewing PETER H. STONE, HEIST: SUPERLOBBYIST JACK ABRAMOFF, HIS REPUBLICAN ALLIES, AND THE BUYING OF WASHINGTON [2006]); Sarah Smith, Letter to the Editor, *The K Street Project*, N.Y. TIMES, Feb. 18, 2007, sec. 7, at 5. Norman Ornstein, reply to Sarah Smith's Letter to the Editor.

138 David D. Kirkpatrick, *Use of Bundlers Raises New Risks for Campaigns*, N.Y. TIMES, Aug. 31, 2007.

139 PHILLIPS, *supra* note 113, at 321–27. *See also* DAVID CAY JOHNSTON, PERFECTLY LEGAL: THE COVERT CAMPAIGN TO RIG OUR TAX SYSTEM TO BENEFIT THE SUPER RICH-AND CHEAT EVERYBODY ELSE (Portfolio 2003);

CHARLES LEWIS AND THE CENTER FOR PUBLIC INTEGRITY, THE BUYING OF THE PRESIDENT 2004 (Perennial 2004).

140 See Trevor Potter and Bryson B. Morgan, *The History of Undisclosed Spending in U.S. Elections & How 2012 Became the "Dark Money" Election*, 27 ND J. L. ETHICS & PUB POL'Y 383 (2013).

141 Reich, *supra* note 37, at 17.

142 *See* Hunter v. Pittsburgh, 207 U.S. 161 (1907).

143 *See* San Antonio Independent School District v. Rodriguez, 411 U.S. 1 (1973).

144 *See* Euclid v. Ambler Realty Co., 272 U.S. 365 (1926).

145 Personal Responsibility and Work Opportunity Reconciliation Act of 1996, 1996 Enacted H.R. 3734, 104 Enacted H.R. 3734, 110 Stat. 2105, 2162 *and see* Hein v. Freedom from Religion Found., Inc., 551 U.S. 587 (2007).

146 *See* Religious Land Use and Institutionalized Persons Act of 2000, 42 U.S.C.S. sec. 2000cc-1(a)(1)-(2); *and see* Patricia E. Salkin and Amy Lavine, *The Genesis of RLUIPA and Federalism: Evaluating the Creation of a Federal Statutory Right and Its Impact on Local Government*, 40 URB. LAWYER 195 (2008).

147 *See* C. VANN WOODWARD, THE STRANGE CAREER OF JIM CROW 74–83 (Oxford Univ. Press 1955).

148 *See* JOSEPH A. SCHUMPETER, CAPITALISM, SOCIALISM AND DEMOCRACY 61 (Harper & Brothers 1942).

149 *Toward a More Responsible Two-Party System*, *supra* note 68.

150 *See* Gibson, *supra* note 2; *see also* James L. Gibson, *Enigmas of Intolerance: Fifty Years After Stouffer's Communism, Conformity, and Civil Liberties*, 4 PERSP. ON POL. 21 (2006); ROBERT WEISSBERG, POLITICAL TOLERANCE: BALANCING COMMUNITY AND DIVERSITY 185–224 (Sage Publications 1998); MICHAEL WALZER, ON TOLERATION (Yale Univ. Press 1997).

151 NANCY BERMEO, ORDINARY PEOPLE IN EXTRAORDINARY TIMES: THE CITIZENRY AND THE BREAKDOWN OF DEMOCRACY 5–6 (Princeton Univ. Press 2003).

152 *Id.* at 168; THE BREAKDOWN OF DEMOCRATIC REGIMES (Johns Hopkins Univ. Press, Juan J. Linz and Alfred Stepan, eds. 1984).

153 *See* BERMEO, *supra* note 151; THE BREAKDOWN OF DEMOCRATIC REGIMES, *supra* note 152.

154 Josh Barbanel, *Examining the Vote; How the Ballots Were Examined*, N.Y. TIMES, July 15, 2001, sec. 1, at 16; David Barstow and Don Van Natta Jr., *How Bush Took Florida: Mining the Overseas Absentee Vote*, N.Y. TIMES, July 15, 2001, sec. 1, at 1; Richard L. Berke, *Examining the Vote: News Analysis; Who Won Florida? The Answer Emerges, but Surely Not the Final Word*, N.Y. TIMES, Nov. 12, 2001, at A16; Richard L. Berke, *Democrats Seek Inquiry on Florida Vote Count*, N.Y. TIMES, July 16, 2001, at A11; Richard L. Berke, *Lieberman Put Democrats in Retreat on Military Vote*, N.Y. TIMES, July 15, 2001, sec. 1, at 16; C. J. Chivers, *House Republicans Pressed Pentagon for E-Mail Addresses of Sailors*, N.Y. TIMES, July 15, 2001, sec. 1, at 19; Michael Cooper, *Timely but Tossed Votes Were Slow to Get to the Ballot Box*, N.Y. TIMES, July 15, 2001, sec. 1, at 19;

Ford Fessenden and John M. Broder, *Study of Disputed Florida Ballots Finds Justices Did Not Cast the Deciding Vote*, N.Y. TIMES, Nov. 12, 2001, at 1; Archie Tse, *The Confusing Ballots*, N.Y. TIMES, Nov. 12, 2001, at A16; Ford Fessenden, *Ballots Cast by Blacks and Older Voters Were Tossed in Far Greater Numbers*, N.Y. TIMES, Nov. 12, 2001, at A17; Ford Fessenden, *Examining the Vote: The Method; How the Consortium of News Organizations Conducted the Ballot Review*, N.Y. TIMES, Nov. 12, 2001, at A17.

155 Bush v. Gore, 531 U.S. 98 (2000).

156 GREG PALAST, THE BEST DEMOCRACY MONEY CAN BUY: AN INVESTIGATIVE REPORTER EXPOSES THE TRUTH ABOUT GLOBALIZATION, CORPORATE CONS, AND HIGH FINANCE FRAUDSTERS 7–12 (Pluto Press 2002).

157 *See* Carl Hulse, *With Promises of a Better-Run Congress, Democrats Take on Political Risks*, N.Y. TIMES, Dec. 27, 2006, at A23.

158 *See generally* AMY CHUA, WORLD ON FIRE: HOW EXPORTING FREE MARKET DEMOCRACY BREEDS ETHNIC HATRED AND GLOBAL INSTABILITY (Doubleday 2003); SUSAN L. WOODWARD, BALKAN TRAGEDY: CHAOS AND DISSOLUTION AFTER THE COLD WAR (Brookings Inst. Press 1995).

159 RICHARD HOFSTADTER, THE PARANOID STYLE IN AMERICAN POLITICS AND OTHER ESSAYS (Univ. of Chicago Press 1964).

160 *See, e.g.*, Laird v. Tatum, 408 U.S. 1 (1972) (finding Army data gathering of domestic demonstrations did not present a justifiable controversy); see DANIEL J. SOLOVE, *The Digital Person: Technology and Privacy in the Information Age 180* (New York Univ. Press 2004).

161 Famous images of the civil rights movement showed use of fire hoses on demonstrators. Many were murdered at the time. *See also* Scheuer v. Rhodes, 416 U.S. 232 (1974); VIOLENCE IN AMERICA: AN ENCYCLOPEDIA 261 (Scribner, Ronald Gottesman and Richard Maxwell Brown, eds. 1999); VIOLENCE IN AMERICA: HISTORICAL AND COMPARATIVE PERSPECTIVES (GPO, Hugh Davis Graham and Ted Robert Gurr, eds. 1969).

162 *See* Schiller v. City of N.Y., 2008 U.S. Dist. LEXIS 4253 (S.D.N.Y. Jan. 23, 2008).

163 *See* Peter Kornbluh, *Chile and the United States: Declassified Documents Relating to the Military Coup*, GEO WASH.: THE NAT'L SECURITY ARCHIVE (Sept. 11, 1973), http://www2.gwu.edu/~nsarchiv/NSAEBB/NSAEBB8/nsaebb8i.htm; Kate Doyle and Peter Kornbluh, *CIA and Assassinations: The Guatemala 1954 Documents*, GEO WASH.: THE NAT'L SECURITY ARCHIVE, http://www2.gwu.edu/~nsarchiv/NSAEBB/NSAEBB4/. *See also* STEPHEN KINZER, ALL THE SHAH'S MEN: AN AMERICAN COUP AND THE ROOTS OF MIDDLE EAST TERROR (John Wiley & Sons 2003).

164 Fiorina, *supra* note 75, at 539–40. *See also* Ian Shapiro, *The State of Democratic Theory*, in POLITICAL SCIENCE: THE STATE OF THE DISCIPLINE, *supra* note 75, 235 at 251–55.

165 *Id.* at 541.

166 *See* Rosenbloom v. Metromedia, 403 U.S. 29, 86 (1971) (Marshall, J., dissenting).

167 Stephen E. Gottlieb, *Brown v. Board of Education and the Application of American Tradition to Racial Division*, 34 SUFFOLK U. L. REV. 281, 287–98 (2001).

168 Putnam, *E Pluribus Unum, supra* note 1, at 138. *See also* HUGH DONALD FORBES, ETHNIC CONFLICT: COMMERCE, CULTURE, AND THE CONTACT HYPOTHESIS (Yale Univ. Press 1997); GORDON W. ALLPORT, THE NATURE OF PREJUDICE 250–67 (Addison-Wesley Publishing Co. 1954).

169 Elliot Aronson, *Stateways can Change Folkways, in* BIGOTRY, PREJUDICE, AND HATRED: DEFINITIONS, CAUSES, AND SOLUTIONS 185 (Prometheus Books, Robert M. Baird and Stuart E. Rosenbaum, eds. 1992); PHYLLIS A. KATZ AND DALMAS A. TAYLOR, ELIMINATING RACISM: PROFILES IN CONTROVERSY 362–63 (Plenum Press 1988); Mark A. Chesler, *Contemporary Sociological Theories of Racism, in* TOWARDS THE ELIMINATION OF RACISM 36 (Pergamon Press, Phyllis A. Katz, ed. 1976).

170 KARL W. DEUTSCH, NATIONALISM AND SOCIAL COMMUNICATION: AN INQUIRY INTO THE FOUNDATIONS OF NATIONALITY 97–125 (MIT Press 1962); *and see* RUPERT EMERSON, FROM EMPIRE TO NATION: THE RISE TO SELF-ASSERTION OF ASIAN AND AFRICAN PEOPLES 329–59 (Beacon Press 1960); Cooper v. Aaron, 358 U.S. 1, 9, 11 (1958).

171 CHARLES C. MOSKOS AND JOHN SIBLEY BUTLER, ALL THAT WE CAN BE: BLACK LEADERSHIP AND RACIAL INTEGRATION THE ARMY WAY (Basic Books 1997). *See also* Peter Karsten, *Who Volunteered for Service in World War II?, in* MILITARY IN AMERICA: FROM THE COLONIAL ERA TO THE PRESENT, 335–37 (Free Press, Peter Karsten, ed. 1980); Larry Ingraham, *The American Enlisted Man in the All-Volunteer Army, in Id.* at 461–63.

172 ASHUTOSH VARSHNEY, ETHNIC CONFLICT AND CIVIC LIFE: HINDUS AND MUSLIMS IN INDIA 173–78, 289–90 & *passim* (Yale Univ. Press 2002).

173 MICHELLE ALEXANDER, THE NEW JIM CROW: MASS INCARCERATION IN THE AGE OF COLORBLINDNESS (New Press 2010): Memorandum from Daniel Patrick Moynihan on the "status of Negroes" to President Nixon, *reproduced* in Peter Kihss, *"Benign Neglect" on Race Is Proposed by Moynihan,* N.Y. TIMES, Mar. 1, 1970.

174 Putnam, *E Pluribus Unum, supra* note 1, at 139.

CHAPTER 8. THREAT OF FORCE

1 On the KKK, *see* WYN CRAIG WADE, THE FIERY CROSS: THE KU KLUX KLAN IN AMERICA 324–25 (Oxford Univ. Press 1987); on the Mafia, *see* JAMES JACOBS, MOBSTERS, UNIONS AND FEDS: THE MAFIA AND THE AMERICAN LABOR MOVEMENT (New York Univ. Press 2005).

2 WOODY HOLTON, UNRULY AMERICANS AND THE ORIGINS OF THE CONSTITUTION 145–55 (Hill and Wang 2007).

3 U.S. Constitution, Art. I, sec. 8, cl. 16; *and see* 1 THE RECORDS OF THE FEDERAL CONVENTION OF 1787, at 114 (Yale Univ. Press, Max Farrand, ed. 1966) (remarks of Gerry, July 25, 1787).

4 United States v. Cruikshank, 92 U.S. 542 (1876); *and see* Civil Rights Cases, 109 U.S. 3 (1883), also known as United States v. Stanley; CHARLES LANE, THE DAY

FREEDOM DIED: THE COLFAX MASSACRE, THE SUPREME COURT, AND THE BETRAYAL OF RECONSTRUCTION (Henry Holt & Co. 2008).

5 *See* ROBERT KESSLER, THE BUREAU: THE SECRET HISTORY OF THE FBI 132–48 (St. Martin's Press 2002); John C. McWilliams, *Review of Racial Matters: The FBI's Secret File on Black America, 1960–1972 by Kenneth O'Reilly*, 95:5 AM. HIST. REV. 1653, 1654 (Dec. 1990); Stanley Coben, *J. Edgar Hoover* (review essay), 34:3 J. OF SOC. HIST. 703, 705 (Spring 2001); Theodore Kornweibel Jr., *Review of Secrecy and Power: The Life of J. Edgar Hoover by Richard Gid Powers*, 20:2 PRESIDENTIAL STUD. Q. 436, 437 (Spring 1990).

6 Juliet Lapidos, *Meet the New N.R.A. President*, TAKING NOTE: N.Y. TIMES EDITORS Blog, May 3, 2013, 11:01 a.m., http://takingnote.blogs.nytimes. com/2013/05/03/meet-the-new-n-r-a-president/.

7 KENNETH S. STERN, A FORCE UPON THE PLAIN: THE AMERICAN MILITIA MOVEMENT AND THE POLITICS OF HATE 81–82 (Univ. of Oklahoma Press 1997).

8 *Terror from the Right: Plots, Conspiracies and Racist Rampages Since Oklahoma City*, Southern Poverty Law Center, http://www.splcenter.org/get-informed/publications/terror-from-the-right (visited on Feb. 11, 2015).

9 *Id.*

10 *See, e.g., Saddam's judge flees to Britain*, EXPRESS, Mar. 17, 2007; *Argentina; Peron Extradition Request Issued; Other Development*, FACTS ON FILE WORLD NEWS DIGEST, Mar. 8, 2007, at 146E2; Editorial, *For Professional Marshals*, THE BOSTON GLOBE, Mar. 5, 2007, at A8; Neal Matthews, *"Monkey" on His Back; Edward Humes Steps into the Evolution-Creationist Brouhaha—and Then He Unloads the Big Guns*, SAN DIEGO UNION-TRIBUNE, Feb. 25, 2007, at Books-1; Edward Humes, *From Ape to Adam? That's Distorting Darwin*, STAR LEDGER (Newark, New Jersey), Feb. 21, 2007, at 15; Randy Richmond, *Bid Made to Jail Winnicki; Human Rights Agency Says the White Supremacist Broke a Federal Release Condition*, LONDON FREE PRESS (Ontario) Jan. 12, 2007, at B4; Jomar Canlas with Katrice Jalbuen, *Chief Justice Urges Justice for Slain Judge; Ok's Arming*, MANILA TIMES (Philippines), Jan. 23, 2007; Bill Cormier, *Argentines Protest Threats in "Dirty War" Trials*, SUN-SENTINEL (Fort Lauderdale, Florida), Jan. 19, 2007, at 18A; Richard Boudreaux and Rushdi Abu Alouf, *Palestinian Premier Ends Tour after Judge Is Slain*, LOS ANGELES TIMES, Dec. 14, 2006, at A3.

11 *See, e.g.,* Somini Sengupta, *As Nepal Shakes Up Ancient Order, All Is Up in the Air*, N.Y. TIMES, Dec. 17, 2006, at 28; Seth Mydans, *Coup May Allow Thais to Take New Tack on Insurgency*, N.Y. TIMES, Sept. 24, 2006, at 12; C. J. Chivers, *In One Chechen's Humiliation, Questions about Rule of Law*, N.Y. TIMES, Aug. 30, 2006, at A1; Seth Mydans, *27 Years Later, a Formal Inquiry Begins into Khmer Rouge Atrocities*, N.Y. TIMES, Aug. 6, 2006, at A6; Saad Hariri, *My Country Needs Help*, WALL STREET JOURNAL, Jan. 25, 2007, at A19; Joseph A. Mussomeli, *The Worst Genocide Ever*, WALL STREET JOURNAL, Aug. 1, 2006, at A12; Greg Jaffe, Carla Anne Robbins, and Roger Thurow, *The Abu Ghraib Fallout: Prisoner Abuse Could Undercut U.S.*

Credibility—Prison Pictures Bolster Belief That America Has Set Itself Above the Law in Terror War, WALL STREET JOURNAL, May 10, 2004, at A10; Philip Gourevitch, *Crimes Against Humanity Persist on U.N. Watch*, WALL STREET JOURNAL, Dec. 22, 1999, at A18; Mary Anastasia O'Grady, *The Americas: Public Distrust of Mexican Justice Cripples Progress*, WALL STREET JOURNAL, Nov. 1, 1996, at A13; Deroy Murdock, *The Americas: Guatemalan Electorate Clamors for an End to Impunity*, WALL STREET JOURNAL, Jan. 5, 1996, at A9.

12 John M. Glionna, *Cliven Bundy II? Utah Protesters Prepare for New Face-Off with Feds ATV Protest Ride*, LOS ANGELES TIMES, May 9, 2014, http://www.latimes.com/nation/la-na-utah-blm-militia-bundy-20140509-story.html#page=1.

13 JOHN A. WOOD, THE PANTHERS AND THE MILITIAS 32–33 (Univ. Press of America 2002) (quoting Robert Luttwak).

14 *See* STERN, *supra* note 7, at 19–34.

15 Dean M. Kelley, of the National Council of Churches, quoted in *Id.* at 59.

16 *Id.* at 123, 211–12 & 238.

17 *Id.* at 211–12.

18 *Id.* at 213.

19 *See* Juan J. Linz, THE BREAKDOWN OF DEMOCRATIC REGIMES: CRISES, BREAKDOWN AND REEQUILIBRATION 39 & 59 (Johns Hopkins Univ. Press 1978); Explanatory Report, par. 11, incorporated as part III of European Commission For Democracy Through Law (Venice Commission), GUIDELINES ON PROHIBITION AND DISSOLUTION OF POLITICAL PARTIES AND ANALOGOUS MEASURES, adopted by the Venice Commission at its 41st plenary session (Venice, Dec. 10–11, 1999), *available at* http://www.venice.coe.int/docs/2000/CDL-INF(2000)001-e.pdf, revised and incorporated in CODE OF GOOD PRACTICE IN THE FIELD OF POLITICAL PARTIES adopted by the Venice Commission at its 77th Plenary Session (Venice, Dec. 12–13, 2008) and Explanatory Report adopted by the Venice Commission at its 78th Plenary Session (Venice, Mar. 13–14, 2009) 2008, *available at* http://www.venice.coe.int/docs/2009/CDL-AD(2009)002-e.asp.

20 *Id.* at 85.

21 *See* NANCY BERMEO, ORDINARY PEOPLE IN EXTRAORDINARY TIMES: THE CITIZENRY AND THE BREAKDOWN OF DEMOCRACY 38, 170 & *passim* (Princeton Univ. Press 2003).

22 *See* JENNIFER S. HOLMES, TERRORISM AND DEMOCRATIC STABILITY (Manchester Univ. Press 2001).

23 ROBERT DAHL, A PREFACE TO DEMOCRATIC THEORY (Univ. of Chicago Press 1956).

24 Terrorist groups in the United States have been tracked by: The National Memorial Institute for the Prevention of Terrorism [MIPT], originally maintained at www.mipt.org, subsequently maintained by the U.S. government National Counterterrorism Center [NCTC]; NCTC interactive calendar available at http://www.nctc.gov/; Global Terrorism Database at the University of Maryland at http://www.start.umd.edu/gtd/. The FBI at www.fbi.gov is searchable for Terror. *See also* Linda

Bloom, As Internet Grows, So Does Number of Hate Sites, Oct. 2000, http://gbgm-umc.org/programs/antihate/webhate.stm (visited on June 8, 2012), also suggesting the Southern Poverty Law Center and Anti-Defamation League as widely cited and respected.

25 THOMAS HOBBES, LEVIATHAN 99–100 (Clarendon Press 1929) (1651).

26 U.S. CONST., art. I, 8, pars. 15, 16; Id., 2d Amend.

27 Max Weber, *Politics as a Vocation* in FROM MAX WEBER: ESSAYS IN SOCIOLOGY, 78 (Routledge, H. H. Gerth and C. Wright Mills, eds. 1991).

28 WOOD, *supra* note 13; Chip Berlet and Matthew N. Lyons, *Citizen Militias Can Become Violent*, in THE MILITIA MOVEMENT 59, at 64–65 (Greenhaven Press, Charles P. Cozic, ed. 1997); Zachary Elkins, *Rewrite the Second Amendment*, N.Y. TIMES, Apr. 5, 2013, at A23.

29 *See* Stathis N. Kalyvas, *International System and Technologies of Rebellion: How the End of the Cold War Shaped Internal Conflict*, 104 AMER. POL. SCI. REV. 415 (2010); James D. Fearon and David D. Laitin, *Ethnicity, Insurgency, and Civil War*, 97 AMER. POL. SCI. REV. 75, 85 (Feb. 2003); Gary King and Langche Zeng, *Research Note: Improving Forecasts of State Failure*, 53 WORLD POL. 623, 637 & 652 (July 2001).

30 *See* LANE, THE DAY FREEDOM DIED, *supra* note 4; 1898 WILMINGTON RACE RIOT COMM'N, FINAL REPORT, May 31, 2006 (North Carolina Department of Cultural Resources), *available at* http://www.history.ncdcr.gov/1898-wrrc/report/report.htm (visited June 8, 2012); C. VAN WOODWARD, THE STRANGE CAREER OF JIM CROW (1955) (Oxford Univ. Press, Commemorative ed. 2001).

31 Philip Taft and Philip Ross, *American Labor Violence: Its Causes, Character and Outcome*, *in* VIOLENCE IN AMERICA: HISTORICAL AND COMPARATIVE PERSPECTIVES 221 (GPO, Staff Report to the National Commission on the Causes and Prevention of Violence, Hugh Davis Graham and Ted Robert Gurr, eds. 1969). Christopher Waldrep, *Word and Deed: The Language of Lynching, 1820–1953, in* LETHAL IMAGINATION: VIOLENCE AND BRUTALITY IN AMERICAN HISTORY 228 (New York Univ. Press, Michael A. Bellesiles, ed. 1999) (photograph of lynched labor organizers).

32 *See* Scott Shane and Ron Nixon, *The Fourth Branch: In Washington, Contractors Take on Biggest Role Ever*, N.Y. TIMES, Feb. 4, 2007, sec. 1, at 1; Marc Santora and James Glanz, *Five American Security Employees Killed in Baghdad Helicopter Attack*, NEW YORK TIMES, Jan. 24, 2007, at A10; Ted Koppel, *These Guns for Hire*, NEW YORK TIMES, May 22, 2006, at A21.

33 *See, e.g., The Iran-Contra Report; key Sections of Document: The Making of a Political Crisis*, N.Y. TIMES, Nov. 19, 1987, at A14; Stephen Engelberg, *Congress Considers Cutbacks in Intelligence Budget*, N.Y. TIMES, Sept. 27, 1986, sec. 1, at 19.

34 CULLEN MURPHY, ARE WE ROME: THE FALL OF AN EMPIRE AND THE FATE OF AMERICA 59–90 (Houghton Mifflin 2007); Daniel Bergner, *The Other Army*, N.Y. TIMES MAGAZINE, Aug. 14, 2005, at 29; Robert Fisk and Severin Carrell, *Occupiers Spend Millions on Private Army of Security Men*, Mar. 29, 2004 (Information

Clearing House), http://www.informationclearinghouse.info/article5976.htm (visited on Mar. 30, 2007).

35 Dana Milbank, *How to Save America: Restore the Draft*, WASHINGTON POST, Nov. 29, 2013, *available at* http://www.washingtonpost.com/opinions/dana-milbank-restore-conscription-restore-america/2013/11/29/8d5f7ef8–5935–11e3–8304-caf30787c0a9_story.html.

36 *See* Hamdan v. Rumsfeld, 548 U.S. 557, 593 (2006) (on breadth of Authorization for Use of Military Force). *See also* Mary Ellen O'Connell, *The International Law of Drones*, ASIL INSIGHT, vol. 14, no. 37, Nov. 12, 2010, http://www.asil.org/insights101112.cfm.

37 *See* Alan Cowell, *Rights Group Criticizes U.S. Over "Outsourcing" in Iraq*, N.Y. TIMES, May 24, 2006, at A16.

38 Art. I, sec. 8, par. 11.

39 *See* 42 U.S.C. 1983; *and see* Norwood v. Harrison, 413 U.S. 455, 465 (1973) Lugar v. Edmondson Oil Co., 457 U.S. 922 (1982).

40 *See* Foreign Assistance Act of 1974, Dec. 30, 1974, 93 P.L. 559, 88 Stat. 1795, repealed and replaced by Intelligence Oversight Act, 50 U.S.C. sec. 413(a)(1), (b), Public Law 96–450, Intelligence Authorization Act for Fiscal Year 1981, Oct. 14, 1980; Executive Order 12,333 (1981).

41 Foreign Intelligence Surveillance Act, 50 U.S.C. 1801ff., Oct. 25, 1978, P.L. 95–511, Title I, sec. 101, 92 Stat. 1783 as amended.

42 SELECT COMM. TO STUDY GOVERNMENTAL OPERATIONS WITH RESPECT TO INTELLIGENCE ACTIVITIES, FINAL REPORT, S. DOC. NO. 94–755, 94th Cong. 2d sess. (1976) (GPO 1976) (the Church Committee Report).

43 *See* DAVID COLE AND JULES LOBEL, LESS SAFE, LESS FREE: WHY AMERICA IS LOSING THE WAR ON TERROR 23–28, 33–40, 60–63 & 135 (New Press 2007); Vincent Martin Bonventre and Amanda Hiller, *High Court Studies: Public Law at the New York Court of Appeals: An Update on Developments, 2000*, 64 ALB. L. REV. 1355, 1359 (2001).

44 *See, e.g.*, Simon Romero, *Settling of Crisis Makes Winners of Andes Nations, While Rebels Lose Ground*, N.Y. TIMES, Mar. 9, 2008, at A12; Simon Romero, *Lawmakers in Colombia Urge Firing of Mediator*, N.Y. TIMES, May 26, 2007, at A3; Simon Romero, *Colombian Government Is Ensnared in a Paramilitary Scandal*, N.Y. TIMES, Jan. 21, 2007, sec. 1, at 15.

45 Simon Romero, *Living in Exile Isn't What It Used to Be*, N.Y. Times, Oct. 7, 2007, sec. 4, at 16; James Dao, *Word for Word/The "Dirty War"; Ally or Enemy? America Couldn't Get a Fix on Post-Coup Argentina*, N.Y. Times, Aug. 25, 2002, sec. 4, at 5; Tim Golden, *Can the Truth Help Salvador Outlive Hate?*, N.Y. Times, Mar. 21, 1993, sec. 4, at 1; Amnesty International, Guatemala: Accountable Intelligence or recycled repression? Abolition of the EMP and Effective Intelligence Reform (Amnesty International), June 9, 2003, http://www.amnesty.org/en/library/info/AMR34/031/2003 (visited May 2, 2008) (Guatemela).

46 Jeffrey Gettleman, *3-Way Battles Again Jolt Eastern Congo*, N.Y. TIMES, Oct. 25, 2007, at A3.

47 *See* Sanil Dasgupta, *Beyond Iraq; Paramilitaries on the March*, N.Y. Times, Apr. 6, 2003, sec. 4, at 7.

48 *See* United States v. Turner, 720 F.3d 411 (2d Cir. 2013); Editorial, *For Professional Marshals*, BOSTON GLOBE, Mar. 5, 2007, at A8; Lenese C. Herbert, *Can't You See What I'm Saying? Making Expressive Conduct a Crime in High-Crime Areas*, 9 GEO. J. POVERTY LAW & POL'Y 135, 150–151 (2002); Bradley Graham, *Colombian Supreme Court Overturns Extraditon Pact With U.S.*, WASHINGTON POST, June 27, 1987, at A16; *Mourning Latest Victim, Colombia Will Seek to Extradite Drug Figures*, N.Y. Times, Aug. 20, 1989, sec. 1, at 1; *and see* sources cited *supra* note 11.

49 *See* Erwin Chemerinsky, *An Independent Analysis of the Los Angeles Police Department's Board of Inquiry Report on the Rampart Scandal*, 34 LOY. L.A. L. REV. 545 (2005).

50 *Id.* at 549–50.

51 *Id.* at 549n.

52 *Id.* at 550–51.

53 Samuel R. Gross and Barbara O'Brien, *Frequency and Predictors of False Conviction: Why We Know So Little, and New Data on Capital Cases*, 5 J. EMPIRICAL LEGAL STUD. 927, 931–32 (2008).

54 Richard Perez Pena, *Supervision of Troopers Faulted in Evidence Tampering Scandal*, N.Y. Times, Feb. 4, 1997, at B1.

55 COMM'N TO INVESTIGATE ALLEGATIONS OF POLICE CORRUPTION AND THE ANTI-CORRUPTION PROCEDURES OF THE POLICE DEP'T, CITY OF NEW YORK (THE "MOLLEN COMM'N"), COMM'N REPORT (1994), *available at* http://www.parc.info/clientfiles/Special%20Reports/4%20-%20Mollen%20Commission%20-%20NYPD.pdf; INDEPENDENT COMM'N ON THE LOS ANGELES POLICE DEPARTMENT (THE "CHRISTOPHER COMM'N"), REPORT (1991), *available at* http://www.parc.info/client_files/Special%20Reports/1%20-%20Chistopher%20Commision.pdf; H.R. Doc. No. 102–242(I), at 136–138 tit. Omnibus Crime Control Act of 1991 (Oct. 7, 1991), 1991 WL 206794, *available at* http://web2.westlaw.com/find/default.wl?cite=1991+WL+206794&rs=WLW13.04&vr=2.0&rp=%2ffind%2fdefault.wl&sv=Full&fn=_top&mt=208; NATIONAL COMM'N ON LAW OBSERVANCE AND ENFORCEMENT (THE "WICKERSHAM COMM'N"), REPORT ON LAWLESSNESS IN LAW ENFORCEMENT 5 (GPO 1931), *and see* Miranda v. Ariz., 384 U.S. 436, 447 (1966).

56 PAUL CHEVIGNY, POLICE POWER: POLICE ABUSE IN NEW YORK CITY (Pantheon 1969).

57 Peter Neufeld, *Ask a Policeman*, N.Y. Times, Dec. 24, 2006, sec. 4, at 8.

58 *Id.*

59 Alice Mcquillan, *Grand Jury's Out: Brooklyn D.A. Accused of Failing to Indict Cops Who Kill*, VILLAGE VOICE, Feb. 25–Mar. 2, 2004.

60 392 U.S. 1 (1968).

61 *United States v. Singleton*, 144 F.3d 1343 (10 Cir. 1998), vacated at 165 F.3d 1297 (10th Cir. 1999) (en banc).

62 *See* NEW YORK ADVISORY COMMITTEE TO THE U.S. COMMISSION ON CIVIL RIGHTS, REPORT, CIVIL RIGHTS IMPLICATIONS OF POST-SEPTEMBER 11 LAW ENFORCEMENT PRACTICES IN NEW YORK 18–19 (2004), *available at* http://www.law.umaryland.edu/marshall/usccr/documents/cr122004024309.pdf (describing testimony of Dennis D. Parker); *Id.*, at 31 (describing testimony of David Harris); DAVID A. HARRIS, PROFILES IN INJUSTICE: WHY RACIAL PROFILING CANNOT WORK (New Press 2002).

63 *See* MICHELLE ALEXANDER, THE NEW JIM CROW: MASS INCARCERATION IN THE AGE OF COLORBLINDNESS 7 & 96 (New Press 2010); Prison Inmates at Midyear 2009—Statistical Tables, Bureau of Justice Statistics 19 (June 2010), http://www.bjs.gov/content/pub/pdf/pim09st.pdf.

64 Theodore J. Lowi, *Our Millennium: Political Science Confronts the Global Corporate Economy*, at 11–13 (presidential address to the 18th Congress of the International Political Science Association, Quebec, Canada, July 2000) (available from the IPSA, and copy in possession of the author).

65 THE FEDERALIST NO. 51, at 322 (James Madison) (New American Library, Clinton Rossiter, ed. 1961).

66 STEVEN PINKER, THE BETTER ANGELS OF OUR NATURE: WHY VIOLENCE HAS DECLINED 680–82 (Viking 2011); *and see* Peter Singer, *Kinder and Gentler*, N.Y. Times, Oct. 9, 2011, Book Rev., at 1 (reviewing PINKER, BETTER ANGELS).

67 Lizette Alvarez and Cara Buckley, *Zimmerman Is Acquitted in Trayvon Martin Killing*, N.Y. Times, July 14, 2013, at A1.

68 Keyishian v. Bd. of Regents, 385 U.S. 589, 592 (1967).

69 William J. Stuntz, *Local Policing After the Terror*, 111 YALE L.J. 2137 (2002) (for a very interesting suggestion). *See also* William J. Stuntz, *The Uneasy Relationship Between Criminal Procedure and Criminal Justice*, 107 YALE L.J. 1, 5 (1997).

70 See Political Instability Task Force (PITF) State Failure Problem Set 1955–2012, Integrated Network for Societal Conflict Research (INSCR) (May 2, 2013), http://www.systemicpeace.org/inscr/inscr.htm.

71 *See* G. BINGHAM POWELL, CONTEMPORARY DEMOCRACIES: PARTICIPATION, STABILITY, AND VIOLENCE 163–66 & 173–74 (Harvard Univ. Press 1982).

72 STERN, A FORCE UPON THE PLAIN, *supra* note 7, at 155–56.

73 *See* David Pion-Berlin, *The Armed Forces and Politics: Gains and Snares in Recent Scholarship*, 30 LATIN AMERICAN RESEARCH REVIEW 147, 155 (1995) (reviewing nine books), *available at* http://www.jstor.org/stable/2504091; Liisa North and José Nun, *A Military Coup Is a Military Coup . . . or Is It?*, 11 CANADIAN JOURNAL OF POLITICAL SCIENCE / REVUE CANADIENNE DE SCIENCE POLITIQUE, 165, 172 (1978) (reviewing three books), *available at* http://www.jstor.org/stable/3230525.

CHAPTER 9. BREAKDOWN BY COURT ORDER

1 Goldstein v. Superior Court, 45 Cal. 4th 218, 222 (Cal. 2008).

2 Brief of Appellee-Respondent in Van de Kamp v. Goldstein, 555 U.S. 335 (2009), 2008 WL 4080370 at 1 (citations omitted).

3 Van de Kamp v. Goldstein, 555 U.S. 335, 339 (2009).

4 Brief of Appellee-Respondent, *supra* note 2, at 4.

5 *See* United States v. Singleton, 144 F.3d 1343 (10th Cir. 1998), rev'd 165 F.3d 1297 (10th Cir. *en banc* 1999) because the criminal "justice" system relied on such bribes.

6 Giglio v. United States, 405 U.S. 150 (1972).

7 See *Giglio*, 405 U.S. at 154; Brady v. Maryland, 373 U.S. 83, 87 (1963).

8 1989–90 LOS ANGELES COUNTY GRAND JURY REPORT: INVESTIGATION OF THE INVOLVEMENT OF JAIL HOUSE INFORMANTS IN THE CRIMINAL JUSTICE SYSTEM IN LOS ANGELES COUNTY (Cal. Comm'n on the Fair Admin. of Justice), June 16, 1990, *available at* http://www.ccfaj.org/documents/reports/jailhouse/ expert/1989-1990%20LA%20County%20Grand%20Jury%20Report.pdf, at 6.

9 *Id.* at 7–31, *and see especially* 27–28 on the complicity of law enforcement.

10 Brief of Appellee-Respondent, *supra* note 2, at 6 (citations omitted).

11 1989–90 LOS ANGELES COUNTY GRAND JURY REPORT, *supra* note 8, at 92–96, 103, 111–19, 140–45. On knowledge of abuse of the use of informants and failure to act, *see id.* at 74–122.

12 Van de Kamp v. Goldstein, 555 U.S. 335 (2009).

13 *Id.* at 348.

14 *Id.* at 339.

15 The Constitution, Art. III, sec. 1 ("Judges"); 28 USCS sec. 1 (June 25, 1948, ch 646, 62 Stat. 869) ("Justice").

16 Connick v. Thompson, 131 S. Ct. 1350, 1358 n.5 (2011).

17 *Connick*, 131 S. Ct. at 1370 (Ginsburg, J., dissenting).

18 Ashcroft v. Iqbal, 556 U.S. 662 (2009).

19 *Id.* at 695 (Souter, J., dissenting) (citations omitted).

20 *See* NEW YORK ADVISORY COMMITTEE TO THE U.S. COMMISSION ON CIVIL RIGHTS, CIVIL RIGHTS IMPLICATIONS OF POST-SEPTEMBER 11 LAW ENFORCEMENT PRACTICES IN NEW YORK (Mar. 2004).

21 *Compare* F.R.C.P. 8(a)(2) and JAMES WM. MOORE, MOORE'S FEDERAL PRACTICE 8-25–8-26 (LEXIS Pub. 3d ed. 2013) *with* Ashcroft v. Iqbal, 556 U.S., at 678.

22 *See* Ashcroft v. Iqbal, 556 U.S. at 691–695 (Souter, J., dissenting).

23 *Compare id.* at 680–81, *with id.* at 694–98 (Souter, J., dissenting).

24 *Id.* at 680–81.

25 *Id.* at 681.

26 On the earlier struggle, *see* STEPHEN E. GOTTLIEB, MORALITY IMPOSED: THE REHNQUIST COURT AND LIBERTY IN AMERICA 57–58 (New York Univ. Press 2000); Stephen E. Gottlieb, *Sandra Day O'Connor's Position on Discrimination*, 4 MARGINS: MARYLAND'S L. J. ON RACE, RELIGION, GENDER & CLASS 241

(2004); Stephen E. Gottlieb, *Reformulating the Motive/Effects Debate in Constitutional Adjudication*, 33 WAYNE L. REV. 97 (1986). On Justice Scalia's view *see* Justice Dennis D. Dorin, *Far Right of the Mainstream: Racism, Rights, and Remedies from the Perspective of Justice Antonin Scalia's McCleskey Memorandum*, 45 MERCER L. REV. 1035, 1038 (1994); DAVID A. SCHULTZ AND CHRISTOPHER E. SMITH, THE JURISPRUDENTIAL VISION OF JUSTICE ANTONIN SCALIA 195 (Rowman & Littlefield 1996).

27 Clinton v. Jones, 520 U.S. 681 (1997).

28 Van de Kamp v. Goldstein, 555 U.S. 335 (2009); Connick v. Thompson, 131 S. Ct. 1350, 1358 n.5 (2011).

29 Bell Atl. Corp. v. Twombly, 550 U.S. 544 (2007).

30 Raymond H. Brescia, *The* Iqbal *Effect: The Impact of New Pleading Standards in Employment and Housing Discrimination Litigation*, 100 KY. L. J. 235, 284–87 (2011–12).

31 Bell Atl. Corp. v. Twombly, *supra* note 29.

32 Brescia, *supra* note 30.

33 *See supra* note 26.

34 Ashcroft v. al-Kidd, 131 S. Ct. 2074 (2011).

35 *See* Atwater v. City of Lago Vista, 532 U.S. 318 (2001); *id.* at 372 (O'Connor, J., dissenting).

36 Ashcroft v. al-Kidd, 131 S. Ct., at 2084 (quoting the court below at 580 F.3d, at 972).

37 *Id.* 131 S. Ct. at 2089 (Ginsburg, J., concurring in the judgment) *and see* Al-Kidd v. Gonzales, 2006 U.S. Dist. LEXIS 70283, 2 (D. Idaho Sept. 27, 2006).

38 James E. Pfander, *Resolving the Qualified Immunity Dilemma: Constitutional Tort Claims For Nominal Damages*, 111 COLUM. L. REV. 1601 (2011) (difficulties with constitutional claims). On immunity doctrine, *see* Reichle v. Howards, 132 S. Ct. 2088, 2093 (U.S. 2012); Cullen v. Pinholster, 131 S. Ct. 1388, 1399 (2011). On source of "good faith" and "clearly established" exceptions, *see* Wood v. Strickland, 420 U.S. 308, 321 (1975). *But see* Millbrook v. United States, 133 S. Ct. 1441 (U.S. 2013); Levin v. United States, 133 S. Ct. 1224 (U.S. 2013).

39 On the exclusionary rule, *see* Andrew E. Taslitz, *Hypocrisy, Corruption, and Illegitimacy: Why Judicial Integrity Justifies the Exclusionary Rule*, 10 OHIO ST. J. CRIM. L. 419 (2013); Stephen E. Gottlieb, *Feedback from the Fourth Amendment: Is the Exclusionary Rule an Albatross around the Judicial Neck*, 67 KY L. J. 1007 (1979).

40 *See* Boumediene v. Bush, 553 U.S. 723 (2008); *id.* at 801 (Roberts, C.J. dissenting); *id.* at 826 (Scalia, J., dissenting).

41 *See* Hamdan v. Rumsfeld, 548 U.S. 557 (2006); *id.* at 655 (Scalia, J., dissenting); *id.* at 678 (Thomas, J., dissenting); *id.* at 725 (Alito, J., dissenting).

42 DA's Office v. Osborne, 557 U.S. 52 (2009); *and see* Skinner v. Switzer, 131 S. Ct. 1289, 1300 (2011) (Thomas, J., dissenting).

43 DA's Office v. Osborne, 557 U.S., at 71, citing House v. Bell, 547 U.S. 518, at 554–555 (2006). *See also* McQuiggin v. Perkins, 133 S. Ct. 1924, 1937 (2013) (Scalia, J., dissenting).

44 DA's Office v. Osborne, 557 U.S. at 71; House v. Bell, 547 U.S. at 540–48, 554–555; *id.* at 555 (Roberts, C.J., concurring in the judgment in part and dissenting in part).

45 See remarks of James Madison, proposing Bill of Rights, 1 ANNALS OF CONG. 454 (U.S. H. Rep., 1st Cong, 1st Sess., June 8, 1789).

46 See chapter 5.

47 Citizens United v. FEC, 558 U.S. 310 (2010).

48 Holder v. Hall, 512 U.S. 874, 896–03 (1994) (Thomas, J., concurring in the judgment).

49 497 U.S. 62, 65 (1990).

50 Rutan v. Republican Party, 497 U.S. 62, 105 (1990).

51 Bush v. Vera, 517 U.S. 952, 964, 967–68 (1996).

52 League of United Latin Am. Citizens v. Perry, 548 U.S. 399 (2006) [hereinafter *LULAC*].

53 *Id.* at 492–93.

54 *Id.* at 511–12.

55 *Id.* at 419–20.

56 42 USCS sec. 1973.

57 42 U.S.C. sec. 1973(b).

58 *LULAC, supra* note 52, at 510 (Roberts, J., dissenting in part).

59 *Id.* at 517.

60 *Id.* at 515–18.

61 *Id.* at 513.

62 N.Y. State Bd. of Elections v. Lopez Torres, 552 U.S. 196 (2008).

63 N. Y. Elect. L. secs. 6–106, 6–124.

64 Lopez-Torres v. New York State Board of Elections, 462 F.3d 161, 178 (2d Cir. 2006).

65 New York State Bd. of Elections v. López Torres, 552 U.S., at 206.

66 Washington State Grange v. Wash. State Republican Party, 552 U.S. 442 (2008).

67 *See* Eu v. San Francisco Cnty. Democratic Cent. Comm., 489 U.S. 214, 227 (1989); Tashjian v. Republican Party of Conn., 479 U.S. 208, 224–25 (1986); Cousins v. Wigoda, 419 U.S. 477, 489–91 (1975).

68 *See* Brief Amicus Curiae of James MacGregor Burns, *et al*, Tashjian v. Republic Party of Conn., 479 U.S. 208 (1986), submitted by the author as counsel for amici curiae, *and see* Republican Party of State of Conn. v. Tashjian, 770 F.2d 265, 286–88 (2d Cir. 1985) (Oakes, J., concurring).

69 Crawford v. Marion County Election Bd., 553 U.S. 181 (2008).

70 Harper v. Virginia State Bd. of Elections, 383 U.S. 663 (1966).

71 *Crawford*, 553 U.S. at 230n (Souter, J., dissenting).

72 Richard L. Hasen, *Why Judge Posner Changed His Mind on Voter ID Laws*, DAILY BEAST, Oct. 23, 2013, http://www.thedailybeast.com/articles/2013/10/23/why-judge-posner-is-right-on-voter-id-laws.html.

73 Davis v. FEC, 554 U.S. 724 (2008).

74 Brunner v. Ohio Republican Party, 555 U.S. 5 (2008).

75 Bartlett v. Strickland, 556 U.S. 1, 44 (2009).

76 Northwest Austin Mun. Util. Dist. No. One v. Holder, 557 U.S. 193 (2009).

77 Shelby County v. Holder, 133 S. Ct. 2612 (2013).

78 Civil Rights Act of 1957, 71 Stat. 634 (authorizing voting rights suits); Civil Rights Act of 1960, 74 Stat. 86 (authorizing, *inter alia* registration by federal officials).

79 *See* South Carolina v. Katzenbach, 383 U.S. 301, 313–14 (1966).

80 42 U.S.C. 1973(a); 42 USCS sec. 1973b(f)(2).

81 42 U.S.C. secs. 1973b and 1973c.

82 42 U.S.C. 1973c(b).

83 Shelby County v. Holder, 133 S. Ct. 2612 (2013).

84 521 U.S. 507 (1997).

85 *Shelby County,* 133 S. Ct., at 2622, 2624.

86 *Id.* at 2623, 2624.

87 U.S. CONST., Amend. XIV, sec. 1.

88 *Shelby County,* 133 S. Ct. at 2624–30.

89 GEORGE ORWELL, ANIMAL FARM (1945).

90 Randall v. Sorrell, 548 U.S. 230 (2006) (rejecting contribution limits as too low).

91 Ariz. Free Enter. Club's Freedom Club PAC v. Bennett, 131 S. Ct. 2806 (2011); Davis v. FEC, 554 U.S. 724 (2008).

92 Citizens United v. FEC, 558 U.S. 310 (2010).

93 Federal Corrupt Practices Act of 1907, 59 P.L. 36; 34 Stat. 864; 59 Cong. Ch. 420, Jan. 26, 1907. *And see* 2 U.S.C. sec. 441b.

94 GARY C. JACOBSON, MONEY IN CONGRESSIONAL ELECTIONS (Yale Univ. Press 1980) is one of the seminal works. *See also* John R. Johannes and Margaret Latus Nugent, *Conclusion: Reforms and Values, in* MONEY, ELECTIONS AND DEMOCRACY, 270–74 (Westview Press, Margaret Latus Nugent and John R. Johannes, eds. 1990), based on a meeting split between the political scientists, favoring competition and funds to enable it, and journalists, seeking to restrict flow of funds.

95 *See* RAYMOND A. BAUER, ITHIEL DE SOLA POOL, AND LEWIS ANTHONY DEXTER, AMERICAN BUSINESS AND PUBLIC POLICY: THE POLITICS OF FOREIGN TRADE (Atherton Press 1963).

96 Randall v. Sorrell, 548 U.S. 230, 248–249, 255–56, 261 (2006) (Breyer, J., plurality opinion); *but see id.,* 548 U.S. at 268, 269n, 271 (Thomas, J., concurring); *id.,* 548 U.S. at 279n (Stevens, J., dissenting); *id.,* 548 at 281, 287–88 (Souter, J., dissenting); *and see* United States Term Limits v. Thornton, 514 U.S. 779, 922 (1995) (Thomas, J., dissenting),

97 Caperton v. A. T. Massey Coal Co., 556 U.S. 868 (2009).

98 On neutral and nonpartisan election administration, compare Paul Krugman, *Hack the Vote,* N.Y. Times, Dec. 2, 2003, A31; David L. Dill, *Diebold,* VerifiedVoting.org Newsletter, vol. 1, no. 11, Sept. 22, 2003, available at http://www.verifiedvoting.org; Farhad Manjoo, *Will the Election Be Hacked?,* SALON.COM, Feb. 9, 2004, http://www.salon.com/tech/feature/2004/02/09/voting_machines/index.html. On security flaws

and concealment, see Robert S. Boynton, THE TYRANNY OF COPYRIGHT?, N.Y. Times, Jan. 25, 2004.

99 On monopoly pricing claims among local exchange, ISP and DSL carriers, *see* Pac. Bell Tel. Co. v. linkLine Communs., Inc., 555 U.S. 438 (2009); Bell Atl. Corp. v. Twombly, 550 U.S. 544 (2007), *and see* FCC Launches Broad Rulemaking on How Best to Protect and Promote the Open Internet; Seeks Public Input over the Next Four Months to Find Most Viable Approach, 2014 FCC LEXIS 1704 (Federal Communications Commission, May 15, 2014).

100 On corporate control, see What General Welfare Means, *infra* this chapter, *and see* Golan v. Holder, 132 S. Ct. 873 (U.S. 2012); Citizens United v. FEC, 558 U.S. 310 (2010). On deference to government, *see* Clapper v. Amnesty Int'l USA, 133 S. Ct. 1138 (2013); Holder v. Humanitarian Law Project, 130 S. Ct. 2705 (2010).

101 THE FEDERALIST NOS. 47–48, at 300–12 (James Madison) (New American Library, Clinton Rossiter, ed. 1961).

102 *E.g.*, Hamdan v. Rumsfeld, 548 U.S. 557, 690–91 (2006) (Thomas, J., dissenting).

103 Clapper v. Amnesty Int'l USA, 133 S. Ct. 1138 (2013).

104 Boumediene v. Bush, 553 U.S. 723, 742–44, 765 (2008).

105 Hein v. Freedom from Religion Found., Inc., 551 U.S. 587 (2007).

106 City of Arlington v. FCC, 133 S. Ct. 1863, 1877 (2013) (Roberts, C.J., dissenting); Decker v. Northwest Envtl. Def. Ctr., 133 S. Ct. 1326 (2013) (Scalia, J., concurring and dissenting in part); Talk Amer., Inc. v. Mich. Bell Tel. Co., 131 S. Ct. 2254 (U.S. 2011) (Scalia, J., concurring); Free Enter. Fund v. Pub. Co. Accounting Oversight Bd., 130 S. Ct. 3138 (2010).

107 Parents Involved in Cmty. Sch. v. Seattle Sch. Dist. No. 1, 551 U.S. 701, 795, 797 (2007) (Kennedy, J., concurring in part and in the judgment).

108 Ian Haney-López, *Intentional Blindness* 87 N.Y.U. L. REV. 1779, 1871–72 (2012); Cedric Merlin Powell, *Harvesting Conceptions of Equality: Opportunity, Results, and Neutrality* 31 ST. LOUIS U. PUB. L. REV. 225, 270 (2012).

109 551 U.S. 701.

110 *See, e.g.*, Missouri ex rel. Gaines v. Canada, 305 U.S. 337 (1938); Sipuel v. Board of Regents, 332 U.S. 631 (1948); Sweat v. Painter, 339 U.S. 629 (1950); McLauren v. Oklahoma State Regents, 339 U.S. 637 (1950); *and see* Morgan v. Virginia, 328 U.S. 373 (1946).

111 *McLauren,* 339 U.S. at 641.

112 Shelley v. Kramer, 334 U.S. 1 (1948).

113 Brown v. Board of Educ., 347 U.S. 483 (1954).

114 Nixon v. Herndon, 273 U.S. 536 (1927); Nixon v. Condon, 286 U.S. 73 (1932); Smith v. Allwright, 321 U.S. 649 (1944); Terry v. Adams, 345 U.S. 461 (1953).

115 Green v. County School Board, 391 U.S. 430, 437–38 (1968).

116 *See* Swann v. Charlotte-Mecklenburg Bd. of Educ., 402 U.S. 1 (1971); Keyes v. School District No. 1, 413 U.S. 189 (1973).

117 Parents Involved in Cmty. Sch. v. Seattle Sch. Dist. No. 1, 551 U.S. 701 (2007). *See also* Fisher v. Univ. of Tex., 133 S. Ct. 2411 (2013).

118 *See, e.g.*, Baker v. F & F Inv. Co., 489 F.2d 829, 831–832 (7th Cir. Ill. 1973).

119 MELVIN L. OLIVER AND THOMAS M. SHAPIRO, BLACK WEALTH/WHITE WEALTH: A NEW PERSPECTIVE ON RACIAL INEQUALITY 17–18, 51–52, 150 & 174 (Routledge 1995); DOUGLAS S. MASSEY AND NANCY A. DENTON, AMERICAN APARTHEID: SEGREGATION AND THE MAKING OF THE UNDERCLASS 54–55 (Harvard Univ. Press 1993); KENNETH T. JACKSON, CRABGRASS FRONTIER: THE SUBURBANIZATION OF THE UNITED STATES 203–15 (Oxford Univ. Press 1985); Florence Wagman Roisman, *The Lessons of American Apartheid: The Necessity and Means of Promoting Residential Racial Integration*, 81 IOWA L. REV. 479, 486 (1995) (review of DOUGLAS S. MASSEY AND NANCY A. DENTON, AMERICAN APARTHEID); CHARLES ABRAMS, FORBIDDEN NEIGHBORS: A STUDY OF PREJUDICE IN HOUSING 229–37 (Harper 1955); NATIONAL COMM'N ON URBAN PROBLEMS, BUILDING THE AMERICAN CITY 101 (GPO 1969). For related legal developments, see Social Security Act of 1935, Pub. L. No. 74–271, sec. 210, 49 Stat. 620 (1935); *see also* Fair Labor Standards Act of 1938, Pub. L. No. 75–718, secs. 6(a),3(b)–(f), 52 Stat. 1060 (1938). *See also* MARC LINDER, MIGRANT WORKERS AND MINIMUM WAGES: REGULATING THE EXPLOITATION OF AGRICULTURAL LABOR IN THE UNITED STATES 165–67 (Westview Press 1992); NADJA ZALOKAR, THE ECONOMIC STATUS OF BLACK WOMEN: AN EXPLORATORY INVESTIGATION (U.S. Commission on Civil Rights 1990); Mary C. King, *Occupational Segregation by Race and Sex, 1940–88*, MONTHLY LAB. REV. 30–36 (1992). For a summary of these developments, see STEPHEN E. GOTTLIEB, BRIAN H. BIX, TIMOTHY D. LYTTON, AND ROBIN L. WEST, JURISPRUDENCE CASES AND MATERIALS: AN INTRODUCTION TO THE PHILOSOPHY OF LAW AND ITS APPLICATIONS 1025–27 (LexisNexis, 2d ed. 2006).

120 418 U.S. 717 (1974).

121 Dayton Bd. of Education v. Brinkman, 433 U.S. 406, 413 (1977).

122 *See* Vance v. Ball State Univ., 133 S. Ct. 2434 (2013); Univ. of Tex. Southwestern Med. Ctr. v. Nassar, 133 S. Ct. 2517 (2013).

123 Parents Involved in Cmty. Sch. v. Seattle Sch. Dist. No. 1, 551 U.S. 701, 745–746 (2007).

124 KARL DEUTSCH, NATIONALISM AND SOCIAL COMMUNICATION: AN INQUIRY INTO THE FOUNDATIONS OF NATIONALITY 97–152 (MIT Press 1962).

125 Parents Involved, 551 U.S., at 711, 733–34; *id.* at 813 & 820 (Breyer, J., dissenting).

126 *Id.*, 551 U.S. at 715–16.

127 Stephen E. Gottlieb, Brown v. Board of Education *and the Application of American Tradition to Racial Division*, 34 SUFFOLK U. L. REV. 281 (2001).

128 Hein v. Freedom from Religion Found., Inc., 551 U.S. 587 (2007).

129 *Id.* at 598 citing Allen v. Wright, 468 U.S. 737, 751 (1984).

130 Youngstown Sheet & Tube Co. v. Sawyer, 343 U.S. 579, 635–38 (1952) (Jackson, J., concurring).

131 Ariz. Christian Sch. Tuition Org. v. Winn, 131 S. Ct. 1436 (2011).

132 *Id.*, 131 S. Ct. at 1440.

133 On designation of credits as tax expenditures, see *id.*, 131 S. Ct. at 1452n (Kagan, J., dissenting).

134 *Id.* at 1461 (Kagan, J., dissenting).

135 *Id.* at 1450 (Kagan, J., dissenting).

136 Lamb's Chapel v. Center Moriches Union Free Sch. Dist., 508 U.S. 384 (1993); Zobrest v. Catalina Foothills Sch. Dist., 509 U.S. 1 (1993); Rosenberger v. Rector & Visitors of the Univ. of Va., 515 U.S. 819 (1995); Agostini v. Felton, 521 U.S. 203 (1997); Mitchell v. Helms, 530 U.S. 793 (2000); Good News Club v. Milford Cent. Sch., 533 U.S. 98 (2001); *but see* Santa Fe Indep. Sch. Dist. v. Doe, 530 U.S. 290 (2000).

137 Zelman v. Simmons-Harris, 536 U.S. 639 (2002).

138 Epperson v. Arkansas, 393 U.S. 97, 106 (1968).

139 *Compare* W. Va. State Bd. of Educ. v. Barnette, 319 U.S. 624 (1943) *and* Sherbert v. Verner, 374 U.S. 398 (1963) *with* Emp't Div., Dep't of Human Res. v. Smith, 494 U.S. 872 (1990).

140 *See* Brief of the Claremont Institute Center for Constitutional Jurisprudence as Amicus Curiae in Support of Petitioners, at 5–9, Zelman v. Simmons-Harris, 536 U.S. 639 (2002); Brief for the Catholic League for Religious and Civil Rights as Amicus Curiae Supporting Petitioners, Zelman v. Simmons-Harris. *See also* STEVEN M. TELES, THE RISE OF THE CONSERVATIVE LEGAL MOVEMENT: THE BATTLE FOR CONTROL OF THE LAW (Princeton Univ. Press 2008); HANS J. HACKER, THE CULTURE OF CONSERVATIVE CHRISTIAN LITIGATION (Roman & Littlefield 2005).

141 Locke v. Davey, 540 U.S. 712 (2004).

142 Davey v. Locke, 299 F.3d 748, 751 (9th Cir. 2002).

143 Locke v. Davey, 540 U.S. at 726–27 (Scalia, J., dissenting).

144 *See id.* at 720 (2004).

145 Brown v. Legal Foundation of Washington, 538 U.S. 216 (2003); Phillips v. Washington Legal Foundation, 524 U.S. 156 (1998).

146 *See* GUIDO CALABRESI, COSTS OF ACCIDENTS: A LEGAL AND ECONOMIC ANALYSIS (Yale Univ. Press 1970).

147 Ronald H. Coase, *The Problem of Social Cost*, 3 J. L. & ECON. 1 (1960), *available at* http://www.jstor.org/stable/724810.

148 550 U.S. 544 (2007).

149 Bell Atl. Corp. v. Twombly, 550 U.S. 544, 558 (2007).

150 *Id.* at 596.

151 Leegin Creative Leather Prods. v. PSKS, Inc., 551 U.S. 877 (2007).

152 *Id.* 551 U.S. at 881.

153 *Id.* 551 U.S. at 914 (Breyer, J., dissenting).

154 *Id.* 551 U.S. at 916.

155 21 U.S.C. sec. 360k(a).

156 Medtronic, Inc. v. Lohr, 518 U.S. 470 (1996).

157 *Id.*

158 *Id.* at 500. On provisions assuming state liability, *see* 21 U.S.C. sec. 360h(d); 21 U.S.C. sec. 360k(b).

159 *Medtronic,* 518 U.S. at 487–88.

160 Margaret Jane Porter, *The* Lohr *Decision: FDA Perspective and Position*, 52 FOOD & DRUG L. J. 7, 11 (1997).

161 Riegel v. Medtronic, Inc., 552 U.S. 312, 326–27 (2008).

162 *Id.* at 326.

163 *Id.*

164 Bruesewitz v. Wyeth LLC, 131 S. Ct. 1068 (2011).

165 42 USC sec. 300aa-22(b)(1).

166 Bruesewitz v. Wyeth, 131 S. Ct. at 1075.

167 *Id.* at 1087 (Sotomayor, J., dissenting).

168 PLIVA, Inc. v. Mensing, 131 S. Ct. 2567 (2011).

169 MacPherson v. Buick Motor Co., 217 N.Y. 382, 389 (N.Y. 1916).

170 Stoneridge Inv. Partners, LLC v. Scientific-Atlanta, Inc., 552 U.S. 148 (2008).

171 Linda Greenhouse, *Supreme Court Limits Lawsuits by Shareholders*, N.Y. Times, Jan. 16, 2008.

172 Janus Capital Group, Inc. v. First Derivative Traders, 131 S. Ct. 2296, 2302 (2011).

173 Credit Suisse Sec. (USA) LLC v. Billing, 551 U.S. 264, 276 (2007).

174 *Id.* 551 U.S. at 287 (Thomas, J., dissenting).

175 *Id.* 551 U.S. at 286–87 (Stevens, J., concurring in the judgment).

176 Exxon Shipping Co. v. Baker, 554 U.S. 471 (2008).

177 *Id.* 554 U.S. at 515; State Farm Mut. Auto. Ins. Co. v. Campbell, 538 U.S. 408, 429 (2003) (Scalia, J. dissenting); *id.* (Thomas, J., dissenting); *id.* at 430 (Ginsburg, dissenting); BMW of North America, Inc. v. Gore, 517 U.S. 559, 598–99 (1996) (Scalia, J., dissenting).

178 Exxon Shipping Co. v. Baker, 554 U.S. at 499.

179 *See* American Express Company v. Italian Colors Restaurant, 133 S. Ct. 2304, 2313 (2013) (Kagan, dissenting).

180 9 U.S.C. sec. 2.

181 Buckeye Check Cashing, Inc. v. Cardegna, 546 U.S. 440 (2006).

182 . *Id.* at 446.

183 *See* Watters v. Wachovia Bank, 127 S.Ct. 1559 (2007).

184 AT&T Mobility LLC v. Concepcion, 131 S. Ct. 1740 (2011).

185 Discover Bank v. Superior Ct., 36 Cal. 4th 148, 162–63, 113 P. 3d 1100, 1110 (2005).

186 AT&T Mobility LLC v. Concepcion, 131 S. Ct. 1740, 1753 (2011). *See also* Stolt-Nielsen S. A. v. AnimalFeeds Int'l Corp., 130 S. Ct. 1758 (U.S. 2010).

187 Wal-Mart Stores, Inc. v. Dukes, 131 S. Ct. 2541 (2011).

188 *See, e.g.*, Alexander v. Sandoval, 532 U.S. 275 (2001); United States v. Armstrong, 517 U.S. 456 (1996); *id.* at 476 (Stevens, J., dissenting); McCleskey v. Kemp, 481 U.S. 279, 298 (1987); Personnel Adm'r v. Feeney, 442 U.S. 256, 279 (1979); Washington v. Davis, 426 U.S. 229 (1976); *Provisions: The Civil Rights Act of 1991*, CONG. Q., Dec. 7, 1991, at 3620; Dennis D. Dorin, *Far Right of the Mainstream: Racism, Rights, and Remedies from* *the Perspective of Justice Antonin Scalia's* McCleskey *Memorandum,* 45 MERCER L. REV. 1035, 1038 (1994); DAVID A. SCHULTZ AND CHRISTOPHER E. SMITH, THE JURISPRUDENTIAL VISION OF JUSTICE ANTONIN SCALIA 195 (Rowman & Littlefield 1996).

189 14 Penn Plaza LLC v. Pyett, 556 U.S. 247 (2009).

190 *See* 29 USCS sec. 623(c).

191 14 Penn Plaza LLC v. Pyett, 556 U.S. at 274–75 (Stevens, J., dissenting).

192 *Id.* 556 U.S. at 266.

193 *Id.* 556 U.S. at 276n (Stevens, J., dissenting).

194 550 U.S. 618 (2007).

195 Lilly Ledbetter Fair Pay Act of 2009, 42 USCS sec. 2000e-5(e)(3), P.L. 111–2, sec. 2, 123 Stat. 5.

196 551 U.S. 158 (2007).

197 29 U.S.C. sec. 213(a)(15) (2004).

198 See Social Security Act of 1935, Pub. L. No. 74–271, sec. 210, 49 Stat. 620 (1935); Fair Labor Standards Act of 1938, Pub. L. No. 75–718, secs. 6(a), 3(b)–(f), 52 Stat. 1060 (1938); LINDER, MIGRANT WORKERS, *supra* note 119, at 165–67; ZALOKAR, ECONOMIC STATUS OF BLACK WOMEN, *supra* note 119; Mary C. King, *Occupational Segregation by Race and Sex, 1940–88,* 115 MONTHLY LAB. REV. 30–36 (1992).

199 Chamber of Commerce of United States v. Brown, 554 U.S. 60 (2008); Cal Gov Code secs. 16645.2 and 16645.7.

200 Schindler Elevator Corp. v. United States ex rel. Kirk, 131 S. Ct. 1885 (2011).

201 John Donne, *No Man is an Island, in* JOHN DONNE, DEVOTIONS UPON EMERGENT OCCASIONS (1624).

202 *See* KEVIN PHILLIPS, WEALTH AND DEMOCRACY 171–200 & 283–90 (Random House 2002).

203 *See* chapter 6; *and see also* American Political Science Association, Task Force on Inequality and American Democracy, American Democracy in an Age of Rising Inequality, http://www.apsanet.org/Files/Task%20Force%20Reports/taskforcereport. pdf; INEQUALITY AND AMERICAN DEMOCRACY: WHAT WE KNOW AND WHAT WE NEED TO LEARN (Russell Sage Foundation, Lawrence R. Jacobs and Theda Skocpol, eds. 2005, research reports for the APSA Task Force on Inequality and American Democracy).

204 *Id.*

205 *Id.*

206 *Id.*

207 554 U.S. 570 (2008).

208 District of Columbia v. Heller, 554 U.S. 570, 625, 635–36 (2008).

209 561 U.S. 742 (2010).

210 *Id.* 561 U.S. at 750 (Alito, J., plurality opinion); *and see id.* 561 U.S. at 805 (Thomas, J., concurring).

211 *Id.* 554 U.S. at 621.

212 *Id.* 554 U.S. at 620, citing *Presser v. Illinois*, 116 U.S. 252 (1886).

213 *See* United States v. Mosley, 238 U.S. 383, 387 (1915); *and see generally* Maj. Gen. Carl Schurz, Report on the Condition of the South, Ex. Doc. No. 2, U.S. Sen, 39th Cong., 1st Session (1865); 42 U.S.C. 1985; Enforcement Act of May 31, 1870 (16 Stat. 141).

214 District of Columbia v. Heller, 554 U.S. 570, 620–21 (2008).

215 See the discussion of Private militias in chapter 8.

216 STEVEN PINKER, THE BETTER ANGELS OF OUR NATURE: WHY VIOLENCE HAS DECLINED 680–82 (Viking 2011).

217 *See generally* GIUSEPPE DI PALMA, TO CRAFT DEMOCRACIES: AN ESSAY ON DEMOCRATIC TRANSITIONS (U. California Press 1990).

218 Prigg v. Pennsylvania, 41 U.S. 539, 624 (1842).

219 *E.g., District of Columbia v. Heller*, 554 U.S. 570 (2008); *McDonald v. City of Chicago*, 130 S. Ct. 3020 (2010).

220 Gibbons v. Ogden, 22 U.S. 1, 194 (1824).

221 *See* Cooley v. Bd. of Wardens, 53 U.S. 299, 319–20 (12 How.) 299 (1852); Ogden v. Saunders, 25 U.S. (12 Wheat.) 213 (1827).

222 See *Nat'l Fed'n of Indep. Bus. v. Sebelius*, 132 S. Ct. at 2615 (Ginsburg, J., dissenting in part) quoting from 2 RECORDS OF THE FEDERAL CONVENTION OF 1787, at 131–132, par. 8 (Yale Univ. Press, Max Farrand, ed. 1966) (instructions to Committee of Detail); *see also d.*, vol. 1, at 21, 53–54, 229, 236; 2 *Id.* at 25–27.

223 Nat'l Fed'n of Indep. Bus. v. Sebelius, 132 S. Ct. at 2612–14 (Ginsburg, J., dissenting).

224 *Id.*

225 See text *supra* at notes 161–68, 176–78 & 181–84.

226 The Virginia Resolution (Dec. 21, 1798) reprinted in 5 THE FOUNDERS' CONSTITUTION 135 (Liberty Fund, Philip B. Kurland and Ralph Lerner, eds. 1987), *available at* http://www.yale.edu/lawweb/avalon/virres.htm, and the Kentucky Resolution of Nov. 10, 1799, reprinted in The Founders' Constitution, *supra* at note 134, *available at* http://avalon.law.yale.edu/18th_century/kenres.asp; *and see* H. Jefferson Powell, *The Principles of '98: An Essay in Historical Retrieval*, 80 VA. L. REV. 689 (1994).

227 Riegel v. Medtronic, Inc., 552 U.S. 312, 333 (2008) (Ginsburg, J., dissenting), overruling Medtronic, Inc. v. Lohr, 518 U.S. 470 (1996). *See also* Bruesewitz v. Wyeth LLC, 131 S. Ct. 1068 (2011); PLIVA, Inc. v. Mensing, 131 S. Ct. 2567 (2011).

228 Rapanos v. United States, 547 U.S. 715 (2006).

229 *Id.* at 763; Brief of the States of New York, Michigan, *et al* as Amici Curiae in Support of Respondents, Rapanos v. United States, 547 U.S. 715 (2006), 2004 U.S. Briefs 1034 (U.S. Jan. 13, 2006).

230 Buckeye Check Cashing, Inc. v. Cardegna, 546 U.S. 440 (2006).

231 AT&T Mobility LLC v. Concepcion, 131 S. Ct. 1740 (2011).

232 *See generally*, RICHARD KLUGER, SIMPLE JUSTICE: THE HISTORY OF BROWN V. BOARD OF EDUCATION AND BLACK AMERICA'S STRUGGLE FOR EQUALITY (Knopf 1976).

233 *See* chapter 1, text in notes 110–12; Brown v. Board of Education, 347 U.S. 483 (1954); Plessy v. Ferguson, 163 U.S. 537 (1896).

234 Parents Involved in Cmty. Sch. v. Seattle Sch. Dist. No. 1, 551 U.S. 701 (2007).

235 Roe v. Wade, 410 U.S. 113 (1973); Ruth Bader Ginsburg, *Speaking in a Judicial Voice*, 67 N.Y.U. L. REV. 1185, 1198–1200, 1205, 1208 (1992).

236 *See* Planned Parenthood v. Casey, 505 U.S. 833 (1992); Stenberg v. Carhart, 530 U.S. 914 (2000); Gonzales v. Carhart, 550 U.S. 124 (2007); 18 U.S.C.S. sec. 1531.

237 Ginsburg, *Judicial Voice, supra* note 235, at 1202–03 & 1207; Bowers v. Hardwick, 478 U.S. 186 (1986); Romer v. Evans, 517 U.S. 620 (1996); Lawrence v. Texas, 539 U.S. 558 (2003). *See also* Ledbetter v. Goodyear Tire & Rubber Co., 550 U.S. 618 (2007); Long Island Care at Home, Ltd. v. Coke, 551 U.S. 158 (2007).

238 133 S. Ct. 2675 (2013).

239 ALEXANDER M. BICKEL, THE LEAST DANGEROUS BRANCH: THE SUPREME COURT AT THE BAR OF POLITICS 127–33 (Bobbs-Merrill 1962).

240 *See* Robert Post, *The Supreme Court Opinion as Institutional Practice: Dissent, Legal Scholarship, and Decisionmaking in the Taft Court*, 85 MINN. L. REV. 1267, 1273 (2001) (describing the effect of the Judiciary Act of 1925 giving the Court control over its docket through the writ of certiorari).

241 Alexander M. Bickel, *The Original Understanding and the Segregation Decision*, 69 HARV. L. REV. 1 (1955).

242 GERALD ROSENBERG, THE HOLLOW HOPE: CAN COURTS BRING ABOUT SOCIAL CHANGE? (Univ. of Chicago Press 1991).

243 For critical evaluations of the issues raised by Rosenberg's argument, and his response, *see* LEVERAGING THE LAW: USING THE COURTS TO ACHIEVE SOCIAL CHANGE (P. Lang, David A. Schultz, ed. 1998); *and see* David Schultz and Stephen Gottlieb, *Legal Functionalism and Social Change: A Reassessment of Rosenberg's The Hollow Hope*, in *id.* at 169. *See also* Joseph Daniel Ura, *The Nature of Supreme Court Power*, L. & POL. BK REV., v. 24, no. 5 (2014) (book review).

244 ROSENBERG, *supra* note 242, at 49–54.

245 *Id.*

246 See WALTER F. MURPHY, CONGRESS AND THE COURT: A CASE STUDY IN THE AMERICAN POLITICAL PROCESS (Univ. of Chicago Press 1962).

247 *Id.*

248 *See, e.g.,* Erica Frankenberg, Chungmei Lee, and Gary Orfield, *A Multiracial Society with Segregated Schools: Are We Losing the Dream?*, The Civil Rights Project Harvard Univ. (Jan. 2003), *available at* http://www.civilrightsproject.harvard.edu/research/reseg03/AreWeLosingtheDream.pdf (visited June 22, 2007).

249 MICHELLE ALEXANDER, THE NEW JIM CROW: MASS INCARCERATION IN THE AGE OF COLORBLINDNESS (New Press 2010); *see also* INVISIBLE PUNISHMENT: THE COLLATERAL CONSEQUENCES OF MASS IMPRISONMENT (New Press, Marc Mauer and Meda Chesney-Lind, eds. 2002).

250 On the chilling events leading to United States v. Cruikshank, 92 U.S. 542 (1876), *see* LEEANNA KEITH, THE COLFAX MASSACRE: THE UNTOLD STORY OF BLACK

POWER, WHITE TERROR, AND THE DEATH OF RECONSTRUCTION (Oxford Univ. Press 2008); CHARLES LANE, THE DAY FREEDOM DIED: THE COLFAX MASSACRE, THE SUPREME COURT, AND THE BETRAYAL OF RECONSTRUCTION (Henry Holt & Company 2008); both reviewed in Kevin Boyle, *White Terrorists*, N.Y. TIMES BOOK REV., May 18, 2008, at 24, a succinct and devastating account.

251 ALEXANDER, *supra* note 249, at 6–8, 175 & *passim*; *and see* Mark Mauer and Ryan Scott King, *Schools and Prisons: Fifty Years After Brown v. Board of Education*, THE SENTENCING PROJECT, http://www.sentencingproject.org/doc/publications/rd_brownvboard.pdf (noting "there are now nine times as many African Americans in prison or jail as on the day of the Brown decision").

252 *See* Joanne Scott and Susan P. Sturm, *Courts as Catalysts: Rethinking the Judicial Role in New Governance*, 13 COLUM. J. EUROPEAN L. 565 (2007), Columbia Public Law Research Paper No. 07–146, *available at* http://ssrn.com/abstract=982281 (suggesting another mechanism of judicial power).

253 Stephen E. Gottlieb, *Rebuilding the Right of Association: The Right to Hold a Convention as a Test Case*, 11 HOFSTRA L. REV. 191, 196–203 & 223–30 (1983).

254 *Id.*

255 Gordon E. Baker, *The Unfinished Reapportionment Revolution*, *in* POLITICAL GERRYMANDERING AND THE COURTS 11 (Agathon Press, Bernard Grofman, ed. 1990).

256 On judicial development of property rules, *see* Raymond H. Brescia, *The Cost of Inequality: Social Distance, Predatory Contact, and the Financial Crisis*, 66 NEW YORK U. ANN. SURV. OF AM. L. 641, 711–12 (2011); on role of preemption doctrine, *see id.* at 714–15.

257 Miguel Garcia-Posada and Juan S.Mora-Sanguinetti, Firm Size and Judicial Efficacy: Evidence for the New Civil Procedures in Spain (Feb. 19, 2013). Banco de Espana Working Paper No. 1303, *available at* http://ssrn.com/abstract=2220654 or http://dx.doi.org/10.2139/ssrn.2220654.

258 For dependence of markets on legal infrastructures, *see* William W. Bratton, *Berle and Means Reconsidered at the Century's Turn*, 26 J. CORP. L. 737, 769 (2001), *available at* http://ssrn.com/abstract=255999. On the importance of the courts, *see id.* at 740.

259 Marc Galanter, *Why the "Haves" Come Out Ahead: Speculations on the Limits of Legal Change*, 9 LAW & SOC'Y REV. 95 (1974).

260 *See, e.g.*, section *supra* "What General Welfare Means," and *see infra* notes 261–265.

261 Robert L. Rabin, *Federal Regulation in Historical Perspective*, 38 STAN. L. REV. 1189, 1192 (1986).

262 *See, e.g.*, JAMES CEASER, PRESIDENTIAL SELECTION: THEORY AND DEVELOPMENT 107 (Princeton Univ. Press 1979) (quoting Thomas Jefferson); *and see supra* note 71.

263 *See, e.g.*, Lucas v. South Carolina Coastal Council, 505 U.S. 1003 (1992).

264 *See, e.g.*, Circuit City Stores v. Adams, 532 U.S. 105 (2001).

265 *See, e.g.*, American Express Company v. Italian Colors Restaurant, 133 S. Ct. 2304 (2013).

266 *See, e.g.*, Plessy v. Ferguson, 163 U.S. 537 (1896); Dred Scott v. Sanford, 60 U.S. 393 (1856); The Civil Rights Cases, 109 U.S. 3 (1883); United States v. Cruikshank, 92 U.S. 542 (1875).

CHAPTER 10. JUDICIAL INTERPRETATION FOR DEMOCRACY

1 STEPHEN BREYER, ACTIVE LIBERTY: INTERPRETING OUR DEMOCRATIC CONSTITUTION (Knopf 2005) though without discussing *Carolene Products.* I asked Breyer about that after he spoke at a national meeting. I took his lengthy response about having forgotten, as a tactful way of avoiding discussions among the justices.

2 *See* Shelby County v. Holder, 133 S. Ct. 2612 (2013) (striking down part of the Voter Rights Act); *but see* Vieth v. Jubelirer, 541 U.S. 267, 311–12 (2004) (Kennedy, J., concurring).

3 Rejecting par. 3 of *Carolene Products* n. 4, *see* Parents Involved in Community Schools v. Seattle School District No. 1, 551 U.S. 701 (2007); Adarand Constructors v. Pena, 515 U.S. 200, 218 (1995); *id.* at 223–24; *and see* Gregory v. Ashcroft, 501 U.S. 452, 468–69 (1991); Video: Ginsburg explains Stone as inspiration for Fisher dissent (Constitutional Center), Sept. 9, 2013, http://blog.constitutioncenter.org/2013/09/video-ginsburg-explains-stone-as-inspiration-for-fisher-dissent/; Regents of Univ. of Cal. v. Bakke, 438 U.S. 265, 487–91 (1978); Adam Winkler, *Sounds of Silence: The Supreme Court and Affirmative Action*, 28 LOY. L.A. L. REV. 923, 933–34 (1995), *available at* http://digitalcommons.lmu.edu/llr/vol28/iss3/8; *but see id.* at 949.

4 *See* Holder v. Hall, 512 U.S. 874, 896–97 (1994) (Thomas, J., concurring in the judgment).

5 *See Parents Involved in Cmty. Sch.*, 551 U.S. at 726 (Roberts, C.J., plurality opinion).

6 *See* Lamb's Chapel v. Ctr. Moriches Union Free Sch. Dist., 508 U.S. 384, 398 (1993) (Scalia, J. concurring in the judgment).

7 *See, e.g.*, Dickerson v. United States, 530 U.S. 428, 450 (2000) (Scalia, J., dissenting).

8 *See, e.g.*, McDonald v. City of Chicago, 130 S. Ct. 3020, 3057 (2010) (Scalia, J., concurring); William H. Rehnquist, *The Notion of a Living Constitution*, 54 TEX. L. REV. 693 (1976); *and cf.* William J. Brennan, Jr., *The Constitution of the United States: Contemporary Ratification*, 43 THE NAT'L LAWYERS GUILD PRACTITIONER 1 (1986); Thurgood Marshall, *The Constitution's Bicentennial: Commemorating the Wrong Document?* 40 VANDERBILT L. REV. 1337 (1987).

9 *See, e.g.*, Gonzales v. Carhart, 550 U.S. 124, 169 (2007) (Thomas, C. concurring).

10 STEPHEN E. GOTTLIEB, MORALITY IMPOSED: THE REHNQUIST COURT AND LIBERTY IN AMERICA 24, 29 & 36 (New York Univ. Press 2000).

11 *See* H. JEFFERSON POWELL, THE MORAL TRADITION OF AMERICAN CONSTITUTIONALISM: A THEOLOGICAL INTERPRETATION 100–05, 189, 231–34 & 254–55 (Duke Univ. Press 1993).

12 *Id.* at 159–64.

13 *See, e.g.,* Rehnquist, *Living Constitution, supra* note 8, at 706; SUE DAVIS, JUSTICE REHNQUIST AND THE CONSTITUTION (Princeton Univ. Press 1989); Nancy Maveety, *The Populist of the Adversary Society: The Jurisprudence of Justice Rehnquist,* 13 J. CONTEMP. L. 221 (1987). *See also* Texas v. Johnson, 491 U.S. 397, 421 (1989) (Rehnquist, dissenting). *See also* Antonin Scalia, *The Doctrine of Standing as an Essential Element of the Separation of Powers,* 17 SUFFOLK U. L. REV. 881, 894–96 (1983).

14 *See supra* chapters 5–8.

15 On competition, *see supra* chapters 5 and 9; *but see* Herbert H. Werlin, *Corruption's Challenge to Global Governance: A Selective Balance Sheet,* NEW GLOBAL STUDIES, vol. 3, no. 2 (2009) (criticizing this two dimensional reduction of Dahl as incomplete), http://www.bepress.com/ngs/vol3/iss2/art3/?sending=10784. On inclusion, *see supra* chapters 8 and 9. On federalism, *see supra* chapters 5 and 9. On concentrated wealth, *see supra* chapters 7 and 9.

16 Miller v. Alabama, 132 S. Ct. 2455, 2464 (2012); Muller v. Oregon, 208 U.S. 412, 420–421 (1908); *but see* Perry v. New Hampshire, 132 S. Ct. 716, 738 (2012) (Sotomayor, J., dissenting). *See also* JOHN MONAHAN AND LAURENS WALKER, SOCIAL SCIENCE IN LAW (Foundation Press, 7th ed. 2009).

17 See U.S. CONST., art. III, sec. 2; THE RECORDS OF THE FEDERAL CONVENTION OF 1787 (Yale Univ. Press, Max Farrand, rev. ed. 1966) (hereinafter Farrand), vol. 1, at 97–98 (in Convention on June 4, 1787); *id.,* vol. 2, at 430 (in Convention on Aug. 27, 1787).

18 3 Farrand 85 (commas added).

19 See Robert Post, *Theorizing Disagreement: Reconceiving the Relationship between Law and Politics,* 98 CALIF. L. REV. 1319, 1348 (2010).

20 *See* Antonin Scalia, *Common-Law Courts in a Civil-Law System: The Role of United States Federal Courts in Interpreting the Constitution and Laws,* in A MATTER OF INTERPRETATION: FEDERAL COURTS AND THE LAW 3–47 (Princeton Univ. Press, Amy Gutmann, ed. 1997); Stephen Breyer, *On the Uses of Legislative History in Interpreting Statutes,* 65 S. CAL. L. REV. 845 (1992); Antonin Scalia, *The Rule of Law as a Law of Rules,* 56 U. CHICAGO L. REV. 1175 (1989); Clarence Thomas, *The Higher Law Background of the Privileges or Immunities Clause of the Fourteenth Amendment,* 12 HARVARD J. OF L. & PUBLIC POLICY 63 (1989); Clarence Thomas, *Toward a "Plain Reading" of the Constitution—the Declaration of Independence in Constitutional Interpretation,* 30 HOWARD L. J. 983 (1987); Thurgood Marshall, *The Constitution's Bicentennial: Commemorating the Wrong Document?,* 40 VANDERBILT L. REV. 1337 (1987); William J. Brennan, Jr., *The Constitution of the United States: Contemporary Ratification,* 43 THE NATIONAL LAWYERS GUILD PRACTITIONER 1 (1986); Rehnquist, *Living Constitution, supra* note 8.

21 Philip Bobbitt, *Constitutional Fate,* 58 TEX. L. REV. 695, at 707–11 (1980), expanded into PHILIP BOBBITT, CONSTITUTIONAL FATE (Oxford U. Press 1984); Richard H. Fallon, Jr., *A Constructivist Coherence Theory of Constitutional*

Interpretation, 100 HARV. L. REV. 1189, 1240 (1987). See also Gary Lawson, *Classical Liberal Constitution or Classical Liberal Construction?* N.Y.U. J. L. & LIBERTY (forthcoming), Boston Univ. School of Law, Law and Economics Research Paper No. 14-2, *available at* http://ssrn.com/abstract=2375787 or http://dx.doi.org/10.2139/ssrn.2375787 (Jan. 7, 2014).

22 Kevin M. Stack, *The Divergence of Constitutional and Statutory Interpretation*, 75 U. COLO. L. REV. 1 (2004).

23 McDonald v. City of Chicago, 130 S. Ct. 3020, 3057–58 (2010); *id.* at 3063 (2010) (Thomas, J., concurring); Scalia, *Common-Law Courts, supra* note 20; Rehnquist, *Living Constitution, supra* note 8.

24 Randy E. Barnett, *An Originalism for Nonoriginalists*, 45 LOY. L. REV. 611, 613 (1999).

25 *See* James Melton, Zachary Elkins, Tom Ginsburg and Kalev Leetaru, *On the Interpretability of Law: Lessons from the Decoding of National Constitutions*, 43 BRIT. J. OF POL. SCI. 399 (2012), *available at* CJO 2012 doi:10.1017/S0007123412000361.

26 Michael Stokes Paulsen, *Does the Constitution Prescribe Rules for its Own Interpretation?*, 103 NW. U. L. REV. 857 (2009).

27 *Compare* H.L.A. Hart, *Positivism and the Separation of Law and Morals*, 71 HARV. L. REV. 593 (1958) *with* Lon L. Fuller, *Positivism and Fidelity to Law—A Reply to Professor Hart*, 71 HARV. L. REV. 630 (1958); *and see* Jeremy Waldron, *Hart's Equivocal Response to Fuller*, 83 N.Y.U. L. REV. 1135 (2008).

28 *See* AKHIL REED AMAR, AMERICA'S UNWRITTEN CONSTITUTION: THE PRECEDENTS AND PRINCIPLES WE LIVE BY 37 (Basic Books 2012); BRUCE A. ACKERMAN, WE THE PEOPLE: TRANSFORMATIONS 88 (Harvard Univ. Press 1998); POWELL, MORAL TRADITION, *supra* note 11, at 251–52; JOHN HART ELY, DEMOCRACY AND DISTRUST (Harvard Univ. Press 1980).

29 See also S. COMM. ON THE JUDICIARY, NOMINATION OF ANTHONY M. KENNEDY TO BE ASSOCIATE JUSTICE OF THE SUPREME COURT OF THE UNITED STATES: HEARINGS BEFORE THE S. COMM. ON THE JUDICIARY, 100th Cong., 1st sess., Dec. 14, 15, and 16, 1987, at 111 (GPO 1989).

30 ANTONIN SCALIA AND BRYAN GARNER, READING LAW: THE INTERPRETATION OF LEGAL TEXTS, 88 (Thomson/West 2012); Scalia, *Common-Law Courts, supra* note 20, at 129–49. *See* McDonald v. City of Chicago, 130 S. Ct. 3020, 3058 (2010) (Scalia, J., concurring); Romer v. Evans, 517 U.S. 620, 636 (1996) (Scalia, J., dissenting); Payne v. Tennessee, 501 U.S. 808, 834–835 (1991) (Scalia, J., concurring); *and see* sources, *supra* note 13.

31 *See* Barnett, *supra* note 24, 45 LOY. L. REV. at 637.

32 *See* Randy E. Barnett, *Constitutional Legitimacy*, 103 COLUM. L. REV. 111 (2003); Randy E. Barnett, *The Misconceived Assumption about Constitutional Assumptions*, 103 NW. U. L. REV. 615, 617–18, 638 (2009).

33 See John Rawls, A THEORY OF JUSTICE, 115–16 (Harvard Univ. Press 1971); Joel Feinberg, *Civil Disobedience in the Modern World*, 2 HUMANITIES IN SOCIETY 37

(1979); and see Barnett, *Misconceived Assumption, supra* note 32, 103 NW. U. L. REV. at 642–43; Randy E. Barnett, *Constitutional Legitimacy without Consent,* 90 ARSP [ARCHIV FÜR RECHTS-UND SOZIALPHILOSOPHIE] 197–200 & 208 (2004).

34 *See* John Locke, THE SECOND TREATISE OF GOVERNMENT, ch. II, par. 4, ch. VIII, pars. 95–96 (1690); *and see* JAMES S. FISHKIN, TYRANNY AND LEGITIMACY: A CRITIQUE OF POLITICAL THEORIES (Johns Hopkins Univ. Press 1979).

35 See H. Jefferson Powell, *The Original Understanding of Original Intent,* 98 HARV. L. REV. 885, 888 (1985); *and see* BOBBITT, CONSTITUTIONAL FATE, *supra* note 21, at 31–32 & 37.

36 ZACHARY ELKINS, TOM GINSBURG, AND JAMES MELTON, THE ENDURANCE OF NATIONAL CONSTITUTIONS 51–53 (Cambridge U. Press 2009). *See also* Barnett, *Originalism for Nonoriginalists, supra* note 24, 45 LOY. L. REV. at 630–36.

37 *See* 1 FARRAND, *supra* note 17, at 541 (Rufus King on July 6, 1787, on consequences in 1937); ELKINS, GINSBURG, AND MELTON, *supra* note 36, at 51–53. *See also* Barnett, *Originalism for Nonoriginalists, supra* note 24, 45 LOY. L. REV. at 630–36.

38 See Scalia, *Common-Law Courts, supra* note 20, at 38–41.

39 See also Andrew B. Coan, *The Irrelevance of Writtenness in Constitutional Interpretation,* 158 U. PA. L. REV. 1025, 1028 & 1032–34 (2010); see *id.* at 1034–36.

40 Donald O. Dewey, *James Madison Helps Clio Interpret the Constitution,* 15 AMER. J. OF LEG. HIST. 38, 40–43 (1971).

41 Barnett, *Originalism for Nonoriginalists, supra* note 24, 45 LOY. L. REV. at 630–36.

42 *See* Dewey, *supra* note 40.

43 On the variants, *see* Bobbitt, *Constitutional Fate, supra* note 21, 58 TEX. L. REV. at 700–07. On external sources of language, *see* H.L.A. Hart, THE CONCEPT OF LAW (Oxford Univ. Press, 2d ed. 1994); H.L.A. Hart, *Positivism and the Separation of Law and Morals,* 71 HARV. L. REV. 593 (1958); Lon L. Fuller, *Positivism and Fidelity to Law—A Reply to Professor Hart,* 71 HARV. L. REV. 630 (1958), and RONALD DWORKIN, TAKING RIGHTS SERIOUSLY 81 (Harvard Univ. Press 1978). On historical meaning, *compare* Barnett, *Originalism for Nonoriginalists, supra* note 24, 45 LOY. L. REV. *with* Paul Brest, *The Misconceived Quest for the Original Understanding,* 60 BOS. U. L. REV. 204, 237–38 (1980); William Nelson, *History and Neutrality in Constitutional Adjudication,* 72 VA. L. REV. 1237 (1986).

44 *See* Bobbitt, *Constitutional Fate, supra* note 21, 58 TEX. L. REV. at 700; *see also* Powell, *Original Understanding, supra* note 35.

45 *See* SAMUEL JOHNSON, DICTIONARY OF THE ENGLISH LANGUAGE (London 1755); Jesse Sheidlower, *The Forgotten Founding Father: Noah Webster's Obsession and the Creation of an American Culture,* N.Y. TIMES BOOK REV., May 29, 2011, at 17.

46 *See* GORDON S. WOOD, THE CREATION OF THE AMERICAN REPUBLIC, 1776–1787 (Pub. for Inst. of Early Amer. Hist. & Culture by Univ. North Carolina Press 1969).

47 Powell, *Original Understanding, supra* note 35; Bobbitt, *Constitutional Fate, supra* note 21, 58 TEX. L. REV. 695.

48 James Madison to Charles J. Ingersoll, June 25, 1831, Founders Online, National Archives, http://founders.archives.gov/documents/Madison/99-02-02-2374 (visited Dec. 27, 2013). See also Donald O. Dewey, *James Madison Helps Clio Interpret the Constitution*, 15 AMER. J. OF LEG. HIST. 38, 52–53 (1971).

49 ALEXANDER M. BICKEL, THE LEAST DANGEROUS BRANCH: THE SUPREME COURT AT THE BAR OF POLITICS 16 (Bobbs-Merrill 1962).

50 *Id.*; *see also* JOHN HART ELY, DEMOCRACY AND DISTRUST: A THEORY OF JUDICIAL REVIEW (Harvard Univ. Press 1980).

51 *Id.*

52 2 FARRAND, *supra* note 17, at 73 (James Wilson on July 21, 1787).

53 *See* Frederick Schauer, *Precedent*, 39 STAN. L. REV. 571, 601–02 (1987).

54 *See* Bobbitt, *Constitutional Fate, supra* note 21, 58 TEX. L. REV. at 711–16.

55 Art. III, sec. 2, par. 1, "The judicial Power shall extend to all Cases . . . arising under this Constitution."

56 *See* 1 FARRAND, *supra* note 17, at 19 (remarks of Edmund Randolph, May 29, 1787); *id.* at 290 (remarks of Alexander Hamilton, June 18, 1787).

57 Bobbitt, *Constitutional Fate, supra* note 21, 58 TEX. L. REV. at 721.

58 McCulloch v. Maryland, 17 U.S. 316, 407, 415 (1819).

59 Crandall v. Nevada, 73 U.S. 35 (1867); Saenz v. Roe, 526 U.S. 489 (1999).

60 *See* Immigration & Naturalization Service v. Chadha, 462 U.S. 919, 957 (1983).

61 *See* Alden v. Maine, 527 U.S. 706 (1999); College Sav. Bank v. Fla. Prepaidpostsecondary Ed. Expense Bd., 527 U.S. 666 (1999); Florida Prepaid Postsecondary Educ. Expense Bd. v. College Sav. Bank, 527 U.S. 627 (1999); Seminole Tribe of Florida v. Florida, 517 U.S. 44, 53–54 (1996).

62 BREYER, ACTIVE LIBERTY, *supra* note 1, at 6.

63 ALEXANDER BICKEL, THE MORALITY OF CONSENT 11 (Yale Univ. Press 1975); Bobbitt, *Constitutional Fate, supra* note 21, 58 TEX. L. REV. at 723–25.

64 Gibbons v. Ogden, 22 U.S. 1 (1824).

65 McCulloch v. Maryland, 17 U.S. 316 (1819).

66 Charles River Bridge v. Warren Bridge, 36 U.S. 420 (1837).

67 Prigg v. Pennsylvania, 41 U.S. 539 (1842).

68 Stephen E. Gottlieb, *Compelling Governmental Interests: An Essential But Unanalyzed Term in Constitutional Adjudication*, 68 B.U. L. REV. 917 (1988).

69 In Bendix Autolite Corp. v. Midwesco Enterprises, Inc., 486 U.S. 888, 897 (1988) (Scalia, J., concurring in the judgment).

70 Stephen E. Gottlieb, *The Paradox of Balancing Significant Interests*, 45 HASTINGS L. J. 825 (1994).

71 Kennedy v. Mendoza-Martinez, 372 U.S. 144, 160 (1963).

72 James Bradley Thayer, *The Origin and Scope of the American Doctrine of Constitutional Law*, 7 HARV. L. REV. 129 (1893); West Virginia State Bd. of Educ. v.

Barnette, 319 U.S. 624, 670 (1943) (Frankfurter, J., dissenting); BICKEL, LEAST DANGEROUS BRANCH, *supra* note 49, at 16.

73 *Cf.* Michael Stokes Paulsen, *Does the Constitution Prescribe Rules for Its Own Interpretation?*, 103 NW. U. L. REV. 857 (2009).

74 RICHARD A. POSNER, LAW, PRAGMATISM AND DEMOCRACY 234–47 (Harvard Univ. Press 2003).

75 *See* Gottlieb, *Compelling Governmental Interests, supra* note 68.

76 *Compare* Bobbitt, *Constitutional Fate, supra* note 21, 58 TEX L. REV. at 726–50 *with* Gottlieb, *Compelling Governmental Interests, supra* note 68. *See also* POWELL, MORAL TRADITION, *supra* note 11, at 182–292; Robin L. West, *Are There Nothing but Texts in this Class? Interpreting the Interpretive Turns in Legal Thought*, 76 CHI-KENT L. REV. 1125 (2000); Robin West, *Progressive and Conservative Constitutionalism*, 88 MICH. L. REV. 641 (1990).

77 FRIEDRICH NIETZSCHE, THUS SPOKE ZARATHUSTRA (Barnes & Noble Classics 2007) (1883–1885).

78 See San Antonio Indep. Sch. Dist. v. Rodriguez, 411 U.S. 1, 49–50 (1973).

79 *See, e.g.*, Clarence Thomas, *The Higher Law Background of the Privileges or Immunities Clause of the Fourteenth Amendment*, 12 HARV. J. L. & PUB. POL'Y 63 (1989).

80 WOOD, CREATION OF THE AMERICAN REPUBLIC, *supra* note 46, at 24–25, 167–68.

81 *See* Locke, SECOND TREATISE, *supra* note 34.

82 Michael H. v. Gerald D., 491 U.S. 110, 163n (1989).

83 *See* POWELL, MORAL TRADITION, *supra* note 11 at 182–292.

84 *See* Feinberg, *Civil Disobedience, supra* note 33, 2 HUMAN. IN SOC'Y at 45–58; *but see* William Van Alstyne, *Clashing Visions of a "Living" Constitution: Of Opportunists and Obligationists*, 2010–11 CATO SUP. CT. REV. 13. On the source of moral obligations, *see* DAVID HUME, AN ENQUIRY CONCERNING THE PRINCIPLES OF MORALS 125–36 (1751) (Open Court Pub. Co. 1966). *See also* James E. Fleming, *Living Originalism and Living Constitutionalism as Moral Readings of the American Constitution*, 92 B.U. L. REV. 1171 (2012).

85 Moore v. East Cleveland, 431 U.S. 494, 503 (1977).

86 *Compare* Exxon Shipping Co. v. Baker, 554 U.S. 471 (2008) *with id.* at 515 (Scalia, J., concurring), *and* Pac. Mut. Life Ins. Co. v. Haslip, 499 U.S. 1, 25 (1991) (Scalia, J., concurring in the judgment).

87 Dep't of Revenue v. Davis, 553 U.S. 328 (2008); United Haulers Ass'n v. Oneida-Herkimer Solid Waste Mgmt. Auth., 550 U.S. 330, 344, 342 (2007); Edmonson v. Leesville Concrete Co., 500 U.S. 614 (1991).

88 Pac. Mut. Life Ins. Co. v. Haslip, 499 U.S. 1, 25 (1991) (Scalia, J., concurring in the judgment).

89 Souter in Washington v. Glucksberg, 521 U.S. 702, 766 (1997) (Souter, J., concurring).

90 Bobbitt, *Constitutional Fate, supra* note 21, 58 TEX L. REV. at 726. See Lawrence B. Solum, *The Unity of Interpretation*, 90 B.U. L. REV. 551, 567–78 (2010); Andrew B. Coan, *The Irrelevance of Writtenness in Constitutional Interpretation*, 158 U. PA. L. REV. 1025 (2010).

91 Coan, *The Irrelevance of Writtenness, supra* note 90, 158 U. PA. L. REV. at 1090.

92 *See* Ran Hirschl, *The New Constitutionalism and the Judicialization of Pure Politics Worldwide*, 75 FORDHAM L. REV. 721, 752 (2006); Richard Albert, *Why Judicial Review: A Preliminary Typology of Scholarly Arguments*, INT'L J. CONST. L. BLOG, Mar. 25, 2013, http://www.iconnectblog.com/2013/03/why-judicial-review.

93 *See* Bond v. United States, 131 S. Ct. 2355, 2367 (2011); Alden v. Maine, 527 U.S. 706, 736 (1999); *and compare* Nat'l League of Cities v. Usery, 426 U.S. 833 (1976) *with* Garcia v. San Antonio Metro. Transit Auth., 469 U.S. 528 (1985).

94 *Cf.* Paulsen, *Rules for Its Own Interpretation, supra* note 73.

95 Stern v. Marshall, 131 S. Ct. 2594 (2011); Arizona Christian Sch. Tuition Org. v. Winn, 131 S. Ct. 1436 (2011); *and cf.* McDonald v. City of Chicago, 130 S. Ct. 3020, 3095n (2010) (Stevens, J., dissenting).

96 U.S. CONST., art. I, sec. 2, par. 3.

97 U.S. CONST., art. II, sec. 1,pars. 2–4.

98 U.S. CONST., Amends. XIII, XIV, XV, XIX, XXIV and XXVI.

99 CHARLES L. BLACK, JR., STRUCTURE AND RELATIONSHIP IN CONSTITU-TIONAL LAW (Louisiana State Univ. Press 1969); *and see* Bobbitt, *Constitutional Fate, supra* note 21, 58 TEX L. REV. at 721–25.

100 *See* Wesberry v. Sanders, 376 U.S. 1, 8 (1964).

101 United States v. Carolene Products Co., 304 U.S. 144, 152n. 4 (1938).

102 BLACK, STRUCTURE AND RELATIONSHIP, *supra* note 99.

103 Stephen E. Gottlieb, *Introduction: Overriding Public Values, in* PUBLIC VALUES IN CONSTITUTIONAL LAW 1 (Univ. Michigan Press, Stephen E. Gottlieb, ed. 1993).

104 Abraham Lincoln, Gettysburg Address, Nov. 19, 1863.

105 *See* JAMES KENT, COMMENTARIES ON AMERICAN LAW, vol. 2, at 338 (Blackstone Publishing Co., William M. Lacy, ed. 1889); SIR EDWARD COKE, THE REPORTS OF SIR EDWARD COKE, vol. 6, at 280 (J. Butterworth and Son, John Henry Thomas and John Farquhar Fraser, eds. 1826); CHARLES VINER, A GENERAL ABRIDGMENT OF LAW AND EQUITY, ALPHABETICALLY DIGESTED UNDER PROPER TITLES; WITH NOTES AND REFERENCES TO THE WHOLE, vol. 15, at 534–35 (G. G. J. & J. Robinson, 1793); American Print Works v. Lawrence, 21 N.J. Law. (3 Zab.) 248, 258–59 (1847); Respublica v. Sparhawk, 1 U.S. (Dal.) 357, 362–63 (Pa. 1788).

106 Alexander Hamilton, *The Vindication [of the funding system] No. III, in* SELECTED WRITINGS AND SPEECHES OF ALEXANDER HAMILTON 331, 333 (American Enterprise Inst. for Pub. Pol'y Research, Morton J. Frisch, ed. 1985).

107 WOOD, CREATION OF THE AMERICAN REPUBLIC, *supra* note 46, esp. the final chapter, *The Federalist Science of Politics*.

108 Kathleen Sullivan, *Categorization, Balancing and Government Interests*, in PUBLIC VALUES IN CONSTITUTIONAL LAW, *supra* note 103, at 241.

109 For the previous Court, see GOTTLIEB, MORALITY IMPOSED, *supra* note10, at 29. On trying to build answers without considering consequences, *see* Gottlieb, *Paradox of Balancing, supra* note 70.

110 Republican Party v. White, 536 U.S. 765, 777–778 (2002).

111 See "direct horizontal" and "indirect effects" of constitutional law, *supra* chapter 4.

112 Karl E. Klare, *Legal Culture and Transformative Constitutionalism*, 14 S. AFR. J. ON HUM. RTS. 146, 150 (1998). *See also* Katharine G. Young and Julieta Lemaitre, *The Comparative Fortunes of the Right to Health: Two Tales of Justiciability in Colombia and South Africa*, 26 HARV. HUM. RTS. J. 179, 198 (2013); Arnon D. Siegel, *Section 1983 Remedies for the Violation of Supremacy Clause Rights*, 97 YALE L.J. 1827, 1833 (1988); *and see* Stephen Macedo, *Transformative Constitutionalism and the Case of Religion: Defending the Moderate Hegemony of Liberalism*, 26 POL. THEORY 56 (1998); Pius Langa, Chief Justice of South African Constitutional Court, Lecture at the University of Stellenbosch, South Africa: Transformative Constitutionalism (Oct. 9, 2006), *available at* http://law.sun.ac.za/LangaSpeech.pdf (discussing recent criticism).

113 *See* GUISEPPE DI PALMA, TO CRAFT DEMOCRACIES: AN ESSAY ON DEMOCRATIC TRANSITIONS (Univ. of California Press 1990).

114 *E.g.*, Dred Scott v. Sanford, 60 U.S. (19 How.) 393 (1856); Prigg v. Pennsylvania, 41 U.S. (16 Pet.) 539 (1842); *and see* ERIC L. MCKITRICK, ANDREW JOHNSON AND RECONSTRUCTION (Univ. of Chicago Press 1960).

115 *See We Stand in Solidarity to Defend Marriage and the Family and Society Founded upon Them* (Freedom Federation), June 20, 2013, http://www.lc.org/media/9980/attachments/pr_ltr_marriage_solidarity_statement_062013.pdf; GERALD N. ROSENBERG, THE HOLLOW HOPE: CAN COURTS BRING ABOUT SOCIAL CHANGE? (Univ. of Chicago Press 1991).

116 *See* WOOD, CREATION OF THE AMERICAN REPUBLIC, *supra* note 46 at 24–25.

117 Holder v. Hall, 512 U.S. 874, 913 (1994) (Thomas, J., concurring in the judgment).

118 *See* text *infra* at note 129.

119 *See* ROBERT A. DAHL, POLYARCHY: PARTICIPATION AND OPPOSITION 4 (Yale Univ. Press 1971).

120 *See* BREYER, ACTIVE LIBERTY, *supra* note 1.

121 *See* Holder v. Hall, 512 U.S. at 913 (Thomas, J., concurring in the judgment).

122 POSNER, LAW, PRAGMATISM AND DEMOCRACY, *supra* note 74, at 158–213; *and see* JOSEPH A. SCHUMPETER, CAPITALISM, SOCIALISM AND DEMOCRACY 269–83 (Harper, 3d ed. 1950).

123 *See* DAHL, POLYARCHY, *supra* note 119, at 3–4. *See also* Niels Petersen, *The Principle of Democratic Teleology in International Law*, 34 BROOKLYN J. INT'L L. 33, 37–40 (2008).

124 DAHL, POLYARCHY, *supra* note 119, at 4.

125 *Cf.* Frederick Schauer, *Judicial Review of the Devices of Democracy*, 94 COLUM. L. REV. 1326 (1994).

126 See Ross Douthat, *Democrats Get a Gift from the Roberts Court*, N.Y. Times, June 30, 2013, at SR11.

127 *See, e.g.*, Shelby County v. Holder, 133 S. Ct. 2612 (2013); Arizona Free Enter. Club's Freedom Club PAC v. Bennett, 131 S. Ct. 2806 (2011); Citizens United v. FEC, 558 U.S. 310 (2010); League of United Latin Am. Citizens v. Perry, 548 U.S. 399 (2006).

128 Schauer, *Judicial Review, supra* note 125.

129 CHARLES A. MILLER, THE SUPREME COURT AND THE USES OF HISTORY (Harvard Univ. Press 1969). *See also* Paul Horwitz, *The Past, Tense: The History of Crisis—And the Crisis of History—In Constitutional Theory*, 61 ALB. L. REV. 459 (1997); Paul Finkelman, *Intentionalism, the Founders, and Constitutional Interpretation*, 75 Tex. L. Rev. 435 (1996) (review of JACK N. RAKOVE, ORIGINAL MEANINGS: POLITICS AND IDEAS IN THE MAKING OF THE CONSTITUTION [1996]).

130 Stephen E. Gottlieb, *Rebuilding the Right of Association: The Right to Hold a Convention as a Test Case*, 11 HOFSTRA LAW REVIEW 191, 196–203 & 223–30 (1983).

131 Frye v. United States, 293 F. 1013, 1014 (D.C. Cir. 1923).

132 Daubert v. Merrell Dow Pharms., 509 U.S. 579, 592–93 (1993).

133 *Id.*

134 David L. Faigman, *The Law's Scientific Revolution: Reflections and Ruminations on the Law's Use of Experts in Year Seven of the Revolution*, 57 WASH & LEE L. REV. 661 (2000).

135 *See Daubert, supra* note 132; DAVID L. FAIGMAN, CONSTITUTIONAL FICTIONS: A UNIFIED THEORY OF CONSTITUTIONAL FACTS 169–70 (Oxford Univ. Press 2008); Faigman, *supra* note 134.

136 John Monahan and Laurens Walker, *A Judges' Guide to Using Social Science*, 43 COURT REVIEW 156, 158 (2007). *See also* John Monahan and Laurens Walker, *Social Authority: Obtaining, Evaluating, and Establishing Social Science in Law*, 134 U. PA. L. REV. 477, 498–512 (1986).

137 Monahan and Walker, *Social Authority, supra* note 136, 134 U. PA. L. REV. at 496–97.

138 JOHN STUART MILL, ON LIBERTY 19–67 (Bobbs-Merrill 1956) (1859).

139 *See* VICKI JACKSON AND MARK TUSHNET, COMPARATIVE CONSTITUTIONAL LAW 1638–61 (Foundation Press, 2d ed. 2006). *See, e.g., Lüth Case*, BVerfGE 7, 198 at 208 (1958), translation from DONALD P. KOMMERS, THE CONSTITUTIONAL JURISPRUDENCE OF THE FEDERAL REPUBLIC OF GERMANY (Duke Univ. Press 2d ed. 1997), at 365. The translation in KOMMERS AND MILLER, 3d ed. rev. & exp., *supra* note 34, at 445–46, is slightly different but to the same effect. *See* Peter E. Quint, *Free Speech and Private Law in German Constitutional Theory*, 48 MD. L. REV. 247 (1989).

140 Lugar v. Edmundson Oil Co., 457 U.S. 922 (1982); New York Times v. Sullivan, 376 U.S. 254 (1964); Shelley v. Kraemer, 334 U.S. 1 (1948); Terry v. Adams, 345 U.S. 461 (U.S. 1953).

141 United States v. Windsor, 133 S. Ct. 2675 (2013).

142 *Id.*

143 Shelby County v. Holder, 133 S. Ct. 2612 (2013).

ABOUT THE AUTHOR

Stephen E. Gottlieb is Jay and Ruth Caplan Professor of Law at Albany Law School. Widely known for his work on constitutional law and honored with distinguished chairs at five law schools, he served on the Board of the New York Civil Liberties Union, on the New York Advisory Committee to the United States Commission on Civil Rights, in the Legal Services Program, and in the Peace Corps (in Iran) and practiced corporate law. A Princeton and Yale Law School graduate, he also founded a political action committee.